D0470569

CompTIA Security+™
Certification Practice Exams

(Exam SY0-301)

Daniel Lachance
Glen E. Clarke

McGraw-Hill is an independent entity from CompTIA. This publication and CD may be used in assisting students to prepare for the CompTIA Security+ exam. Neither CompTIA nor McGraw-Hill warrant that use of this publication and CD will ensure passing any exam. CompTIA® and CompTIA Security+™ are trademarks or registered trademarks of CompTIA in the United States and/or other countries. All other trademarks are trademarks of their respective owners.

McGraw Hill

New York Chicago San Francisco Lisbon London Madrid
Mexico City Milan New Delhi San Juan Seoul Singapore Sydney Toronto

The McGraw·Hill Companies

Cataloging-in-Publication Data is on file with the Library of Congress

McGraw-Hill books are available at special quantity discounts to use as premiums and sales promotions, or for use in corporate training programs. To contact a representative, please e-mail us at bulksales@mcgraw-hill.com.

CompTIA Security+™ Certification Practice Exams (Exam SY0-301)

Copyright © 2011 by The McGraw-Hill Companies. All rights reserved. Printed in the United States of America. Except as permitted under the Copyright Act of 1976, no part of this publication may be reproduced or distributed in any form or by any means, or stored in a database or retrieval system, without the prior written permission of publisher, with the exception that the program listings may be entered, stored, and executed in a computer system, but they may not be reproduced for publication.

All trademarks or copyrights mentioned herein are the possession of their respective owners and McGraw-Hill makes no claim of ownership by the mention of products that contain these marks.

1 2 3 4 5 6 7 8 9 0   DOC DOC   1 0 9 8 7 6 5 4 3 2 1

ISBN: Book p/n 978-0-07-177117-7 and CD p/n 978-0-07-177118-4
of set 978-0-07-177120-7

MHID: Book p/n 0-07-177117-4 and CD p/n 0-07-177118-2
of set 0-07-177120-4

Sponsoring Editor Meghan Riley Manfre	**Technical Editor** Bobby Rogers	**Production Supervisor** Jean Bodeaux
Editorial Supervisor Jody McKenzie	**Copy Editor** Robert Campbell	**Composition** Cenveo Publisher Services
Project Manager Harleen Chopra, Cenveo Publisher Services	**Proofreader** Carol Shields	**Illustration** Cenveo Publisher Services
Acquisitions Coordinator Stephanie Evans	**Indexer** Jack Lewis	**Art Director, Cover** Jeff Weeks

Information has been obtained by McGraw-Hill from sources believed to be reliable. However, because of the possibility of human or mechanical error by our sources, McGraw-Hill, or others, McGraw-Hill does not guarantee the accuracy, adequacy, or completeness of any information and is not responsible for any errors or omissions or the results obtained from the use of such information.

For Janet, Trinity, and Roman for unwavering encouragement and support of my career choice.

—Daniel Lachance

ABOUT THE AUTHORS

Daniel Lachance, MCITP, MCTS, CNI, IBM Certified Instructor, CompTIA A+®, CompTIA Network+®, CompTIA Security+™, is a technical trainer for Global Knowledge and has delivered classroom training in a wide variety of products for the past 17 years. Throughout his career he has also developed custom applications and planned, implemented, troubleshot, and documented various network configurations.

Glen E. Clarke, MCSE, MCDBA, MCSD, MCT, CCENT, CEH, CHFI, SCNP, CISSO, CompTIA A+, CompTIA Network+, CompTIA Security+, is an independent trainer and consultant, focusing on network security and security auditing services. Glen spends most of his time delivering certified courses on Windows Server, SQL Server, Exchange Server, Visual Basic.NET, and ASP.NET. Glen also teaches a number of security-related courses covering topics such as ethical hacking and countermeasures, computer forensics and investigation, information systems security officer, vulnerability testing, firewall design, and packet analysis topics.

Glen is an experienced author and technical editor whose published work has been nominated for a referenceware excellence award in 2003 and 2004. Glen has authored many certification titles, including *CompTIA Network+ Certification Study Guide, Fourth Edition*, *Mike Meyers' CompTIA Network+ Certification Passport, Third Edition*, and *CCENT Certification All-In-One For Dummies* (Wiley; he has also co-authored the bestselling *A+ Certification All-In-One For Dummies* (Wiley).

When he's not working, Glen loves to spend quality time with his wife, Tanya, and their four children, Sara, Brendon, Ashlyn, and Rebecca. He is an active member of the High Technology Crime Investigation Association (HTCIA). You can visit Glen online at www.gleneclarke.com, or contact him at glenclarke@ accesswave.ca.

About the Technical Editor

Bobby E. Rogers is a principal information security analyst with Dynetics, Inc., a national technology firm specializing in the certification and accreditation process for the U.S. government. He also serves as a penetration testing team lead for various government and commercial engagements. Bobby recently retired from the U.S.

Air Force after almost 21 years, where he served as a computer networking and security specialist and designed and managed networks all over the world. His IT security experience includes several years working as a network administrator, system administrator, information assurance manager, penetration tester, and auditor. He has held several positions of responsibility for network security in both the Department of Defense and private company networks. His duties have included perimeter security, client-side security, security policy development, security training, computer crime investigations, and security auditing. As a trainer, he has taught a wide variety of IT-related subjects in both makeshift classrooms in desert tents and formal training centers. Bobby is also an accomplished author, having written numerous IT articles in various publications and training materials for the U.S. Air Force. He has also authored numerous security training videos.

He has a Bachelor of Science degree in computer information systems from Excelsior College and two Associates in Applied Science degrees from the Community College of the Air Force. Bobby's professional IT certifications include A+, Security+, ACP, CCNA, CCAI, CIW, CIWSA, MCP+I, MCSA (Windows 2000 and 2003), MCSE (Windows NT4, 2000, and 2003), MCSE: Security (Windows 2000 and 2003), CISSP, CIFI, CEH, CHFI, and CPTS. He is also a certified trainer.

About LearnKey

LearnKey provides self-paced learning content and multimedia delivery solutions to enhance personal skills and business productivity. LearnKey claims the largest library of rich streaming-media training content that engages learners in dynamic media-rich instruction complete with video clips, audio, full-motion graphics, and animated illustrations. LearnKey can be found on the Web at www.LearnKey.com.

CONTENTS AT A GLANCE

1	Network Basics and Terminology	1
2	Introduction to Security Terminology	19
3	Security Policies and Standards	37
4	Types of Attacks	53
5	System Security Threats	71
6	Mitigating Security Threats	89
7	Implementing System Security	111
8	Securing the Network Infrastructure	131
9	Wireless Networking	157
10	Authentication	177
11	Access Control	197
12	Introduction to Cryptography	221
13	Managing a PKI Infrastructure	245
14	Physical Security	265
15	Risk Analysis	281
16	Disaster Recovery	303
17	Introduction to Computer Forensics	327
18	Security Assessments and Audits	349

19   Understanding Monitoring and Auditing   373

20   Practice Exam   395

A   About the CD-ROM   459

      Index   463

CONTENTS

Acknowledgments . . . . *xiii*

Preface . . . . *xv*

Introduction . . . . *xvii*

1   Network Basics and Terminology **1**

Questions 2

Quick Answer Key 7

In-Depth Answers 8

2   Introduction to Security Terminology **19**

Questions 20

Quick Answer Key 25

In-Depth Answers 26

3   Security Policies and Standards **37**

Questions 38

Quick Answer Key 43

In-Depth Answers 44

4   Types of Attacks **53**

Questions 54

Quick Answer Key 59

In-Depth Answers 60

5   System Security Threats **71**

Questions 72

Quick Answer Key 77

In-Depth Answers 78

6 Mitigating Security Threats **89**
Questions 90
Quick Answer Key 96
In-Depth Answers 97

7 Implementing System Security **111**
Questions 112
Quick Answer Key 117
In-Depth Answers 118

8 Securing the Network Infrastructure **131**
Questions 132
Quick Answer Key 139
In-Depth Answers 140

9 Wireless Networking **157**
Questions 158
Quick Answer Key 163
In-Depth Answers 164

10 Authentication **177**
Questions 178
Quick Answer Key 183
In-Depth Answers 184

11 Access Control **197**
Questions 198
Quick Answer Key 205
In-Depth Answers 206

12 Introduction to Cryptography **221**
Questions 222
Quick Answer Key 229
In-Depth Answers 230

13 **Managing a PKI Infrastructure** **245**

    Questions 246

    Quick Answer Key 252

    In-Depth Answers 253

14 **Physical Security** **265**

    Questions 266

    Quick Answer Key 270

    In-Depth Answers 271

15 **Risk Analysis** **281**

    Questions 282

    Quick Answer Key 288

    In-Depth Answers 289

16 **Disaster Recovery** **303**

    Questions 304

    Quick Answer Key 311

    In-Depth Answers 312

17 **Introduction to Computer Forensics** **327**

    Questions 328

    Quick Answer Key 334

    In-Depth Answers 335

18 **Security Assessments and Audits** **349**

    Questions 350

    Quick Answer Key 357

    In-Depth Answers 358

19 **Understanding Monitoring and Auditing** **373**

    Questions 374

    Quick Answer Key 380

    In-Depth Answers 381

20 Practice Exam **395**

    Questions 396

    Quick Answer Key 416

    In-Depth Answers 417

A About the CD-ROM **459**

    System Requirements 460

    Installing And Running Masterexam 460

    Electronic Book 461

    Help 461

    Removing Installation(s) 461

    Technical Support 461

    Index **463**

ACKNOWLEDGMENTS

I would like to make known the stellar team that contributed to this book's existence. All of the following people were given raw materials that were forged into a refined product, this book.

The dedication of the skilled staff at McGraw-Hill cannot be overstated; Tim Green, Meghan Riley, and Stephanie Evans from the Acquisitions team, Melinda Lytle for her work in print production, Jody McKenzie for her editorial supervision, Bob Campbell's work as copy editor, and Harleen Chopra's work as production project manager. These professionals exhibited saintly patience with me, and I thank them.

I would like to thank Glen Clarke for his guidance in crafting a meaningful body of text, and for never running out of interesting things to talk about. To the technical editor, Bobby Rogers, for catching even the minutest problematic detail in the text—thank you for making me look better.

Finally, to my wife Janet for enduring my obsession with this book, and to Roman and Trinity and the rest of my family for listening to my continuous technobabble.

—Daniel Lachance

elcome to *CompTIA Security+™ Certification Practice Exams!* This book serves as a preparation tool for the CompTIA Security+ Exam (Exam SY0-301) as well as for your work in the IT security field.

The objective of this book is to prepare you for the CompTIA Security+ Exam by familiarizing you with the technology and body of knowledge tested on the exam. Because the primary focus of this book is to help you pass the test, we don't always cover every aspect of the related technology. Some aspects of the technology are only covered to the extent necessary to help you understand what you need to know to pass the exam, but we hope this book will serve you as a valuable professional resource after your exam as well.

In This Book

This book is organized in such a way as to serve as an in-depth review for the CompTIA Security+ Exam for both experienced IT security professionals and newcomers to security technologies. Each chapter covers a major aspect of the exam, with practice questions to test your knowledge of specific exam objectives.

In Every Chapter

Each chapter contains components that call your attention to important items and reinforce salient points. Take a look at what you'll find in every chapter:

- Every chapter begins with **Certification Objectives**, a list of the official CompTIA exam objectives covered in that chapter.
- Twenty to thirty practice **Questions**, similar to those found on the actual exam, are included in every chapter. By answering these questions, you'll test your knowledge while becoming familiar with the structure of the exam questions.

- The **Quick Answer Key** follows the Questions and allows you to easily check your answers.
- **In-Depth Answers** at the end of every chapter include explanations for the correct and incorrect answer choices and provide an opportunity for review of the exam topics.

Practice Exams

Of the 800+ questions included in this book, 300 are organized into three practice exams of 100 questions each. Like the questions organized by objectives, the practice exams also include detailed explanations for the correct and incorrect answer choices.

On the CD

For more information on the CD-ROM, please see the Appendix "About the CD-ROM" at the back of the book.

Exam Readiness Checklist

At the end of the Introduction you will find an Exam Readiness Checklist. This table has been constructed to allow you to reference the official CompTIA Security+ objectives and refer to the order in which these objectives are covered in this book. This checklist also allows you to gauge your level of expertise on each exam objective at the outset of your studies. This should allow you to check your progress and make sure you spend the time you need on more difficult or unfamiliar sections. The objectives are listed as CompTIA has presented them with the corresponding book chapter and question number reference.

The CompTIA Security+™ Exam (Exam SY0-301)

The CompTIA Security+ Exam is a vendor-neutral exam validating skills in risk identification and management, the application of physical and digital security controls for devices and networks, disaster recovery, and the adherence to rules set forth by legal and regulatory bodies. This certification is aimed at individuals with a minimum of two years of experience in IT administration focusing on security.

The CompTIA Security+ Exam consists of six domains (categories). CompTIA represents the relative importance of each domain within the body of knowledge required for an entry-level IT professional taking this exam.

1.0 Network Security	21%
2.0 Compliance and Operational Security	18%
3.0 Threats and Vulnerabilities	21%
4.0 Application, Data, and Host Security	16%
5.0 Access Control and Identity Management	13%
6.0 Cryptography	11%

Your CompTIA Security+ certification is valid for three years from the date you are certified, after which you must take the most current version of the exam to keep your certification. Detailed information regarding the CompTIA Security+ certification and exam is available at www.comptia.org.

Organization and Design of This Book

CompTIA Security+™ Certification Practice Exams (Exam SY0-301) is a battery of practice test questions organized by the official exam objectives. The first 19 chapters contain over 500 questions that cover all of the objectives for the SY0-301 exam. The last chapter is a complete practice exam. The accompanying CD contains an additional practice exam in a simulated testing environment, and a third practice exam is available for free download via the web.

This book was developed and written in conjunction with the *CompTIA Security+*™ *Certification Study Guide,* by Glen E. Clarke. The order the objectives are presented in is identical, as are the chapter titles. These books were designed to work together as a comprehensive program for self-study.

Strategies for Use

There are a variety of ways in which this book can be used, whether used simultaneously with the *CompTIA Security+*™ *Certification Study Guide* or as a stand-alone test prep tool.

With the Study Guide: Taking a chapter-by-chapter approach, you can opt to read a Study Guide chapter and then practice what you have learned with the questions in the corresponding Practice Exams chapter, and alternate between books throughout your course of study.

The Practice Exams book alone: Using the Practice Exams book after you have read the Study Guide, or as a stand-alone test prep tool, you can work through the book cover to cover and take the three practice exams as the final step in your preparation.

Or, by means of the Exam Readiness Checklist, which comes next, you can gauge your level of expertise and determine which objectives to focus on and work through the book by objectives. The Exam Readiness Checklist notes which questions pertain to which objectives, allowing you to tailor your review.

Exam Readiness Checklist

Official Objective	Chapter Number	Question Number
1.0 Network Security	9	22
1.1 Explain the security function and purpose of network devices and technologies	1 5 8 17	1, 2, 3, 9, 19, 23, 24, 25 15 1, 2, 3, 4, 5, 6, 7, 8, 11, 14, 21, 27, 29, 30 13, 15, 18
1.2 Apply and implement secure network administration principles	8 19	2, 5, 9, 10, 13, 15, 20, 28 2, 3, 4, 5, 6, 9, 10, 11, 12, 13, 14, 15, 17, 18, 20, 21, 22, 23, 24, 25, 27, 28, 30
1.3 Distinguish and differentiate network design elements and compounds	1 7 8 10	19, 24, 25 17, 24, 25, 26 18, 22, 23, 26 2, 3, 5, 7, 19
1.4 Implement and use common protocols	1 12 17 18 13	4, 5, 6, 10, 11, 13, 14, 15, 16, 18, 20, 21, 22, 26, 27 2, 3, 4, 18 19, 25 19 10
1.5 Identify commonly used default network ports	1 12	4, 11, 12, 17 1, 5
1.6 Implement wireless network in a secure manner	9	2, 3, 4, 6, 8, 9, 10
2.0 Compliance and Operational Security	2 14	1, 3, 16, 17, 19 2, 4, 5, 15, 17
2.1 Explain risk-related concepts	3 11 15 17 18	1, 2, 3, 4, 5, 6, 7, 8, 10, 11, 12, 13, 14, 15, 17, 18, 19, 20, 21 10, 12, 26, 27 1, 2, 3, 4, 5, 6, 7, 8, 10, 11, 12, 13, 14, 15, 16, 17, 18, 19, 22, 27, 29, 30 26 5
2.2 Carry out appropriate risk mitigation strategies	15	9, 20, 21, 23, 24, 25, 26, 28
2.3 Execute appropriate incident response procedures	17	1, 2, 3, 4, 5, 6, 7, 8, 9, 10, 11, 16, 17, 20, 21, 23, 24, 27, 28, 29, 30

Exam Readiness Checklist

Official Objective	Chapter Number	Question Number
2.4 Explain the importance of security-related awareness and training	3	9, 11, 16
2.5 Compare and contrast aspects of business continuity	16	3, 4, 5, 6, 8, 9, 10, 11, 12, 14, 16, 17, 18, 19, 23, 24, 26, 27, 28, 29, 30
2.6 Explain the impact and proper use of environmental controls	14	1, 5, 6, 7
2.7 Execute disaster recovery plans and procedures	16	1, 2, 7, 10, 13, 15, 20, 21, 22, 25
2.8 Exemplify the concepts of confidentiality, integrity, and availability (CIA)	2	2, 7, 9, 10, 14, 15, 18, 20, 21, 24, 25
3.0 Threats and Vulnerabilities	2 4	5 11, 12, 14
3.1 Analyze and differentiate among types of malware	5	1, 2, 3, 4, 5, 6, 7, 8, 9, 10, 13, 16, 17, 18, 19, 20, 21
3.2 Analyze and differentiate among types of attacks	4	1, 3, 4, 6, 7, 8, 9, 10, 12, 13, 20, 21, 22
3.3 Analyze and differentiate among types of social engineering attacks	4	2, 5, 14
3.4 Analyze and differentiate among types of wireless attacks	9	5, 12, 14, 15, 16, 17, 24, 27
3.5 Analyze and differentiate among types of application attacks	4	3, 4, 6, 8, 11, 15, 16, 17, 18, 19
3.6 Analyze and differentiate among types of mitigation and deterrent techniques	6 8 14 18 19	2, 4, 5, 6, 7, 10, 11, 13, 14, 16, 17, 18, 19, 23, 24, 25, 26, 27 3, 4, 5, 12, 16, 17, 19, 24, 25 3, 8, 9, 10, 11, 12, 13, 14, 15, 16, 19, 21 29 1, 6, 7, 8, 16, 19, 26, 29
3.7 Implement assessment tools and techniques to discover security threats and vulnerabilities	15 18	3, 4, 5 1, 2, 3, 4, 6, 7, 9, 10, 11, 12, 14, 15, 16, 22

Exam Readiness Checklist

Official Objective	Chapter Number	Question Number
3.8 Within the realm of vulnerability assessments, explain the proper use of penetration testing versus vulnerability scanning	18	2, 4, 8, 9, 11, 15, 17, 21, 24, 27, 28
4.0 Application, Data, and Host Security		
4.1 Explain the importance of application security	6	1, 3, 8, 9, 12, 15, 20, 21, 22, 28
4.2 Carry out appropriate procedures to establish host security	7	1, 2, 5, 7, 9, 11, 13, 14, 15, 16, 18, 19, 22, 27
4.3 Explain the importance of data security	7 14	3, 4, 5, 6, 7, 8, 9, 10, 12, 20, 21, 23, 24 18, 20
5.0 Access Control and Identity Management		
5.1 Explain the function and purpose of authentication services	10 18	1, 4, 5, 8, 9, 10, 22 23, 25, 30
5.2 Explain the fundamental concepts and best practices related to authentication, authorization, and access control	2 10 11	5, 6, 7, 8, 11, 12, 13, 22, 23 6, 10, 11, 12, 13, 14, 15, 16, 17, 18, 19, 20, 21, 23, 24 1, 4, 5, 7, 11, 14, 15, 16, 17, 20, 22, 23, 24, 28
5.3 Implement appropriate security controls when performing account management	11 18	1, 2, 3, 6, 8, 9, 13, 18, 19, 21, 25 26
6.0 Cryptography		
6.1 Summarize general cryptography concepts	12 13 17 18	6, 8, 9, 10, 11, 13, 14, 15, 16, 17, 20, 21, 22, 23, 24, 25, 26, 27, 28, 29, 30 1, 2, 3, 4, 5, 6, 7, 8, 9, 10, 11, 12, 13, 14, 15, 16, 17, 18, 19, 20, 21, 22, 23, 24 12, 14, 22 13, 18, 20
6.2 Use and apply appropriate cryptographic tools and products	9 12	2, 3, 7, 9, 20, 21, 25 1, 2, 3, 4, 7, 12, 19

1

Network Basics and Terminology

CERTIFICATION OBJECTIVES

- ❑ **1.1** Explain the security function and purpose of network devices and technologies
- ❑ **1.3** Distinguish and differentiate network design elements and compounds
- ❑ **1.4** Implement and use common protocols
- ❑ **1.5** Identify commonly used default network ports

QUESTIONS

Proper implementation of network security requires a sound knowledge of network hardware as well as of the TCP/IP protocol suite. Switches control network traffic by creating VLANs and by remembering which MAC addresses are plugged into which switch ports. Routers use routing tables to forward network traffic to the proper destination network. Command-line tools such as IPCONFIG, PING, and TRACERT aid in testing and troubleshooting a TCP/IP network.

1. You are asked to ensure that Ethernet switches allow computers with specific physical network cards to connect to the wired network. What type of network address will the switches examine?
   A. SSID
   B. IP address
   C. NetBIOS computer name
   D. MAC address

2. What can be done on a network switch to secure the network?
   A. Disable unused ports.
   B. Use SCP instead of TELNET for administration.
   C. Enable RC4 encryption.
   D. Configure each port for half-duplex.

3. As a security consultant, you have been asked to recommend a secure cabling solution for a military installation. Which cable type is considered the most secure?
   A. STP (shielded twisted pair)
   B. Multimode fiber
   C. Coaxial
   D. UTP (unshielded twisted pair)

4. After performing a routine network scan, you notice that a vast majority of Windows 7 desktop computers show TCP port 25 as being in a "listening" state. What should you do next?
   A. Nothing—Windows 7 requires port 25 for workgroup computing.
   B. Turn off all computers immediately—they are infected.
   C. Uninstall the web service from each affected desktop.
   D. Uninstall the mail service from each affected desktop.

5. Which of the following are TCP/IP mail protocols? (Choose three.)
   A. SNMP
   B. SMTP
   C. IMAP
   D. POP
   E. Windows Mail

6. Using a protocol analyzer, your colleague Maria notices a small amount of ICMP network traffic. VoIP has recently been implemented on the network. She is concerned that this traffic implies a network attack is under way. What should you tell her?
   A. Utilities such as PING and TRACERT use ICMP.
   B. This is not normal—immediately notify the network administrator.
   C. This is VoIP traffic.
   D. Utilities such as SNMP use ICMP.

7. You are the network administrator for a small clothing company. The majority of business revenues are derived from clothing sales from the company's web site. Recently the web server has crashed more than once and the business owners have expressed concern about lost sales due to server failures. A second web server has already been purchased. You are asked what else is needed to ensure customers can make online purchases even if one web server is busy or has crashed. Which of the following is the best economic solution?
   A. Purchase a second router and Internet connection, and configure the second server to use only the second Internet connection.
   B. Configure both web servers to use NetBIOS computer names.
   C. Configure a network load balancer to distribute traffic to an available web server.
   D. Enable NAT on the router.

8. Which network tool would a malicious user benefit from as a result of initiating a MAC flooding attack on a network switch?
   A. Crimper
   B. Port scanner
   C. PING
   D. Packet sniffer

9. Your wiring closet consists of three 24-port Ethernet switches all linked together. Computers from the Accounting department are plugged into each Ethernet switch, as are computers from the Research department. Your manager asks you to ensure computers in the Accounting department are on a different network than computers in the Research department. What could you do? (Choose two.)
   A. Replace the Ethernet switches with Ethernet hubs.
   B. Configure all Accounting computers on the same TCP/IP subnet (e.g., 192.268.2.0 /24) and configure all Research computers on their own TCP/IP subnet (e.g., 192.168.3.0 /16).
   C. Configure an Accounting VLAN that includes the Accounting computers and a Research VLAN that includes the Research computers.
   D. Configure all Accounting computers on the same TCP/IP subnet (e.g., 192.168.2.0 /24) and configure all Research computers on their own TCP/IP subnet (e.g., 192.168.3.0 /24).

10. What type of address is fe80::dca6:d048:cba6:bd06?
   A. IPv4
   B. IPv6
   C. MAC
   D. DMZ

11. Which of the following statements regarding DNS are true? (Choose two.)
   A. It resolves NetBIOS computer names to IP addresses.
   B. Client to server queries use TCP port 53.
   C. It resolves FQDNs to IP addresses.
   D. Given an IP address, DNS can return a FQDN.

12. Which protocol uses TCP port 443?
   A. FTPS
   B. HTTP
   C. HTTPS
   D. SSH

13. You are troubleshooting TCP/IP settings on a workstation. The workstation IP address is 10.17.6.8/24, the DNS server setting is set to 199.126.129.86, and the default gateway setting is set to 10.17.5.6. The router has a public IP address of 199.126.129.76/24 and a private internal IP address of 10.17.5.6/24. This workstation is the only station on the network that cannot connect to the Internet. What should you do?
   A. Change the DNS server setting to 10.17.5.6.
   B. Change the router private internal IP address to 10.17.6.6.
   C. Change the workstation IP address to 10.17.5.8.
   D. Change the default gateway setting to 199.126.129.76.

14. You need a server to store router configuration files. The server must not require a username or password. Which type of server is the best choice?
   A. Windows file server
   B. FTP
   C. TFTP
   D. FTPS

15. Which TCP/IP protocol is designed to synchronize time between computers?
   A. SNMP
   B. Windows time sync
   C. NTP
   D. SMTP

16. Which TCP/IP protocol gives administrators a remote command prompt to a network service?
- A. POP
- B. ARP
- C. UDP
- D. TELNET

17. While capturing network traffic, you notice some packets destined for UDP port 69. What type of network traffic is this?
- A. FTP
- B. TFTP
- C. SNMP
- D. IMAP

18. Which TCP/IP protocols use encryption to secure data transmissions?
- A. SCP, DNS, SSH
- B. SSH, SCP, TELNET
- C. HTTPS, FTP, SSH
- D. SSH, SCP, FTPS

19. Which of the following network connectivity devices function primarily using computer MAC addresses? (Choose two.)
- A. Router
- B. Bridge
- C. Hub
- D. Switch

20. Which of the following are considered TCP/IP transport protocols? (Choose two.)
- A. HTTP
- B. TCP
- C. TELNET
- D. UDP

21. Your Vancouver users cannot connect to a corporate web server housed in Seattle, but they can connect to Internet web sites. The network technicians in Seattle insist the web server is running because Seattle users have no problem connecting to the Seattle web server. From the Vancouver network, you ping the Seattle web server but do not get a reply. Which tool should you use next?
- A. TRACERT
- B. IPCONFIG
- C. TELNET
- D. HTTP

22. A workstation has an IP address of 169.254.46.86. The server administrators realize the DHCP service is offline, so they start the DHCP service. What command should be used next on the workstation to immediately obtain a valid TCP/IP configuration?
   A. PING -T
   B. TRACERT
   C. NETSTAT -A
   D. IPCONFIG /RENEW

23. Which of the following is a security best practice for configuring an Ethernet switch?
   A. Disable unused ports and assign MAC addresses to enabled ports.
   B. Disable unused ports and configure enabled ports for half-duplex.
   C. Disable unused ports and configure additional VLANs.
   D. Disable unused ports and configure enabled ports for full-duplex.

24. Which network device has the ability to filter network traffic based on layer 3 and layer 4 addresses?
   A. Hub
   B. Switch
   C. Router
   D. Bridge

25. Due to past network failures, you would like an alternative method (besides the Internet) to remotely connect to your business network. Which of the following devices is a valid option?
   A. DSL modem
   B. Cable modem
   C. Modem
   D. Switch

26. Which of the following is not a valid IP address that you could assign to a workstation?
   A. 1.67.255.5
   B. 192.166.43.254
   C. 1.0.0.1
   D. 127.0.0.1

27. The process by which IP addresses are resolved to network card hardware addresses is called what?
   A. Proxy
   B. DNS
   C. WINS
   D. ARP

QUICK ANSWER KEY

1. D		**10.** B		**19.** B, D	
2. A		**11.** C, D		**20.** B, D	
3. B		**12.** C		**21.** A	
4. D		**13.** C		**22.** D	
5. B, C, D		**14.** C		**23.** A	
6. A		**15.** C		**24.** C	
7. C		**16.** D		**25.** C	
8. D		**17.** B		**26.** D	
9. C, D		**18.** D		**27.** D	

IN-DEPTH ANSWERS

1. You are asked to ensure that Ethernet switches allow computers with specific physical network cards to connect to the wired network. What type of network address will the switches examine?

   A. SSID

   B. IP address

   C. NetBIOS computer name

   D. MAC address

   ☑ **D.** MAC addresses are specific to a physical network card.

   ☒ **A, B, and C** are incorrect. A is incorrect because an SSID identifies a wireless network. B is incorrect because an IP address is not tied to a specific physical network card. C is incorrect because NetBIOS computer names are 15-byte computer names that are not tied to a physical network card.

2. What can be done on a network switch to secure the network?

   A. Disable unused ports.

   B. Use SCP instead of TELNET for administration.

   C. Enable RC4 encryption.

   D. Configure each port for half-duplex.

   ☑ **A.** Disabling unused switch ports reduces the possibility of somebody plugging a computer into an empty wall jack and gaining access to the network.

   ☒ **B, C, and D** are incorrect. B is incorrect because SCP is not used to administer switches. C is incorrect because even though RC4 is an encryption algorithm, it is not enabled on switches. D is incorrect because a half-duplex port has to do with network speed, not security.

3. As a security consultant, you have been asked to recommend a secure cabling solution for a military installation. Which cable type is considered the most secure?

   A. STP (shielded twisted pair)

   B. Multimode fiber

C. Coaxial

D. UTP (unshielded twisted pair)

> ☑ **B.** Fiber optic cabling is the most secure cable type because it is much more difficult to "tap into" light waves (the data stream) than it is to tap into standard copper wires carrying electronic pulses.
>
> ☒ **A, C,** and **D** are incorrect. These are all incorrect because they are copper wire-based cables.

4. After performing a routine network scan, you notice that a vast majority of Windows 7 desktop computers show TCP port 25 as being in a "listening" state. What should you do next?

A. Nothing—Windows 7 requires port 25 for workgroup computing.

B. Turn off all computers immediately—they are infected.

C. Uninstall the web service from each affected desktop.

D. Uninstall the mail service from each affected desktop.

> ☑ **D.** TCP port 25 is reserved for the SMTP mail service.
>
> ☒ **A, B,** and **C** are incorrect. **A** is incorrect because workgroup computing with file and printer sharing does not use port 25. **B** is incorrect because a service running at port 25 does not necessarily mean that the machine is infected. **C** is incorrect because web servers normally use ports 80 and, if using encryption, 443.

5. Which of the following are TCP/IP mail protocols? (Choose three.)

A. SNMP

B. SMTP

C. IMAP

D. POP

E. Windows Mail

> ☑ **B, C,** and **D.** SMTP is used for outbound mail transfer. IMAP is a mail retrieval protocol as is POP, but POP is much more popular.
>
> ☒ **A** and **E** are incorrect. **A** is incorrect because SNMP is a network management protocol. **E** is incorrect because Windows Mail is not a TCP/IP protocol, although it is an application in Windows Vista.

6. Using a protocol analyzer, your colleague Maria notices a small amount of ICMP network traffic. VoIP has recently been implemented on the network. She is concerned that this traffic implies a network attack is under way. What should you tell her?

A. Utilities such as PING and TRACERT use ICMP.

B. This is not normal—immediately notify the network administrator.

C. This is VoIP traffic.

D. Utilities such as SNMP use ICMP.

> ☑ **A.** ICMP is a network congestion and reporting protocol that utilities such as PING and TRACERT use as their transport.
>
> ☒ **B, C,** and **D** are incorrect. **B** is incorrect because small amounts of ICMP network traffic should be expected on most networks. **C** is incorrect because VoIP hardware and software do not use ICMP. **D** is incorrect because SNMP uses UDP as a transport, not ICMP.

7. You are the network administrator for a small clothing company. The majority of business revenues are derived from clothing sales from the company's web site. Recently the web server has crashed more than once and the business owners have expressed concern about lost sales due to server failures. A second web server has already been purchased. You are asked what else is needed to ensure customers can make online purchases even if one web server is busy or has crashed. Which of the following is the best economic solution?

A. Purchase a second router and Internet connection, and configure the second server to use only the second Internet connection.

B. Configure both web servers to use NetBIOS computer names.

C. Configure a network load balancer to distribute traffic to an available web server.

D. Enable NAT on the router.

> ☑ **C.** A load balancer distributes network traffic to multiple available hosts.
>
> ☒ **A, B,** and **D** are incorrect. **A** is incorrect because in addition to the second purchased web server, purchasing a second router and Internet connection is not economical. **B** is incorrect because servers should never use the same NetBIOS computer names. **D** is incorrect because NAT allows a single public IP address to be shared by multiple internal hosts.

8. Which network tool would a malicious user benefit from as a result of initiating a MAC flooding attack on a network switch?

A. Crimper

B. Port scanner

C. PING

D. Packet sniffer

☑ **D.** MAC flood attacks send enough frames with different source MAC addresses to a switch to exhaust its MAC table memory, thus forcing some switches to flood all frames to all ports (much like a hub would), which means a packet sniffer would be able to capture all network traffic on that switch.

☒ **A, B,** and **C** are incorrect. **A** is incorrect because a crimper is used to join RJ-45 connectors to UTP or STP cables. **B** is incorrect because port scanners do not need to see all network traffic to function. **C** is incorrect because PING does not rely on seeing all network traffic.

---

9. Your wiring closet consists of three 24-port Ethernet switches all linked together. Computers from the Accounting department are plugged into each Ethernet switch, as are computers from the Research department. Your manager asks you to ensure computers in the Accounting department are on a different network than computers in the Research department. What could you do? (Choose two.)

A. Replace the Ethernet switches with Ethernet hubs.

B. Configure all Accounting computers on the same TCP/IP subnet (e.g., 192.268.2.0 /24) and configure all Research computers on their own TCP/IP subnet (e.g., 192.168.3.0 /16).

C. Configure an Accounting VLAN that includes the Accounting computers and a Research VLAN that includes the Research computers.

D. Configure all Accounting computers on the same TCP/IP subnet (e.g., 192.168.2.0 /24) and configure all Research computers on their own TCP/IP subnet (e.g., 192.168.3.0 /24).

☑ **C and D.** Grouping the Accounting and Research computers each into their own VLAN means Accounting and Research computers would be on different networks. If Accounting computers were on the 192.168.2.0 /24 network and Research computers were on the 192.168.3.0 /24 network, the computers would be on the same physical network but on *different* logical networks.

☒ **A and B** are incorrect. **A** is incorrect because Ethernet hubs would not put Accounting and Research computers on different networks. **B** is incorrect because 192.268.2.0/24 is not a valid TCP/IP network.

10. What type of address is fe80::dca6:d048:cba6:bd06?

    A. IPv4

    B. IPv6

    C. MAC

    D. DMZ

> ☑ **B.** IPv6 addresses are hexadecimal (base 16) addresses with each portion separated with a colon. Double colons can be used as shorthand for :0000:.
>
> ☒ **A, C,** and **D** are incorrect. **A** is incorrect because IPv4 addresses are decimal values separated with periods, for example, 145.76.56.87. **C** is incorrect because MAC addresses are much shorter; they are only 48 bits long and might appear as something similar to 00-24-D6-9B-08-8C. **D** is incorrect because DMZ is not a type of address.

11. Which of the following statements regarding DNS are true? (Choose two.)

    A. It resolves NetBIOS computer names to IP addresses.

    B. Client to server queries use TCP port 53.

    C. It resolves FQDNs to IP addresses.

    D. Given an IP address, DNS can return a FQDN.

> ☑ **C** and **D.** DNS is used to resolve FQDNs (fully qualified domain names) such as www.mhprofessional.com to an IP address. The reverse is also true. An IP address such as 22.33.44.55 could be used to return an FQDN (this is called a DNS reverse lookup).
>
> ☒ **A** and **B** are incorrect. **A** is incorrect because WINS servers, not DNS servers, resolve NetBIOS computer names to IP addresses. **B** is incorrect because client requests use UDP port 53.

12. Which protocol uses TCP port 443?

    A. FTPS

    B. HTTP

    C. HTTPS

    D. SSH

> ☑ **C.** HTTPS (Hypertext Transfer Protocol Secure) uses TCP port 443.
>
> ☒ **A, B,** and **D** are incorrect. **A** is incorrect because FTPS uses TCP ports 989 and 990. **B** is incorrect because HTTP uses TCP port 80. **D** is incorrect because SSH uses TCP port 22.

13. You are troubleshooting TCP/IP settings on a workstation. The workstation IP address is 10.17.6.8/24, the DNS server setting is set to 199.126.129.86, and the default gateway setting is set to 10.17.5.6. The router has a public IP address of 199.126.129.76/24 and a private internal IP address of 10.17.5.6/24. This workstation is the only station on the network that cannot connect to the Internet. What should you do?

   A. Change the DNS server setting to 10.17.5.6.

   B. Change the router private internal IP address to 10.17.6.6.

   C. Change the workstation IP address to 10.17.5.8.

   D. Change the default gateway setting to 199.126.129.76.

> ☑ **C.** The workstation IP address is currently on a different subnet from the default gateway. Changing the workstation IP address to 10.17.5.8 would allow communication with the default gateway.
>
> ☒ **A, B,** and **D** are incorrect. **A** is incorrect because the question does not specifically state name resolution as being a problem. **B** is incorrect because this station is the only one experiencing connectivity issues, so there is no reason to modify the router configuration. **D** is incorrect because a workstation's default gateway must be on the same subnet as its IP address.

14. You need a server to store router configuration files. The server must not require a username or password. Which type of server is the best choice?

   A. Windows file server

   B. FTP

   C. TFTP

   D. FTPS

> ☑ **C.** TFTP (Trivial FTP) allows storage of files without requiring a username or password.
>
> ☒ **A, B,** and **D** are incorrect. These all normally require a username and password.

15. Which TCP/IP protocol is designed to synchronize time between computers?

   A. SNMP

   B. Windows time sync

   C. NTP

   D. SMTP

☑ **C.** NTP (Network Time Protocol) synchronizes time between computers over UDP port 123.

☒ **A, B,** and **D** are incorrect. **A** is incorrect because SNMP is a network management protocol using UDP port 161. **B** is incorrect because Windows time sync is not a TCP/IP protocol. **D** is incorrect because SMTP is a mail transfer protocol using TCP port 25.

16. Which TCP/IP protocol gives administrators a remote command prompt to a network service?

A. POP

B. ARP

C. UDP

D. TELNET

☑ **D.** TELNET gives administrators a remote command prompt to a network service.

☒ **A, B,** and **C** are incorrect. **A** is incorrect because POP (Post Office Protocol) is a mail retrieval protocol. **B** is incorrect because ARP (Address Resolution Protocol) resolves IP addresses to MAC addresses. **C** is incorrect because UDP (User Datagram Protocol) is a connectionless TCP/IP transport protocol.

17. While capturing network traffic, you notice some packets destined for UDP port 69. What type of network traffic is this?

A. FTP

B. TFTP

C. SNMP

D. IMAP

☑ **B.** TFTP (Trivial File Transfer Protocol) uses UDP port 69.

☒ **A, C,** and **D** are incorrect. **A** is incorrect because FTP uses TCP ports 20 and 21. **C** is incorrect because SNMP uses UDP port 161. **D** is incorrect because IMAP uses TCP port 143.

18. Which TCP/IP protocols use encryption to secure data transmissions?

A. SCP, DNS, SSH

B. SSH, SCP, TELNET

C. HTTPS, FTP, SSH

D. SSH, SCP, FTPS

> ☑ **D.** SSH (Secure Shell), SCP (Secure Copy) and FTPS (File Transfer Protocol Secure) encrypt data transmissions.
>
> ☒ **A, B,** and **C** are incorrect. **A** is incorrect because DNS (Domain Name Service) does not encrypt data. **B** is incorrect because TELNET does not encrypt data. **C** is incorrect because FTP does not encrypt data.

19. Which of the following network connectivity devices function primarily using computer MAC addresses? (Choose two.)

A. Router

B. Bridge

C. Hub

D. Switch

> ☑ **B** and **D.** Bridges and switches optimize network usage by remembering which network segments MAC addresses (network cards) are connected to.
>
> ☒ **A** and **C** are incorrect. **A** is incorrect because a router is primarily concerned with software network addresses, such as IP addresses. **C** is incorrect because hubs do not look at any type of address within a transmission.

20. Which of the following are considered TCP/IP transport protocols? (Choose two.)

A. HTTP

B. TCP

C. TELNET

D. UDP

> ☑ **B** and **D.** TCP (Transmission Control Protocol) and UDP (User Datagram Protocol) are both considered to be transport protocols. TCP is a connection-oriented (a session is established before transmitting data) and acknowledged transport (each transmission gets an acknowledgment packet), whereas UDP is connectionless and unacknowledged. Because of reduced overhead, UDP is faster.
>
> ☒ **A** and **C** are incorrect. They are both application protocols, not transport protocols.

21. Your Vancouver users cannot connect to a corporate web server housed in Seattle, but they can connect to Internet web sites. The network technicians in Seattle insist the web server is running because Seattle users have no problem connecting to the Seattle web server. From the Vancouver network, you ping the Seattle web server but do not get a reply. Which tool should you use next?

A. TRACERT

B. IPCONFIG

C. TELNET

D. HTTP

☑ **A.** TRACERT (Trace Route) to the Seattle web server will send a reply from each router along the path so that you can identify where the transmission is failing.

☒ **B, C,** and **D** are incorrect. **B** is incorrect because users can connect to other Internet web sites. **C** is incorrect because TELNET does not identify network transmission problems. **D** is incorrect because HTTP is the application protocol used between web browsers and web servers.

22. A workstation has an IP address of 169.254.46.86. The server administrators realize the DHCP service is offline, so they start the DHCP service. What command should be used next on the workstation to immediately obtain a valid TCP/IP configuration?

A. PING -T

B. TRACERT

C. NETSTAT -A

D. IPCONFIG /RENEW

☑ **D.** IPCONFIG should be used with the /RENEW parameter to get an IP address from the DHCP server.

☒ **A, B,** and **C** are incorrect. **A** is incorrect because PING only checks whether a host is online or not. **B** is incorrect because TRACERT is used to verify the path a packet takes to a destination by sending replies from each router along the path. **C** is incorrect because NETSTAT displays network statistics for the local computer.

23. Which of the following is a security best practice for configuring an Ethernet switch?

   A. Disable unused ports and assign MAC addresses to enabled ports.

   B. Disable unused ports and configure enabled ports for half-duplex.

   C. Disable unused ports and configure additional VLANs.

   D. Disable unused ports and configure enabled ports for full-duplex.

> ☑ **A.** Disabling unused switch ports prevents unwanted network connections. Assigning specific MAC addresses to specific switch ports allows you to control which stations can connect to which switch ports.
>
> ☒ **B, C,** and **D** are incorrect. **B** is incorrect because half-duplex network speed is not considered a security best practice. **C** is incorrect because additional VLANs are not always applicable to all networks. **D** is incorrect because full-duplex network speed is not considered a security best practice.

24. Which network device has the ability to filter network traffic based on layer 3 and layer 4 addresses?

   A. Hub

   B. Switch

   C. Router

   D. Bridge

> ☑ **C.** A router has the ability to allow or reject network traffic based on values such as IP addresses, protocol numbers, or port numbers.
>
> ☒ **A, B,** and **D** are incorrect. **A** is incorrect because a hub does not examine anything in a packet. **B** is incorrect because most switches (Layer 2 switches) examine MAC addresses and not port numbers. **D** is incorrect because bridges only examine MAC addresses within a packet.

25. Due to past network failures, you would like an alternative method (besides the Internet) to remotely connect to your business network. Which of the following devices is a valid option?

   A. DSL modem

   B. Cable modem

   C. Modem

   D. Switch

☑ **C.** A modem allows remote connectivity to networks over the PSTN (public switched telephone network). Modems convert digital computer signals to analog signals so that the transmission can travel over analog telephone lines. The reverse occurs using a modem on the receiving end of the transmission.

☒ **A, B,** and **D** are incorrect. **A** and **B** are incorrect because both DSL and cable modems connect to the Internet. **D** is incorrect because a switch only connects devices on a LAN.

26. Which of the following is not a valid IP address that you could assign to a workstation?

A. 1.67.255.5

B. 192.166.43.254

C. 1.0.0.1

D. 127.0.0.1

☑ **D.** 127.0.0.1 is reserved for local loopback testing (to test your own TCP/IP stack), so you cannot use this as a workstation IP address.

☒ **A, B,** and **C** are incorrect. These are all valid IP addresses.

27. The process by which IP addresses are resolved to network card hardware addresses is called what?

A. Proxy

B. DNS

C. WINS

D. ARP

☑ **D.** ARP (Address Resolution Protocol) is a TCP/IP protocol where, given an IP address, the corresponding MAC address can be learned via broadcast.

☒ **A, B,** and **C** are incorrect. **A** is incorrect because proxy servers retrieve Internet content on behalf of an internal computer. **B** is incorrect because DNS resolves FQDNs to IP addresses. **C** is incorrect because WINS resolves NetBIOS computer names to IP addresses.

$$\frac{14}{27} \quad 55\%$$

1) D   22) D

2) A   23) C   A   Disable unused ports.
                                          assign MAC Address
                                          to enabled por

3) B   24) C

4) C, D   unneeded mail server 25) A   C   modem / dial up

5) B, C, D   26) C D   127.0.0.1 loopback ilon
                                       IP address not use

6) A   27) A D

7) C   ARP

8) B D   Packet sniffer

9) B, C

10) B

11) D, C ?

12) C

13) C

14) B C   TFTP

15) D C   NTP

16) C D   Telnet

17) B

18) C D   SSH, SCP, FTPS

19) C, D, B   UDP, TCP Switch, Bridge

20) A, B, D   UDP, TCP

21) A

2

Introduction to Security Terminology

CERTIFICATION OBJECTIVES

❑   **2.8**   Exemplify the concepts of confidentiality, integrity, and availability (CIA)

❑   **5.2**   Explain the fundamental concepts and best practices related to authentication, authorization, and access control

QUESTIONS

Information Security strives to prevent, detect, and properly respond to security breaches. CIA (Confidentiality, Integrity, and Availability) is defined as keeping the correct data safe and available for those parties that should have access to it. Identification could be your user logon name or the photo on an employee ID card. Authentication involves proving that a person or entity is who or what he says he is. This can be done with knowledge of an access code or password, possession of an access card or certificate, or a more physical trait such as a fingerprint. Knowing when these security principles are applicable is key, not only for the Security+ exam, but equally important in your day-to-day activities as an IT security professional.

1. You are the network administrator for a pharmaceutical firm. Last month, the company hired a third party to conduct a security audit. From the audit findings, you learn that customer's confidential medical data is not properly secured. Which security concept has been ignored?
   A. Due diligence
   B. Due care
   C. Due process
   D. Separation of duties

2. The security administrator for an office has controlled access to a file in order to limit unauthorized modifications to the file. Which goal of information security is being reached?
   A. Confidentiality
   B. Integrity
   C. Availability
   D. Accountability

3. Which of the following is the best example of the Custodian security role?
   A. Human Resources department employee
   B. Server Backup Operator
   C. CEO
   D. Law enforcement employee responsible for signing out evidence
   E. Cook in the cafeteria

4. In keeping up with the latest computer security threats, you find a web site offering a tool that can give a malicious user full administrative rights to a remote Windows computer. How would you classify this tool?
   A. Boot sector virus
   B. Vulnerability
   C. Denial of service
   D. Exploit

5. Franco, an accountant, accesses a shared network folder containing travel expense documents to which he has read and write access. What is this an example of?

    A. Privilege escalation

    B. Due care

    C. Authorization

    D. Authentication

6. Which security role is responsible for establishing access to data and enforcing related policies, laws, or regulations?

    A. Custodian

    B. Data Owner

    C. Data User

    D. Database Administrator

7. Using the Windows EFS (Encrypting File System) feature to encrypt payroll files on a file server is an example of what?

    A. Integrity

    B. Availability

    C. Confidentiality

    D. Legality

8. Alfonse supplies his e-mail address and password when logging on to his computer each morning. What is his e-mail address an example of?

    A. Authentication

    B. Biometrics

    C. Identification

    D. Authorization

9. You decide to install two e-mail servers in a cluster so that e-mail service will still function if one of the servers fails. What principle does this apply to?

    A. Least privilege

    B. Confidentiality

    C. Availability

    D. Job rotation

10. A computer room at a secure facility is shielded. What principles does this apply to? (Choose three.)

    A. Confidentiality

    B. Integrity

    C. Availability

    D. Vulnerability

11. A large corporation requires new employees to present their driver's license and passport to a security officer before receiving a company-issued laptop. Which security principle does presenting their ID this map to?

   A. Authorization

   B. Confidentiality

   C. Identification

   D. Custodian

12. What security principle requires a user to prove she really is who she says she is before allowing access to data?

   A. Availability

   B. Vulnerability

   C. Auditing

   D. Authentication

13. Which of the following is the best example of Authentication?

   A. Each morning a network administrator visits various web sites looking for the newest Windows Server vulnerabilities.

   B. Before two systems communicate with one another across a network, they exchange PKI certificates to ensure they share a common ancestor.

   C. A file server has two power supplies in case one fails.

   D. An application has some unintended behavior that could allow a malicious user to write to the Windows registry.

14. Which of the following is the best example of confidentiality?

   A. You ensure your virus scanner has an up-to-date virus signature database.

   B. You add more RAM to your computer so that less data will potentially end up in Windows swap file.

   C. You enable the Windows firewall.

   D. You encrypt D:\Projects using Windows Encrypting File System.

15. As the network administrator, you occasionally use a protocol analyzer to view network traffic on the corporate network. In doing so, you are surprised that you can see the contents of most network transmissions. Which security principle does this fact violate?

   A. Authentication

   B. Nonrepudiation

   C. Availability

   D. Confidentiality

16. Trinity is the new network administrator for a legal firm. She studies the existing file server folder structures and permissions and quickly realizes the previous administrator did not properly secure legal documents in these folders. She sets the appropriate file and folder permissions to ensure only the appropriate users can access the data, based on corporate policy. What security role has Trinity undertaken?

    A. Custodian

    B. Data Owner

    C. User

    D. Power User

17. A doctor heading a small rural medical clinic asks his receptionist to install a wireless router for their small network. The receptionist purchases and installs the wireless router with default settings. Their network consists of three Windows 7 workstations, one of which runs a medical application that links to an urban server using a modem to retrieve patient medical records. A few weeks later, after a security audit, the doctor is forced to remove the wireless router to prevent the possibility of lawsuits. Which of the following best describes this violation of information security?

    A. Malpractice

    B. Due diligence

    C. Due care

    D. Due process

18. Which of the following best applies to data availability?

    A. Ensuring wireless users know the wireless encryption code to access the wireless network

    B. Distributing USB flash drives to employees so that they can take work documents home

    C. Replacing your existing 100 Mbps Ethernet switches with 1000 Mbps Ethernet switches

    D. Configuring the two server hard disks with a RAID 1 disk mirror

19. While determining how to best ensure web servers are secure from Internet attacks, you explore the possibility of a web server cluster. To which of the following does this apply?

    A. Due process

    B. Due care

    C. Due diligence

    D. Vulnerability

20. You have the misfortune of experiencing a worm virus on your corporate network. Being the network administrator, you follow corporate procedure and unplug your network from the router to ensure the problem does not spread beyond your infected network. Which security principle have you adhered to?

    A. Due care

    B. Due diligence

    C. Due process

    D. Vulnerability

21. Your company stores human resources backup tapes in a locked drawer in a filing cabinet in a secured area of the building. A disgruntled IT employee manages to gain access to the backup tapes. This employee takes the tapes home and restores the data to her hard disk. She also modifies one document and copies it back to tape. That night she carefully returns the backup tapes to their original location. Which of the following security goals have been violated? (Choose two.)

   A. Break and enter

   B. Integrity

   C. Confidentiality

   D. Exploit

22. From the following list, which best describes authentication?

   A. Logging in to a TFTP server with a username and password

   B. Using a username, password, and token card to connect to the corporate VPN

   C. Checking corporate webmail on a secured web site at http://owa.acme.com after supplying credentials

   D. Copying files from a server to a USB flash drive

23. The senior security officer for your company wishes to implement accountability on the server. Which of the following should you implement to achieve this goal?

   A. Encryption

   B. RAID

   C. Auditing

   D. Permissions

24. What methods could be used to implement confidentiality?

   A. RAID

   B. Encryption

   C. Backups

   D. Auditing

25. Which of the following tasks can help with availability?

   A. Auditing

   B. Authentication

   C. Backups

   D. Encryption

QUICK ANSWER KEY

1.	B	10.	A, B, C	19.	C
2.	B	11.	C	20.	A
3.	B	12.	D	21.	B, C
4.	D	13.	B	22.	B
5.	C	14.	D	23.	C
6.	B	15.	D	24.	B
7.	C	16.	A	25.	C
8.	C	17.	C		
9.	C	18.	D		

IN-DEPTH ANSWERS

1. You are the network administrator for a pharmaceutical firm. Last month, the company hired a third party to conduct a security audit. From the audit findings, you learn that customer's confidential medical data is not properly secured. Which security concept has been ignored?

A. Due diligence

B. Due care

C. Due process

D. Separation of duties

☑ **B. Due care** means taking steps to address a security problem, such as ensuring client data is kept confidential.

☒ **A, C,** and **D** are incorrect. **A** is incorrect because due diligence is the act of understanding security risks. **C** is incorrect because due process are actions taken as a result of a violation of a due care policy. **D** is incorrect because separation of duties addresses internal issues resulting from one person having too much control of a business process.

2. The security administrator for an office has controlled access to a file in order to limit unauthorized modifications to the file. Which goal of information security is being reached?

A. Confidentiality

B. Integrity

C. Availability

D. Accountability

☑ **B. Integrity** ensures that data is not tampered with or modified inappropriately.

☒ **A, C,** and **D** are incorrect. **A** is incorrect because confidentiality prevents unauthorized access to data even before modifications can be made. **C** does not apply because the question refers to file modifications, not whether or not the file is always available. **D** is incorrect because accountability makes people responsible for their actions such as through authentication or auditing.

3. Which of the following is the best example of the Custodian security role?

A. Human Resources department employee

B. Server Backup Operator

C. CEO

D. Law enforcement employee responsible for signing out evidence

E. Cook in the cafeteria

> ☑ **B.** Custodians are responsible for maintaining access to and integrity of data.
>
> ☒ **A, C, D,** and **E** are incorrect. All are incorrect because taking care of access to and integrity of data is not the direct responsibility of CEOs, cooks, HR staff, or law enforcement staff.

4. In keeping up with the latest computer security threats, you find a web site offering a tool that can give a malicious user full administrative rights to a remote Windows computer. How would you classify this tool?

A. Boot sector virus

B. Vulnerability

C. Denial of service

D. Exploit

> ☑ **D.** An exploit takes advantage of a vulnerability. In this example the vulnerability grants the malicious tool administrative access.
>
> ☒ **A, B,** and **C** are incorrect. **A** is incorrect because a boot sector virus infects the boot sector of a hard disk. **B** is incorrect because the question asks specifically about a tool that takes advantage of a vulnerability. **C** is incorrect because a denial of service attack renders a system unusable.

5. Franco, an accountant, accesses a shared network folder containing travel expense documents to which he has read and write access. What is this an example of?

A. Privilege escalation

B. Due care

C. Authorization

D. Authentication

> ☑ **C.** Franco is accessing an item that he has legitimate access to—this is authorization.
>
> ☒ **A, B,** and **D** are incorrect. **A** is incorrect because Franco is not increasing his rights to the shared network folder. **B** is incorrect because due care means acting on known security issues. **D** is incorrect because authentication means proving you are who you say you are.

6. Which security role is responsible for establishing access to data and enforcing related policies, laws, or regulations?

   A. Custodian

   B. Data Owner

   C. Data User

   D. Database Administrator

   ☑ **B.** The Data Owner establishes and to a degree enforces security access to data.

   ☒ **A, C,** and **D** are incorrect. **A** is incorrect because the Custodian maintains, not establishes, integrity of the data. **C** is incorrect; the Data User simply uses (reads and perhaps writes) the data. **D** is incorrect because the Database Administrator is not a formal security role.

7. Using the Windows EFS (Encrypting File System) feature to encrypt payroll files on a file server is an example of what?

   A. Integrity

   B. Availability

   C. Confidentiality

   D. Legality

   ☑ **C.** Confidentiality involves ensuring data is only readable by authorized persons; folder encryption with EFS does just that.

   ☒ **A, B,** and **D** are incorrect. **A** is incorrect because integrity involves making sure data is correct. **B** is incorrect because availability involves making sure data is always available to the appropriate parties when they need it (for example, backups or redundant hard disks). **D** is incorrect because encrypting folders is not legally required for all companies.

8. Alfonse supplies his e-mail address and password when logging on to his computer each morning. What is his e-mail address an example of?

   A. Authentication

   B. Biometrics

   C. Identification

   D. Authorization

☑ **C.** Identification means somehow stating who (or what) you are; in this case, an e-mail address.

☒ **A, B,** and **D** are incorrect. **A** is incorrect because authentication would occur after identification and often requires additional information, in this case, a password. **B** is incorrect because e-mail addresses and passwords are not physical characteristics. **D** is incorrect because authorization occurs after authentication, which occurs after identification.

9. You decide to install two e-mail servers in a cluster so that e-mail service will still function if one of the servers fails. What principle does this apply to?

   A. Least privilege

   B. Confidentiality

   C. Availability

   D. Job rotation

☑ **C.** Availability. Data is useless if the people that need it cannot get to it.

☒ **A, B,** and **D** are incorrect. **A** is incorrect because least privilege refers to only giving people the rights they need to perform a role and nothing more. **B** does not apply because confidentiality keeps data private. **D** is incorrect because job rotation entails personnel changing job roles at certain times.

10. A computer room at a secure facility is shielded. What principles does this apply to? (Choose three.)

   A. Confidentiality

   B. Integrity

   C. Availability

   D. Vulnerability

☑ **A, B,** and **C.** Confidentiality requires that data be kept private. Integrity assures data is correct and has not been tampered with. Availability ensures data is accessible and is not lost. A shielded computer room prevents outsiders from gaining access to data in the computer room, thus assuring data is private, not tampered with, and available to those who need it.

☒ **D** is incorrect. A shielded computer room is not a vulnerability.

11. A large corporation requires new employees to present their driver's license and passport to a security officer before receiving a company-issued laptop. Which security principle does presenting their ID this map to?

    A. Authorization

    B. Confidentiality

    C. Identification

    D. Custodian

    ☑ **C.** Providing a driver's license and passport means you are providing identification.

    ☒ **A, B,** and **D** are incorrect. **A** is incorrect because we are not exercising our right to access corporate data. **B** is incorrect because we are not preventing unauthorized access to private data. **D** is incorrect because we are not protecting and maintaining data.

12. What security principle requires a user to prove she really is who she says she is before allowing access to data?

    A. Availability

    B. Vulnerability

    C. Auditing

    D. Authentication

    ☑ **D.** Authentication requires users to prove who they are before allowing access to resources.

    ☒ **A, B,** and **C** are incorrect. **A** does not apply to proving who you are, it applies to always having access to data. **B** refers to a weakness of some kind. **C,** auditing, refers to logging activity.

13. Which of the following is the best example of Authentication?

    A. Each morning a network administrator visits various web sites looking for the newest Windows Server vulnerabilities.

    B. Before two systems communicate with one another across a network, they exchange PKI certificates to ensure they share a common ancestor.

    C. A file server has two power supplies in case one fails.

    D. An application has some unintended behavior that could allow a malicious user to write to the Windows registry.

☑ **B.** Exchanging PKI certificates before allowing communication is an example of system authentication.

☒ **A, C,** and **D** are incorrect. **A** is incorrect because it describes due diligence. **C** is incorrect because it describes availability. **D** is incorrect because it describes a vulnerability.

14. Which of the following is the best example of confidentiality?

A. You ensure your virus scanner has an up-to-date virus signature database.

B. You add more RAM to your computer so that less data will potentially end up in Windows swap file.

C. You enable the Windows firewall.

D. You encrypt D:\Projects using Windows Encrypting File System.

☑ **D.** Encrypting data prevents unauthorized access to that data.

☒ **A, B,** and **C** are incorrect. **A** is incorrect because an up-to-date virus scanner does not directly imply confidentiality. **B** is incorrect because, although potentially preventing data from ending up in the swap file might serve to limit who can access certain data, encrypting is a much better example of confidentiality. **C** is incorrect because enabling a firewall, compared to encryption, is not the best example of confidentiality.

15. As the network administrator, you occasionally use a protocol analyzer to view network traffic on the corporate network. In doing so, you are surprised that you can see the contents of most network transmissions. Which security principle does this fact violate?

A. Authentication

B. Nonrepudiation

C. Availability

D. Confidentiality

☑ **D.** Confidentiality is violated because most network traffic is being transmitted in clear text. Network encryption of some kind should be used to secure the traffic.

☒ **A, B,** and **C** are incorrect. **A** does not apply, since we aren't violating authentication in any way. **B** is incorrect because nonrepudiation means a user or system cannot refute the validity of a transaction. **C** is not applicable, since clear text network transmissions do not directly relate to data availability.

16. Trinity is the new network administrator for a legal firm. She studies the existing file server folder structures and permissions and quickly realizes the previous administrator did not properly secure legal documents in these folders. She sets the appropriate file and folder permissions to ensure only the appropriate users can access the data, based on corporate policy. What security role has Trinity undertaken?

    A. Custodian

    B. Data Owner

    C. User

    D. Power User

    ☑ **A.** The Custodian performs data protection and maintenance duties based on established security policies, which Trinity is doing in this case.

    ☒ **B, C,** and **D** are incorrect. **B** is incorrect because she is not the Data Owner; the legal firm is. **C** does not apply because she is not a User accessing the data to perform her job duties. **D** is incorrect; Power User is not recognized as a standard security role in the industry.

17. A doctor heading a small rural medical clinic asks his receptionist to install a wireless router for their small network. The receptionist purchases and installs the wireless router with default settings. Their network consists of three Windows 7 workstations, one of which runs a medical application that links to an urban server using a modem to retrieve patient medical records. A few weeks later, after a security audit, the doctor is forced to remove the wireless router to prevent the possibility of lawsuits. Which of the following best describes this violation of information security?

    A. Malpractice

    B. Due diligence

    C. Due care

    D. Due process

    ☑ **C.** Due care involves protecting confidential data; the opposite occurred in this example.

    ☒ **A, B,** and **D** are incorrect. **A** is incorrect because malpractice is not a violation of information security. **B** is incorrect because, although due diligence applies in the sense of researching and being aware of the risk, actively exposing sensitive data is a violation of due care. **D** is incorrect because due process does not apply to violating security policies and best practices. Due process implements appropriate consequences for failure to comply with policies.

18. Which of the following best applies to data availability?

   A. Ensuring wireless users know the wireless encryption code to access the wireless network

   B. Distributing USB flash drives to employees so that they can take work documents home

   C. Replacing your existing 100 Mbps Ethernet switches with 1000 Mbps Ethernet switches

   D. Configuring the two server hard disks with a RAID 1 disk mirror

> ☑ **D.** A RAID 1 disk mirror duplicates all disk writes to the second disk. If one disk fails, data is still available on the other disk, thus ensuring high availability.
>
> ☒ **A, B**, and **C** are incorrect. **A** is incorrect because the ability to connect to a wireless network is important to get to data, but does not offer better data availability than RAID 1. **B** is incorrect because, unless the USB flash drives are encrypted, data confidentially is being violated. **C** might allow quicker access to data, but it does not guarantee a higher level of data availability.

19. While determining how to best ensure web servers are secure from Internet attacks, you explore the possibility of a web server cluster. To which of the following does this apply?

   A. Due process

   B. Due care

   C. Due diligence

   D. Vulnerability

> ☑ **C.** Researching and performing risk assessment are both due diligence actions.
>
> ☒ **A, B**, and **D** are incorrect. **A** and **B** do not apply because due process and due care have nothing to do with evaluating options and performing a risk assessment. **D** simply refers to a weakness and not to mitigating that weakness.

20. You have the misfortune of experiencing a worm virus on your corporate network. Being the network administrator, you follow corporate procedure and unplug your network from the router to ensure the problem does not spread beyond your infected network. Which security principle have you adhered to?

   A. Due care

   B. Due diligence

   C. Due process

   D. Vulnerability

☑ **A.** Following documented security policies means you have performed due care.

☒ **B, C**, and **D** are incorrect. **B** is incorrect because due diligence does not apply to acting on existing procedures. **C** is incorrect because due process involves consequences of failing to adhere to documented security policies. **D** is not a security principle; it is a weakness.

21. Your company stores human resources backup tapes in a locked drawer in a filing cabinet in a secured area of the building. A disgruntled IT employee manages to gain access to the backup tapes. This employee takes the tapes home and restores the data to her hard disk. She also modifies one document and copies it back to tape. That night she carefully returns the backup tapes to their original location. Which of the following security goals have been violated? (Choose two.)

    A. Break and enter

    B. Integrity

    C. Confidentiality

    D. Exploit

☑ **B** and **C**. Because data has been tampered with, integrity has been violated. Confidentiality has not been adhered to, since an unauthorized employee had access to sensitive data.

☒ **A** and **D** are incorrect. **A** may violate the law, but it is not a security goal. **D** is not applicable because an exploit takes advantage of a vulnerability.

22. From the following list, which best describes authentication?

    A. Logging in to a TFTP server with a username and password

    B. Using a username, password, and token card to connect to the corporate VPN

    C. Checking corporate webmail on a secured web site at http://owa.acme.com after supplying credentials

    D. Copying files from a server to a USB flash drive

☑ **B.** Proving who you are with something you know (username, password) and something you have (token card) is authentication.

☒ **A, C**, and **D** are incorrect. **A** is incorrect because TFTP servers cannot authenticate users. **C** is incorrect because secure web sites use HTTPS, not HTTP. **D** is incorrect because copying files would be an example of authorization, not authentication.

23. The senior security officer for your company wishes to implement accountability on the server. Which of the following should you implement to achieve this goal?

A. Encryption

B. RAID

C. Auditing

D. Permissions

☑ **C.** Auditing tracks usage and makes users accountable for their actions.

☒ **A, B,** and **D** are incorrect. **A** is incorrect because encryption implements confidentiality. **B** is incorrect because RAID implements availability. **D** is incorrect because permissions simply allow or deny access to a resource.

24. What methods could be used to implement confidentiality?

A. RAID

B. Encryption

C. Backups

D. Auditing

☑ **B.** Confidentiality restricts who can access private data. Only the appropriate parties can decrypt encrypted data.

☒ **A, C,** and **D** are incorrect. **A** is incorrect because RAID relates to disk performance or availability. **C** does not imply confidentiality. Data backups make that data available should there be a problem with the live data. **D** is incorrect because auditing tracks user actions and makes users accountable for those actions.

25. Which of the following tasks can help with availability?

A. Auditing

B. Authentication

C. Backups

D. Encryption

☑   **C.** If data is deleted, modified or corrupted, it can be retrieved from backup so that the data is made available.

☒   **A, B,** and **D** are incorrect. **A** is incorrect because auditing does not make data available; it logs activity. **B** is incorrect because authentication identifies users or computers so that they can potentially access data, but the data is not made available because of this. **D** does not apply; encrypted data can only be decrypted by the appropriate parties, so the data is kept private.

3

Security Policies
and Standards

CERTIFICATION OBJECTIVES

☐   **2.1**   Explain risk-related concepts

☐   **2.4**   Explain the importance of security-related awareness and training

QUESTIONS

Security policies are a requirement in many businesses to achieve certification compliance with standards bodies, particularly if a business is interested in government contracts. Policies must clearly document how people are expected to behave. These policies could range from proper sensitive document disposal to how complex user passwords must be. Adhering to regulations and standards such as the use of PII (Personally Identifiable Information) is critical—phone numbers, e-mail addresses, and fingerprints are all examples of PII. Without education and awareness, employees may fail to comply with these policies, which could expose a company to legal action or loss of business.

1. Which of the following best describes proper usage of PII? (Choose two.)
   A. Law enforcement tracking an Internet offender using an IP address
   B. Distributing an e-mail contact list to marketing firms
   C. Logging in to a secured laptop using a fingerprint scanner
   D. Due diligence

2. A company security policy states that under no circumstances are jokes to be sent using the company e-mail system. Which type of security policy is this?
   A. Password
   B. Privacy
   C. Acceptable use
   D. Guideline

3. You are asked to configure a VPN appliance. Which item will help determine how the VPN appliance should be configured?
   A. Microsoft HCL
   B. VPN performance baseline
   C. VPN security log
   D. VPN security policy

4. Users are required to change their passwords every 60 days. In addition, their passwords must contain at least two numeric characters and one uppercase letter. Which type of policy would dictate these settings?
   A. Acceptable use
   B. Privacy
   C. VPN
   D. Password

5. Your company restricts firewall administrators from modifying firewall logs. Only IT security personnel are allowed to do this. What is this an example of?
   A. Due care
   B. Separation of duties

    C. Principle of least privilege

    D. Acceptable use

6. You are the network administrator for a legal firm. Users in Vancouver must be able to view trade secrets for patent submission. You share a network folder called "Trade Secrets" and allow the following NTFS permissions:

    Vancouver_Staff—Read, List Folder Contents
    Executives—Write
    IT_Admins—Full Control

Regarding Vancouver employees, which principle is being adhered to?

    A. Job rotation

    B. Least privilege

    C. Mandatory vacations

    D. Separation of duties

7. Your local ISP provides a PDF file stating a 99.97 percent service availability for T1 connectivity to the Internet. How would you classify this type of documentation?

    A. Top Secret

    B. Acceptable use policy

    C. Service level agreement

    D. Availability

8. Your colleague Glen purchases a second-hand router. After powering it on, he realizes the router configuration from the previous owner is still in effect. Which security policy did the previous owner ignore?

    A. Confidentiality

    B. PII

    C. Secure equipment disposal

    D. Privacy

9. The Accounts Payable department notices large out-of-country purchases made using a corporate credit card. After discussing the matter with Juan, the employee whose name is on the credit card, they realize somebody has illegally obtained the credit card details. You also learn that he recently received an e-mail from what appeared to be the credit card company asking him to sign in to their web site to validate his account, which he did. How could this have been avoided?

    A. Provide credit card holders with smart cards.

    B. Tell users to increase the strength of online passwords.

    C. Install a workstation-based firewall.

    D. Provide security awareness training to employees.

10. Which of the following statements are true? (Choose two.)
   A. Security labels are used for data classifications such as Restricted and Top Secret.
   B. PII is applicable only to biometric authentication devices.
   C. Forcing user password changes is considered change management.
   D. A person's signature on a check is considered PII.

11. Which of the following best illustrates potential security problems related to social networking sites?
   A. Other users can easily see your IP address.
   B. Talkative employees can expose a company's intellectual property.
   C. Malicious users can use your pictures for steganography.
   D. Your credit card number is easily stolen.

12. You are the network security auditor assigned to audit a plastic toy manufacturing plant. The manufacturing equipment is on a completely isolated network and is configured by plugging a serial cable from an employee's laptop into the equipment controller. The employee takes her laptop home at night, where she and her two teenage children live. What is the most likely method of infecting this isolated network?
   A. If network cables in the wiring closet are close enough together, data can jump to other cables that might be on the isolated network.
   B. Teenagers using a word processor on the laptop could inadvertently create a macro virus.
   C. A laptop operating system update could render the equipment controller useless.
   D. Her teenagers could download infected MP3s using P2P software.

13. Which of the following is a newly discovered software exploit that has no current remedy?
   A. Vulnerability
   B. Worm
   C. Trojan
   D. Zero-day exploit

14. What do revolving building doors that require a security pass to enter, but nothing to exit, help prevent?
   A. Phishing
   B. Tailgating
   C. Dumpster diving
   D. Shoulder surfing

15. Your company implements a strict password policy where most users cannot remember their own passwords. During mandatory password change every 30 days, users simply use their previous password. How can users be prevented from doing this?

   A. Force password changes more often.

   B. Force password changes less often.

   C. Loosen other restrictions, but disallow using any form of the previous password.

   D. Loosen other restrictions, but disallow using any form of their username.

16. A newly revised security policy states that company data on USB flash drives must be encrypted using the company's file encryption solution. What security concern does this address?

   A. Data handling

   B. Principle of least privilege

   C. Separation of duties

   D. Due diligence

17. You are installing a POS (point of sale) solution at a retail outlet. After testing the POS software, you realize that the software illegally retains all magnetic strip data from customer payment cards. Which of the following applies to this situation? (Choose two.)

   A. The retained data is considered PII.

   B. The POS software does not comply with the law.

   C. The retained data should be encrypted.

   D. POS systems should not connect to the Internet.

18. You are the network administrator for a call center that is downsizing. In the next month, some employees will begin working from home and will use a VPN connection to the corporate network. The CIO (Chief Information Officer) expresses security concerns and asks for any recommendations you might have. What might you say?

   A. The only thing employees need is an Internet connection, their own computer, and a USB headset with a microphone.

   B. Employees should install antivirus software on their home PCs.

   C. Employees should be given corporate computers that have been secured by the IT department to take home.

   D. Employees should be given IP phones to facilitate working from home.

19. As the IT security officer, you establish a security policy requiring that users protect all paper documents so that sensitive client, vendor, or company data is not stolen. What type of policy is this?

   A. Privacy

   B. Acceptable use

    C. Clean desk

    D. Password

20. What is the primary purpose of enforcing a mandatory vacation policy?

    A. To adhere to government regulation

    B. To ensure employees are refreshed

    C. To allow other employees to experience other job roles

    D. To prevent improper activity

21. A departmental manager is implementing a policy whereby employees enhance their skill set by periodically occupying different job roles. What is this called?

    A. Mandatory vacations

    B. Due diligence

    C. Rotation of duties

    D. Least privilege

QUICK ANSWER KEY

1.	A, C	**8.**	C	**15.**	C
2.	C	**9.**	D	**16.**	A
3.	D	**10.**	A, D	**17.**	A, B
4.	D	**11.**	B	**18.**	C
5.	B	**12.**	D	**19.**	C
6.	B	**13.**	D	**20.**	D
7.	C	**14.**	B	**21.**	C

IN-DEPTH ANSWERS

1. Which of the following best describes proper usage of PII? (Choose two.)
   A. Law enforcement tracking an Internet offender using an IP address
   B. Distributing an e-mail contact list to marketing firms
   C. Logging in to a secured laptop using a fingerprint scanner
   D. Due diligence

   ☑ **A and C.** Proper use of PII means not divulging a person or entity's personal information to other parties. Tracking criminals using IP addresses and logging in with a fingerprint scanner are proper uses of PII.

   ☒ **B and D** are incorrect. **B** is incorrect because sending an e-mail contact list to marketing firms violates the privacy of those users in the contact list; it is an improper use of PII. **D** is incorrect because due diligence refers to conducting proper research and procedures and has nothing to do with the proper use of personal information.

2. A company security policy states that under no circumstances are jokes to be sent using the company e-mail system. Which type of security policy is this?
   A. Password
   B. Privacy
   C. Acceptable use
   D. Guideline

   ☑ **C.** Acceptable use policies state what is allowed and what is not, such as jokes being sent.

   ☒ **A, B, and D** are incorrect. **A** is incorrect because password policies are used to control all aspects of passwords such as password length. **B** does not apply because privacy policies are designed to protect personal confidential information. **D** is incorrect because there is no such thing as a guideline policy.

3. You are asked to configure a VPN appliance. Which item will help determine how the VPN appliance should be configured?
   A. Microsoft HCL
   B. VPN performance baseline
   C. VPN security log
   D. VPN security policy

☑ **D.** A VPN security policy will state how VPNs are to be used, and also how they will be configured.

☒ **A, B,** and **C** are incorrect. **A** is incorrect because the Microsoft HCL simply lists what hardware is compatible with a Microsoft operating system. **B** is incorrect because performance baselines are used to gauge abnormal activity. **C** is incorrect because VPN security logs do not directly dictate how VPN appliances should be configured.

4. Users are required to change their passwords every 60 days. In addition, their passwords must contain at least two numeric characters and one uppercase letter. Which type of policy would dictate these settings?

   A. Acceptable use

   B. Privacy

   C. VPN

   D. Password

☑ **D.** Password policies require that passwords meet specific criteria such as password length or complexity.

☒ **A, B,** and **C** are incorrect. **A** is incorrect because acceptable use policies focus primarily on conduct, not on passwords. **B** does not apply because privacy policies protect private information. **C** is incorrect because VPN policies cover the use and possible configuration of VPNs.

5. Your company restricts firewall administrators from modifying firewall logs. Only IT security personnel are allowed to do this. What is this an example of?

   A. Due care

   B. Separation of duties

   C. Principle of least privilege

   D. Acceptable use

☑ **B.** Separation of duties requires more than one person to complete a process such as controlling a firewall and its logs.

☒ **A, C,** and **D** are incorrect. **A** is incorrect because due care means implementing policies to correct security problems. **C** is incorrect because the principle of least privilege requires users to only have the rights they need to do their jobs. Although this does apply in this case, **B** is a much stronger fit. **D** is incorrect because acceptable use refers to proper conduct when using company assets.

6. You are the network administrator for a legal firm. Users in Vancouver must be able to view trade secrets for patent submission. You share a network folder called "Trade Secrets" and allow the following NTFS permissions:

> Vancouver_Staff—Read, List Folder Contents
> Executives—Write
> IT_Admins—Full Control

Regarding Vancouver employees, which principle is being adhered to?

A. Job rotation

B. Least privilege

C. Mandatory vacations

D. Separation of duties

> ☑ **B.** The principle of least privilege states we should only allow people access to do what their job requires, such as Vancouver staff members having only read access to trade secrets.
>
> ☒ **A, C, and D** are incorrect. **A** is incorrect because job rotation refers to periodically having different people occupy job roles for a variety of reasons, such as employee skill enhancement or exposure to a wider range of business processes. **C** is incorrect because mandatory vacations are used to ensure employees are not involved in improper activity. **D** is incorrect because the question specifically asks about one entity, Vancouver employees.

7. Your local ISP provides a PDF file stating a 99.97 percent service availability for T1 connectivity to the Internet. How would you classify this type of documentation?

A. Top Secret

B. Acceptable use policy

C. Service level agreement

D. Availability

> ☑ **C.** SLAs (service level agreements) formally define an expected level of service, such as 99.97 percent availability.
>
> ☒ **A, B, and D** are incorrect. **A** is incorrect because the SLA information is not considered confidential. **B** is incorrect because acceptable use policies are defined for and within an organization, not by external businesses. **D** is incorrect because availability is not a type of documentation.

8. Your colleague Glen purchases a second-hand router. After powering it on, he realizes the router configuration from the previous owner is still in effect. Which security policy did the previous owner ignore?

   A. Confidentiality

   B. PII

   C. Secure equipment disposal

   D. Privacy

> ☑ **C.** Secure equipment disposal policies dictate the proper way to decommission and dispose of computer equipment, such as wiping router configurations.
>
> ☒ **A, B,** and **D** are incorrect. **A** is incorrect because confidentiality is not a type of security policy, although it is a goal of information security. **B** is incorrect because PII applies to people (personally identifiable information), not equipment. **D** is incorrect because privacy policies do not govern the disposal of computer equipment.

9. The Accounts Payable department notices large out-of-country purchases made using a corporate credit card. After discussing the matter with Juan, the employee whose name is on the credit card, they realize somebody has illegally obtained the credit card details. You also learn that he recently received an e-mail from what appeared to be the credit card company asking him to sign in to their web site to validate his account, which he did. How could this have been avoided?

   A. Provide credit card holders with smart cards.

   B. Tell users to increase the strength of online passwords.

   C. Install a workstation-based firewall.

   D. Provide security awareness training to employees.

> ☑ **D.** If Juan had been aware of phishing scams, he would have ignored the e-mail message.
>
> ☒ **A, B,** and **C** are incorrect. **A** is incorrect. Smart cards allow users to authenticate to a resource but would not have prevented this problem. **B** is incorrect because even the strongest password means nothing if the user willingly types it in. **C** is incorrect because, although very important, a workstation-based firewall will not prevent phishing scams.

10. Which of the following statements are true? (Choose two.)

   A. Security labels are used for data classifications such as Restricted and Top Secret.

   B. PII is applicable only to biometric authentication devices.

C. Forcing user password changes is considered change management.

D. A person's signature on a check is considered PII.

☑ **A** and **D**. Restricted and Top Secret are examples of security data labeling. A signature on a check is considered PII, since it is a personal characteristic.

☒ **B** and **C** are incorrect. **B** is incorrect because PII applies also to other personal traits such as speech, handwriting, tattoos, and so on. **C** is incorrect because change management ensures standardized procedures are applied to the entire life cycle of IT configuration changes.

11. Which of the following best illustrates potential security problems related to social networking sites?

A. Other users can easily see your IP address.

B. Talkative employees can expose a company's intellectual property.

C. Malicious users can use your pictures for steganography.

D. Your credit card number is easily stolen.

☑ **B**. People tend to speak more freely on social networking sites than anywhere else. Exposing important company information could pose a problem.

☒ **A, C,** and **D** are incorrect. **A** is incorrect because knowing a computer's IP address has nothing to do with social networking risks. **C** is incorrect because secretly embedding messages in pictures is not a threat tied specifically to social networks. **D** is incorrect because credit card numbers are not normally stolen through social networks.

12. You are the network security auditor assigned to audit a plastic toy manufacturing plant. The manufacturing equipment is on a completely isolated network and is configured by plugging a serial cable from an employee's laptop into the equipment controller. The employee takes her laptop home at night, where she and her two teenage children live. What is the most likely method of infecting this isolated network?

A. If network cables in the wiring closet are close enough together, data can jump to other cables that might be on the isolated network.

B. Teenagers using a word processor on the laptop could inadvertently create a macro virus.

C. A laptop operating system update could render the equipment controller useless.

D. Her teenagers could download infected MP3s using P2P software.

☑ **D.** Files downloaded through P2P (Peer to Peer) file sharing programs are often infected.

☒ **A, B,** and **C** are incorrect. **A** is incorrect because network data cannot "jump" from one cable to the other. **B** is not applicable, since it would be difficult to inadvertently create a macro virus—some intent would have to be there. **C** is incorrect because operating system updates normally correct security problems, not cause them.

13. Which of the following is a newly discovered software exploit that has no current remedy?

A. Vulnerability

B. Worm

C. Trojan

D. Zero-day exploit

☑ **D.** A zero-day exploit means the software vendor and most others are not aware of it, and therefore no remedy exists.

☒ **A, B,** and **C** are incorrect. **A** is incorrect because a vulnerability is a security flaw. An exploit takes advantage of that flaw. **B** is incorrect because computer worms are self-replicating and may be known by the vendor. **C** is incorrect because Trojan viruses mask themselves as being useful when they are in fact malicious. Newly discovered worms or Trojans could initially be zero-day exploits.

14. What do revolving building doors that require a security pass to enter, but nothing to exit, help prevent?

A. Phishing

B. Tailgating

C. Dumpster diving

D. Shoulder surfing

☑ **B.** Following somebody into a restricted area without their knowledge is known as tailgating.

☒ **A, C,** and **D** are incorrect. **A** is incorrect because phishing refers to an attempt acquire sensitive information from a person. **C** is incorrect because dumpster diving refers to sifting through trash to locate sensitive information. **D** is incorrect because shoulder surfing means directly observing somebody, for example, watching while someone enters their bank card PIN.

15. Your company implements a strict password policy where most users cannot remember their own passwords. During mandatory password change every 30 days, users simply use their previous password. How can users be prevented from doing this?

   A. Force password changes more often.

   B. Force password changes less often.

   C. Loosen other restrictions, but disallow using any form of the previous password.

   D. Loosen other restrictions, but disallow using any form of their username.

   ☑ **C.** Disallowing previous passwords and loosening up other restrictions (such as password length) will encourage users to properly adhere to password policies.

   ☒ **A, B,** and **D** are incorrect. **A** and **B** are both incorrect because forcing password changes more or less often will have no effect on users using their previous passwords; they will simply keep doing it more or less often because the password policy is too strict. **D** is incorrect because the scenario did not specify anything about the username being used as the password.

16. A newly revised security policy states that company data on USB flash drives must be encrypted using the company's file encryption solution. What security concern does this address?

   A. Data handling

   B. Principle of least privilege

   C. Separation of duties

   D. Due diligence

   ☑ **A.** Data handling is defined as keeping data secure and legal, such as by encryption.

   ☒ **B, C,** and **D** are incorrect. **B** is incorrect because it is a principle that states users should have only the rights required to do their jobs, nothing more. **C** is incorrect because separation of duties prevents one person from overseeing an entire business process. **D** is incorrect because due diligence refers to researching and risk assessment.

17. You are installing a POS (point of sale) solution at a retail outlet. After testing the POS software, you realize that the software illegally retains all magnetic strip data from customer payment cards. Which of the following applies to this situation? (Choose two.)

   A. The retained data is considered PII.

   B. The POS software does not comply with the law.

   C. The retained data should be encrypted.

   D. POS systems should not connect to the Internet.

> ☑ **A** and **B**. PII refers to any type of personal information, including magnetic strip data from a payment card. POS software should never store all magnetic strip data; therefore, the POS software does not comply with the law.
>
> ☒ **C** and **D** are incorrect. **C** is incorrect because not only should all of the magnetic strip data not be encrypted, it should not be stored at all. **D** does not apply to this situation since Internet connectivity was not mentioned.

18. You are the network administrator for a call center that is downsizing. In the next month, some employees will begin working from home and will use a VPN connection to the corporate network. The CIO (Chief Information Officer) expresses security concerns and asks for any recommendations you might have. What might you say?

   A. The only thing employees need is an Internet connection, their own computer, and a USB headset with a microphone.

   B. Employees should install antivirus software on their home PCs.

   C. Employees should be given corporate computers that have been secured by the IT department to take home.

   D. Employees should be given IP phones to facilitate working from home.

> ☑ **C**. To address security concerns, the best answer is to ensure users are not left to secure their own computers.
>
> ☒ **A**, **B**, and **D** are incorrect. **A** is incorrect because the employee's home computer and its lack of security have not even been addressed. **B** is incorrect because, while antivirus software is very important, it is not the only thing needed to secure a computer, nor should non-IT employees be tasked with installing it. **D** is incorrect because IP telephones will not be enough for call center personnel to connect to a corporate network through a VPN.

19. As the IT security officer, you establish a security policy requiring that users protect all paper documents so that sensitive client, vendor, or company data is not stolen. What type of policy is this?

   A. Privacy

   B. Acceptable use

   C. Clean desk

   D. Password

☑ C. A clean desk policy requires paper documents to be safely stored (and not left on desks) to prevent malicious users from acquiring them.

☒ A, B, and D are incorrect. A is incorrect because privacy policies are designed to protect data personal data. B is incorrect because acceptable use policies govern the proper use of corporate assets. D is incorrect because password policies control all aspects of passwords for authentication, not securing paper documents.

20. What is the primary purpose of enforcing a mandatory vacation policy?

A. To adhere to government regulation

B. To ensure employees are refreshed

C. To allow other employees to experience other job roles

D. To prevent improper activity

☑ D. Knowledge that vacation time is mandatory means employees are less likely to engage in improper business practices. A different employee filling that job role is more likely to notice irregularities.

☒ A, B, and C are incorrect. A is not the primary purpose of mandatory vacations, as they pertain to security policies. B is incorrect, although refreshed employees tend to be more productive. C is incorrect; it is one definition for a job rotation policy.

21. A departmental manager is implementing a policy whereby employees enhance their skill set by periodically occupying different job roles. What is this called?

A. Mandatory vacations

B. Due diligence

C. Rotation of duties

D. Least privilege

☑ C. Rotation of duties allows employees to learn more about the business as a whole while enhancing their skills.

☒ A, B, and D are incorrect. A allows another employee to occupy a job role, which makes noticing irregularities much easier. B requires procedures and research be carried out properly. D refers to granting only those rights and permissions that people need to do their jobs.

4

Types of Attacks

CERTIFICATION OBJECTIVES

❑　**3.2**　Analyze and differentiate among types of attacks

❑　**3.3**　Analyze and differentiate among types of social engineering attacks

❑　**3.5**　Analyze and differentiate among types of application attacks

QUESTIONS

Understanding different types of attacks is an important topic for any security professional in the work force, but is also important for the Security+ certification exam. You are sure to receive questions related to different types of attacks on the Security+ certification exam!

Social engineering attacks involve the hacker contacting a person through e-mail, a phone call, or maybe a conversation in person, and trying to trick the person into compromising security. You also need to be familiar with the different types of network attacks, such as buffer overflow attacks, which are very popular today, and SQL injection attacks, which are typically performed against web sites that have been developed without considering programming best practices. You also should be familiar with the different password attacks for the exam, such as a dictionary attack, a hybrid attack, and a brute-force attack. This chapter is designed to help review these critical points!

1. You are inspecting a user's system after she has complained about the slow Internet usage. After analyzing the system you notice that the MAC address of the default gateway in the ARP cache is referencing the wrong MAC address. What type of attack has occurred?
   A. Brute force
   B. DNS poisoning
   C. Buffer overflow
   D. ARP poisoning

2. You want to implement a security control that limits the amount of tailgating in a high-security environment. Which of the following protective controls would you use?
   A. Swipe cards
   B. Mantrap
   C. Locked door
   D. CMOS settings

3. Which of the following descriptions best describes a buffer overflow attack?
   A. Injecting database code into a web page
   B. Using a dictionary file to crack passwords
   C. Sending too much data to an application that allows the hacker to run arbitrary code
   D. Altering the source address of a packet

4. You are analyzing web traffic in transit to your web server and you notice someone logging on with a username of "Bob" with a password of "pass' or 1=1--". Which of the following describes what is happening?
   A. Buffer overflow
   B. A SQL injection attack

C.   Brute-force attack

D.   Denial of service

5.   A user on your network receives an e-mail from the bank stating that there has been a security incident at the bank. The e-mail continues by asking the user to log on to her bank account by following the link provided and verify that her account has not been tampered with. What type of attack is this?

A.   Phishing

B.   Denial of service

C.   Dictionary attack

D.   Buffer overflow

6.   What type of attack involves the hacker modifying the source IP address of the packet?

A.   Brute force

B.   Buffer overflow

C.   Spoofing

D.   SQL injection

7.   Which of the following files might a hacker modify after gaining access to your system in order to achieve DNS redirection?

A.   /etc/passwd

B.   Hosts

C.   SAM

D.   Services

8.   What type of attack involves the hacker sending too much data to a service or application that typically results in the hacker gaining administrative access to the system?

A.   SQL injection

B.   Brute force

C.   Eavesdrop

D.   Buffer overflow

9.   Which of the following methods could be used to prevent ARP poisoning on the network? (Choose two.)

A.   Static ARP entries

B.   Patching

C.   Antivirus software

D.   Physical security

E.   Firewall

10. As a network administrator, what should you do to help prevent buffer overflow attacks from occurring to your systems?
   A. Static ARP entries
   B. Antivirus software
   C. Physical security
   D. Patching

11. Which of the following is the term for a domain name that is registered and deleted repeatedly as to avoid paying for the domain name?
   A. DNS redirection
   B. Domain poisoning
   C. Domain kiting
   D. Domain name system

12. You receive many calls from customers stating that your web site seems to be slow in responding. You analyze the traffic and notice that you are receiving a number of malformed requests on that web server at a very high rate. What type of attack is occurring?
   A. Eavesdrop
   B. Denial of service
   C. Man-in-the-middle
   D. Social engineer

13. What type of attack is a smurf attack?
   A. Distributed denial of service (DDoS)
   B. Denial of service (DoS)
   C. Eavesdrop
   D. Man-in-the-middle

14. Your manager has ensured that a policy is implemented that requires all employees to shred sensitive documents. What type of attack is your manager hoping to prevent?
   A. Tailgating
   B. Denial of service
   C. Social engineering
   D. Dumpster diving

15. What type of attack involves the hacker inserting client-side script into the web page?
   A. XSS
   B. DNS poisoning

    C. ARP poisoning

    D. SQL injection

16. Your manager has read about SQL injection attacks and is wondering what can be done to protect against them for your in-house-developed applications. What would you recommend?

    A. Patching

    B. Antivirus

    C. Input validation

    D. Firewall

17. A hacker is sitting in an Internet cafe and ARP poisons everyone connected to the wireless network so that all traffic passes through the hacker's laptop before she routes the traffic to the Internet. What type of attack is this?

    A. Replay

    B. Man-in-the-middle

    C. DNS poison

    D. Spoofing

18. Which of the following best describes a zero-day attack?

    A. An attack that modifies the source address of the packet

    B. An attack that changes the computer's system date to 00/00/00

    C. An attack that never happens

    D. An attack that uses an exploit that the product vendor is not aware of yet

19. What type of file on your hard drive stores preferences from web sites?

    A. Cookie

    B. Hosts

    C. LMHOSTS

    D. System.dat

20. What type of attack involves the hacker disconnecting one of the parties from the communication and continues the communication while impersonating that system?

    A. Man-in-the-middle

    B. Denial of service

    C. SQL injection

    D. Session hijacking

21. What type of password attack involves the use of a dictionary file and modifications of the words in the dictionary file?

   A. Dictionary attack

   B. Brute-force attack

   C. Hybrid attack

   D. Modification attack

22. Which of the following countermeasures is designed to protect against a brute-force password attack?

   A. Patching

   B. Account lockout

   C. Password complexity

   D. Strong passwords

QUICK ANSWER KEY

1.	D	9.	A, D	17.	B
2.	B	10.	D	18.	D
3.	C	11.	C	19.	A
4.	B	12.	B	20.	D
5.	A	13.	A	21.	C
6.	C	14.	D	22.	B
7.	B	15.	A		
8.	D	16.	C		

IN-DEPTH ANSWERS

1. You are inspecting a user's system after she has complained about the slow Internet usage. After analyzing the system you notice that the MAC address of the default gateway in the ARP cache is referencing the wrong MAC address. What type of attack has occurred?

   A. Brute force

   B. DNS poisoning

   C. Buffer overflow

   D. ARP poisoning

   ☑ **D.** ARP poisoning is when the hacker alters the ARP cache in order to redirect communication to a particular IP address to the wrong MAC address. This is a very popular attack with wireless networks.

   ☒ **A, B,** and **C** are incorrect. **A** is incorrect because brute-force attack is a type of password attack that involves the hacker calculating all potential passwords. **B** is incorrect because DNS poisoning is when the attacker poisons the DNS cache so that the DNS server gives out the wrong IP address. **C** happens when too much data is sent to an application or service causing the data to go beyond the buffer area (memory). The result of a buffer overflow is that the hacker typically gets administrative access to the system.

2. You want to implement a security control that limits the amount of tailgating in a high-security environment. Which of the following protective controls would you use?

   A. Swipe cards

   B. Mantrap

   C. Locked door

   D. CMOS settings

   ☑ **B.** Tailgating is the concept that someone tries to slip through a secured door after you open it. A mantrap is a way to help prevent tailgating by having an area between two locked doors—the second door does not open until the first door closes. This allows you to watch who enters the building with you.

   ☒ **A, C,** and **D** are incorrect. **A** is incorrect because swipe cards are a mechanism to unlock doors, but they do not prevent someone from tailgating. The same goes for a **C**—a locked door does not prevent someone from tailgating through the door after you open it. **D** is incorrect because CMOS settings are a way to implement a level of security to prevent someone from booting from a CD and bypassing the security of the local system.

3. Which of the following descriptions best describes a buffer overflow attack?

   A. Injecting database code into a web page

   B. Using a dictionary file to crack passwords

   C. Sending too much data to an application that allows the hacker to run arbitrary code

   D. Altering the source address of a packet

   ☑ **C.** A buffer overflow attack is when a hacker sends more data to an application or service that what it is expecting. The extra data that is sent flows out of the area of memory (the buffer) assigned to the application. It has been found that if the hacker can write information beyond the buffer he can run whatever code he wants. Hackers typically write code that gives them remote shell access to the system with administrative capabilities.

   ☒ **A, B,** and **D** are incorrect. **A** is an example of a SQL injection attack. **B** is known as a dictionary attack—a form of password attack. **D** is known as spoofing.

4. You are analyzing web traffic in transit to your web server and you notice someone logging on with a username of "Bob" with a password of "pass' or 1=1--". Which of the following describes what is happening?

   A. Buffer overflow

   B. A SQL injection attack

   C. Brute-force attack

   D. Denial of service

   ☑ **B.** A SQL injection attack is when the hacker inserts database (SQL) statements into an application, such as a web site, that manipulates the way the application executes. In this example, the hacker is trying to bypass the logon by typing "pass' or 1=1--" into the password box.

   ☒ **A, C,** and **D** are incorrect. **A** is incorrect because buffer overflow happens when the hacker sends too much data to an application, not SQL code to the application. **C** is incorrect because a brute-force attack is a type of password attack that calculates all potential passwords. **D** is incorrect because denial of service is when the hacker tries to overload your system so that it cannot service valid request from clients.

5. A user on your network receives an e-mail from the bank stating that there has been a security incident at the bank. The e-mail continues by asking the user to log on to her bank account by following the link provided and verify that her account has not been tampered with. What type of attack is this?

   A. Phishing

   B. Denial of service

   C. Dictionary attack

   D. Buffer overflow

   ☑ **A.** Phishing is when the hacker e-mails a victim and hopes she clicks the link that leads her to a fake site (typically a bank). At this point the hacker hopes the user types information into the fake site (such as bank account information) that he can use to gain access to her real account.

   ☒ **B, C,** and **D** are incorrect. **B** is incorrect because denial of service is when the hacker overloads your system so that it cannot service a valid request. **C** is a type of password attack that reads a text file and uses all words in the text file as password attempts. **D** happens when the hacker sends too much data to an application and gets remote shell access to the system.

6. What type of attack involves the hacker modifying the source IP address of the packet?

   A. Brute force

   B. Buffer overflow

   C. Spoofing

   D. SQL injection

   ☑ **C.** A spoof attack is when the hacker modifies the source address of the packet. IP spoofing is when the source IP address is modified, MAC spoofing is when the source MAC address is modified, and e-mail spoofing is when the hacker alters the source e-mail address of the message.

   ☒ **A, B,** and **D** are incorrect. **A** is incorrect because a brute-force attack is a type of password attack that calculates all potential passwords. **B** happens when the hacker sends too much data to an application and gets remote shell access to the system. **D** is when the hacker inserts database (SQL) statements into an application, such as a web site, that manipulates the way the application executes.

7. Which of the following files might a hacker modify after gaining access to your system in order to achieve DNS redirection?

A. /etc/passwd

B. Hosts

C. SAM

D. Services

☑ **B.** The hosts file on the local hard drive of the computer is used to resolve fully qualified domain names (FQDNs) to IP addresses and could be used to redirect an unsuspecting person to the wrong site.

☒ **A, C,** and **D** are incorrect. **A** is incorrect because the /etc/passwd file is where passwords are stored in Linux. **C** is incorrect because the SAM file is where the user accounts in Windows are stored. **D** is incorrect because the services file is a file that maps ports to actual friendly names of services.

8. What type of attack involves the hacker sending too much data to a service or application that typically results in the hacker gaining administrative access to the system?

A. SQL injection

B. Brute force

C. Eavesdrop

D. Buffer overflow

☑ **D.** A buffer overflow attack involves the hacker sending too much data to an application to gain administrative access to the system.

☒ **A, B,** and **C** are incorrect. **A** is incorrect because SQL injection is when the hacker inserts database (SQL) statements into an application, such as a web site, that manipulates the way the application executes. **B** is incorrect because a brute-force attack is a type of password attack that calculates all potential passwords. **C** is incorrect because an eavesdrop attack is when the hacker listens in on a conversation or captures traffic off the network with a packet analyzer such as Wireshark.

9. Which of the following methods could be used to prevent ARP poisoning on the network? (Choose two.)

A. Static ARP entries

B. Patching

C. Antivirus software

D. Physical security

E. Firewall

☑ **A and D.** ARP poisoning can be countered by adding static ARP entries to your ARP cache and by implementing physical security so that unauthorized persons cannot gain access to the network and poison everyone's ARP cache.

☒ **B, C, and E** are incorrect. **B** is incorrect because patching a system will not prevent ARP poisoning, because patching a system is used to remove vulnerabilities in software. **C** is incorrect because antivirus software will not prevent ARP poisoning, as there is no virus involved. **E** is incorrect because a firewall is not the solution either, because you will need to ensure that ARP messages can reach all the stations and this will allow ARP poisoning messages.

10. As a network administrator, what should you do to help prevent buffer overflow attacks from occurring to your systems?

A. Static ARP entries

B. Antivirus software

C. Physical security

D. Patching

☑ **D.** The best countermeasure to buffer overflow attacks is to ensure that you keep up to date with system and application patches. As the vendor finds the vulnerabilities, that vendor will fix the issues through a patch.

☒ **A, B, and C** are incorrect. **A** is incorrect because static ARP entries will help protect against ARP poisoning, **B** is incorrect because antivirus software will protect against viruses and other malicious software as long as you keep the virus definitions up to date, and **C** is incorrect because physical security will help control who gets physical access to an asset such as a server—but buffer overflow attacks are typical network-based attacks where physical access to the asset is not required by the hacker.

11. Which of the following is the term for a domain name that is registered and deleted repeatedly as to avoid paying for the domain name?

A. DNS redirection

B. Domain poisoning

C. Domain kiting

D. Domain name system

> ☑ **C.** Domain kiting is a vulnerability in the domain name system where the hacker registers a DNS name but does not have to pay for the five-day grace period. After a few days he deletes the name and recreates it to get the five-day grace period again.
>
> ☒ **A, B,** and **D** are incorrect. **A** is incorrect because DNS redirection is the concept of the hacker ensuring your system is given an incorrect IP address for a DNS name. **B** is incorrect because domain poisoning is a method of ensuring your system is given the wrong IP address for a specific domain name, and **D** is incorrect, as it is the method of resolving FQDNs to IP addresses.

12. You receive many calls from customers stating that your web site seems to be slow in responding. You analyze the traffic and notice that you are receiving a number of malformed requests on that web server at a very high rate. What type of attack is occurring?

A. Eavesdrop

B. Denial of service

C. Man-in-the-middle

D. Social engineer

> ☑ **B.** The fact that you are receiving a high number of request a very high rate is a great indication that someone is trying to perform a denial of service (DoS) attack on your system. The results of a DoS could be to keep your system so busy servicing bogus requests that it cannot service valid request from customers, or the hacker may try to crash your system.
>
> ☒ **A, C,** and **D** are incorrect. **A** is incorrect because eavesdropping is a passive-type attack, which involves the hacker capturing traffic—not sending traffic to your system. **C** is incorrect because a man-in-the-middle attack involves the hacker inserting himself or herself into a conversation so that all traffic passes through the hacker. **D** is incorrect because a social engineering attack is when someone tries to trick you into compromising security through social contact (e-mail or phone call).

13. What type of attack is a smurf attack?

A. Distributed denial of service (DDoS)

B. Denial of service (DoS)

C. Eavesdrop

D. Man-in-the-middle

☑ **A.** A smurf attack is a distributed denial of service (DDoS), which is a DoS attack involving multiple systems. The smurf attack involved the hacker pinging a number of systems but spoofing the address of the ping packet so that all those systems would reply to an intended victim. The victim would be overburdened with the ping replies that it would cause a denial of service.

☒ **B, C,** and **D** are incorrect. **B** is incorrect because a denial of service (DoS) attack involves only one system doing the attack, but the smurf attack has many systems doing the attack. **C** is incorrect because eavesdropping is a passive-type attack, which involves the hacker capturing traffic. **D** is incorrect because a man-in-the-middle attack involves the hacker inserting himself or herself into a conversation so that all traffic passes through the hacker.

14. Your manager has ensured that a policy is implemented that requires all employees to shred sensitive documents. What type of attack is your manager hoping to prevent?

A. Tailgating

B. Denial of service

C. Social engineering

D. Dumpster diving

☑ **D.** Dumpster diving is when the hacker goes through a company's garbage trying to locate information that can help him perform an attack or gain access to the company assets.

☒ **A, B,** and **C** are incorrect. **A** is incorrect because tailgating is when someone tries to sneak past a locked door after you have opened it for yourself. **B** is incorrect because denial of service is when a hacker overloads a system causing it to become unresponsive or crash, and **C** is incorrect because social engineering is when the hacker tries to trick someone into compromising security through social contact—such as phone call or e-mail.

15. What type of attack involves the hacker inserting client-side script into the web page?

A. XSS

B. DNS poisoning

C. ARP poisoning

D. SQL injection

☑ **A.** Cross-site scripting is an attack that involves the hacker inserting script code into a web page so that it is then processed and executed by a client system.

☒ **B, C,** and **D** are incorrect. **B** is incorrect because DNS poisoning is when the hacker can insert incorrect IP address information into DNS, thus leading the victim to the wrong site. **C** is incorrect because ARP poisoning is when the hacker inserts incorrect MAC addresses into the ARP cache, thus leading systems to the hacker's system. **D** is incorrect because SQL injection is inserting SQL code into an application in order to manipulate the underlying database or system.

16. Your manager has read about SQL injection attacks and is wondering what can be done to protect against them for your in-house-developed applications. What would you recommend?

   A. Patching

   B. Antivirus

   C. Input validation

   D. Firewall

☑ **C.** A SQL injection attack involves the hacker inserting database code into an application (such as a web site) where it is not expected. The best countermeasure to this is to have your programmers validate any information (check its accuracy) passed into an application.

☒ **A, B,** and **D** are incorrect. **A** is incorrect because although patching a system solves a lot of problems, it will not solve a SQL injection attack for applications that you build. **B** is incorrect because antivirus software is not going to help you in this instance either, because this is not a virus problem—it is a problem based on your own coding habits. **D** is incorrect because firewalls are not going to help you because you need to allow people access to the application and the problem is not about the type of traffic reaching the system—the problem is about the data that is being inserted into the application.

17. A hacker is sitting in an Internet cafe and ARP poisons everyone connected to the wireless network so that all traffic passes through the hacker's laptop before she routes the traffic to the Internet. What type of attack is this?

   A. Replay

   B. Man-in-the-middle

   C. DNS poison

   D. Spoofing

☑ **B.** When a hacker poisons everyone's ARP cache in order to have them send any data destined for the Internet through her system, this is known as a man-in-the-middle attack because the hacker is receiving all traffic before it is sent out to the Internet. The hacker will do this in order to see what you are doing on the Internet and hopefully capture sensitive information.

☒ **A, C,** and **D** are incorrect. **A** is incorrect because a replay attack involves the hacker capturing traffic and then replaying that traffic at a later time. **C** is incorrect because DNS poisoning involves the hacker modifying the DNS cache in order to lead you to the wrong web sites, and **D** is incorrect because spoofing is the altering of a source address to make a packet look as if it is coming from somewhere different.

18. Which of the following best describes a zero-day attack?

    A. An attack that modifies the source address of the packet

    B. An attack that changes the computer's system date to 00/00/00

    C. An attack that never happens

    D. An attack that uses an exploit that the product vendor is not aware of yet

☑ **D.** A zero-day attack is considered a new exploit that the vendor is not aware of yet, but the hacking community is very aware of.

☒ **A, B,** and **C** are incorrect. **A** is incorrect because an attack that involves the source address being modified is known as a spoof attack. **B** and **C** are incorrect because there is no such attack as one that modifies the system date to 00/00/00 and an attack that never happens is not really an attack.

19. What type of file on your hard drive stores preferences from web sites?

    A. Cookie

    B. Hosts

    C. LMHOSTS

    D. System.dat

☑ **A.** A cookie is a text file on the hard drive of your system that stores preferences for specific web sites.

☒ **B, C,** and **D** are incorrect. **B** is incorrect because the hosts file stores the FQDNs and matching IP addresses, **C** is incorrect because the LMHOSTS file in Windows stores the computer names and matching IP addresses, and **D** is incorrect because the system.dat file is a registry file for Windows 9x systems.

20. What type of attack involves the hacker disconnecting one of the parties from the communication and continues the communication while impersonating that system?

A. Man-in-the-middle

B. Denial of service

C. SQL injection

D. Session hijacking

☑ **D.** Session hijacking involves the hacker taking over a conversation by impersonating one of the parties involved in the conversation after the hacker kicks that party off. The hacker typically does a DoS attack in order to kick one of the parties out of the communication.

☒ **A, B,** and **C** are incorrect. **A** is incorrect because a man-in-the-middle attack involves the hacker inserting himself or herself into a conversation so that all traffic passes through the hacker. **B** is incorrect because denial of service is when a hacker overloads a system causing it to become unresponsive or crash. **C** is incorrect because SQL injection is inserting SQL code into an application in order to manipulate the underlining database or system.

21. What type of password attack involves the use of a dictionary file and modifications of the words in the dictionary file?

A. Dictionary attack

B. Brute-force attack

C. Hybrid attack

D. Modification attack

☑ **C.** A hybrid password attack is when the hacker uses a dictionary file and then the software uses modifications of the dictionary words by placing numbers at the end of each word.

☒ **A, B,** and **D** are incorrect. **A** is incorrect because although a dictionary attack does use a dictionary file, it only uses the entries found in the file and does not try modifications of the words in the file. **B** is incorrect because a brute-force attack mathematically calculates each possible password and does not use a file at all. **D** is incorrect because there is no such thing as a modification attack.

22. Which of the following countermeasures is designed to protect against a brute-force password attack?

   A. Patching

   B. Account lockout

   C. Password complexity

   D. Strong passwords

☑ **B.** Because brute-force attacks mathematically calculate all possible passwords, if you give the hacker enough time he will crack passwords, including complex passwords. The key point here is you need to take the time away from the hacker, and how you do that is to enable account lockout—after a certain number of bad logon attempts the account is locked.

☒ **A, C,** and **D** are incorrect. **A** is incorrect because patching will not protect against any type of password attack, while **C** and **D** are incorrect because strong passwords and password complexity (which are the same thing), constitute a countermeasure to dictionary attacks—not brute-force attacks.

5

System Security Threats

CERTIFICATION OBJECTIVES

❑　**1.1**　Explain the security function and purpose of network devices and technologies

❑　**3.1**　Analyze and differentiate among types of malware

QUESTIONS

IT Security threats can apply to programs or hardware. Software threats include the exploitation of vulnerabilities and the wide array of malware such as worms and spyware. Hardware threats apply when a malicious entity gains physical access, for example, to a handheld device or a server hard disk. Physical security threats could include employees being tricked into allowing unauthorized persons into a secured area such as a server room. Identifying these threats is an important step in properly applying security policies.

1. Which type of threat is mitigated by shredding paper documents?
   A. Rootkit
   B. Spyware
   C. Shoulder surfing
   D. Physical

2. Which of the following statements are true? (Choose two.)
   A. Worms log all typed characters to a text file.
   B. Worms propagate themselves to other systems.
   C. Worms can carry viruses.
   D. Worms infect the hard disk MBR.

3. One of your users, Janet, reports that when she visits web sites, pop-up advertisements appear incessantly. After further investigation, you learn one of the web sites she had visited had infected Flash code. Janet asks what the problem was—what do you tell her caused the problem?
   A. Cross-site scripting attack
   B. Worm
   C. Adware
   D. Spyware

4. Which description *best* defines a computer virus?
   A. A computer program that replicates itself
   B. A file with a .VBS file extension
   C. A computer program that gathers user information
   D. A computer program that runs malicious actions

5. An exploit connects to a specific TCP port and presents the invoker with an administrative command prompt. What type of attack is this?
   A. Botnet
   B. Trojan
   C. Privilege escalation
   D. Logic bomb

6. Ahmid is a software developer for a high tech company. He creates a program that connects to a chatroom and waits to receive commands that will gather personal user information. Ahmid embeds this program into an .AVI file for a current popular movie and shares this file on a P2P file sharing network. Once Ahmid's program is activated as people download and watch the movie, what will be created?

  A. Botnet

  B. DDoS (distributed denial of service)

  C. Logic bomb

  D. Worm

7. A user reports USB keyboard problems. You check the back of the computer to ensure the keyboard is properly connected and notice a small connector between the keyboard and the computer USB port. After investigation you learn this piece of hardware captures everything a user types in. What type of hardware is this?

  A. Smart card

  B. Trojan

  C. Keylogger

  D. PS/2 converter

8. What is the difference between a rootkit and privilege escalation?

  A. Rootkits propagate themselves.

  B. Privilege escalation is the result of a rootkit.

  C. Rootkits are the result of privilege escalation.

  D. Each uses a different TCP port.

9. Which of the following are true regarding backdoors? (Choose two.)

  A. They are malicious code.

  B. They allow remote users access to TCP port 25.

  C. They are made accessible through rootkits.

  D. They provide access to the Windows root account.

10. You are hosting an IT security meeting regarding physical server room security. A colleague, Tony, suggests adding CMOS hardening to existing server security policies. What kind of security threat is Tony referring to?

  A. Changing the amount of installed RAM

  B. Changing CPU throttling settings

  C. Changing the boot order

  D. Changing power management settings

11. You are the IT security officer for a government department. You are amending the USB security policy. Which items apply to USB security? (Choose two.)

   A. Disallow external USB drives larger than 1TB.

   B. Disable USB ports.

   C. Prevent corporate data from being copied to USB devices unless USB device encryption is enabled.

   D. Prevent corporate data from being copied to USB devices unless USB port encryption is enabled.

12. Which of the following are *not* considered serious cell phone threats? (Choose two.)

   A. Hackers with the right equipment posing as cell towers

   B. Having Bluetooth enabled

   C. Changing the boot order

   D. Spyware

13. What is defined as the transmission of unwelcome bulk messages?

   A. Worm

   B. Ping of death

   C. Spam

   D. DoS (denial of service)

14. Which technology separates storage from the server to disks in a network appliance?

   A. Router

   B. Switch

   C. NAS

   D. Wireless router

15. You are responsible for determining what technologies will be needed in a new office space. Employees will need a single network to share data, traditional voice calls, VoIP calls, voice mailboxes, and other services such as call waiting and call transfer. What type of service provides this functionality?

   A. Ethernet switch

   B. PBX

   C. NAS

   D. Router

16. Botnets can be used to set what type of coordinated attack in motion?

   A. DDoS

   B. Cross-site scripting

   C. Privilege escalation

   D. Rootkit

17. As a Windows administrator, you configure a Windows networking service to run with a specially created account with limited rights. Why would you do this?

   A. To prevent computer worms from entering the network

   B. To prevent a hacker from receiving elevated privileges due to a compromised network service

   C. Because Windows networking services will not run with administrative rights

   D. Because Windows networking services must run with limited access

18. Discovered in 1991, the Michelangelo virus was said to be triggered to overwrite the first 100 hard disk sectors with null data each year on March 6, the date of the Italian artist's birthday. What type of virus is Michelangelo?

   A. Zero day

   B. Worm

   C. Trojan

   D. Logic bomb

19. The Stuxnet attack was discovered in June 2010. Its primary function is to hide its presence while reprogramming industrial computer systems. The attack is believed to be spread through USB flash drives, where it transmits copies of itself to other hosts. To which of the following does Stuxnet apply? (Choose two.)

   A. Rootkit

   B. Spam

   C. Worm

   D. Adware

20. A piece of malicious code uses dictionary attacks against computers to gain access to administrative accounts. The code then links compromised computers together for the purpose of receiving remote commands. What term *best* applies to this malicious code?

   A. Exploit

   B. Botnet

   C. Logic bomb

   D. Backdoor

21. Windows 7 UAC (User Account Control) allows users to change Windows settings, but displays prompts when applications attempt to configure the operating system. Which of the following is addressed by UAC?

   A. Privilege escalation

   B. Adware

   C. Spyware

   D. Worms

22. Which of the following items are affected by spyware? (Choose two.)

  A. Memory

  B. IP address

  C. Computer name

  D. Network bandwidth

23. Juanita uses the Firefox web browser on her Linux workstation. She reports that her browser home page keeps changing to web sites offering savings on consumer electronic products. Her virus scanner is running and is up to date. What is causing this problem?

  A. Firefox on Linux automatically changes the home page every two days.

  B. Juanita is experiencing a denial of service attack.

  C. Juanita's user account has been compromised.

  D. Juanita's browser configuration is being changed by adware.

24. Which of the following is true regarding Trojan software?

  A. It secretly gathers user information.

  B. It is self-replicating.

  C. It can be propagated through peer-to-peer file sharing networks.

  D. It automatically spreads through Windows file and print sharing networks.

QUICK ANSWER KEY

1.	D	**9.**	A, C	**17.**	B
2.	B, C	**10.**	C	**18.**	D
3.	C	**11.**	B, C	**19.**	A, C
4.	D	**12.**	B, C	**20.**	B
5.	C	**13.**	C	**21.**	A
6.	A	**14.**	C	**22.**	A, D
7.	C	**15.**	B	**23.**	D
8.	B	**16.**	A	**24.**	C

IN-DEPTH ANSWERS

1. Which type of threat is mitigated by shredding paper documents?

    A. Rootkit

    B. Spyware

    C. Shoulder surfing

    D. Physical

    ☑ **D.** Shredding documents prevents physical threats such as theft of those documents or acquiring information from them.

    ☒ **A, B**, and **C** are incorrect. **A** is incorrect because rootkits hide themselves from the OS while allowing privileged access to a malicious user. **B** is incorrect because spyware gathers user computing habits without user knowledge. This can be very valuable to marketing firms. **C** is incorrect because the direct observation of somebody using sensitive information is an example of shoulder surfing.

2. Which of the following statements are true? (Choose two.)

    A. Worms log all typed characters to a text file.

    B. Worms propagate themselves to other systems.

    C. Worms can carry viruses.

    D. Worms infect the hard disk MBR.

    ☑ **B** and **C.** Worms are programs that multiply and spread, and they sometimes carry viruses (the worm is the delivery mechanism).

    ☒ **A** and **D** are incorrect. **A** is incorrect because keyloggers capture data as it is typed. **D** is incorrect because boot sector viruses, not worms, infect the MBR.

3. One of your users, Janet, reports that when she visits web sites, pop-up advertisements appear incessantly. After further investigation, you learn one of the web sites she had visited had infected Flash code. Janet asks what the problem was—what do you tell her caused the problem?

    A. Cross-site scripting attack

    B. Worm

    C. Adware

    D. Spyware

☑ **C.** Adware is responsible for displaying pop-up advertisements pertaining to a user's interest, usually as a result of spyware.

☒ **A, B,** and **D** are incorrect. **A** is incorrect because cross-site scripting attacks are malicious scripts that appear to be from a trusted source. The script runs locally on a user station, usually in the form of a malicious URL that a user is tricked into executing. **B** is incorrect because worms are self-replicating programs that propagate themselves. **D** is incorrect because, although spyware tracks personal user data, the component that results in pop-up advertisements is referred to as adware.

4. Which description *best* defines a computer virus?

    A. A computer program that replicates itself

    B. A file with a .VBS file extension

    C. A computer program that gathers user information

    D. A computer program that runs malicious actions

☑ **D.** Viruses are applications that run malicious actions without user consent.

☒ **A, B,** and **C** are incorrect. **A** is incorrect because worms replicate themselves. **B** is incorrect because a .VBS file extension does not always mean the file is malicious. **C** is incorrect because it defines spyware.

5. An exploit connects to a specific TCP port and presents the invoker with an administrative command prompt. What type of attack is this?

    A. Botnet

    B. Trojan

    C. Privilege escalation

    D. Logic bomb

☑ **C.** Privilege escalation occurs when a user gains higher rights than he should have, either because he was given too many rights, or because of a security flaw.

☒ **A, B,** and **D** are incorrect. **A** is incorrect because a botnet refers to a group of computers under the control of a malicious user. **B** is incorrect because a Trojan is malware that appears to be benign. **D** is incorrect because logic bombs are malware triggered by specific conditions or dates.

6. Ahmid is a software developer for a high tech company. He creates a program that connects to a chatroom and waits to receive commands that will gather personal user information. Ahmid embeds this program into an .AVI file for a current popular movie and shares this file on a P2P file sharing network. Once Ahmid's program is activated as people download and watch the movie, what will be created?

    A. Botnet

    B. DDoS (distributed denial of service)

    C. Logic bomb

    D. Worm

    ☑   **A.** Botnets consist of computers infected with malware that are under hacker control.

    ☒   **B, C,** and **D** are incorrect. **B** is incorrect because DDoS attacks can be facilitated with botnets, but they do not gather personal user information; they render network services unusable by legitimate users. **C** is incorrect because logic bombs are malware triggered by specific conditions. **D** is incorrect because worms replicate and proliferate.

7. A user reports USB keyboard problems. You check the back of the computer to ensure the keyboard is properly connected and notice a small connector between the keyboard and the computer USB port. After investigation you learn this piece of hardware captures everything a user types in. What type of hardware is this?

    A. Smart card

    B. Trojan

    C. Keylogger

    D. PS/2 converter

    ☑   **C.** Hardware keyloggers capture every keystroke and store them in a chip.

    ☒   **A, B,** and **D** are incorrect. **A** is incorrect because smart cards are the size of a credit card, contain a microchip, and are used to authenticate a user. **B** is incorrect because a Trojan is malware posing as legitimate software; the question is referring to hardware. **D** is incorrect because the question refers to a USB keyboard and port, not a PS/2 keyboard.

8. What is the difference between a rootkit and privilege escalation?

    A. Rootkits propagate themselves.

    B. Privilege escalation is the result of a rootkit.

C. Rootkits are the result of privilege escalation.

D. Each uses a different TCP port.

☑ **B.** Rootkits conceal themselves from operating systems and allow remote access with escalated privileges.

☒ **A, C,** and **D** are incorrect. **A** is incorrect because worms propagate themselves, not rootkits. **C** is incorrect because the opposite is true: privilege escalation is the result of a rootkit. **D** does not apply, since privilege escalation does not refer to network software that uses a TCP port.

9. Which of the following are true regarding backdoors? (Choose two.)

A. They are malicious code.

B. They allow remote users access to TCP port 25.

C. They are made accessible through rootkits.

D. They provide access to the Windows root account.

☑ **A** and **C.** Malicious code produces undesired results, such as a rootkit providing access to a backdoor.

☒ **B** and **D** are incorrect. **B** is incorrect; SMTP uses TCP port 25. **D** is incorrect because Windows has an "administrator" account while Unix and Linux have a "root" account.

10. You are hosting an IT security meeting regarding physical server room security. A colleague, Tony, suggests adding CMOS hardening to existing server security policies. What kind of security threat is Tony referring to?

A. Changing the amount of installed RAM

B. Changing CPU throttling settings

C. Changing the boot order

D. Changing power management settings

☑ **C.** Changing the boot order means having the ability to boot through alternative means, thus bypassing any operating system controls.

☒ **A, B,** and **D** are incorrect because they would not compromise server security.

11. You are the IT security officer for a government department. You are amending the USB security policy. Which items apply to USB security? (Choose two.)

A. Disallow external USB drives larger than 1TB.

B. Disable USB ports.

C. Prevent corporate data from being copied to USB devices unless USB device encryption is enabled.

D. Prevent corporate data from being copied to USB devices unless USB port encryption is enabled.

> ☑ **B** and **C**. Disabling USB ports on a system blocks malicious code on infected USB devices. Forcing USB device encryption ensures data confidentiality of departmental data.
>
> ☒ **A** and **D** are incorrect. **A** is incorrect because larger USB drives do not pose more of a threat than smaller USB drives. **D** is incorrect because encryption is not enabled on USB ports; it is enabled on USB devices.

12. Which of the following are *not* considered serious cell phone threats? (Choose two.)

A. Hackers with the right equipment posing as cell towers

B. Having Bluetooth enabled

C. Changing the boot order

D. Spyware

> ☑ **B** and **C**. Enabling Bluetooth itself is not a threat any more than surfing the web is. Most Bluetooth devices have security options such as passwords and device trust lists. You cannot change the "boot order" on a cell phone as you would on a computer system.
>
> ☒ **A** and **D** are incorrect. **A** is incorrect because posing as a cell tower means cell phone information and conversations could be compromised. **D** is incorrect because most modern cell phones have the ability to download apps. As a result, spyware on cell phones has become a serious problem.

13. What is defined as the transmission of unwelcome bulk messages?

A. Worm

B. Ping of death

C. Spam

D. DoS (denial of service)

☑ **C.** Spam affects business productivity by consuming enormous amounts of bandwidth and storage space for unsolicited messages.

☒ **A, B, and D** are incorrect. **A** is incorrect because worms don't send unwelcome messages with the intent of being read (although they do send themselves). **B** does not apply because the ping of death is an older denial of service attack executed by sending many large or malformed ping packets to a host, thus rendering it unusable. **D** does not apply because DoS (denial of service) attacks render systems unusable; spammers want our systems to work so that we can read their junk mail.

14. Which technology separates storage from the server to disks in a network appliance?

   A. Router

   B. Switch

   C. NAS

   D. Wireless router

☑ **C.** NAS (network-attached storage) devices are network appliances that contain disks. Client and server operating systems can access this NAS using various protocols such as TCP/IP or NFS.

☒ **A, B, and D** are incorrect. **A** is incorrect because routers do not have disks. Routers route packets between networks. **B** is incorrect because switches do not have disks; their primary concern is increasing network efficiency by making each port its own collision domain. **D** is incorrect because wireless routers have nothing to do with disk storage.

15. You are responsible for determining what technologies will be needed in a new office space. Employees will need a single network to share data, traditional voice calls, VoIP calls, voice mailboxes, and other services such as call waiting and call transfer. What type of service provides this functionality?

   A. Ethernet switch

   B. PBX

   C. NAS

   D. Router

☑ **B.** PBXs (private branch exchanges) offer telecommunication and data networking services in the form of hardware or software. PBXs may exist at the customer or provider premises.

☒ **A, C,** and **D** are incorrect. **A** is incorrect because Ethernet switches do not offer a full range of telecommunications options such as voice mailboxes and call waiting; instead, they increase the efficiency of a data network. **C** is incorrect because NAS (network-attached storage) is concerned with disk storage. **D** is incorrect because routers transmit data between networks.

16. Botnets can be used to set what type of coordinated attack in motion?

   A. DDoS

   B. Cross-site scripting

   C. Privilege escalation

   D. Rootkit

☑ **A.** Botnets (groups of computers under singular control) can be used to dispatch DDoS (distributed denial of service) attacks against hosts or other networks.

☒ **B, C,** and **D** are incorrect. **B** is incorrect because cross-site scripting attacks trick users into running malicious scripts, often in the form of a URL. **C** is incorrect because privilege escalation means a user having more rights than they normally would have, usually by means of malware. **D** is incorrect because rootkits are malware that grants elevated rights while remaining undetected by the OS.

17. As a Windows administrator, you configure a Windows networking service to run with a specially created account with limited rights. Why would you do this?

   A. To prevent computer worms from entering the network

   B. To prevent a hacker from receiving elevated privileges due to a compromised network service

   C. Because Windows networking services will not run with administrative rights

   D. Because Windows networking services must run with limited access

☑ **B.** In the event that the Windows networking service is compromised, it is important that the service not have full rights to the system.

☒ **A, C,** and **D** are incorrect. **A** is incorrect because worms can enter networks in many ways, including through privilege escalation, but it is not a better reason to run services with limited access than answer B. **C** and **D** are both incorrect because they are untrue.

18. Discovered in 1991, the Michelangelo virus was said to be triggered to overwrite the first 100 hard disk sectors with null data each year on March 6, the date of the Italian artist's birthday. What type of virus is Michelangelo?

    A. Zero day

    B. Worm

    C. Trojan

    D. Logic bomb

> ☑ **D.** Logic bombs trigger malicious code when specific conditions are satisfied, such as a date.
>
> ☒ **A, B**, and **C** are incorrect. **A** is incorrect because zero-day exploits are not triggered by certain conditions; they are exploits that are unknown to most others, and therefore, have no remedy. **B** is incorrect because worms are self-replicating and self-propagating. **C** does not apply; Trojans are malicious code posing as legitimate code.

19. The Stuxnet attack was discovered in June 2010. Its primary function is to hide its presence while reprogramming industrial computer systems. The attack is believed to be spread through USB flash drives, where it transmits copies of itself to other hosts. To which of the following does Stuxnet apply? (Choose two.)

    A. Rootkit

    B. Spam

    C. Worm

    D. Adware

> ☑ **A** and **C.** Stuxnet replicates itself, as worms do, and masks itself while running, as rootkits do.
>
> ☒ **B** and **D** are incorrect. **B** is incorrect because spam refers to the bulk sending of unsolicited e-mail. **D** does not apply because Stuxnet is not triggered by any specific conditions.

20. A piece of malicious code uses dictionary attacks against computers to gain access to administrative accounts. The code then links compromised computers together for the purpose of receiving remote commands. What term *best* applies to this malicious code?

    A. Exploit

    B. Botnet

    C. Logic bomb

    D. Backdoor

☑ **B.** Botnets are collections of computers under the sole control of the attacker.

☒ **A, C,** and **D** are incorrect. **A** does not best describe the scenario, although an exploit can lead to the creation of a botnet. **C** is incorrect because a specific condition is not triggering the code to run. **D** is incorrect because backdoors are typically open doors in computer code that bypass normal authentication mechanisms.

21. Windows 7 UAC (User Account Control) allows users to change Windows settings, but displays prompts when applications attempt to configure the operating system. Which of the following is addressed by UAC?

   A. Privilege escalation
   B. Adware
   C. Spyware
   D. Worms

☑ **A.** UAC limits software to having only standard user rights and requires authorization for code needing elevated rights.

☒ **B, C,** and **D** are incorrect. **B** is incorrect because adware displays advertising messages to users without their permission. **C** is incorrect because spyware is malicious code that monitors computer usage patterns and personal information. **D** does not apply; self-replicating worms should be detected by antivirus software.

22. Which of the following items are affected by spyware? (Choose two.)

   A. Memory
   B. IP address
   C. Computer name
   D. Network bandwidth

☑ **A** and **D.** Spyware is software that gets installed covertly and gathers user information without the user's knowledge. In some cases users may know it is being installed, such as when free software is being installed. Spyware consumes memory resources because it is normally running all the time. Network bandwidth is utilized when the spyware sends data to an external source.

☒ **B** and **C** are incorrect. Neither the IP address nor the computer name is affected by spyware.

23. Juanita uses the Firefox web browser on her Linux workstation. She reports that her browser home page keeps changing to web sites offering savings on consumer electronic products. Her virus scanner is running and is up to date. What is causing this problem?

    A. Firefox on Linux automatically changes the home page every two days.

    B. Juanita is experiencing a denial of service attack.

    C. Juanita's user account has been compromised.

    D. Juanita's browser configuration is being changed by adware.

    ☑ **D.** Adware attempts to expose users to advertisements in various ways, including through pop-ups or changing the web browser home page. Spyware often analyzes user habits so that adware displays relevant advertisements. Some antivirus software also scans for spyware, but not in this case.

    ☒ **A, B,** and **C** are incorrect. **A** is incorrect since Firefox on Linux does not change the home page every two days. Denial of service attacks prevent legitimate access to a network resource; Juanita is not being denied access. This is the reason why **B** is incorrect. **C** is incorrect because the presence of spyware or adware does not imply the user account has been compromised. Often these types of malware are silently installed when visiting web sites or installing freeware.

24. Which of the following is true regarding Trojan software?

    A. It secretly gathers user information.

    B. It is self-replicating.

    C. It can be propagated through peer-to-peer file sharing networks.

    D. It automatically spreads through Windows file and print sharing networks.

    ☑ **C.** Trojans are malicious code that appears to be useful software. For example, a user might use a peer-to-peer file sharing network on the Internet to illegally download pirated software. The software may install and function correctly, but a Trojan may also get installed. This Trojan could create a backdoor method for attackers to gain access to the system.

    ☒ **A, B,** and **D** are incorrect. **A** is incorrect because Trojans don't secretly gather user information, spyware does. **B** is incorrect because Trojans are not self-replicating on Windows file and print sharing or any other network as worms are. **D** is incorrect because Trojans are spread manually.

6

Mitigating Security Threats

CERTIFICATION OBJECTIVES

❑ **3.6** Analyze and differentiate among types of mitigation and deterrent techniques

❑ **4.1** Explain the importance of application security

QUESTIONS

The ability to identify security threats is important. Understanding how to minimize or prevent threats is critical, and often motivated by the potential for loss of revenue, shareholder confidence, or even litigation. Hardening, or minimizing security risk, of computing equipment and software is an important step in the right direction. Applying security settings from a central point such as Group Policy through Active Directory achieves the maximum effect. Application developers must adhere to secure coding guidelines so that their code does not afford malicious users an entry point.

1. The web developers at your company are testing their latest web site code before going live to ensure that it is robust and secure. During their testing they provide malformed URLs with additional abnormal parameters as well as an abundance of random data. What term describes their actions?
   A. Cross-site scripting
   B. Fuzzing
   C. Patching
   D. Debugging

2. The process of disabling unneeded network services on a computer is referred to as what?
   A. Patching
   B. Fuzzing
   C. Hardening
   D. Debugging

3. You are on a conference call with your developers Serena and Thomas, discussing the security of your new travel site. You express concern over a recent article describing how user submissions to web sites may contain malicious code that runs locally when others simply read the post. Serena suggests validating user input before allowing the user submissions. Which problem might validation solve?
   A. Cross-site scripting
   B. Fuzzing
   C. Hardening
   D. Patching

4. Which of the following lessens the probability of success of dictionary password attacks?
   A. Password complexity requirements
   B. Account lockout threshold
   C. Password hints
   D. Enforce password history

5. A RADIUS server is used to authenticate your wireless network users. While creating a new user account, you notice there are many more user accounts than actual users. What should be done?
   A. Delete all accounts not linked to a user.
   B. Disable all accounts not linked to a user.
   C. Verify how accounts are used, and then delete unnecessary accounts.
   D. Verify how accounts are used, and then disable unnecessary accounts.

6. The 802.11n wireless network in your department must be Layer 2 secured. You would like to control which specific wireless devices are allowed to connect. How can you do this?
   A. SIM card
   B. NetBIOS computer name
   C. MAC address
   D. IP address

7. What is the best definition of the IEEE 802.1x standard?
   A. It defines a group of wireless standards.
   B. It defines the Ethernet standard.
   C. It defines network access control only for wireless networks.
   D. It defines network access control for wired and wireless networks.

8. You are hardening a Linux computer and have disabled SSH in favor of Telnet. You ensure passwords are required for Telnet access. What error did you make?
   A. Secure Telnet should have public key authentication enabled.
   B. Only strong passwords should be used with Telnet.
   C. SSH should have been used instead of Telnet.
   D. The Telnet port should have been changed from 23 to 8080.

9. As the IT director of a high school using Group Policy and Active Directory, you plan the appropriate standard security settings for newly deployed Windows 7 workstations. Some teachers require modifications to these settings due to specialized software they use. Which term refers to the standardized security parameters?
   A. Initial baseline configuration
   B. Principle of least privilege
   C. Sysprepped image
   D. Local security policy

10. The periodic assessment of security policy compliance is referred to as what?
    A. Remediation
    B. Hardening
    C. Continuous security monitoring
    D. Trend analysis

11. You are a Windows Server 2008 administrator. You install and configure the NPS (Network Policy Server) role and configure health policies that require all connecting clients to have firewall and spyware software enabled. Clients violating these health policies will receive an IP address placing them on a restricted subnet containing servers with client firewall and spyware software to install. What term accurately refers to the role the servers on this restricted subnet play?

    A. Isolation

    B. Remediation

    C. Validation

    D. Authentication

12. IT security personnel respond to the repeated misuse of an authenticated user's session cookie on an ecommerce web site. The affected user reports that he occasionally uses the site, but not for the transactions in question. The security personnel decide to reduce the amount of time an authentication cookie is valid. What type of attack have they responded to?

    A. DoS

    B. Dictionary

    C. Privilege escalation

    D. Cross-site request forgery

13. A network administrator places a network appliance on the DMZ network and configures it with various security thresholds, each of which will notify the IT group via e-mail. The IT group will then adhere to the Incident Response policy and take action. What will be triggered when any of these thresholds is violated?

    A. Alarm

    B. Alert

    C. Remediation

    D. Input validation

14. A user reports repeated instances of Windows 7 slowing down to the point where she can no longer be productive. You view the Windows event viewer logs for the past month and notice an exorbitant amount of SMTP traffic leaving the local machine each morning between 10 and 11 A.M. What type of analysis was performed to learn of this anomaly?

    A. Forensic

    B. Trend

    C. Network statistical

    D. Vulnerability

15. Roman is developing an application that controls the lighting system in a large industrial complex. A piece of code calls a function that controls a custom-built circuit board. While running his application, Roman's application fails repeatedly due to unforeseen circumstances. Which secure coding guideline did Roman not adhere to?
   A. Packet encryption
   B. Digital signatures
   C. Error handling
   D. Hardening

16. What can be done to harden the Windows operating system? (Choose three.)
   A. Disable system restore points.
   B. Disable unnecessary services.
   C. Patch the operating system.
   D. Configure EFS.
   E. Disable group policy.

17. You are configuring a fleet of Windows 7 laptops for traveling employees, some of whom prefer using USB mice. It is critical that the machines be as secure as possible. What should you configure? (Choose three.)
   A. Disable USB ports.
   B. Require USB device encryption.
   C. Enable and configure the Windows firewall.
   D. Install and configure Antivirus software.
   E. Enable a power management scheme.

18. A shipment of new Windows computers has arrived for Accounting department employees. The computers have the operating system preinstalled but will require additional financial software. In which order should you perform all of the following?
   A. Join the Active Directory domain.
   B. Apply all operating system patches.
   C. Ensure the virus scanner is up to date.
   D. Log in to the Active Directory domain to receive group policy security settings.
   E. Install the additional financial software.

19. Which of the following items can help prevent ARP cache poisoning? (Choose three.)
   A. Use 802.1x security.
   B. Disable ARP.
   C. Patch the operating system.
   D. Configure the use of digital signatures for all network traffic.
   E. Disable unused switch ports.

20. Your intranet provides employees the ability to search through a SQL database for their past travel expenses once they have logged in. One employee from the IT department discovers that if he enters a SQL string such as SELECT * FROM EXPENSES WHERE EMPID = 'x'='x'; it returns all employee travel expense records. What secure coding guideline was ignored?

   A. SQL injection prevention

   B. Input validation

   C. Disabling of SQL indexes

   D. User authentication

21. You capture and examine network traffic weekly to ensure the network is being used properly. In doing so, you notice traffic to TCP port 53 on your server from an unknown IP address. After reviewing your server logs, you notice repeated failed attempts to execute a zone transfer to your server. What type of attack was attempted?

   A. ARP poisoning

   B. Cross-site scripting

   C. DNS poisoning

   D. MAC flooding

22. A network security audit exposes three insecure wireless routers using default configurations. Which security principle has been ignored?

   A. Application patch management

   B. Device hardening

   C. Input validation

   D. Principle of least privilege

23. Which of the following standards must authenticate computing devices before allowing network access?

   A. Router

   B. Hub

   C. IEEE 802.1x

   D. IEEE 802.11n

24. What will prevent frequent repeated malicious attacks against user account passwords?

   A. Minimum password age

   B. Password hints

   C. Password history

   D. Account lockout

25. Which item would *best* apply a standard security baseline to many computers?

    A. A disk image of the operating system

    B. Security templates distributed through group policy

    C. Password settings distributed through group policy

    D. Security templates distributed through local security policy

26. After patching and hardening your computers, how would you determine if your computers are secure?

    A. Performance baseline

    B. Security templates

    C. Penetration testing

    D. Password cracking

27. While hardening a Windows server, you decide to disable a number of services. How can you ensure that the services you are disabling will not adversely affect other services?

    A. Run the NET START 'service name' / DEP command.

    B. Disable the services, let the system run for a few days, and then check the event viewer logs.

    C. Right-click the service and choose Show Dependency Chain.

    D. Double-click the service and view the Dependencies tab.

28. Your company uses Microsoft IIS to host multiple intranet web sites on a two-node cluster. All sites store their configuration and content on drive C:, and log files are stored on D:. All sites share a common application pool. The IT director has asked that you ensure a single hacked web site will not adversely affect other running web sites. What should you do?

    A. Move each web site configuration to a separate hard disk.

    B. Move each web site content to a separate hard disk.

    C. Configure each web site to use its own application pool.

    D. Add a third node to the two-node cluster.

QUICK ANSWER KEY

1.	B	11.	B	21.	C
2.	C	12.	D	22.	B
3.	A	13.	A	23.	C
4.	A	14.	B	24.	D
5.	D	15.	C	25.	B
6.	C	16.	B, C, D	26.	C
7.	D	17.	B, C, D	27.	D
8.	C	18.	C, B, A, D, E	28.	C
9.	A	19.	A, D, E		
10.	C	20.	B		

IN-DEPTH ANSWERS

1. The web developers at your company are testing their latest web site code before going live to ensure that it is robust and secure. During their testing they provide malformed URLs with additional abnormal parameters as well as an abundance of random data. What term describes their actions?

   A. Cross-site scripting

   B. Fuzzing

   C. Patching

   D. Debugging

   ☑ **B.** Fuzzing is a means of injecting data into an application that it does not expect to ensure there are no weaknesses.

   ☒ **A, C,** and **D** are incorrect. **A** is incorrect because cross-site scripts do not ensure applications are secure; rather, they are a type of attack. **C** is incorrect because patching would occur after flaws were discovered. **D** is incorrect because debugging implies software flaws are already known.

2. The process of disabling unneeded network services on a computer is referred to as what?

   A. Patching

   B. Fuzzing

   C. Hardening

   D. Debugging

   ☑ **C.** Hardening includes actions such as disabling unneeded services to make a system more secure.

   ☒ **A, B,** and **D** are incorrect. **A** is incorrect because patches fix problems with software. **B** does not apply because fuzzing refers to testing your own software for vulnerabilities. **D** is incorrect because debugging is the methodical testing of software to identify the cause of a flaw.

3. You are on a conference call with your developers Serena and Thomas, discussing the security of your new travel site. You express concern over a recent article describing how user submissions to web sites may contain malicious code that runs locally when others simply read the post. Serena suggests validating user input before allowing the user submissions. Which problem might validation solve?

    A. Cross-site scripting

    B. Fuzzing

    C. Hardening

    D. Patching

    ☑ **A.** Cross-site scripting attacks take advantage of dynamically generated web pages on sites that allow unvalidated user input. User submissions can be validated to ensure malicious scripts do not exist on the site.

    ☒ **B, C,** and **D** are incorrect. **B** is incorrect because fuzzing is essentially in-house software penetration testing. **C** and **D** are incorrect because hardening and patching serve to protect computing equipment and are not considered problems.

4. Which of the following lessens the probability of success of dictionary password attacks?

    A. Password complexity requirements

    B. Account lockout threshold

    C. Password hints

    D. Enforce password history

    ☑ **A.** Complex password enforcement means dictionary words or username variations, to name just a few, cannot be used as passwords.

    ☒ **B, C,** and **D** are incorrect. **B** is incorrect because account lockout thresholds best mitigate brute-force password attacks. **C** is incorrect because password hints aid the user in remembering their password. **D** is incorrect because, although an important password security consideration, enforcing password history alone will not minimize dictionary attack risks.

5. A RADIUS server is used to authenticate your wireless network users. While creating a new user account, you notice there are many more user accounts than actual users. What should be done?

    A. Delete all accounts not linked to a user.

    B. Disable all accounts not linked to a user.

C. Verify how accounts are used, and then delete unnecessary accounts.

D. Verify how accounts are used, and then disable unnecessary accounts.

> ☑ **D.** Disable only accounts that are not required; other accounts may be needed later. Further investigation is needed to determine if any accounts are used by network services and not users.
>
> ☒ **A, B,** and **C** are incorrect. **A** and **B** are incorrect because accounts are sometimes used for network devices and services. **C** is not the best choice, since accounts not in current use may be needed later.

6. The 802.11n wireless network in your department must be Layer 2 secured. You would like to control which specific wireless devices are allowed to connect. How can you do this?

A. SIM card

B. NetBIOS computer name

C. MAC address

D. IP address

> ☑ **C.** The MAC address is an OSI Layer 2 (Data Link Layer) 48-bit unique hexadecimal address assigned to all network cards and is often used to restrict connecting wireless clients.
>
> ☒ **A, B,** and **D** are incorrect. **A** is incorrect because SIM (Subscriber Identity Module) cards are used in cell phones and not for 802.11n networks. **B** does not apply because NetBIOS computer names apply to OSI layers 4 (the Transport Layer) and 5 (the Session Layer). **D** is incorrect because IP addresses are OSI layer 3 (Network Layer) addresses.

7. What is the best definition of the IEEE 802.1x standard?

A. It defines a group of wireless standards.

B. It defines the Ethernet standard.

C. It defines network access control only for wireless networks.

D. It defines network access control for wired and wireless networks.

☑ **D.** 802.1x applies to wired and wireless networks. 802.1x connectivity devices forward authentication requests to an authentication server before allowing access to a network.

☒ **A, B,** and **C** are incorrect. **A** is incorrect because IEEE 802.11 defines a group of wireless standards. **B** is incorrect because IEEE 802.3 is the Ethernet standard. **C** is incorrect because 802.1x is not exclusive to wireless networks.

8. You are hardening a Linux computer and have disabled SSH in favor of Telnet. You ensure passwords are required for Telnet access. What error did you make?

   A. Secure Telnet should have public key authentication enabled.

   B. Only strong passwords should be used with Telnet.

   C. SSH should have been used instead of Telnet.

   D. The Telnet port should have been changed from 23 to 8080.

☑ **C.** SSH (Secure Shell), unlike Telnet, encrypts all packet payloads and, therefore, should be used when hardening.

☒ **A, B,** and **D** are incorrect. **A** is incorrect because Telnet does not support public key authentication. **B** is also incorrect although it is true that strong passwords should be used if you must use Telnet. **D** is incorrect because not changing the Telnet port does not constitute a configuration error.

9. As the IT director of a high school using Group Policy and Active Directory, you plan the appropriate standard security settings for newly deployed Windows 7 workstations. Some teachers require modifications to these settings due to specialized software they use. Which term refers to the standardized security parameters?

   A. Initial baseline configuration

   B. Principle of least privilege

   C. Sysprepped image

   D. Local security policy

☑ **A.** The initial baseline configuration implies blanket security settings that are the minimum standard.

☒ **B, C,** and **D** are incorrect. **B** does not apply, since the principle of least privilege ensures users have only the rights they require to do their jobs. **C** is incorrect because sysprepping a disk image ensures the installation is unique when it is deployed, but it does not specifically refer to security. **D** is incorrect because local security policy would not be the best way to implement standardized security to more than one computer.

10. The periodic assessment of security policy compliance is referred to as what?

   A. Remediation

   B. Hardening

   C. Continuous security monitoring

   D. Trend analysis

> ☑ C. Continuous security monitoring ensures security policies are adhered to and enforced.
>
> ☒ A, B, and D are incorrect. A is incorrect because remediation implies taking action to correct flaws. B is incorrect because hardening eliminates security risks but has nothing to do with security assessments. D does not apply. Trend analysis refers to collecting data and noticing patterns.

11. You are a Windows Server 2008 administrator. You install and configure the NPS (Network Policy Server) role and configure health policies that require all connecting clients to have firewall and spyware software enabled. Clients violating these health policies will receive an IP address placing them on a restricted subnet containing servers with client firewall and spyware software to install. What term accurately refers to the role the servers on this restricted subnet play?

   A. Isolation

   B. Remediation

   C. Validation

   D. Authentication

> ☑ B. Remediation servers provide a method of correcting security deficiencies.
>
> ☒ A, C and D are incorrect. The servers on the restricted subnet do not isolate, validate, or authenticate the clients on the restricted subnet; the NPS server does.

12. IT security personnel respond to the repeated misuse of an authenticated user's session cookie on an ecommerce web site. The affected user reports that he occasionally uses the site, but not for the transactions in question. The security personnel decide to reduce the amount of time an authentication cookie is valid. What type of attack have they responded to?

   A. DoS

   B. Dictionary

   C. Privilege escalation

   D. Cross-site request forgery

☑ **D.** Cross-site request forgeries involve the malicious use of a trusted party's cookie against a web site.

☒ **A, B,** and **C** are incorrect. **A** is incorrect because DoS (denial of service) attacks render a network service unusable, which is not the case here. **B** is incorrect because dictionary attacks are applied to user accounts to guess passwords. **C** is incorrect because privilege escalation raises the rights a user would normally have. In this example the violated user has the same rights he would normally have during a legitimate transaction.

13. A network administrator places a network appliance on the DMZ network and configures it with various security thresholds, each of which will notify the IT group via e-mail. The IT group will then adhere to the Incident Response policy and take action. What will be triggered when any of these thresholds is violated?

   A. Alarm

   B. Alert

   C. Remediation

   D. Input validation

☑ **A.** An alarm is a warning of danger that requires action (adherence to an Incident Response policy), such as a security threshold that might warn of excessive types of network traffic (which could imply a denial of service attack).

☒ **B, C,** and **D** are incorrect. **B** is incorrect because alerts notify of changes in state that may not always warrant a response, for example, the fact that a workstation has come online. **C** does not apply. Remediation actively corrects a problem; notifying the IT group of a situation in itself does not correct a problem. **D** is incorrect because input validation verifies the integrity of submitted data; this would not be triggered if some activity met a preconfigured threshold.

14. A user reports repeated instances of Windows 7 slowing down to the point where she can no longer be productive. You view the Windows event viewer logs for the past month and notice an exorbitant amount of SMTP traffic leaving the local machine each morning between 10 and 11 A.M. What type of analysis was performed to learn of this anomaly?

   A. Forensic

   B. Trend

   C. Network statistical

   D. Vulnerability

☑ **B.** A trend analysis seeks patterns within data sets, such as events happening around the same time each day.

☒ **A, C,** and **D** are incorrect. **A** is incorrect because forensic analysis seeks legal evidence of wrongdoing that can be used in a court of law, but this scenario does not imply collection of evidence for legal proceedings. **C** is incorrect because network statistic gathering is proactive, but in this case you are reacting to previously gathered data. **D** is not applicable because a vulnerability analysis is proactive and tests for weaknesses; in this case we are reacting to an anomaly.

15. Roman is developing an application that controls the lighting system in a large industrial complex. A piece of code calls a function that controls a custom-built circuit board. While running his application, Roman's application fails repeatedly due to unforeseen circumstances. Which secure coding guideline did Roman not adhere to?

A. Packet encryption

B. Digital signatures

C. Error handling

D. Hardening

☑ **C.** Error handling is a secure coding guideline that requires developers to write code that will capture any unforeseen situations instead of allowing applications to fail.

☒ **A, B,** and **D** are incorrect. **A** is incorrect because the lack of packet encryption would not cause an application to fail; it would simply be insecure. **B** does not apply because digital signatures verify the identity of the sender of a transmission. There is no mention of transmitting data in this case. **D** is incorrect because hardening would minimize security risks in Roman's application, but it would not increase its stability.

16. What can be done to harden the Windows operating system? (Choose three.)

A. Disable system restore points.

B. Disable unnecessary services.

C. Patch the operating system.

D. Configure EFS.

E. Disable group policy.

☑ **B, C,** and **D.** Hardening is defined as making hardware or software less vulnerable to security breaches. Disabling unnecessary services reduces the potential attack surface of an operating system. Patching applies solutions for known flaws and weaknesses. EFS (Encrypting File System) protects files and folders by encrypting them in such a way that parties without the decryption keys cannot decrypt the data.

☒ **A** and **E** are incorrect. **A** is incorrect because system restore points take snapshots of the Windows configuration periodically for the purpose of reverting to those snapshots. This could be used to revert a compromised or infected system back to a stable point in time, so it should not be disabled when hardening. **E** is incorrect because group policy contains many security settings that can be distributed centrally to many computers to harden them.

17. You are configuring a fleet of Windows 7 laptops for traveling employees, some of whom prefer using USB mice. It is critical that the machines be as secure as possible. What should you configure? (Choose three.)

   A. Disable USB ports.

   B. Require USB device encryption.

   C. Enable and configure the Windows firewall.

   D. Install and configure Antivirus software.

   E. Enable a power management scheme.

☑ **B, C,** and **D.** USB device encryption can be enforced to disallow copying of data to USB drives unless the USB device is encrypted. This ensures copied data remains confidential even if the USB drive is lost. The Windows firewall is critical in controlling inbound and outbound network traffic. For example, when connected to public networks, the firewall might block all incoming traffic, but when connected to the Active Directory domain network, the firewall might allow inbound remote control. Antivirus software is always essential to protect operating systems from the enormous amount of known malware.

☒ **A** and **E** are incorrect. **A** is incorrect because some users will need USB ports enabled for their USB mice; also, answer B provides a solution to data copied from the laptop, and answer D protects data copied to the laptop. **E** is incorrect because power management options serve to conserve power, not secure laptops.

18. A shipment of new Windows computers has arrived for Accounting department employees. The computers have the operating system preinstalled, but will require additional financial software. In which order should you perform all of the following?

A. Join the Active Directory domain.

B. Apply all operating system patches.

C. Ensure the virus scanner is up to date.

D. Log in to the Active Directory domain to receive group policy security settings.

E. Install the additional financial software.

☑ **C, B, A, D**, and **E.** (1) The virus scanner must first be updated to protect against malicious code while the system is updating. (2) Applying operating system patches is the second thing to do to ensure any software and security flaws are addressed. (3) Next you would join the computer to the domain, but only after patching and ensuring that there are no viruses. (4) Once the computer is joined to the domain, you should log in to ensure group policy security settings are applied. (5) Finally, the financial software required by Accounting department employees should be installed and tested.

19. Which of the following items can help prevent ARP cache poisoning? (Choose three.)

A. Use 802.1x security.

B. Disable ARP.

C. Patch the operating system.

D. Configure the use of digital signatures for all network traffic.

E. Disable unused switch ports.

☑ **A, D**, and **E.** ARP cache poisoning is a process by which a malicious device sends unsolicited broadcasts including its MAC address and another node's IP address, thus redirecting traffic through itself instead of to that other node. This can only happen if network access is granted. Unused switch ports should be disabled to prevent unauthorized access to the network. 802.1x security requires device authentication before allowing network access. Unauthorized computers should not be able to authenticate to the network. ARP cache poisoning requires having network access to transmit forged ARP broadcast packets. Digital signatures assure the recipient of a transmission that the sender is valid. The can be done in many ways such as by using IPSec (Internet Protocol Security), which can require that computers first authenticate to Active Directory before they can participate in secure transmissions.

> ☒ **B and C are incorrect. B** is incorrect because disabling ARP is not an option; ARP is required in TCP/IP networks to resolve IP addresses to MAC addresses. **C** is incorrect, although it is very important. There are no patches addressing this issue because ARP, by design, is stateless and is required for TCP/IP to function.

20. Your intranet provides employees the ability to search through a SQL database for their past travel expenses once they have logged in. One employee from the IT department discovers that if he enters a SQL string such as SELECT * FROM EXPENSES WHERE EMPID = 'x'='x'; it returns all employee travel expense records. What secure coding guideline was ignored?

A. SQL injection prevention

B. Input validation

C. Disabling of SQL indexes

D. User authentication

> ☑ **B.** Had the SQL query string been properly validated, returning all records would have been prevented.
>
> ☒ **A, C, and D are incorrect. A** is incorrect because SQL injection prevention is not a secure coding guideline. **C** is incorrect because lack of indexes may make searching slower, but it will not prevent the flaw in this example, and it is not considered a secure coding guideline. **D** is incorrect because the question clearly states that users are logging in.

21. You capture and examine network traffic weekly to ensure the network is being used properly. In doing so, you notice traffic to TCP port 53 on your server from an unknown IP address. After reviewing your server logs, you notice repeated failed attempts to execute a zone transfer to your server. What type of attack was attempted?

A. ARP poisoning

B. Cross-site scripting

C. DNS poisoning

D. MAC flooding

> ☑ **C.** DNS (Domain Name Service) poisoning means including incorrect name resolution data with the intent of secretly redirecting users to malicious hosts. TCP port 53 is used by DNS servers to synchronize DNS records, and in this case, to (not from) your server.

☒ **A, B,** and **D** are incorrect. **A** is incorrect because ARP (Address Resolution Protocol) poisoning links IP addresses to incorrect MAC addresses, the result of which is to redirect traffic to a malicious device. The question involves port 53 and zone transfers, which are DNS and not ARP attributes. **B** is incorrect because cross-site scripting injects malicious scripts into normally trustworthy web sites. Web sites use ports 80 and 443, so clearly the question related to DNS, not HTTP (Hypertext Transfer Protocol). **D** does not apply because MAC flooding does not relate in any way to port 53 or zone transfers; MAC flooding attempts to overwhelm a network switch to the point that the switch forwards all traffic to all switch ports.

22. A network security audit exposes three insecure wireless routers using default configurations. Which security principle has been ignored?

A. Application patch management

B. Device hardening

C. Input validation

D. Principle of least privilege

☑ **B.** Had the wireless routers been properly hardened, the default configurations would have been changed to avoid, for instance, lack of MAC filtering, lack of encryption, and use of default admin passwords.

☒ **A, C,** and **D** are incorrect. **A** does not apply because patching may correct security flaws, but it will not normally change default configurations. **C** is incorrect because there is no input being applied to the wireless routers. Input validation is best suited to areas where users can supply data that is sent to a server. **D** is incorrect because granting users only the rights they need is inapplicable to wireless routers but is applicable to network resources.

23. Which of the following standards must authenticate computing devices before allowing network access?

A. Router

B. Hub

C. IEEE 802.1x

D. IEEE 802.11n

☑ **C.** IEEE 802.1x is a standard that authenticates computers against a server before allowing access to wired or wireless networks.

☒ **A, B,** and **D** are incorrect. **A** and **B** are network devices, not standards. **D** is incorrect because IEEE 802.11n is a wireless networking standard with theoretical rates of up to 600 Mbps, but the 802.11n standard does not authenticate computers prior to allowing network access.

24. What will prevent frequent repeated malicious attacks against user account passwords?

A. Minimum password age

B. Password hints

C. Password history

D. Account lockout

☑ **D.** Account lockout locks an account after a predetermined number of incorrect password attempts renders the account unusable for a period of time, thus preventing further password attempts.

☒ **A, B,** and **C** are incorrect. **A** does not apply in this case. Minimum password age ensures users do not reset their current password to an old, easy-to-remember one. This setting would still allow incessant password attempts. **B** is incorrect because password hints simply help the user remember a complex password, not restrict repeated password attempts. **C** is incorrect because password history prevents users from reusing the same passwords, but it does not restrict the number of times hackers can attempt to compromise user accounts.

25. Which item would *best* apply a standard security baseline to many computers?

A. A disk image of the operating system

B. Security templates distributed through group policy

C. Password settings distributed through group policy

D. Security templates distributed through local security policy

☑ **B.** Security templates can contain many security settings, which are best distributed to groups of computers through group policy.

☒ **A, C,** and **D** are incorrect. **A** is incorrect because despite the fact that an image could already be configured with standard security settings, it is tied to the image and is, therefore, not as flexible as security templates and group policy. **C** does not apply because there are many more security items to consider than just password settings. **D** is incorrect because local security policy applies to a single machine only, but in this case we must deploy settings to many computers.

26. After patching and hardening your computers, how would you determine if your computers are secure?

    A. Performance baseline

    B. Security templates

    C. Penetration testing

    D. Password cracking

> ☑ **C.** Penetration testing exploits hardware and software vulnerabilities to determine how secure computing devices or networks really are.
>
> ☒ **A, B,** and **D** are incorrect. **A** is incorrect because performance baselines determine what type of performance can be expected under normal conditions, but they do not directly relate to how secure a system is. **B** is incorrect because security templates are used to apply settings to harden a system, but not to test that security. **D** is incorrect because, although password cracking does test computer security, there are many more aspects of computer security that would be covered in a penetration test.

27. While hardening a Windows server, you decide to disable a number of services. How can you ensure that the services you are disabling will not adversely affect other services?

    A. Run the NET START 'service name' / DEP command.

    B. Disable the services, let the system run for a few days, and then check the event viewer logs.

    C. Right-click the service and choose Show Dependency Chain.

    D. Double-click the service and view the Dependencies tab.

> ☑ **D.** The Dependencies tab in a service's properties lists other services that depend on the one you are considering disabling.
>
> ☒ **A, B,** and **C** are incorrect. **A** and **C** are incorrect because these options do not exist. **B** is incorrect because checking service dependencies is much more reliable and quicker.

28. Your company uses Microsoft IIS to host multiple intranet web sites on a two-node cluster. All sites store their configuration and content on drive C:, and log files are stored on D:. All sites share a common application pool. The IT director has asked that you ensure a single hacked web site will not adversely affect other running web sites. What should you do?

    A. Move each web site configuration to a separate hard disk.

    B. Move each web site content to a separate hard disk.

C. Configure each web site to use its own application pool.

D. Add a third node to the two-node cluster.

☑ **C.** Web sites running in separate application pools prevent one pool from affecting other pools, as in the event of a compromised web site.

☒ **A, B,** and **D** are incorrect. The question clearly states all sites share the same application pool. Each site should have its own application pool for security and stability reasons.

7

Implementing System Security

CERTIFICATION OBJECTIVES

❑   **1.3**   Distinguish and differentiate network design elements and compounds

❑   **4.2**   Carry out appropriate procedures to establish host security

❑   **4.3**   Explain the importance of data security

QUESTIONS

Various forms of malware are created every day. Preventing and removing this malware is more important now than ever, especially as mobile, hand-held devices become increasingly popular. Even on firewall-protected networks, host-based firewalls offer protection from network attacks. Because they are desirable and very easy to steal, mobile devices should encrypt data and have a tracking mechanism such as GPS enabled. Continuing with modern technology trends, cloud computing allows us to have every aspect of our data networking hosted by a third party, often in a virtualized environment. All of these technologies offer enormous advantages that you must weigh against the security risks.

1. Which security measure would protect hard disk contents even if server hard disks were physically stolen?
   A. NTFS permissions
   B. Power-on password
   C. Complex administrative passwords
   D. Encryption

2. Sara's user account is mistakenly deleted when she goes on a twelve-month maternity leave. When she returns, a new account with appropriate NTFS permissions is created for her. When she tries to open her old files she keeps getting "Access Denied" messages. What is the problem?
   A. Sara does not have proper NTFS permissions.
   B. Sara's new user account has a different SID than her old one.
   C. Sara's files are encrypted with her old account.
   D. Sara's account should be made a member of the Power Users group.

3. Carlos has been using his work e-mail address when surfing the web and filling in forms on various web sites. To which potential problem has Carlos exposed himself?
   A. Spam
   B. Phishing
   C. SQL injection
   D. DNS poisoning

4. You are a server virtualization consultant for Not Really There, Inc. During a planning meeting with a client, the issue of virtual machine point-in-time snapshots comes up. You recommend very careful use of snapshots because of the security ramifications. What is your concern?
   A. Snapshots can consume a large amount of disk space.
   B. The use of snapshots could trigger a MAC flood.
   C. Invoked snapshots will mean that virtual machine is temporarily unavailable.
   D. Invoked snapshots will be less patched than the currently running virtual machine.

5. What can be done to harden a mobile, hand-held device? (Choose two.)
   A. Disable Wi-Fi.
   B. Ensure it is used only in physically secured areas.
   C. Set Bluetooth discovery to disabled.
   D. Enable screen lock.

6. A private medical practice hires you to determine the feasibility of cloud computing whereby e-mail and medical applications, as well as patient information, would be hosted by an Internet provider. You are asked to identify possible security issues. (Choose two.)
   A. Data storage is not local but instead on the provider's premises, where other businesses also have access to cloud computing services.
   B. HTTPS will be used to access remote services.
   C. Should the provider be served a subpoena, the possibility of full data disclosure exists.
   D. Data will be encrypted in transit as well as when stored.

7. Which option will protect employee laptops when they travel and connect to wireless networks?
   A. Personal firewall software
   B. MAC address filtering
   C. Virtualization
   D. 802.11n-compliant wireless card

8. What can be done to ensure the confidentiality of sensitive data copied to USB flash drives?
   A. File hash
   B. Encryption
   C. NTFS permissions
   D. Share permissions

9. Which standard is a firmware solution for drive encryption?
   A. TPM
   B. DLP
   C. EFS
   D. NTFS

10. What can be done to protect data after a hand-held device is lost or stolen?
   A. Enable encryption.
   B. Execute a remote wipe.
   C. Enable screen lock.
   D. Disable Bluetooth discovery.

11. How can the specific location of a mobile device be tracked?
    A. IP address
    B. MAC address
    C. SIM card code
    D. GPS

12. What type of software filters unsolicited junk e-mail?
    A. Antispam
    B. Antivirus
    C. Antispyware
    D. Antiadware

13. What type of software works against the collection of personal information?
    A. Antispam
    B. Antivirus
    C. Antispyware
    D. Antiadware

14. Which of the following best protects against operating system defects?
    A. Antivirus software
    B. Firewall software
    C. Encryption
    D. Patching

15. What is the best way to prevent laptop theft?
    A. GPS
    B. Cable lock
    C. Host-based firewall
    D. Antivirus software

16. A server administrator must adhere to legislation that states financial data must be kept secure in the event of a physical security breach. What practices will ensure the administrator complies with the law? (Choose two.)
    A. Apply NTFS permissions.
    B. Store backup tapes in a safe.
    C. Encrypt server hard disks.
    D. Store backup tapes in a locked cabinet.

17. What type of software examines application behavior, logs, and events for suspicious activity?
    A. NIDS
    B. Host-based firewall

C. HIDS

D. Spyware

18. A database administrator requests a method by which malicious activity against a Microsoft SQL database server can be detected. All network traffic to the database server is encrypted. What solution should you recommend?

A. HIDS

B. NIDS

C. IPSec

D. SSL

19. Which of the following are true regarding virtualization? (Choose two.)

A. Each virtual machine has one or more unique MAC addresses.

B. Virtual machine operating systems do not need to be patched.

C. Virtual machines running on the same physical host can belong to different VLANs.

D. A security compromise in one virtual machine means all virtual machines on the physical host are compromised.

20. Cloud computing offers which benefits? (Choose two.)

A. Simple scalability

B. Fewer hardware purchases

C. Better encryption

D. Local data storage

E. No requirement for anti-virus software

21. Julian is responsible for three payroll servers that store data on a SAN. The CFO (Chief Financial Officer) requests observation of access to a group of budget files by a particular user. What should Julian do?

A. Create file hashes for each budget file.

B. Encrypt the budget files.

C. Configure a HIDS to monitor the budget files.

D. Configure file system auditing.

22. Your company has acquired security software that will monitor application usage on all workstations. Before the software can function properly, you must have users run their applications as they normally would for a short period. Why does the security software require this to be done?

A. To update antivirus definitions for application files

B. To establish a normal usage baseline

C. To verify the security software has the required permissions to run

D. To verify licensed software is being used

23. Kevin is a trial lawyer in southern California. He requires secure, high-quality voice communication with clients. What can he do?

A. Use VoIP with packet encryption over the Internet.

B. Use cell phone voice encryption.

C. Use only landline telephones.

D. Use his cell phone on a special voice network for legal professionals.

24. Your IT manager asks you to ensure e-mail messages and attachments do not contain sensitive data that could be leaked to competitors. What type of solution should you propose?

A. Antivirus software

B. NIDS

C. DLP

D. HIDS

25. Your server performance has decreased since the introduction of digitally signing and encrypting all network traffic. You would like to release the servers from this function. Which device should you use?

A. Smart card

B. TPM

C. HSM

D. EFS

26. Your company has decided that all new server hardware will have TPM support. You receive a new server and you enable TPM through the CMOS utility and enable drive encryption using TPM in your operating system. What should you do next?

A. Reboot the server.

B. Enable EFS on the server.

C. Enable IPSec.

D. Back up the TPM keys.

27. You attempt to encrypt a folder on drive D: using EFS, but the encryption option is unavailable. What should you do?

A. Issue the **CONVERT D: /FS:NTFS** command.

B. Add your account to the Administrators group.

C. Enable EFS through Group Policy.

D. Enable TPM in the CMOS utility.

QUICK ANSWER KEY

1.	D	10.	B	19.	A, C
2.	C	11.	D	20.	A, B
3.	A	12.	A	21.	D
4.	D	13.	C	22.	B
5.	C, D	14.	D	23.	B
6.	A, C	15.	B	24.	C
7.	A	16.	B, C	25.	C
8.	B	17.	C	26.	D
9.	A	18.	A	27.	A

IN-DEPTH ANSWERS

1. Which security measure would protect hard disk contents even if server hard disks were physically stolen?

    A. NTFS permissions

    B. Power-on password

    C. Complex administrative passwords

    D. Encryption

    ☑ **D.** Encryption is the best answer because NTFS permissions, power-on password, and complex passwords are all meaningless when someone gains physical access to hard disks.

    ☒ **A, B,** and **C** are incorrect. **A** is incorrect because NTFS permissions are easily circumvented by taking ownership of the disk contents after plugging the disk into another machine. **B** is incorrect because the power-on password is tied to the specific machine, not the hard disk. **C** is incorrect because passwords can be reset if somebody gets local physical access to a hard disk.

2. Sara's user account is mistakenly deleted when she goes on a twelve-month maternity leave. When she returns, a new account with appropriate NTFS permissions is created for her. When she tries to open her old files she keeps getting "Access Denied" messages. What is the problem?

    A. Sara does not have proper NTFS permissions.

    B. Sara's new user account has a different SID than her old one.

    C. Sara's files are encrypted with her old account.

    D. Sara's account should be made a member of the Power Users group.

    ☑ **C.** EFS (Encrypting File System) encrypts files and folders using keys that are unique to the user. Newly created user accounts, even with the same name, will not use the same keys, which means decryption will not occur. A recovery agent is required to decrypt her files.

    ☒ **A, B,** and **D** are incorrect. **A** does not apply, since the question states the appropriate NTFS permissions are put into place. **B** is incorrect, although Sara does have a different SID. The SID does not get used to encrypt files; the user public key does. **D** is incorrect because members of the Power Users group have no special access to EFS-encrypted files.

3. Carlos has been using his work e-mail address when surfing the web and filling in forms on various web sites. To which potential problem has Carlos exposed himself?

A. Spam

B. Phishing

C. SQL injection

D. DNS poisoning

☑ **A.** Despite perhaps being illegal (this is currently a legal gray area), there is money to be made in providing valid e-mail addresses to spammers, and also in spammers sending unsolicited advertisements to those e-mail addresses.

☒ **B, C,** and **D** are incorrect. **B** is incorrect because phishing directs unsuspecting users via what appears to be a legitimate e-mail to false web sites in an attempt to gather private user information. In this case, Carlos is surfing the web, not clicking links in e-mail messages. **C** does not apply because SQL injections are intentionally crafted by malicious users to retrieve more records from a database than they normally should. **D** is incorrect because DNS poisoning has nothing to do with e-mail addresses; instead, it has to do with FQDNs (fully qualified domain names) being directed to malicious sites.

4. You are a server virtualization consultant for Not Really There, Inc. During a planning meeting with a client, the issue of virtual machine point-in-time snapshots comes up. You recommend very careful use of snapshots because of the security ramifications. What is your concern?

A. Snapshots can consume a large amount of disk space.

B. The use of snapshots could trigger a MAC flood.

C. Invoked snapshots will mean that virtual machine is temporarily unavailable.

D. Invoked snapshots will be less patched than the currently running virtual machine.

☑ **D.** Reverting a running virtual machine to an older snapshot could mean going back to a point in time before critical patches or virus scanning updates were applied, thus rendering your virtual machine vulnerable.

☒ **A, B,** and **C** are incorrect. **A** and **C** are not applicable to security, although they are true in fact. **B** is incorrect because MAC address floods are not invoked when reverting to a virtual machine snapshot.

5. What can be done to harden a mobile, hand-held device? (Choose two.)

   A. Disable Wi-Fi.

   B. Ensure it is used only in physically secured areas.

   C. Set Bluetooth discovery to disabled.

   D. Enable screen lock.

   ☑ **C** and **D**. Bluetooth discovery mode makes it possible for anybody within range (ten meters) to see and potentially connect to the mobile device. Screen lock is essential to secure mobile devices; a password or fingerprint scan is used to unlock the screen and make the device usable.

   ☒ **A** and **B** are incorrect. **A** is incorrect because completely disabling Wi-Fi is not a recommended hardening solution. Wi-Fi hardening is more often configured on the wireless access point. Disabling Bluetooth discovery and configuring screen lock are much better hardening options. **B** is incorrect because it is incredibly inconvenient, and convenience is the primary reason for the success of hand-held devices.

6. A private medical practice hires you to determine the feasibility of cloud computing whereby e-mail and medical applications, as well as patient information, would be hosted by an Internet provider. You are asked to identify possible security issues. (Choose two.)

   A. Data storage is not local but instead on the provider's premises, where other businesses also have access to cloud computing services.

   B. HTTPS will be used to access remote services.

   C. Should the provider be served a subpoena, the possibility of full data disclosure exists.

   D. Data will be encrypted in transit as well as when stored.

   ☑ **A** and **C**. Because there are many customers sharing the same cloud computing services, it is reasonable to approach the issue of data storage cautiously. Third-party audit findings may dispel or confirm these fears. Depending on the provider's geographic location, different laws may apply to whether or not data hosted by the provider can legally be disclosed.

   ☒ **B** and **D** are incorrect. **B** is incorrect because HTTPS (Hypertext Transfer Protocol Secure) is considered a secure transmission protocol; HTTP is not. **D** is also incorrect because data encryption does not warrant security concerns, it addresses them.

7. Which option will protect employee laptops when they travel and connect to wireless networks?

    A. Personal firewall software

    B. MAC address filtering

    C. Virtualization

    D. 802.11n-compliant wireless card

    ☑ **A.** Personal firewall software could be configured to prevent all inbound network traffic, which also prevents its discovery on a wired or wireless network.

    ☒ **B, C,** and **D** are incorrect. **B** is incorrect because MAC address filtering is configured on the wireless routers, which would not all be under your control. **C** does not apply, because even virtualized operating systems need firewall protection. **D** is incorrect because an 802.11n-compliant wireless card offers no more protection than an 802.11g-compliant wireless card.

8. What can be done to ensure the confidentiality of sensitive data copied to USB flash drives?

    A. File hash

    B. Encryption

    C. NTFS permissions

    D. Share permissions

    ☑ **B.** Encrypting USB flash drives prevents unauthorized parties from viewing the data.

    ☒ **A, C,** and **D** are incorrect. **A** is incorrect because, although file hashing is important for file integrity (any changes in the file invalidate the file hash), it does not apply to confidentiality. **C** does not apply, since NTFS permissions can be circumvented by taking ownership of files and folders. **D** is incorrect because share permissions only apply across a network.

9. Which standard is a firmware solution for drive encryption?

    A. TPM

    B. DLP

    C. EFS

    D. NTFS

☑   **A.** TPM (Trusted Platform Module) chips can store cryptographic keys or certificates used to encrypt and decrypt drive contents. If the drive were moved to another computer (even one with TPM), the drive would remain encrypted and inaccessible.

☒   **B, C,** and **D** are incorrect. **B** is incorrect because DLP (Data Loss Prevention) refers to fault tolerance and related mechanisms for ensuring data is safe. **C** is incorrect because EFS is purely software, not a firmware chip. **D** is incorrect because NTFS (New Technology File System) uses ACLs (access control lists) to control access to data, but the data is not encrypted.

10. What can be done to protect data after a hand-held device is lost or stolen?

    A. Enable encryption.

    B. Execute a remote wipe.

    C. Enable screen lock.

    D. Disable Bluetooth discovery.

☑   **B.** Remote wipe is an option administrators can exercise to remotely wipe the contents of a hand-held device

☒   **A, C,** and **D** are incorrect. These settings would have to be either set before the device was lost or stolen, or pushed out the next time the device was connected.

11. How can the specific location of a mobile device be tracked?

    A. IP address

    B. MAC address

    C. SIM card code

    D. GPS

☑   **D.** GPS (Global Positioning System) is a common feature in mobile devices that provides coordinates (longitude and latitude) for geographic tracking.

☒   **A, B,** and **C** are incorrect. **A** is incorrect because NAT (Network Address Translation) and proxy servers both mask the originating IP address, thus making it unreliable for tracking devices. **B** is incorrect because the originating device MAC address is only used on a LAN. Once packets leave a LAN, the source MAC address changes as the packet travels through routers. **C** is incorrect because, although SIM (Subscriber Identification Module) cards in mobile devices do register with the nearest cell tower, the location is not as specific as GPS.

12. What type of software filters unsolicited junk e-mail?

    A. Antispam

    B. Antivirus

    C. Antispyware

    D. Antiadware

> ☑   **A.** Spam is unsolicited junk e-mail. Antispam software attempts to filter out these messages, but it sometimes flags legitimate messages as spam.
>
> ☒   **B, C**, and **D** are incorrect. They do not offer protection against unsolicited junk e-mail.

13. What type of software works against the collection of personal information?

    A. Antispam

    B. Antivirus

    C. Antispyware

    D. Antiadware

> ☑   **C.** Spyware gathers personal information and computer usage habits without user knowledge.
>
> ☒   **A, B**, and **D** are incorrect. **A** is incorrect because antispam software reduces the amount of junk e-mail in a mail user's inbox. **B** is incorrect because antivirus software prevents the propagation of malware such as worms and Trojans. **D** is incorrect because adware does not collect personal information, but it does display advertisements selected on the basis of personal information.

14. Which of the following best protects against operating system defects?

    A. Antivirus software

    B. Firewall software

    C. Encryption

    D. Patching

> ☑   **D.** Patching addresses specific operating system defects.
>
> ☒   **A, B**, and **C** are incorrect. These are all very important and are critical security components, but the question asks the best protection against bugs in the operating system.

15. What is the best way to prevent laptop theft?

A. GPS

B. Cable lock

C. Host-based firewall

D. Antivirus software

☑ **B.** A cable lock is a steel cable designed to secure a laptop to a secure object, such as a desk.

☒ **A, C,** and **D** are incorrect. **A** is incorrect because GPS (Global Positioning System) allows tracking the laptop but does not prevent its theft. **C** and **D** are software security prevention techniques, but they do nothing to protect equipment physically.

16. A server administrator must adhere to legislation that states financial data must be kept secure in the event of a physical security breach. What practices will ensure the administrator complies with the law? (Choose two.)

A. Apply NTFS permissions.

B. Store backup tapes in a safe.

C. Encrypt server hard disks.

D. Store backup tapes in a locked cabinet.

☑ **B and C.** In the event of a physical security breach, data will be kept secure in a safe. If server hard disks are stolen, encryption will ensure the data cannot be decrypted by unauthorized parties.

☒ **A and D** are incorrect. **A** is incorrect because NTFS permissions are easily defeated locally (not across the network). **D** is incorrect because such storage is not as secure as storing backup tapes in a safe and encrypting server hard disks.

17. What type of software examines application behavior, logs, and events for suspicious activity?

A. NIDS

B. Host-based firewall

C. HIDS

D. Spyware

☑ **C.** HIDS (host-based intrusion detection system) software monitors applications, logs, and events for suspicious activity.

☒ **A, B,** and **D** are incorrect. **A** is incorrect because an NIDS (network intrusion detection system) examines network packets to identify suspicious network activity, not application-specific anomalies. **B** is incorrect because host-based firewalls either allow or deny inbound and outbound packets. **D** is incorrect because spyware gathers personal user information. Spyware is not designed to look at logs and application events.

18. A database administrator requests a method by which malicious activity against a Microsoft SQL database server can be detected. All network traffic to the database server is encrypted. What solution should you recommend?

 A. HIDS

 B. NIDS

 C. IPSec

 D. SSL

☑ **A.** Host-based intrusion detection systems are application specific (such as to a SQL database). Encryption presents no problems, since HIDS runs on the target computer.

☒ **B, C,** and **D** are incorrect. **B** does not apply, since network intrusion detection systems do not single out suspicious application activity; instead, they attempt to single out suspect network activity. **C** is incorrect because IPSec (IP Security) encrypts and digitally signs packets; it does not apply to specific applications. **D** does not apply. SSL (Secure Sockets Layer) is used to secure HTTP network traffic.

19. Which of the following are true regarding virtualization? (Choose two.)

 A. Each virtual machine has one or more unique MAC addresses.

 B. Virtual machine operating systems do not need to be patched.

 C. Virtual machines running on the same physical host can belong to different VLANs.

 D. A security compromise in one virtual machine means all virtual machines on the physical host are compromised.

☑ **A** and **C.** Each virtual machine does have a unique MAC address that is configurable by the virtual machine administrator. Virtual machines running on the same host can connect to different VLANs (physical or internal); this is simply a virtual network configuration setting.

☒ **B and D are incorrect. B** is incorrect because virtualized operating systems must be patched. **D** is incorrect because, as with physical hosts, a compromised machine does not imply full access to all other machines.

20. Cloud computing offers which benefits? (Choose two.)

A. Simple scalability

B. Fewer hardware purchases

C. Better encryption

D. Local data storage

E. No requirement for anti-virus software

☑ **A and B.** Scalability with cloud computing is simple because a third party takes care of hardware, software, software licensing, and so on. Because a third party is hosting some (or all) of your IT services, you will require fewer hardware resources.

☒ **C, D, and E are incorrect. C** is incorrect because the question does not specify what (if any) type of encryption either party is using. **D** is incorrect because cloud computing normally implies data storage is hosted by the provider, not locally. **E** is incorrect because, even for firms relying exclusively on cloud computing, their employees will still use a computing device to connect to cloud services and, therefore, will still need antivirus software.

21. Julian is responsible for three payroll servers that store data on a SAN. The CFO (Chief Financial Officer) requests observation of access to a group of budget files by a particular user. What should Julian do?

A. Create file hashes for each budget file.

B. Encrypt the budget files.

C. Configure a HIDS to monitor the budget files.

D. Configure file system auditing.

☑ **D.** File system auditing should be configured for budget file access by the employee in question.

☒ **A, B, and C are incorrect. A** does not apply because file hashing is useful only in determining if a file has changed, not if anybody in particular accessed the file. **B** does not apply when you must observe file access; encryption is used for data confidentiality. **C** is incorrect because HIDS looks for abnormal activity; Julian was only asked to observe file access.

22. Your company has acquired security software that will monitor application usage on all workstations. Before the software can function properly, you must have users run their applications as they normally would for a short period. Why does the security software require this to be done?

 A. To update antivirus definitions for application files

 B. To establish a normal usage baseline

 C. To verify the security software has the required permissions to run

 D. To verify licensed software is being used

 ☑ **B.** In order to detect abnormal behavior, the security software must know what is normal in this environment.

 ☒ **A, C,** and **D** are incorrect. **A** is incorrect because the antivirus software will update its own virus definitions. **C** is inapplicable; this is normally done by the installation routine. **D** is incorrect because checking software license compliance would not require users to use the software for a short period.

23. Kevin is a trial lawyer in southern California. He requires secure, high-quality voice communication with clients. What can he do?

 A. Use VoIP with packet encryption over the Internet.

 B. Use cell phone voice encryption.

 C. Use only landline telephones.

 D. Use his cell phone on a special voice network for legal professionals.

 ☑ **B.** Cell phone voice encryption software ensures that your voice calls are confidential after establishing a secure session with the other cell phone. The encrypted voice is transmitted through the cell phone's data channel as opposed to the normal voice channel.

 ☒ **A, C,** and **D** are incorrect. **A** is incorrect because VoIP is very time sensitive such that encrypting and decrypting each packet over the Internet means VoIP will suffer from delay. **C** is incorrect because landline phones are not considered secure. **D** does not apply, since there is no such voice network.

24. Your IT manager asks you to ensure e-mail messages and attachments do not contain sensitive data that could be leaked to competitors. What type of solution should you propose?

 A. Antivirus software

 B. NIDS

C.   DLP

D.   HIDS

☑   **C.** DLP (data loss prevention) hardware and software solutions perform deep content inspection of data (such as e-mail bodies and attachments) to prevent information leakage.

☒   **A, B,** and **D** are incorrect. **A** does not apply because antivirus software scans for viruses, not company secrets. **B** and **D** are incorrect because they both look for abnormalities (NIDS on the network, HIDS on a host).

---

25. Your server performance has decreased since the introduction of digitally signing and encrypting all network traffic. You would like to release the servers from this function. Which device should you use?

A.   Smart card

B.   TPM

C.   HSM

D.   EFS

☑   **C.** HSM (hardware security module) devices are designed to handle cryptographic duties, thus allowing servers to focus on other tasks.

☒   **A, B,** and **D** are incorrect. **A** is incorrect because smart cards are an authentication mechanism used to identify users and do not remove server cryptographic responsibilities. **B** does not apply because TPM chips are used to encrypt and decrypt disk contents, not network traffic. **D** is incorrect because EFS (Encrypting File System) is not a device; it is software.

---

26. Your company has decided that all new server hardware will have TPM support. You receive a new server and you enable TPM through the CMOS utility and enable drive encryption using TPM in your operating system. What should you do next?

A.   Reboot the server.

B.   Enable EFS on the server.

C.   Enable IPSec.

D.   Back up the TPM keys.

☑ **D.** TPM stores keys, certificates, and passwords used for disk encryption in a chip. In the event the chip or motherboard fails, it is important to have a copy of keys so that disk contents can be decrypted.

☒ **A, B,** and **C** are incorrect. **A** is incorrect because rebooting the server is not required by all operating systems using TPM. **B** is incorrect because, although EFS (Encrypting File System) can be used in conjunction with TPM, enabling it is not the next thing you should do. **C** does not apply, since the question refers to TPM disk encryption, not IP (Internet Protocol) encryption.

27. You attempt to encrypt a folder on drive D: using EFS, but the encryption option is unavailable. What should you do?

    A. Issue the **CONVERT D: /FS:NTFS** command.

    B. Add your account to the Administrators group.

    C. Enable EFS through Group Policy.

    D. Enable TPM in the CMOS utility.

☑ **A.** EFS (Encrypting File System) requires NTFS file systems.

☒ **B, C,** and **D** are incorrect. **B** is incorrect because you do not need to be in the Administrators group to encrypt a folder. **C** is incorrect because EFS does not need to be enabled through Group Policy. **D** is incorrect because TPM is not required for EFS to function.

8

Securing the Network Infrastructure

CERTIFICATION OBJECTIVES

❑   1.1   Explain the security function and purpose of network devices and technologies

❑   1.2   Apply and implement secure network administration principles

❑   1.3   Distinguish and differentiate network design elements and compounds

❑   3.6   Analyze and differentiate among types of mitigation and deterrent techniques

QUESTIONS

Firewalls are an integral part of computer networks and come in various forms such as NAT firewalls, packet filtering firewalls, and proxy servers. Some firewalls perform deep packet inspection, whereas others examine only packet headers. Intrusion detection analyzes and identifies suspicious activity. Intrusion prevention extends this detection by attempting to block the suspicious activity. Both can be performed for a network or for a specific host. Besides firewalling, it's also important to remember basic network security options, including switch port security, placement of network devices, and changing default configurations.

1. You are a guest at a hotel offering free Wi-Fi Internet access to guests. You connect to the wireless network at full signal strength and obtain a valid TCP/IP configuration. When you try to access Internet web sites, a web page displays instead asking for a code before allowing access to the Internet. What type of network component is providing this functionality?
   A. DHCP Server
   B. NAT
   C. Proxy Server
   D. Switch

2. You are configuring a wireless router at a car repair shop so that waiting customers can connect to the Internet. You want to ensure wireless clients can connect to the Internet but cannot connect to internal computers owned by the car repair shop. Where should you plug in the wireless router?
   A. LAN
   B. Port 24 on the switch
   C. Port 1 on the switch
   D. DMZ

3. What will detect network or host intrusions and take actions to prevent the intrusion from succeeding?
   A. IPS
   B. IDS
   C. IPSec
   D. DMZ

4. What technology uses a single external IP address to represent many computers on an internal network?
   A. IPSec
   B. DHCP

    C. NAT

    D. NIDS

5. You must purchase a network device that supports content filtering and virus defense for your LAN. What should you choose?

    A. NAT router

    B. HIPS

    C. Web security gateway

    D. Packet filtering firewall

6. You have been asked to somehow separate Engineering departmental network traffic from Accounting departmental traffic due to a decrease in network throughput. What should you use?

    A. VLAN

    B. DMZ

    C. NAT

    D. VPN

7. Given the following LAN firewall rule set, which is the best description?
Allow inbound TCP 3389
Allow outbound TCP 80
Allow outbound TCP 443

    A. LAN users can connect to external FTP sites. External users can use RDP to connect to LAN computers.

    B. LAN users can connect to external SMTP servers. External users can use LDAP to connect to LAN computers.

    C. LAN users can connect to external web servers. External uses can use RDP to connect to LAN computers.

    D. LAN users can connect to external proxy servers. External users can use IPSec to connect to LAN computers.

8. Which tool would allow you to capture and view network traffic?

    A. Vulnerability scanner

    B. Port scanner

    C. Protocol analyzer

    D. NAT

9. You are reviewing router configurations to ensure they comply with corporate security policies. You notice the routers are configured to load their configurations using TFTP and also that TCP port 22 is enabled. What security problem exists with these routers?

   A. Telnet should be disabled.
   B. Telnet should have a password configured.
   C. TFTP is an insecure protocol.
   D. Telnet should limit concurrent logins to 1.

10. A router must be configured to only allow traffic from certain hosts. How can this be accomplished?

    A. ACL
    B. Subnet
    C. Proxy server
    D. NAT

11. Which technologies allow analysis of network traffic? (Choose two.)

    A. Port scanner
    B. Sniffer
    C. DMZ
    D. NIDS

12. What term describes the network between the two firewalls in this illustration?

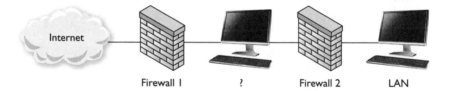

Internet   Firewall 1   ?   Firewall 2   LAN

    A. Proxy server
    B. NAT
    C. DMZ
    D. NIDS

13. You have received a new VPN concentrator to allow traveling users' access to LAN B. Where in this illustration should you place the VPN concentrator?

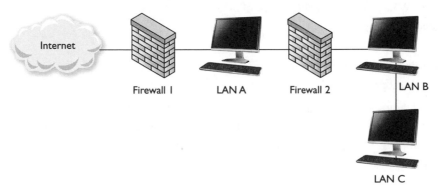

A. Internet

B. LAN A

C. LAN B

D. LAN C

14. Sylvia's workstation has been moved to a new cubicle. On Monday morning, Sylvia reports that even though the network card is plugged into the network jack, there is no link light on the network card. What is the problem?

A. The workstation has an APIPA address. Issue the IPCONFIG / RENEW command.

B. The default gateway has not been set.

C. Sylvia must first log on to the domain.

D. Since the MAC address has changed, switch port security has disabled the port.

15. You need a method of authenticating Windows 7 workstations before allowing local LAN access. What should you use?

A. VPN concentrator

B. Router

C. 802.1x switch

D. Proxy server

16. An attacker sends thousands of TCP SYN packets with unreachable source IP addresses to a server. After consuming server resources with this traffic, legitimate traffic can no longer reach the server. What can prevent this type of attack?
    A. Packet filtering firewall
    B. Proxy server
    C. Antivirus software
    D. SYN flood protection

17. A junior IT employee links three network switches together such that each switch connects to the two others. As a result, the network is flooded with useless traffic. What can prevent this situation?
    A. Web application firewall
    B. Loop protection
    C. SYN flood guard
    D. Router ACL

18. Your boss asks that specific HTTP traffic be monitored and blocked. What should you use?
    A. Web application firewall
    B. Protocol analyzer
    C. Packet filtering firewall
    D. NAT

19. A high school principal insists on preventing student access to known malware web sites. How can this be done?
    A. DMZ
    B. URL filtering
    C. DNS forwarding
    D. 802.1x switch

20. Which of the following scenarios best describes implicit deny?
    A. Allow network access if it is 802.1x authenticated.
    B. Block outbound network traffic destined for TCP port 25.
    C. Block network traffic unless specifically permitted.
    D. Allow network traffic unless specifically forbidden.

21. A university student has a wired network connection to a restrictive university network. At the same time, the student is connected to a Wi-Fi hotspot for a nearby coffee shop that allows unrestricted Internet access. What potential problem exists in this case?
    A. The student computer could link coffee shop patrons to the university network.
    B. The student computer could override the university default gateway setting.

    C. Encrypted university transmissions could find their way onto the Wi-Fi network.

    D. Encrypted coffee shop transmissions could find their way onto the university network.

22. Which network device encrypts and decrypts network traffic over an unsafe network to allow access to private LANs?

    A. Proxy server

    B. IPSec

    C. VPN concentrator

    D. TPM

23. You suspect malicious activity on your DMZ. In an effort to identify the offender, you have intentionally configured an unpatched server to attract further attention. What term describes what you have configured?

    A. Honeynet

    B. Logging server

    C. Exploit

    D. Honeypot

24. Your NIDS incorrectly reports legitimate network traffic as being suspicious. What is this known as?

    A. False positive

    B. Explicit false

    C. False negative

    D. Implicit false

25. Your corporate network access policy states that all connecting devices require a host-based firewall and an antivirus scanner as well as having the latest operating system updates. You would like to prevent noncompliant devices from connecting to your network. What solution should you consider?

    A. NIDS

    B. NAC

    C. VLAN

    D. HIDS

26. Which of the following are true regarding NAT? (Choose two.)

    A. The NAT client is unaware of address translation.

    B. The NAT client is aware of address translation.

    C. Internet hosts are unaware of address translation.

    D. Internet hosts are aware of address translation.

27. You are a sales executive for a real estate firm. One of your clients calls you wondering why you have not e-mailed them critical documentation regarding a sale. You check your mail program to verify the message was sent two days ago. You also verify the message was not sent back to you as undeliverable. You tell your client that you did in fact send the message. What should you next tell your client?

    A. Clean your mailbox—there is no room for new incoming mail.

    B. Wait a few hours—Internet e-mail is slow.

    C. NAT might have prevented the message from being delivered.

    D. Check your junk mail; antispam software sometimes incorrectly identifies legitimate mail as spam.

28. You are an IT network consultant. You install a new wireless network for a hotel. What must you do to prevent wireless network users from gaining administrative access to wireless routers?

    A. Apply MAC filtering.

    B. Disable SSID broadcasting.

    C. Change the admin password.

    D. Enable WPA.

29. You are an IT specialist with a law enforcement agency. You have tracked illegal Internet activity down to an IP address. Detectives would like to link a person to the IP address in order to secure an arrest warrant. Which of the following are true regarding this situation? (Choose two.)

    A. The IP address might be that of a NAT router or a proxy server.

    B. The IP address could not have been spoofed; otherwise, it would not have reached its destination.

    C. IP addresses can be traced to a regional ISP.

    D. IP addresses are unique for every individual device connecting to the Internet.

30. Your IT security director asks you to configure packet encryption for your internal network. She expresses concerns about how existing packet filtering firewall rules might affect this encrypted traffic. How would you respond to her concerns?

    A. Encrypted packets will not be affected by existing packet filtering firewall rules.

    B. Encrypted packet headers could prevent outbound traffic from leaving the internal network.

    C. Encrypted packet payloads will prevent outbound traffic from leaving the internal network.

    D. Inbound encrypted traffic will be blocked by the firewall.

QUICK ANSWER KEY

1.	C	11.	B, D	21.	A
2.	D	12.	C	22.	C
3.	A	13.	B	23.	D
4.	C	14.	D	24.	A
5.	C	15.	C	25.	B
6.	A	16.	D	26.	A, C
7.	C	17.	B	27.	D
8.	C	18.	A	28.	C
9.	C	19.	B	29.	A, C
10.	A	20.	C	30.	B

IN-DEPTH ANSWERS

1. You are a guest at a hotel offering free Wi-Fi Internet access to guests. You connect to the wireless network at full signal strength and obtain a valid TCP/IP configuration. When you try to access Internet web sites, a web page displays instead asking for a code before allowing access to the Internet. What type of network component is providing this functionality?

    A. DHCP Server

    B. NAT

    C. Proxy Server

    D. Switch

    ☑ **C.** Proxy servers retrieve content for connected clients and can also require authentication before doing so.

    ☒ **A, B,** and **D** are incorrect. **A** is incorrect because DHCP (Dynamic Host Configuration Protocol) provides to clients a valid IP address, subnet mask, default gateway, DNS (Domain Name Service) server, and so on; there is no mechanism for authentication. **B** is also incorrect because NAT (Network Address Translation) uses a single public IP address to represent all internal computers. Like DHCP, NAT does not authenticate connections. **D** is incorrect because switches isolate network conversations between hosts and track which computers are plugged into which switch port using the machine's MAC address.

2. You are configuring a wireless router at a car repair shop so that waiting customers can connect to the Internet. You want to ensure wireless clients can connect to the Internet but cannot connect to internal computers owned by the car repair shop. Where should you plug in the wireless router?

    A. LAN

    B. Port 24 on the switch

    C. Port 1 on the switch

    D. DMZ

    ☑ **D.** A DMZ (demilitarized zone) is a network allowing external unsecure access to resources while preventing direct access to internal resources. If the wireless router is plugged into the DMZ, this will provide Internet access to customers while disallowing them access to internal business computers. Plugging the wireless router into the internal LAN would also allow Internet access, but would place customers on a business LAN.

> ☒ **A, B,** and **C** are incorrect. **A** would allow customer access to internal computers and is therefore incorrect. **B** and **C** are incorrect because ports 24 and 1 on a switch generally have no special DMZ meaning any more than any other port does, although some network devices do have specially designated DMZ ports.

3. What will detect network or host intrusions and take actions to prevent the intrusion from succeeding?

A. IPS

B. IDS

C. IPSec

D. DMZ

> ☑ **A.** An IPS (intrusion prevention system) actively monitors network or system activity for abnormal activity and also takes steps to stop it. Abnormal activity can be detected by checking for known attack patterns (signature-based) or variations beyond normal activity (anomaly-based).
>
> ☒ **B, C,** and **D** are incorrect. **B** does not apply in this case. Like an IPS, an IDS (intrusion detection system) monitors network or system activity for irregular activity, but does not attempt to stop this activity. **C** is incorrect because IPSec (IP Security) provides data confidentially and integrity to network transmissions and does not detect or prevent intrusions. **D** is incorrect because a DMZ does not detect or prevent attacks; it is a network segment hosting services (and ideally an IPS) that are accessible to an untrusted network.

4. What technology uses a single external IP address to represent many computers on an internal network?

A. IPSec

B. DHCP

C. NAT

D. NIDS

> ☑ **C.** NAT runs on a router and allows computers on an internal network to access an external network using only a single external IP address. NAT routers track outbound connections in order to deliver inbound traffic to the originating internal host.

☒ **A, B,** and **D** are incorrect. **A** is incorrect because IPSec provides a means of encrypting and digitally signing network packets and has nothing to do with translating IP addresses. **B** and **D** are incorrect because DHCP and NIDS do not use a single IP address on behalf of internal computers. DHCP provides a valid TCP/IP configuration for network nodes. An NIDS (network intrusion detection system) analyzes network traffic to identify and report network attacks

5. You must purchase a network device that supports content filtering and virus defense for your LAN. What should you choose?

   A. NAT router

   B. HIPS

   C. Web security gateway

   D. Packet filtering firewall

☑ **C.** Web security gateways can perform deep packet inspection (content) to filter network traffic. They also include the ability to detect and deal with malware.

☒ **A, B,** and **D** are incorrect. **A** is incorrect because NAT does not support content filtering or virus protection; it merely analyzes and modifies packet headers. **B** is incorrect because an HIPS (host intrusion prevention system) detects and stops attacks on a computer system and does not monitor the content of LAN network traffic. **D** does not apply, since packet filtering firewalls only look at packet headers to allow or deny traffic; they do not analyze packet payloads.

6. You have been asked to somehow separate Engineering departmental network traffic from Accounting departmental traffic due to a decrease in network throughput. What should you use?

   A. VLAN

   B. DMZ

   C. NAT

   D. VPN

☑ **A.** Virtual local area networks (VLANs) create separate broadcast domains in the same way a router physically separates two network segments. Both the Engineering and Accounting departments should be configured on their own VLANs, thus separating their network traffic.

☒ **B, C,** and **D** are incorrect. **B** is incorrect because a DMZ does not isolate departmental traffic; it is a network between a private LAN and an unsafe external network such as the Internet. Network services such as e-mail or web servers that must be reachable from the external network reside in the DMZ. Network services on the private LAN are kept unreachable from the external network. **C** is incorrect because NAT devices are not designed to separate busy networks; they are designed to allow many internal computers access to an external network using only one IP address. **D** is not applicable. VPNs (virtual private networks) allow external connectivity to a private LAN over an untrusted network such as the Internet via an encrypted data stream, but they are not used to separate networks to increase throughput.

7. Given the following LAN firewall rule set, which is the best description?
Allow inbound TCP 3389
Allow outbound TCP 80
Allow outbound TCP 443

   A. LAN users can connect to external FTP sites. External users can use RDP to connect to LAN computers.

   B. LAN users can connect to external SMTP servers. External users can use LDAP to connect to LAN computers.

   C. LAN users can connect to external web servers. External uses can use RDP to connect to LAN computers.

   D. LAN users can connect to external proxy servers. External users can use IPSec to connect to LAN computers.

   ☑ **C.** Connecting to external web servers means connecting to HTTP (port 80) for unencrypted sites and HTTPS (port 443) for encrypted sites. RDP (Remote Desktop Protocol) uses port 3389.

   ☒ **A, B,** and **D** are incorrect. **A** is incorrect because FTP uses TCP ports 20 and 21. **B** is incorrect because SMTP uses TCP port 25. **D** is incorrect because IPSec uses UDP port 500 in addition to specific protocol IDs that would have to be allowed through the firewall.

8. Which tool would allow you to capture and view network traffic?

   A. Vulnerability scanner

   B. Port scanner

C. Protocol analyzer

D. NAT

> ☑ **C.** Protocol analyzers capture and view network traffic by placing the network card into promiscuous mode. In a switched environment you will only capture network traffic involving your machine in addition to multicast and broadcast packets. Enable port monitoring or mirroring on your switch to view all network activity on the switch.
>
> ☒ **A, B,** and **D** are incorrect. **A** does not apply. The question refers to capturing and viewing traffic, not scanning the network for vulnerable hosts. **B** is incorrect because port scanning identifies services running on a host, but it does not capture network traffic. **D** is incorrect because NAT connects internal computers to an external network using a single IP address.

9. You are reviewing router configurations to ensure they comply with corporate security policies. You notice the routers are configured to load their configurations using TFTP and also that TCP port 22 is enabled. What security problem exists with these routers?

A. Telnet should be disabled.

B. Telnet should have a password configured.

C. TFTP is an insecure protocol.

D. Telnet should limit concurrent logins to 1.

> ☑ **C.** TFTP (Trivial File Transfer Protocol) transmits data (such as router configurations) in clear text. TFTP does not have an authentication mechanism; therefore, anybody with network access could have access to all router configurations. It would be more secure to store router configurations locally on the router and to secure the router with the appropriate passwords.
>
> ☒ **A, B,** and **D** are incorrect because Telnet was not implied in the question. SSH (Secure Shell) uses TCP port 22.

10. A router must be configured to only allow traffic from certain hosts. How can this be accomplished?

A. ACL

B. Subnet

C. Proxy server

D. NAT

☑ **A.** ACLs (access control lists) are router settings that allow or deny various types of network traffic from or to specific hosts.

☒ **B, C,** and **D** are incorrect. **B** does not apply. A subnet cannot restrict network traffic. Routers can be used to divide larger networks into smaller subnets. **C** is incorrect because the question specifically states configuring a router, and proxy hosts should have routing disabled. Proxy servers do have the ability to limit network access from certain hosts, though. **D** is incorrect because NAT (Network Address Translation) routers do not restrict network traffic from certain hosts; instead, they use a single external IP address to allow many internal computers access to an external network.

11. Which technologies allow analysis of network traffic? (Choose two.)

   A. Port scanner

   B. Sniffer

   C. DMZ

   D. NIDS

☑ **B** and **D.** Sniffers use network card promiscuous mode to capture all network traffic instead of only traffic addresses to the host running the sniffer. Switches isolate each port from one another, so sniffers will not see all switch network traffic unless a switch port is configured to do so. NIDSs (network intrusion detection systems) are placed on the network strategically so that they can analyze all network traffic to identify and report on suspicious activity.

☒ **A** and **C** are incorrect. **A** is incorrect because port scanners identify running services on network hosts. Port scanners do not analyze all network traffic; they are directed to scan one or more hosts. **C** is incorrect because a DMZ does not analyze network traffic, although sniffers and NIDS are very important to use in a DMZ. A DMZ is a network containing hosts that are accessible to external users. Firewalls limit access from the DMZ to internal resources.

12. What term describes the network between the two firewalls in this illustration?

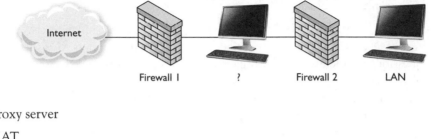

Firewall 1   ?   Firewall 2   LAN

A. Proxy server

B. NAT

C. DMZ

D. NIDS

☑ **C.** A DMZ hosts services that are externally accessible while preventing access to internal LANs. Firewall 1 could ensure that only appropriate traffic enters the DMZ. Firewall 2 could be enabled with NAT to allow LAN users' access to the Internet while blocking any traffic initiated from outside of the LAN.

☒ **A, B,** and **D** are incorrect. The question refers to a network, not a single device on a network.

13. You have received a new VPN concentrator to allow traveling users' access to LAN B. Where in this illustration should you place the VPN concentrator?

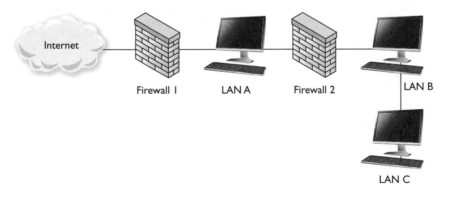

Firewall 1   LAN A   Firewall 2   LAN B

LAN C

A. Internet

B. LAN A

C. LAN B

D. LAN C

> ☑ **B.** To allow traveling users to connect to LAN B, the VPN concentrator should be placed in the DMZ (LAN A). Placing the VPN concentrator on LAN B is not recommended because it would allow direct access to an internal LAN from the Internet. Firewall 1 should be configured to allow inbound VPN traffic to the VPN concentrator. Firewall 2 should be configured to allow only authenticated VPN users into LAN B.
>
> ☒ **A, C,** and **D** are incorrect. **A** is incorrect because we want the VPN concentrator behind firewall 1 so that firewall 1 can control which packets get sent to the VPN device. **C** and **D** are both incorrect because placing the VPN device on LAN B or C would open a direct line from the Internet to LAN B.

14. Sylvia's workstation has been moved to a new cubicle. On Monday morning, Sylvia reports that even though the network card is plugged into the network jack, there is no link light on the network card. What is the problem?

A. The workstation has an APIPA address. Issue the IPCONFIG / RENEW command.

B. The default gateway has not been set.

C. Sylvia must first log on to the domain.

D. Since the MAC address has changed, switch port security has disabled the port.

> ☑ **D.** This is the only choice that would result in an unlit link light on a network card.
>
> ☒ **A, B,** and **C** are incorrect. **A** and **B** are incorrect because an APIPA (Automatic Private IP Addressing) or lack of a default gateway entry would only result in limited network connectivity; the network card link light would still be lit. **C** is incorrect because domain connectivity is not possible without a network link.

15. You need a method of authenticating Windows 7 workstations before allowing local LAN access. What should you use?

A. VPN concentrator

B. Router

C. 802.1x switch

D. Proxy server

☑ **C.** The 802.1x protocol defines how devices must first be authenticated before getting LAN access.

☒ **A, B,** and **D** are incorrect. **A** is incorrect because a VPN device allows remote access to a LAN, not local access. **B** is incorrect because routers do not authenticate devices. **D** is incorrect because LAN access is needed before connecting to a proxy server.

16. An attacker sends thousands of TCP SYN packets with unreachable source IP addresses to a server. After consuming server resources with this traffic, legitimate traffic can no longer reach the server. What can prevent this type of attack?

A. Packet filtering firewall

B. Proxy server

C. Antivirus software

D. SYN flood protection

☑ **D.** SYN flood protection prevents the described DoS (denial of service) attack by limiting the number of half-open TCP (Transmission Control Protocol) connections. A normal TCP conversation follows a three-way handshake whereby a SYN packet is sent to the target, who responds with a SYN-ACK packet. The originator then sends an ACK packet to complete the handshake. A large number of SYN packets consume server resources.

☒ **A, B,** and **C** are incorrect. **A** is incorrect because packet filtering firewalls can allow or deny packets based on IP addresses, ports, protocol ID, and so on, but they cannot prevent SYN floods. **B** is not applicable, since proxy servers do not check for half-open TCP handshakes; they retrieve external content for internal clients. **C** is incorrect because antivirus software scans for malware, not DoS attacks.

17. A junior IT employee links three network switches together such that each switch connects to the two others. As a result, the network is flooded with useless traffic. What can prevent this situation?

A. Web application firewall

B. Loop protection

C. SYN flood guard

D. Router ACL

☑ **B.** Loop protection is a switch feature that prevents uplink switch ports from switching to "forwarding" mode, thus preventing bridging loops.

☒ **A, C,** and **D** are incorrect. **A** does not apply. Web application firewalls have nothing to do with switches; they monitor HTTP conversations to prevent inappropriate activity. **C** is incorrect because SYN floods are not a result of improperly wired switches; they are specific to TCP. **D** is incorrect because router ACLs do not correct problems stemming from incorrectly linked switches.

18. Your boss asks that specific HTTP traffic be monitored and blocked. What should you use?

   A. Web application firewall

   B. Protocol analyzer

   C. Packet filtering firewall

   D. NAT

☑ **A.** Web application firewalls can stop inappropriate HTTP activity according to a configured policy.

☒ **B, C,** and **D** are incorrect. **B** is incorrect because protocol analyzers can capture network traffic and generate reports, but they do not block any type of traffic. **C** is incorrect because packet filtering firewalls do not perform deep packet inspection; that is, they only examine packet headers and not packet payloads, which is where HTTP content exists. **D** is incorrect because NAT does not block specific types of network traffic, it changes the source IP address for outbound packets to be its external IP address.

19. A high school principal insists on preventing student access to known malware web sites. How can this be done?

   A. DMZ

   B. URL filtering

   C. DNS forwarding

   D. 802.1x switch

☑ **B.** URL filtering examines where traffic is going and compares that against a list of allowed and forbidden sites to allow or prevent access. This can be done on a dedicated network appliance, or it could simply be server software.

☒ **A, C,** and **D** are incorrect. **A** is incorrect because a DMZ does not control access to web sites; it is a network hosting services to external users and exists between a private network and a public network. **C** is incorrect because, if a DNS server receives a specific DNS query that it cannot answer and DNS forwarding is configured, it will direct the query to DNS servers that can resolve the specific request. This will not prevent students from visiting malware web sites. **D** is incorrect because 802.1x switches do not perform detailed packet analysis; they simply authenticate devices against an authentication server before granting network access.

20. Which of the following scenarios best describes implicit deny?

    A. Allow network access if it is 802.1x authenticated.
    B. Block outbound network traffic destined for TCP port 25.
    C. Block network traffic unless specifically permitted.
    D. Allow network traffic unless specifically forbidden.

    ☑ **C.** Implicit denial applies when there is no setting explicitly stating network traffic is allowed.

    ☒ **A, B,** and **D** are incorrect. **A** is incorrect because this is an example of explicit allow. **B** is incorrect because it is an example of explicit deny. **D** is incorrect because it describes implicit allowance.

21. A university student has a wired network connection to a restrictive university network. At the same time, the student is connected to a Wi-Fi hotspot for a nearby coffee shop that allows unrestricted Internet access. What potential problem exists in this case?

    A. The student computer could link coffee shop patrons to the university network.
    B. The student computer could override the university default gateway setting.
    C. Encrypted university transmissions could find their way onto the Wi-Fi network.
    D. Encrypted coffee shop transmissions could find their way onto the university network.

    ☑ **A.** Many operating systems automatically create a network connection between networks when two network interfaces are detected. This would link network segments together in a single broadcast domain, but create multiple collision domains. This means, for example, that a coffee shop patron could get a valid TCP/IP configuration from a university DHCP server.

☒ **B, C,** and **D** are incorrect. **B** is incorrect because being connected to two networks simultaneously will not override a networks default gateway settings. **C** and **D** are incorrect because there is no problem with encrypted data finding its way onto either network; only authorized parties can decrypt the transmissions.

22. Which network device encrypts and decrypts network traffic over an unsafe network to allow access to private LANs?
    A. Proxy server
    B. IPSec
    C. VPN concentrator
    D. TPM

☑ **C.** VPNs (virtual private networks) are encrypted tunnels established over an unsafe network with the goal of safely connecting to a private LAN.

☒ **A, B,** and **D** are incorrect. **A** is incorrect because proxy servers do not encrypt or decrypt network traffic; they retrieve content based on client requests. **B** is incorrect because IPSec is not a network device; it is a software method of encrypting and digitally signing packets. **D** is incorrect because a TPM (Trusted Platform Module) chip is a device storing keys or passphrases used to encrypt and decrypt disk contents, not network traffic.

23. You suspect malicious activity on your DMZ. In an effort to identify the offender, you have intentionally configured an unpatched server to attract further attention. What term describes what you have configured?
    A. Honeynet
    B. Logging server
    C. Exploit
    D. Honeypot

☑ **D.** A honeypot is designed to attract the attention of hackers or malware in an effort to learn how to mitigate the risk or to identify the offender.

☒ **A, B,** and **C** are incorrect. **A** is incorrect because the question states a single computer was configured, not an entire network. **B** is incorrect because a logging server would never be left intentionally unpatched. **C** is incorrect because an exploit takes advantage of a vulnerability. An intentional vulnerability has been created, but not an exploit.

24. Your NIDS incorrectly reports legitimate network traffic as being suspicious. What is this known as?

A. False positive

B. Explicit false

C. False negative

D. Implicit false

☑ **A.** Reporting there is a problem when in truth there is not is known as a false positive.

☒ **B, C,** and **D** are incorrect. **B** and **D** are incorrect because they are not terms commonly used in IT security. **C** is incorrect because false negatives mean no problem is stated as existing when in fact one does. The question states the exact opposite.

25. Your corporate network access policy states that all connecting devices require a host-based firewall and an antivirus scanner as well as having the latest operating system updates. You would like to prevent noncompliant devices from connecting to your network. What solution should you consider?

A. NIDS

B. NAC

C. VLAN

D. HIDS

☑ **B.** Network Access Control (NAC) ensures connecting devices are compliant with configured health requirements before allowing network access. This can be done with 802.1x network equipment such as a switch, or it can be done with software such as a VPN server checking connecting clients.

☒ **A, C,** and **D** are incorrect. **A** is incorrect because an NIDS (network intrusion detection system) analyzes network packets looking for abnormal activity; it does not check whether or not connecting devices meet health requirements. **C** is incorrect because VLANs do not verify client health compliance; they segment larger broadcast domains into smaller ones to maximize network throughput. **D** is incorrect because HIDSs (host-based intrusion detection systems) seek problems by analyzing data received by a host as well as its logs and local activity.

26. Which of the following are true regarding NAT? (Choose two.)

    A. The NAT client is unaware of address translation.

    B. The NAT client is aware of address translation.

    C. Internet hosts are unaware of address translation.

    D. Internet hosts are aware of address translation.

    ☑ **A** and **C.** The NAT client simply sees the NAT router as its default gateway. Beyond that, it has no idea that for outbound packets its source IP address is being changed to that of the NAT router's public interface. To Internet hosts, the traffic appears to come from the NAT router's public interface (which it really does); there is no indication of IP address translation.

    ☒ **B** and **D** are incorrect. NAT is transparent to clients and Internet hosts.

27. You are a sales executive for a real estate firm. One of your clients calls you wondering why you have not e-mailed them critical documentation regarding a sale. You check your mail program to verify the message was sent two days ago. You also verify the message was not sent back to you as undeliverable. You tell your client that you did in fact send the message. What should you next tell your client?

    A. Clean your mailbox—there is no room for new incoming mail.

    B. Wait a few hours—Internet e-mail is slow.

    C. NAT might have prevented the message from being delivered.

    D. Check your junk mail; antispam software sometimes incorrectly identifies legitimate mail as spam.

    ☑ **D.** Assuming the message was sent according to the sender's system two days ago and the sender did not receive an undeliverable message, the most likely answer is that it was flagged as junk mail by the receiver's mail system.

    ☒ **A, B,** and **C** are incorrect. **A** is not the best answer. Although mail servers can hold e-mail until a user cleans out his mailbox, this is not as likely as the message having been flagged by antispam software. **B** is incorrect because the Internet is not that slow. **C** is incorrect because NAT simply changes IP addresses in packet headers. This would not prevent e-mail from getting to its destination.

28. You are an IT network consultant. You install a new wireless network for a hotel. What must you do to prevent wireless network users from gaining administrative access to wireless routers?

A. Apply MAC filtering.

B. Disable SSID broadcasting.

C. Change the admin password.

D. Enable WPA.

☑ **C.** Wireless routers ship with a standard admin username and password. It is critical that the wireless router admin password be changed to prevent unauthorized admin access.

☒ **A, B,** and **D** are incorrect. **A** is incorrect because MAC (Media Access Control) address filtering controls which wireless devices can connect to a wireless network, but it would not prevent admin access to a wireless router using a default admin password. **B** is also incorrect because disabling SSID (Station Set Identifier) broadcasting prevents wireless clients from seeing the wireless network name when they are within range, but it does not prevent admin access to an unsecured wireless router. **D** does not apply because encrypting wireless network traffic with WPA (Wi-Fi Protected Access) might secure wireless traffic, but it does not secure the wireless router itself.

29. You are an IT specialist with a law enforcement agency. You have tracked illegal Internet activity down to an IP address. Detectives would like to link a person to the IP address in order to secure an arrest warrant. Which of the following are true regarding this situation? (Choose two.)

A. The IP address might be that of a NAT router or a proxy server.

B. The IP address could not have been spoofed; otherwise, it would not have reached its destination.

C. IP addresses can be traced to a regional ISP.

D. IP addresses are unique for every individual device connecting to the Internet.

☑ **A** and **C.** NAT routers and proxy servers change the source IP address of packets going to the Internet to be that of their public interface, so on the Internet the packets appear to have originated from those hosts; the internal IP address of a client behind the NAT router or proxy server is not known. Law enforcement could obtain a warrant to examine the logs on a NAT router or proxy server to identify internal clients, but privacy laws in some countries prevent Internet service providers from disclosing this information.

☒ **B** and **D** are incorrect. **B** is incorrect because IP addresses can be spoofed (faked) easily with freely available software. Packets with spoofed source IP addresses will reach their destination, but responses will not reach the originator; instead, they will go to the spoofed IP address. **D** is untrue and therefore incorrect. Most networks around the planet have a NAT router (or multiple layers of NAT routers) to allow internal clients using a nonunique IP address access to the Internet. The NAT router modifies the source IP address in outbound packets to be that of its public interface, and it tracks this change so that any responses to the sent packet can be delivered to the internal client.

30. Your IT security director asks you to configure packet encryption for your internal network. She expresses concerns about how existing packet filtering firewall rules might affect this encrypted traffic. How would you respond to her concerns?

A. Encrypted packets will not be affected by existing packet filtering firewall rules.

B. Encrypted packet headers could prevent outbound traffic from leaving the internal network.

C. Encrypted packet payloads will prevent outbound traffic from leaving the internal network.

D. Inbound encrypted traffic will be blocked by the firewall.

☑ **B.** Packet headers include addressing information such as IP and port addresses. These are used to get a packet to its destination. Packet filtering firewalls allow or deny traffic based on IP or port addresses, to name just a few criteria. If, for example, packets headers containing port addresses are encrypted, packet filtering firewalls may block traffic this when perhaps it should be allowed.

☒ **A**, **C**, and **D** are incorrect. **A** is incorrect because it is an ambiguous statement. We must consider what portions of a packet are being encrypted, and we must consider the specific firewall rules in question. **C** is incorrect because packet filtering firewalls do not examine packet payload, only the headers. **D** does not apply—the question discusses encrypting internal traffic; there is no mention of allowing inbound encrypted traffic.

9
Wireless Networking

CERTIFICATION OBJECTIVES

❑   **1.6**   Implement wireless network in a secure manner

❑   **3.4**   Analyze and differentiate among types of wireless attacks

❑   **6.2**   Use and apply appropriate cryptographic tools and products

QUESTIONS

The popularity of wireless network connectivity has introduced a wide array of security concerns. Bluetooth wireless networks are personal networks designed for short ranges and are useful for transferring data among handheld devices. Wi-Fi networks have a greater range than Bluetooth and are used by computers. Knowing when to apply various wireless standards can help insulate your wireless network from unauthorized access.

1. While reviewing wireless router logs, you notice wireless network usage by unfamiliar systems. How can you control which systems connect to your wireless network?
   A. Change the SSID.
   B. Disable DHCP.
   C. Change the wireless router admin password.
   D. Enable MAC address filtering.

2. Enabling WPA on a WLAN provides what? (Choose two.)
   A. Confidentiality
   B. Integrity
   C. Availability
   D. Authorization

3. In addition to encrypting wireless traffic, you configure your wireless router to require connecting users to authenticate against a RADIUS server. What type of security have you configured?
   A. WEP
   B. TKIP
   C. WPA2 Personal
   D. WPA2 Enterprise

4. You decide to capture network traffic with a sniffer while connected to a busy public Wi-Fi hotspot. After several minutes you realize you can see only your own network traffic in addition to broadcasts and multicasts. Why can you not see anybody else's wireless network traffic?
   A. WPA encryption is in use.
   B. The SSID is not broadcasting.
   C. MAC filtering is enabled.
   D. Isolation mode is enabled.

5. A curious IT professional drives through an industrial park late at night while scanning for unsecured wireless networks with a PDA. What is this called?
   A. Network scanning
   B. War driving

    C. War dialing

    D. War chalking

6. To which of the following security concerns does EAP apply?

    A. Virus scanning

    B. Hard disk encryption

    C. Network authentication

    D. Firewall rules

7. Which mechanism requires only a server-side PKI certificate to encrypt user authentication traffic?

    A. EAP

    B. PEAP

    C. LEAP

    D. EAP-TLS

8. You are configuring access to a wireless LAN on a Windows 7 laptop. When you list available wireless networks, you notice multiple listings for "Other Network." What wireless router option is in use for these "Other Networks"?

    A. Disable SSID broadcast

    B. MAC address filtering

    C. WEP

    D. WPA

9. Which wireless encryption protocol uses counter mode to make pattern detection difficult?

    A. CCMP

    B. CHAP

    C. WEP

    D. RSA

10. You are conducting a wireless site survey at a client site. The client expresses a desire to keep wireless transmissions secure. There is a single 802.11n wireless router with omnidirectional antennae in the server room at one end of the building. WPA2 enterprise and MAC filtering have been configured. What additional security issue should you address?

    A. WPA2 Personal should be used.

    B. MAC filtering is useless; MAC addresses are easily spoofed.

    C. Move the wireless router to the center of the building.

    D. Upgrade the wireless router to 802.11m.

11. What can be done to secure a wireless network?

    A. Decrease power transmission level to cover only intended area.

    B. Use a wireless encryption standard such as 802.3.

    C. Change the DHCP-supplied default gateway address.

    D. Configure wireless router admin access to use HTTP.

12. A Windows 7 user in your company issues the command **netsh wlan set hostednetwork mode=allow ssid=AcmeWLAN key=password** on her company wireless laptop. What best describes the security problem created by this user?

    A. The user has Administrative rights in Windows 7.

    B. The key is not complex enough.

    C. The user has created a rogue access point.

    D. The SSID name is invalid.

13. You are the wireless network administrator. Users report unstable wireless 802.11g network connectivity. After careful examination you realize 2.4 GHz wireless phones and Bluetooth devices are interfering with the Wi-Fi signal. Which choice offers the best solution?

    A. Replace the 802.11g network with 802.11n.

    B. Cease using all 2.4 GHz wireless phones and Bluetooth devices.

    C. Purchase a high-gain antenna for your wireless router.

    D. Change the Wi-Fi channel used by your wireless router.

14. A hacker configures a rogue access point to appear as a legitimate Wi-Fi hotspot. Which term best describes this configuration?

    A. Evil twin

    B. Bad rogue

    C. War driving

    D. War chalking

15. Which of the following refers to unsolicited messages sent to nearby Bluetooth devices?

    A. Bluespamming

    B. Bluejacking

    C. Bluehacking

    D. Bluedriving

16. Which of the following refers to unauthorized data access of a Bluetooth device over a Bluetooth wireless network?

    A. Bluejacking

    B. Bluesnarfing

    C. Packet sniffing

    D. Port scanning

17. You are working at a client site to solve wireless performance issues. In doing so you notice WEP is configured on the client's wireless routers. What type of attack might this network be susceptible to?
   A. DDoS
   B. IV attack
   C. ARP poisoning
   D. Dictionary attack

18. How can you control whether or not all wireless devices will see your WLAN name?
   A. Disable SSID broadcasting.
   B. Block packet sniffing.
   C. Reduce transmission power level.
   D. Change antenna placement.

19. Which of the following items could interfere with an 802.11g wireless network?
   A. Remote garage door opener
   B. Microwave oven
   C. Television infrared remote
   D. Cell phone

20. In securing a wireless network, you decide to enable EAP-TLS to authorize wireless client access to the wireless LAN. What should you do next?
   A. Install a public key certificate on the client and a smartcard on the server.
   B. Install a smartcard on the client and a public key certificate on the server.
   C. Install MS-CHAP on the client and a public key certificate on the server.
   D. Install a smart card on the client and MS-CHAP on the server.

21. TKIP is used primarily by which wireless standard?
   A. 802.11n
   B. WEP
   C. WPA
   D. 802.1x

22. You are a Wi-Fi IT specialist. Users report that the new 802.11g network is not running at the advertised 54 Mbps. What should you tell your wireless users?
   A. 802.11g runs at 11 Mbps.
   B. Wireless encryption will be disabled to increase bandwidth.
   C. Wi-Fi bandwidth is shared by all users connected to the same wireless network.
   D. SSID broadcasting will be disabled to increase bandwidth.

23. Which standard requires stations to authenticate prior to gaining network access?
   A. 802.11a
   B. 802.11b
   C. 802.1x
   D. 802.3

24. You are securing your Wi-Fi network infrastructure. You configure network monitoring software with a list of valid wireless access point MACs allowed on the network. What type of threat will this enable you to detect?
   A. Rogue access points
   B. War driving
   C. Bluesnarfing
   D. Bluejacking

25. You are configuring a wireless network for your home office. Which options are applicable to a home network? (Choose two.)
   A. WPA2 PSK
   B. WPA2 Enterprise
   C. EAP-TLS
   D. WPA PSK

26. A traveling user calls the help desk regarding her wireless connectivity problem. When she attempts to connect to a visible wireless network at full strength, it eventually times out with no further messages. What is the problem?
   A. The user does not have the WPA2 PSK configured on her station.
   B. MAC address filtering is blocking her wireless network card.
   C. The user needs an external antenna for her wireless card.
   D. She must enter the SSID.

27. You are enjoying a cup of coffee at the local coffee shop when all of a sudden your cell phone displays an anonymous message complimenting you on your Hawaiian shirt. What are you a victim of?
   A. Bluetoothing
   B. Bluesnarfing
   C. Bluejacking
   D. Bluedriving

QUICK ANSWER KEY

1.	D	10.	C	19.	B
2.	A, B	11.	A	20.	B
3.	D	12.	C	21.	C
4.	D	13.	D	22.	C
5.	B	14.	A	23.	C
6.	C	15.	B	24.	A
7.	B	16.	B	25.	A, D
8.	A	17.	B	26.	B
9.	A	18.	A	27.	C

IN-DEPTH ANSWERS

1. While reviewing wireless router logs, you notice wireless network usage by unfamiliar systems. How can you control which systems connect to your wireless network?

   A. Change the SSID.

   B. Disable DHCP.

   C. Change the wireless router admin password.

   D. Enable MAC address filtering.

   ☑ **D.** MAC addresses are unique 48-bit hexadecimal identifiers for network cards. You can configure a list of allowed MAC addresses on your wireless router to limit which devices can connect.

   ☒ **A, B,** and **C** are incorrect. **A** is incorrect because changing the SSID does not allow you to directly control which systems can connect; it changes the name of the wireless network. **B** is not applicable, since disabling DHCP on the wireless router cannot control which machines connect; it requires each device to have a manual TCP/IP configuration. **C** is incorrect because changing the wireless router admin password does not prevent connectivity to a wireless LAN.

2. Enabling WPA on a WLAN provides what? (Choose two.)

   A. Confidentiality

   B. Integrity

   C. Availability

   D. Authorization

   ☑ **A** and **B.** WPA (Wi-Fi Protected Access) encrypts packets on a wireless network to prevent unauthorized viewing of data (confidentiality), and it verifies that received data has not been tampered with (integrity).

   ☒ **C** and **D** are incorrect. **C** is incorrect because availability relates to continuous access to data, not WPA. **D** is also incorrect because WPA secures wireless traffic, it does not check access rights to a network resource (authorization).

3. In addition to encrypting wireless traffic, you configure your wireless router to require connecting users to authenticate against a RADIUS server. What type of security have you configured?

   A. WEP

   B. TKIP

   C. WPA2 Personal

   D. WPA2 Enterprise

☑ **D.** WPA2 (Wi-Fi Protected Access version 2) Enterprise uses an authentication server to control access to a wireless network.

☒ **A, B,** and **C** are incorrect. **A** is incorrect because WEP (Wired Equivalent Privacy) does encrypt traffic, but cannot authenticate connecting users against an authentication server. **B** is incorrect because TKIP (Temporal Key Integrity Protocol) secures wireless networks by changing the encryption key per packet. **C** is incorrect because the question refers to an authentication server. WPA Personal simply uses a passphrase to secure the network; it cannot authenticate connecting users to a server.

4. You decide to capture network traffic with a sniffer while connected to a busy public Wi-Fi hotspot. After several minutes you realize you can see only your own network traffic in addition to broadcasts and multicasts. Why can you not see anybody else's wireless network traffic?

   A. WPA encryption is in use.

   B. The SSID is not broadcasting.

   C. MAC filtering is enabled.

   D. Isolation mode is enabled.

☑ **D.** Wireless isolation mode prevents wireless clients on the same WLAN (wireless LAN) from seeing each other.

☒ **A, B,** and **C** are incorrect. While they are relevant when securing a wireless network, none of them prevents a wireless client from seeing another client's network traffic.

5. A curious IT professional drives through an industrial park late at night while scanning for unsecured wireless networks with a PDA. What is this called?

   A. Network scanning

   B. War driving

C. War dialing

D. War chalking

> ☑ **B.** War driving entails searching for wireless networks, often from within a moving vehicle.
>
> ☒ **A, C,** and **D** are incorrect. **A** is incorrect because, although network scanning is occurring, the act of scanning for wireless networks is called war driving. **C** is incorrect because war dialing involves using a modem to dial phone numbers until telephony equipment answers the call. **D** is incorrect because war chalking refers to scanning for and charting (for example, writing in chalk on the sidewalk) open wireless networks.

6. To which of the following security concerns does EAP apply?

A. Virus scanning

B. Hard disk encryption

C. Network authentication

D. Firewall rules

> ☑ **C.** EAP (Extensible Authentication Protocol) is a connecting device network authentication framework supporting methods such as PKI certificates, smartcards, and passwords. Wireless networks that support WPA or WPA2 commonly provide multiple EAP options to choose from for RADIUS authentication of connecting clients.
>
> ☒ **A, B,** and **D** are incorrect. These choices do not apply because they are unrelated to EAP. **A,** virus scanning, checks for malware; **B,** hard disk encryption, ensures only authorized persons can use data on a hard disk; and **D,** firewall rules, control inbound or outbound network traffic.

7. Which mechanism requires only a server-side PKI certificate to encrypt user authentication traffic?

A. EAP

B. PEAP

C. LEAP

D. EAP-TLS

> ☑ **B.** PEAP (Protected Extensible Authentication Protocol) creates a secure channel for user authentication using a server-side PKI certificate initially; then a symmetric session key is used for the remainder of the session.

☒   **A, C,** and **D** are incorrect. **A** is incorrect because EAP is a general framework for securing authentication traffic, but it does not specify whether or not PKI certificates are used. **C** is incorrect because LEAP (Lightweight Extensible Authentication Protocol) is a Cisco wireless authentication protocol that does not involve PKI certificates; usernames are sent in clear text. **D** is incorrect because, although similar to PEAP, EAP-TLS (Extensible Authentication Protocol–Transport Layer Security) requires the client and server to possess PKI certificates to secure authentication traffic.

8. You are configuring access to a wireless LAN on a Windows 7 laptop. When you list available wireless networks, you notice multiple listings for "Other Network." What wireless router option is in use for these "Other Networks"?

   A. Disable SSID broadcast
   B. MAC address filtering
   C. WEP
   D. WPA

☑   **A.** Disabling the SSID (station set identifier) suppresses the wireless network name in beacon packets. When scanning for wireless networks, some tools will not display these networks, but Windows 7 does display them labeled as "Other Network."

☒   **B, C,** and **D** are incorrect. **B** does not apply. MAC (Media Access Control) filtering restricts which wireless client can connect by checking their network card hardware address (MAC address), but it does not control the display of wireless network names. **C** and **D** are incorrect because they encrypt wireless traffic, but do not impact whether a wireless network is visible or not.

9. Which wireless encryption protocol uses counter mode to make pattern detection difficult?

   A. CCMP
   B. CHAP
   C. WEP
   D. RSA

☑   **A.** CCMP (Counter Mode with Cipher Block Chaining Message Authentication Code Protocol) is a WPA2 standard that uses an AES block cipher with counter mode. Counter mode makes pattern detection difficult, thus making this a strong protocol.

☒ **B, C,** and **D** are incorrect. **B** is incorrect because CHAP (Challenge Handshake Authentication Protocol) is not a wireless encryption protocol; it is an authentication mechanism whereby credentials are not sent across the network. **C** is incorrect because WEP is a deprecated wireless security protocol, but it does not use counter mode. **D** is incorrect because RSA (Rivest Shamir Adleman) is a public key algorithm used for digitally signing and encrypting packets, but it does not use counter mode.

10. You are conducting a wireless site survey at a client site. The client expresses a desire to keep wireless transmissions secure. There is a single 802.11n wireless router with omnidirectional antennae in the server room at one end of the building. WPA2 enterprise and MAC filtering have been configured. What additional security issue should you address?

   A. WPA2 Personal should be used.

   B. MAC filtering is useless; MAC addresses are easily spoofed.

   C. Move the wireless router to the center of the building.

   D. Upgrade the wireless router to 802.11m.

   ☑ **C.** Omnidirectional antennae radiate radio signals in all directions, so a wireless router at one end of a building would allow connectivity from outside the building. Placing the wireless router in the center of the building would allow optimal wireless connectivity from within the building while minimizing radiation outside of the building.

   ☒ **A, B,** and **D** are incorrect. **A** is incorrect because WPA2 Personal requires each device to use a key, whereas WPA2 Enterprise uses an authentication server before allowing wireless network access. Using WPA2 Personal would make the network less secure. **B** is incorrect because, although MAC addresses can be spoofed, MAC filtering is not useless, since most users won't know or care about how to spoof a MAC address. **D** is incorrect because the 802.11m standard does not apply to equipment; rather, it applies to the maintenance of 802.11 wireless documentation.

11. What can be done to secure a wireless network?

   A. Decrease power transmission level to cover only intended area.

   B. Use a wireless encryption standard such as 802.3.

   C. Change the DHCP-supplied default gateway address.

   D. Configure wireless router admin access to use HTTP.

☑ **A.** Wireless routers can be configured with a transmit power level (measured in milliwatts). Increasing this value can, to a point, provide better wireless access to clients. Decreasing this value reduces the wireless coverage area, for example, to only include a property where legitimate access is required.

☒ **B, C,** and **D** are incorrect. **B** is incorrect because 802.3 defines the Ethernet standard, not a wireless encryption standard. **C** is also incorrect because changing the default gateway address is pointless; it is still being delivered to clients automatically via DHCP (Dynamic Host Configuration Protocol). **D** is incorrect because HTTP (Hypertext Transfer Protocol) is the default protocol for connecting to and configuring a wireless router. HTTPS (Hypertext Transfer Protocol Secure) would further secure a wireless network beyond HTTP.

12. A Windows 7 user in your company issues the command **netsh wlan set hostednetwork mode=allow ssid=AcmeWLAN key=password** on her company wireless laptop. What best describes the security problem created by this user?

   A. The user has Administrative rights in Windows 7.
   B. The key is not complex enough.
   C. The user has created a rogue access point.
   D. The SSID name is invalid.

☑ **C.** A rogue access point is either a software or hardware wireless access point that can allow unauthorized wireless access to a secure network, or it can pose as a valid access point. In this case a Windows 7 computer with a wireless card will advertise itself as a wireless network named AcmeWLAN.

☒ **A, B,** and **D** are incorrect. **A** does not apply. Users having Windows administrative access is not considered a security problem in all environments. **B** is incorrect because, although it is true, the problem is not the password; the problem is the unauthorized wireless access point. **D** is incorrect because the SSID (station set identifier) name is valid.

13. You are the wireless network administrator. Users report unstable wireless 802.11g network connectivity. After careful examination you realize 2.4 GHz wireless phones and Bluetooth devices are interfering with the Wi-Fi signal. Which choice offers the best solution?

   A. Replace the 802.11g network with 802.11n.
   B. Cease using all 2.4 GHz wireless phones and Bluetooth devices.
   C. Purchase a high-gain antenna for your wireless router.
   D. Change the Wi-Fi channel used by your wireless router.

☑ **D.** The Wi-Fi 2.4 GHz range is divided into smaller bands (channels) that slightly overlap. If the wireless router is set to use channel 6 and other devices are interfering with it, select a channel furthest away from 6, perhaps channel 1 or 11.

☒ **A, B,** and **C** are incorrect. **A** is incorrect because it would not make a difference. 802.11g and 802.11n can both use the 2.4 GHz frequency range. **B** is incorrect and is an extreme solution to a simple problem—it is much easier to change the Wi-Fi channel. **C** is incorrect because a higher-gain antenna would not solve interference problems, although it would increase your wireless coverage area.

14. A hacker configures a rogue access point to appear as a legitimate Wi-Fi hotspot. Which term best describes this configuration?

A. Evil twin

B. Bad rogue

C. War driving

D. War chalking

☑ **A.** Evil twin is the term used to describe the situation in the question. This is a security risk because users are tricked into connecting to what appears to be a legitimate wireless network, when in fact all the network traffic can be controlled and redirected by a malicious user.

☒ **B, C,** and **D** are incorrect. **B** is incorrect because bad rogue is not an industry-standard term. **C** is incorrect because war driving entails being mobile and scanning for wireless networks. **D** is also incorrect because war chalking entails charting (often with chalk on a sidewalk) open wireless networks.

15. Which of the following refers to unsolicited messages sent to nearby Bluetooth devices?

A. Bluespamming

B. Bluejacking

C. Bluehacking

D. Bluedriving

☑ **B.** Bluejacking refers to a Bluetooth user sending an anonymous message to another Bluetooth device such as a cell phone (assuming Bluetooth is enabled). Bluetooth is a short range (10 meters) wireless technology running in the 2.4 GHz range.

☒ **A, C,** and **D** are incorrect because they are not industry-standard terms.

16. Which of the following refers to unauthorized data access of a Bluetooth device over a
Bluetooth wireless network?

    A. Bluejacking

    B. Bluesnarfing

    C. Packet sniffing

    D. Port scanning

    ☑ **B.** Bluesnarfing is the act of connecting to and accessing data from a device over a
Bluetooth wireless connection. It is considered much more invasive than packet sniffing
or port scanning.

    ☒ **A, C,** and **D** are incorrect. **A** is incorrect because Bluejacking does not access data from a
Bluetooth device; instead, Bluejacking sends an unsolicited message to another Bluetooth
device. **C** and **D** do not apply because the question specifies accessing data. Packet sniffing
captures network traffic; it does not access data from a wireless device. Port scanning
enumerates running services on a host but does not access data stored on the host.

17. You are working at a client site to solve wireless performance issues. In doing so you notice
WEP is configured on the client's wireless routers. What type of attack might this network be
susceptible to?

    A. DDoS

    B. IV attack

    C. ARP poisoning

    D. Dictionary attack

    ☑ **B.** IV (initialization vector) attacks are specific to WEP. The clear-text dynamic IV and
static WEP key are included in each packet. Since the IV is a 24-bit value, there are only
16,777,216 possibilities (2 raised to the power of 24) that can be used with a WEP key.
Given enough network traffic, an attacker can eventually derive the WEP key using
freely available tools.

    ☒ **A, C,** and **D** are incorrect. **A** is incorrect because DDoS (distributed denial of service)
attacks flood a host with useless traffic and are not specific to WEP. **C** is incorrect. ARP
poisoning modifies host ARP cache entries with a valid host IP address (for example,
the default gateway IP) matched to the attacker's MAC address. This means the attacker
would receive packets destined for the default gateway. ARP poisoning can happen on any
wired or wireless network once an attacker gains network access. **D** is incorrect because
dictionary attacks apply to any type of network (including wireless networks using WEP);
they use a dictionary in an attempt to crack account passwords.

18. How can you control whether or not all wireless devices will see your WLAN name?

    A. Disable SSID broadcasting.

    B. Block packet sniffing.

    C. Reduce transmission power level.

    D. Change antenna placement.

    ☑ **A.** Disabling SSID broadcasting results in clients not seeing the wireless network name when they are within range. Newer operating systems will detect a wireless network, but the name will not be displayed.

    ☒ **B, C,** and **D** are incorrect. **B** does not apply. Packet sniffing can be detected on the network because a network card is placed into promiscuous mode to capture traffic. This can be detected and controlled, for example, by disabling a switch port, but it has nothing to do with viewing wireless LANs. **C** and **D** are incorrect because reducing power levels or changing antenna placement on a wireless router might reduce the range from which the wireless network is visible, but it could prevent wireless devices (including those within range) from seeing the wireless network.

19. Which of the following items could interfere with an 802.11g wireless network?

    A. Remote garage door opener

    B. Microwave oven

    C. Television infrared remote

    D. Cell phone

    ☑ **B.** Any wireless devices using the 2.4 GHz range, such as a microwave oven, could potentially interfere with an 802.11g Wi-Fi network.

    ☒ **A, C,** and **D** are incorrect. These are all incorrect because they do not use the 2.4 Ghz frequency range. **A** is incorrect because remote garage door openers usually operate in the 300–400 MHz frequency range. **C** is incorrect because infrared remotes rely on line of sight for communication, Wi-Fi does not; it uses radio waves. **D** is incorrect because cell phones in general use the 800–2000 MHz frequency range, depending on the type of cell phone.

20. In securing a wireless network, you decide to enable EAP-TLS to authorize wireless client access to the wireless LAN. What should you do next?

    A. Install a public key certificate on the client and a smartcard on the server.

    B. Install a smartcard on the client and a public key certificate on the server.

    C. Install MS-CHAP on the client and a public key certificate on the server.

    D. Install a smart card on the client and MS-CHAP on the server.

> ☑ **B.** EAP-TLS uses public key cryptography to control network access. Cryptographic keys can be stored on smartcards. Smartcards are not used on servers; they are used on client stations, normally with a PIN, to authenticate to a server that has been configured with a public key certificate.
>
> ☒ **A, C,** and **D** are incorrect. **A** is incorrect because servers do not use smartcards; clients do. **C** and **D** are incorrect since MS-CHAP (Microsoft Challenge Handshake Protocol) is not used with EAP-TLS, it can be used instead of EAP-TLS, although it is less secure.

21. TKIP is used primarily by which wireless standard?

    A. 802.11n

    B. WEP

    C. WPA

    D. 802.1x

> ☑ **C.** TKIP (Temporal Key Integrity Protocol) is used by WPA for encryption and supersedes WEP.
>
> ☒ **A, B,** and **D** are incorrect. **A** does not apply. The 802.11n standard in no way implies TKIP is used; rather, it is a Wi-Fi standard that improves upon the 802.11g Wi-Fi standard. **B** is incorrect because TKIP addresses encryption implementation flaws in WEP. **D** is incorrect because 802.1x specifies client network authentication and is not related to TKIP.

22. You are a Wi-Fi IT specialist. Users report that the new 802.11g network is not running at the advertised 54 Mbps. What should you tell your wireless users?

    A. 802.11g runs at 11 Mbps.

    B. Wireless encryption will be disabled to increase bandwidth.

    C. Wi-Fi bandwidth is shared by all users connected to the same wireless network.

    D. SSID broadcasting will be disabled to increase bandwidth.

☑ **C.** Like a hub, wireless clients share the network bandwidth on a wireless network, so the more wireless clients connected to the same network, the less bandwidth available per client.

☒ **A, B,** and **D** are incorrect. **A** is incorrect because 802.11b runs at 11 Mbps, but 802.11g runs at 54 Mbps. **B** and **D** are incorrect; they would not have as big of an impact on wireless network bandwidth as option **C**.

23. Which standard requires stations to authenticate prior to gaining network access?

A. 802.11a

B. 802.11b

C. 802.1x

D. 802.3

☑ **C.** The IEEE 802.1x standard defines port-based authentication (including wireless) prior to allowing client network access.

☒ **A, B,** and **D** are incorrect. **A** and **B** are incorrect because 802.11a and 802.11b are wireless standards, but they do not specify network authentication. **D** is incorrect because 802.3 defines the Ethernet standard.

24. You are securing your Wi-Fi network infrastructure. You configure network monitoring software with a list of valid wireless access point MACs allowed on the network. What type of threat will this enable you to detect?

A. Rogue access points

B. War driving

C. Bluesnarfing

D. Bluejacking

☑ **A.** Unauthorized (rogue) wireless access points can either allow malicious wireless users unauthorized access to a wired network or fool unsuspecting users to make a connection to what appears to be a legitimate wireless network. There are many methods of detecting rogue access points; in this example the BSSID (Basic Service Set Identifier), or MAC address, of the access point is compared against a list of allowed BSSIDs.

☒ **B, C,** and **D** are incorrect. **B** is incorrect because war driving is the action of scanning for wireless networks. The question states you are configuring valid AP (access point) MACs to prevent a threat. **C** and **D** are incorrect because the question states you are securing a Wi-Fi network, not a Bluetooth network.

25. You are configuring a wireless network for your home office. Which options are applicable to a home network? (Choose two.)

A. WPA2 PSK

B. WPA2 Enterprise

C. EAP-TLS

D. WPA PSK

☑ **A** and **D.** WPA and WPA2 PSK (Preshared Key) are for home use. They both require the same passphrase be configured on the wireless router and connecting wireless clients.

☒ **B** and **C** are incorrect. They do not apply because they are enterprise-class options. **B** is incorrect because WPA2 Enterprise uses a RADIUS server to authenticate connecting wireless users. **C** is incorrect because EAP-TLS authenticates connecting devices using public keys configured on both the client and the authenticating server.

26. A traveling user calls the help desk regarding her wireless connectivity problem. When she attempts to connect to a visible wireless network at full strength, it eventually times out with no further messages. What is the problem?

A. The user does not have the WPA2 PSK configured on her station.

B. MAC address filtering is blocking her wireless network card.

C. The user needs an external antenna for her wireless card.

D. She must enter the SSID.

☑ **B.** MAC address filtering will prevent connections from unauthorized wireless clients.

☒ **A, C,** and **D** are incorrect. **A** is incorrect because the user is not prompted with any further messages. **C** does not apply; the wireless network appears at full strength. **D** does not apply because the user is clicking the visible wireless network; thus, there is no need to enter the SSID.

27. You are enjoying a cup of coffee at the local coffee shop when all of a sudden your cell phone displays an anonymous message complimenting you on your Hawaiian shirt. What are you a victim of?

A. Bluetoothing

B. Bluesnarfing

C. Bluejacking

D. Bluedriving

☑ **C.** The sending of messages to users that did not ask for the message over a Bluetooth network is referred to as Bluejacking.

☒ **A, B,** and **D** are incorrect. **A** and **D** are incorrect because they are not standard industry terms. **B** does not apply to this situation; only a message was sent. Bluesnarfing entails accessing private data on a Bluetooth device.

10

Authentication

CERTIFICATION OBJECTIVES

❑   **1.3**   Distinguish and differentiate network design elements and compounds

❑   **5.1**   Explain the function and purpose of authentication services

❑   **5.2**   Explain the fundamental concepts and best practices related to authentication, authorization, and access control

QUESTIONS

Authentication involves verifying the identity of users and computers. This can be implemented at various levels, such as requiring authentication before gaining network or server access. Multifactor authentication requires more than one method of proving identity, such as knowing a username and password, having a physical card, and knowing the PIN for that card. Network configuration in production environments will present you with many authentication options. This chapter prepares you to make informed decisions regarding these options.

1. Before accessing computer systems, a government agency requires users to swipe a card through a keyboard-embedded card reader and then provide a PIN. What is this an example of?
   A. Bifactor authentication
   B. Biometric authentication
   C. Physical security
   D. Multifactor authentication

2. Your traveling users require secure remote access to corporate database servers. What should you configure for them?
   A. Modem
   B. WLAN
   C. VPN
   D. Intranet

3. You are the network administrator for a national marketing firm. Employees have frequent lengthy telephone conference calls with colleagues from around the country. To reduce costs, you have been asked to recommend replacement telephony solutions. Which of the following might you suggest?
   A. Modem
   B. VoIP
   C. Internet text chat
   D. E-mail

4. You are an IT security consultant auditing a network. During your presentation of audit findings, one of your clients asks what can be used to prevent unauthorized LAN access. How do you answer the question?
   A. NAC
   B. Packet filtering firewall
   C. PKI
   D. SSL

5. What type of server authenticates remote users prior to allowing network access?

   A. File server

   B. Active Directory

   C. RADIUS

   D. Domain controller

6. Which of the following are examples of RADIUS clients? (Choose two.)

   A. VPN client

   B. 802.1x switch

   C. Wireless router

   D. Windows 7 OS

   E. Linux OS

7. Which of the following are true regarding TACACS+? (Choose three.)

   A. It is compatible with TACACS.

   B. It is compatible with RADIUS.

   C. It is a Cisco proprietary protocol.

   D. It can be used as an alternative to RADIUS.

   E. TACACS+ uses TCP.

8. You are the network administrator for a Unix network. You are planning your network security. A secure protocol must be chosen to authenticate all users logging in. Which is a valid authentication protocol choice?

   A. TCP

   B. Telnet

   C. Kerberos

   D. AES

9. A client asks you to evaluate the feasibility of a Linux client and server operating system environment. Their primary concern is having a central database of user and computer accounts capable of secure authentication. What Linux options should you explore?

   A. NFS

   B. SSH

   C. Samba

   D. LDAP

10. You are configuring a Cisco network authentication appliance. During configuration, you are given a list of authentication choices. Which choice provides the best security and reliability?

   A. RADIUS

   B. TACACS

   C. TACACS+

   D. XTACACS

11. A user enters his logon name to gain network access. To which of the following terms would this example apply?

   A. Identification

   B. Authorization

   C. Auditing

   D. Authentication

12. A user enters a logon name and password to gain network access. Which is the best description of this action?

   A. Single-factor authentication

   B. Dual-factor authentication

   C. Multifactor authentication

   D. Quasifactor authentication

13. A corporation has invested heavily in the development of a much sought-after product. To protect their investment, they would like to ensure that only very specific personnel can enter a research facility. Which of the following is considered the most secure?

   A. Building access card

   B. Voice scan

   C. Finger print scanner

   D. Iris scan

14. Which of the following is considered multifactor authentication?

   A. Building access card / voice recognition scan

   B. Building access card / username / password

   C. Username / password / smartcard

   D. Username / password / smartcard / PIN

15. To log on to a secured system, a user must enter a username, password, and passcode. The passcode is generated from a tiny handheld device and displayed on a tiny screen. What type of device is this?

   A. Smartcard

   B. PKI certificate

   C. Hardware token

   D. PDA

16. Which of the following prevents users from having to specify logon credentials when accessing multiple applications?
   A. Single sign-on
   B. Remember my password
   C. Biometric authentication
   D. Multifactor authentication

17. Which authentication protocol replaces RADIUS?
   A. TACACS
   B. TACACS+
   C. XTACACS
   D. Diameter

18. Which of the following best describes the CHAP protocol?
   A. PKI certificates must be used on both ends of the connection.
   B. 802.1x equipment forwards authentication requests to a RADIUS server.
   C. Passwords are never sent over the network.
   D. SSL is used to encrypt the session.

19. You are configuring a WPA2 wireless network connection on a company laptop. The company has implemented a PKI. Which WPA2 network authentication method would be the best choice?
   A. MS-CHAP
   B. Local computer certificate
   C. WPA2 PSK
   D. SSO

20. Which of the following examples best illustrates authentication?
   A. A user accesses a shared folder to which he has been granted permission.
   B. A computer successfully identifies itself to a server prior to user logon.
   C. A network contains two network links to a remote office in case one fails.
   D. A network appliance encrypts all network traffic before transmitting it further.

21. A technician is troubleshooting user access to an 802.1x wireless network called CORP. The same computer was previously given an IP address on the 10.17.7.0/24 network, but now for some reason it has an IP address on the 10.16.16.0/24 network. The technician reports the machine was recently reimaged, and the image uses DHCP. What is the most likely cause of the problem?
   A. The workstation has a static IP address on the 10.16.16.0/24 network.
   B. The technician needs to issue the IPCONFIG /RENEW command.
   C. The workstation time is incorrect.
   D. The workstation needs to have its PKI certificate reinstalled.

22. What type of security problem would Network Access Control best address?
    A. Dictionary attack
    B. ARP cache poisoning
    C. WEP
    D. SQL injection attack

23. A company intranet consists of various internal web servers each using different authentication stores. What would allow users to use the same username and password for all internal web sites?
    A. NAC
    B. SSO
    C. VPN
    D. Smartcard

24. While capturing network traffic you notice clear text credentials being transmitted. After investigating the TCP headers, you notice the destination port is 389. What type of authentication traffic is this?
    A. EAP
    B. EAP-TLS
    C. LDAP
    D. CHAP

QUICK ANSWER KEY

1.	D	9.	D	17.	D
2.	C	10.	C	18.	C
3.	B	11.	A	19.	B
4.	A	12.	A	20.	B
5.	C	13.	D	21.	D
6.	B, C	14.	D	22.	B
7.	C, D, E	15.	C	23.	B
8.	C	16.	A	24.	C

IN-DEPTH ANSWERS

1. Before accessing computer systems, a government agency requires users to swipe a card through a keyboard-embedded card reader and then provide a PIN. What is this an example of?

   A. Bifactor authentication

   B. Biometric authentication

   C. Physical security

   D. Multifactor authentication

   ☑ **D.** Multifactor authentication involves more than one item to authenticate to a system; for example, something you have (a card) and something you know (a PIN).

   ☒ **A, B,** and **C** are incorrect. **A** is incorrect because bifactor authentication is not a standard industry term. **B** is incorrect because biometric authentication requires a unique physical characteristic such as a fingerprint or retinal scan. **C** is incorrect because there is no mention of the computer systems being locked up before users can gain access to them.

2. Your traveling users require secure remote access to corporate database servers. What should you configure for them?

   A. Modem

   B. WLAN

   C. VPN

   D. Intranet

   ☑ **C.** A VPN (virtual private network) creates an encrypted tunnel between a remote access client and a private network over the Internet. This would allow access to corporate database servers.

   ☒ **A, B,** and **D** are incorrect. **A** is incorrect because a modem converts between computer digital signals and analog signaling used by some portions of the PSTN (public switched telephone network) to allow remote access to a private network, but a modem itself does not provide secure remote access. **B** is incorrect because a WLAN (wireless local area network) you configure would have a short range (a few hundred feet) and would not work for traveling users. **D** does not apply to remote traveling users. An intranet is an internal private network that uses Internet technologies such as TCP/IP and HTTP web servers.

3. You are the network administrator for a national marketing firm. Employees have frequent lengthy telephone conference calls with colleagues from around the country. To reduce costs, you have been asked to recommend replacement telephony solutions. Which of the following might you suggest?

   A. Modem

   B. VoIP

   C. Internet text chat

   D. E-mail

> ☑ **B.** VoIP (Voice over Internet Protocol) transmits digitized voice over a TCP/IP network such as the Internet. As such, the only cost to both parties is that of your Internet connection.
>
> ☒ **A, C,** and **D** are incorrect. **A** is incorrect because a modem converts digital signals to analog and vice versa; it is used to connect computers to the PSTN (public switched telephone network) but is not well suited for multiple party conference calls. **C** and **D** are both incorrect because they are not telephony solutions to conference calls.

4. You are an IT security consultant auditing a network. During your presentation of audit findings, one of your clients asks what can be used to prevent unauthorized LAN access. How do you answer the question?

   A. NAC

   B. Packet filtering firewall

   C. PKI

   D. SSL

> ☑ **A.** Network Access Control (NAC) technology can be hardware or software solution that requires user or device authentication prior to gaining network access.
>
> ☒ **B, C,** and **D** are incorrect. **B** is incorrect because packet filtering firewalls analyze packet headers to allow or block traffic already on the network; they don't control who (or what) gains access to the network in the first place. **C** is not a complete answer. In itself, PKI (public key infrastructure) does not control network access. PKI uses public key certificates to authenticate and secure network traffic, including with some NAC solutions. **D** is incorrect because SSL (Secure Sockets Layer) encrypts traffic that is already on the network.

5. What type of server authenticates remote users prior to allowing network access?

A. File server

B. Active Directory

C. RADIUS

D. Domain controller

   ☑ **C. RADIUS** (Remote Authentication Dial In User Service) servers are central user or device authentication points on the network. Authentication can occur in many ways, including EAP (Extensible Authentication Protocol) and CHAP (Challenge Handshake Authentication Protocol).

   ☒ **A, B,** and **D** are incorrect. **A** is incorrect because file servers host shared file and folder resources; they rely on users and devices already having network access. **B** is incorrect because Active Directory is a replicated network database of network resources in a Microsoft domain environment and it does not control network access; it controls network resource access. **D** is not the answer; a Domain Controller partakes in Active Directory database replication.

6. Which of the following are examples of RADIUS clients? (Choose two.)

A. VPN client

B. 802.1x switch

C. Wireless router

D. Windows 7 OS

E. Linux OS

   ☑ **B and C.** Radius clients are network devices such as switches, wireless routers, or VPN concentrators that authenticate connecting devices or users to a RADIUS authentication server to grant network access.

   ☒ **A, D,** and **E** are incorrect. Connecting clients such as VPN client or Windows and Linux operating systems are not considered RADIUS clients; they are access clients. These access clients initially request network access to a RADIUS client, which in turn then checks against a RADIUS server to determine if access is allowed or not.

7. Which of the following are true regarding TACACS+? (Choose three.)

   A. It is compatible with TACACS.

   B. It is compatible with RADIUS.

   C. It is a Cisco proprietary protocol.

   D. It can be used as an alternative to RADIUS.

   E. TACACS+ uses TCP.

   ☑ **C, D**, and **E.** TACACS+ (Terminal Access Controller Access Control System) is a Cisco proprietary network access protocol that uses the reliable TCP (Transmission Control Protocol) transport mechanism. TACACS+ might be used instead of RADIUS because it encrypts the entire packet payload instead of only the password, as well as separating authentication, authorization, and accounting duties.

   ☒ **A** and **B** are incorrect. **A** is incorrect because TACACS and TACACS+ are not compatible, despite their similar names. TACACS is an old network access standard that was used primarily in Unix network environments. **B** is untrue. RADIUS uses the best-effort UDP (User Datagram Protocol) transport, whereas TACACS+ uses the more reliable TCP.

8. You are the network administrator for a Unix network. You are planning your network security. A secure protocol must be chosen to authenticate all users logging in. Which is a valid authentication protocol choice?

   A. TCP

   B. Telnet

   C. Kerberos

   D. AES

   ☑ **C.** Kerberos is an authentication protocol used by many vendors, including Microsoft with Active Directory Services. Clients and servers must securely prove their identity to each other by way of a central third party referred to as a KDC (key distribution center).

   ☒ **A, B,** and **D** are incorrect. **A** is incorrect because TCP is a connection-oriented reliable TCP/IP transport protocol, but it does not perform authentication. **B** is incorrect because Telnet transmits data in clear text, and so it is not secure. It is used to allow administrative remote access to hosts running a Telnet daemon, usually in Unix or Linux environments. **D** is incorrect because AES (Advanced Encryption Standard) is a symmetric key encryption algorithm; it encrypts data transmissions, but it does not authenticate users on a network.

9. A client asks you to evaluate the feasibility of a Linux client and server operating system environment. Their primary concern is having a central database of user and computer accounts capable of secure authentication. What Linux options should you explore?

A. NFS

B. SSH

C. Samba

D. LDAP

> ☑ **D.** A central database that can securely authenticate users or computers sounds like an LDAP (Lightweight Directory Access Protocol)–compliant database. LDAP transmissions can be clear text (TCP port 389) or encrypted (TCP port 636), and the LDAP database can also be replicated among servers. Microsoft Active Directory Services and Novell eDirectory are LDAP compliant.
>
> ☒ **A, B,** and **C** are incorrect. **A** does not apply. NFS (Network File System) is a Unix-based file sharing protocol; there is no central database involved. **B** is also incorrect because SSH (Secure Shell) encrypts remote administrative shell access to a host running an SSH daemon, commonly Unix or Linux. **C** is incorrect because Samba is a Microsoft-compliant file and printer sharing in Unix and Linux environments. Options **A, B,** and **C** may authorize access to LDAP authenticated users, but they themselves do not perform authentication.

10. You are configuring a Cisco network authentication appliance. During configuration, you are given a list of authentication choices. Which choice provides the best security and reliability?

A. RADIUS

B. TACACS

C. TACACS+

D. XTACACS

> ☑ **C.** TACACS+ (Terminal Access Controller Access Control System) is a Cisco proprietary protocol that authenticates connecting users over TCP to a remote authentication server.
>
> ☒ **A, B,** and **D** are incorrect. **A** is incorrect because RADIUS (Remote Authentication Dial In User Service) uses UDP to authenticate users, and only the password in the packet payload is encrypted, unlike TACACS+. UDP is a connectionless, or best-effort, network transport whereby there are no packet receipt acknowledgments. **B** and **D** are incorrect because TACACS+ supersedes them both.

11. A user enters his logon name to gain network access. To which of the following terms would this example apply?

    A. Identification

    B. Authorization

    C. Auditing

    D. Authentication

    ☑ **A.** Specifying a unique attribute of some kind (such as a logon name) is identification.

    ☒ **B, C,** and **D** are incorrect. **B** is incorrect because authorization to network resources can happen only after a user has been identified and authenticated. **C** does not apply. Although a user logon can be audited, the logon process itself does not imply auditing. **D** is incorrect because authentication occurs as a result of correct identification. A logon name uniquely identifies one user from another; all users will be authenticated given they provide their unique credentials.

12. A user enters a logon name and password to gain network access. Which is the best description of this action?

    A. Single-factor authentication

    B. Dual-factor authentication

    C. Multifactor authentication

    D. Quasifactor authentication

    ☑ **A.** The logon name and password combination is known as single-factor authentication (something you know). Higher-security environments will either require additional factors (such as a physical card) or will limit access when single-factor authentication is used.

    ☒ **B, C,** and **D** are incorrect. **B** and **C** are incorrect because dual-factor authentication means using two independent authentication methods such as a token card and username/password combination, whereas multifactor authentication can mean two or more methods of establishing identity. **D** is incorrect because it is not an industry standard term.

13. A corporation has invested heavily in the development of a much sought-after product. To protect their investment, they would like to ensure that only very specific personnel can enter a research facility. Which of the following is considered the most secure?

   A. Building access card

   B. Voice scan

   C. Finger print scanner

   D. Iris scan

> ☑ **D.** Iris scanning is considered one of the most secure of biometric authentication methods. Retinal blood vessel patterns are unique to an individual and are extremely difficult to reproduce.
>
> ☒ **A, B,** and **C** are incorrect. **A** is the least secure authentication method of all the choices; an impersonator would only need to have the building access card in his possession. **B** and **C** are not as secure as retinal scanning; voice and fingerprint scans have been defeated by using high-fidelity MP3 players and by using valid lifted fingerprints.

14. Which of the following is considered multifactor authentication?

   A. Building access card / voice recognition scan

   B. Building access card / username / password

   C. Username / password / smartcard

   D. Username / password / smartcard / PIN

> ☑ **D.** The username and password combination is considered single-factor authentication. Coupled with possessing a smartcard and knowing the PIN to use the smartcard results in multifactor authentication.
>
> ☒ **A, B,** and **C** are incorrect. They are only two-factor authentication.

15. To log on to a secured system, a user must enter a username, password, and passcode. The passcode is generated from a tiny handheld device and displayed on a tiny screen. What type of device is this?

   A. Smartcard

   B. PKI certificate

   C. Hardware token

   D. PDA

☑ **C.** A hardware token displays an authentication passcode that a user enters in addition to other data such as a username and password to gain access to a system or network resource.

☒ **A, B,** and **D** are incorrect. **A** is not applicable because smartcards do not have screens; they have an embedded chip containing personal identification data such as encryption keys or PKI digital certificates. **B** does not apply; a PKI certificate is not a hardware device, it is a software construct issued to a user or computer used to securely identify that entity and to secure transmissions. **D** is incorrect because a PDA (personal digital assistant) is a small handheld computer; it does not specifically display passcodes used for authentication.

16. Which of the following prevents users from having to specify logon credentials when accessing multiple applications?

    A. Single sign-on

    B. Remember my password

    C. Biometric authentication

    D. Multifactor authentication

☑ **A.** Single sign-on (SSO) enables access to many applications while requiring user authentication only once. SSO is often used when users access data from disparate systems to prevent multiple logons.

☒ **B, C,** and **D** are incorrect. **B** is incorrect because some applications offer to "remember your password." This is a security risk and only applies to the application offering this option. **C** and **D** are incorrect because biometric and multifactor authentication do not prevent the prompting of credentials when accessing applications; they simply provide another means of authentication.

17. Which authentication protocol replaces RADIUS?

    A. TACACS

    B. TACACS+

    C. XTACACS

    D. Diameter

☑ **D.** The Diameter protocol adds capabilities to the RADIUS protocol such as using TCP instead of UDP (more reliability) and being more scalable and flexible.

☒ **A, B,** and **C** are incorrect. **A** and **C** are incorrect because the TACACS and XTACACS authentication protocols all predate RADIUS. **B** is incorrect because TACACS+ does not succeed RADIUS; it is an alternative to RADIUS.

18. Which of the following best describes the CHAP protocol?

    A. PKI certificates must be used on both ends of the connection.

    B. 802.1x equipment forwards authentication requests to a RADIUS server.

    C. Passwords are never sent over the network.

    D. SSL is used to encrypt the session.

> ☑ **C.** The Challenge Handshake Authentication Protocol (CHAP) involves a three-way handshake to establish a session after which peers must periodically prove their identity by way of a changing value based on a shared secret. A shared secret (for example, a password) is known by both parties, but is never sent over the network.
>
> ☒ **A, B,** and **D** are incorrect. **A** does not describe CHAP; it describes other authentication and security methods, for example EAP-TLS, which requires the client and server to possess PKI certificates. **B** is incorrect because an 802.1x infrastructure can use CHAP prior to allowing network access, but it does not have to. **D** is incorrect because SSL (Secure Sockets Layer) is used to encrypt transmissions; CHAP is an authentication protocol.

19. You are configuring a WPA2 wireless network connection on a company laptop. The company has implemented a PKI. Which WPA2 network authentication method would be the best choice?

    A. MS-CHAP

    B. Local computer certificate

    C. WPA2 PSK

    D. SSO

> ☑ **B.** A local computer certificate implies a PKI (public key infrastructure). A certificate is issued to users or computers and uniquely identifies those entities. It contains public and private key pairs used to secure network traffic can be used with WPA2 (Wi-Fi Protected Access) wireless networks.
>
> ☒ **A, C,** and **D** are incorrect. **A** is incorrect because MS-CHAP (Microsoft Challenge Handshake Authentication Protocol) is a valid WPA2 network authentication method, but it is not a better choice than PKI certificate authentication. **C** is incorrect because WPA2 PSK (Preshared Key) is not as secure an authentication method as PKI. **D** is incorrect because SSO (single sign-on) is not a configuration setting for WPA2 network authentication.

20. Which of the following examples best illustrates authentication?

    A. A user accesses a shared folder to which he has been granted permission.

    B. A computer successfully identifies itself to a server prior to user logon.

    C. A network contains two network links to a remote office in case one fails.

    D. A network appliance encrypts all network traffic before transmitting it further.

    ☑ **B.** Authentication means proving your identity (user or computer). This can be done via username/password or smartcard and PIN, or else in this case, the computer might have a PKI certificate installed that gets validated against a server with a related PKI certificate.

    ☒ **A, C,** and **D** are incorrect. **A** is not valid because it describes authorization. **C** describes availability, not authentication. **D** is incorrect because the question states all network traffic is encrypted; authentication is not implied here.

21. A technician is troubleshooting user access to an 802.1x wireless network called CORP. The same computer was previously given an IP address on the 10.17.7.0/24 network, but now for some reason it has an IP address on the 10.16.16.0/24 network. The technician reports the machine was recently reimaged, and the image uses DHCP. What is the most likely cause of the problem?

    A. The workstation has a static IP address on the 10.16.16.0/24 network.

    B. The technician needs to issue the IPCONFIG /RENEW command.

    C. The workstation time is incorrect.

    D. The workstation needs to have its PKI certificate reinstalled.

    ☑ **D.** A computer PKI certificate can grant access to an 802.1x-configured wireless network. Without the certificate, the machine is either denied network access or, in this case, placed on a guest VLAN.

    ☒ **A, B,** and **C** are incorrect. **A** does not apply since the question states DHCP is in use. **B** is not likely to resolve the problem; DHCP should have received a correct IP address on first boot after the image was applied. **C** is incorrect, unsynchronized clocks would not put the machine on a different subnet.

22. What type of security problem would Network Access Control best address?

    A. Dictionary attack

    B. ARP cache poisoning

C. WEP

D. SQL injection attack

☑ **B.** ARP cache poisoning involves an attacker modifying host ARP caches with the attacker's MAC address associated with a valid host IP, thus forcing network traffic to the attacker station. This can be very difficult to prevent, so the key lies in controlling access to the network in the first place.

☒ **A, C,** and **D** are incorrect. **A** is incorrect because the best way to address dictionary attacks is to use strong passwords and enable account lockout thresholds. **C** is incorrect because WEP (Wired Equivalent Privacy) is a deprecated wireless encryption standard; NAC (Network Access Control) does not address WEP problems. **D** does not apply in this case. The best way to address SQL injection attacks is for the developer to carefully validate user submitted queries.

---

23. A company intranet consists of various internal web servers each using different authentication stores. What would allow users to use the same username and password for all internal web sites?

A. NAC

B. SSO

C. VPN

D. Smartcard

☑ **B.** SSO (single sign-on) enables users to use only a single username and password to access multiple network resources even if those network resources use different authentication sources.

☒ **A, C,** and **D** are incorrect. **A** is incorrect because NAC (Network Access Control) determines which users or computers are given access to a network. **C** is incorrect because a VPN would not enable the use of one set of credentials for intranet web servers. **D** does not apply, since the question states the use of a username and password.

24. While capturing network traffic you notice clear text credentials being transmitted. After investigating the TCP headers, you notice the destination port is 389. What type of authentication traffic is this?

A. EAP

B. EAP-TLS

C. LDAP

D. CHAP

☑ **C.** LDAP is a standard for accessing a network directory (database), in this case, for authentication purposes. LDAP uses TCP port 389 for clear-text transmissions and TCP port 636 for encrypted transmissions.

☒ **A, B,** and **D** are incorrect because they are not tied to LDAP. **A** is incorrect because EAP (Extensible Authentication Protocol) is an authentication framework with many specific authentication methods, but it is not tied to LDAP. **B** is a specific EAP mechanism using Transport Layer Security (TLS). Certificates containing encryption and decryption keys are required on the server and client. **D** is incorrect because CHAP (Challenge Handshake Authentication Protocol) is an authentication mechanism whereby the shared secret (often a password) is never sent across the network.

11

Access Control

CERTIFICATION OBJECTIVES

❑ **2.1** Explain risk-related concepts

❑ **5.2** Explain the fundamental concepts and best practices related to authentication, authorization, and access control

❑ **5.3** Implement appropriate security controls when performing account management

QUESTIONS

Access control allows a computer system to secure access to resources including the network itself, servers, shared folders, and printers, just to name a few. IT administrators must implement strong password policies, network access rules, and strong file and folder permissions in accordance with established security policies.

1. A network administrator must grant the appropriate network permissions to a new employee. Which of the following is the best strategy?
    A. Give the new employee user account the necessary rights and permissions.
    B. Add the new employee user account to a group. Ensure the group has the necessary rights and permissions.
    C. Give the new employee administrative rights to the network.
    D. Ask the new employee what network rights they would like.

2. In securing your network, you enforce complex user passwords. Users express concern about forgetting their passwords. What should you configure to allay those concerns?
    A. Password expiration
    B. Periodic password change
    C. Password hints
    D. Maximum password length

3. To quickly give a contractor network access, a network administrator adds the contractor account to the Windows Administrators group. Which security principle does this violate?
    A. Separation of duties
    B. Least privilege
    C. Job rotation
    D. Account lockout

4. James is the branch network administrator for ABC, Inc. Recently the company headquarters requested a network security audit, so James performed an audit himself using freely available Linux tools. What is the problem with James' actions?
    A. ABC, Inc. should have sent a network administrator from headquarters to perform the audit.
    B. The Chief Security Officer should have conducted the audit.
    C. Freely available tools are not reliable and should not have been used.
    D. A third party should have been hired to conduct the audit.

5. A secure computing environment labels data with various security classifications. Authenticated users must have clearance to read this classified data. What type of access control model is this?

 A. Mandatory access control

 B. Discretionary access control

 C. Role-based access control

 D. Time of day access control

6. To ease giving access to network resources for employees, you decide there must be an easier way than to grant users individual access to files, printers, computers, and applications. What security model should you consider using?

 A. Mandatory access control

 B. Discretionary access control

 C. Role-based access control

 D. Time of day access control

7. Linda creates a folder called Budget Projections in her home account and shares it with colleagues in her department. Which of the following best describes this type of access control system?

 A. Mandatory access control

 B. Discretionary access control

 C. Role-based access control

 D. Time of day access control

8. You require that users not be logged on to the network after 6 P.M. while you analyze network traffic during non-business hours. What should you do?

 A. Unplug their stations from the network.

 B. Tell users to press CTRL-ALT-DEL to lock their stations.

 C. Configure time of day restrictions to ensure nobody can be logged in after 6 P.M.

 D. Disable user accounts at 6 P.M.

9. One of your users, Matthias, is taking a three-month sabbatical due to a medical condition, after which he will return to work. What should you do with Matthias' user account?

 A. Delete the account and recreate it when he returns.

 B. Disable the account and enable it when he returns.

 C. Export his account properties to a text file for later import and then delete it.

 D. Ensure you have a backup of his account details and delete his account.

10. During an IT security meeting the topic of account lockout surfaces. When you suggest all user accounts be locked for thirty minutes after three incorrect logon attempts, your colleague Phil states this is a serious problem when applied to administrative accounts. What types of issues might Phil be referring to?

    A. Dictionary attacks could break into administrative accounts.

    B. Administrative accounts are much sought after by attackers.

    C. Administrative accounts are placed into administrative groups.

    D. DoS attacks could render administrative accounts unusable.

11. Your VPN appliance is configured to disallow user authentication unless the user or group is listed as allowed. Regarding blocked users, what best describes this configuration?

    A. Implicit allow

    B. Implicit deny

    C. Explicit allow

    D. Explicit deny

12. Margaret is the head of Human Resources for Emrom, Inc. An employee does not wish to use his annual vacation allotment, but Margaret insists it is mandatory. What IT benefit is derived from mandatory vacations?

    A. Irregularities in job duties can be noticed when another employee fills that role.

    B. Users feel recharged after time off.

    C. Emrom, Inc. will not be guilty of labor violations.

    D. There is less security risk when fewer users are on the network.

13. What type of attack is mitigated by strong, complex passwords?

    A. DoS

    B. Dictionary

    C. Brute force

    D. DNS poisoning

14. A government contract requires your computers to adhere to mandatory access control methods and multilevel security. What should you do to remain compliant with this contract?

    A. Patch your current operating system.

    B. Purchase new network hardware.

    C. Use a Trusted OS.

    D. Purchase network encryption devices.

15. Which term is best defined as an object's list of users, groups, processes, and their permissions?

    A. ACE

    B. ACL

    C. Active Directory

    D. Access log

16. Users complain that they must remember passwords for a multitude of user accounts to access software required for their jobs. How can this be solved?

    A. SSO

    B. ACL

    C. PKI

    D. Password complexity

17. What security model uses data classifications and security clearances?

    A. RBAC

    B. DAC

    C. PKI

    D. MAC

18. The permissions for a Windows folder are shown next. Permission inheritance has been disabled. User DLachance attempts to access the folder Jones_Vs_Cowell. What is the result?

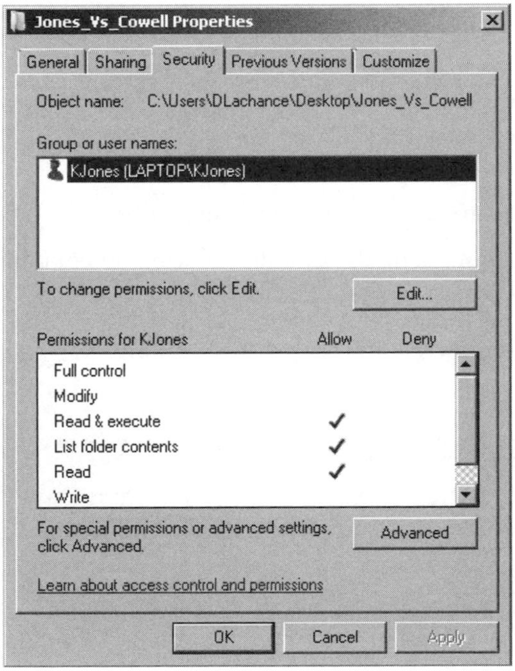

    A. JLachance is denied access due to explicit denial.

    B. JLachance is allowed access due to being in the Everyone group.

    C. JLachance is denied access due to implicit denial.

    D. JLachance is allowed access due to implicit allowal.

19. What security problem exists with the password policy shown here?

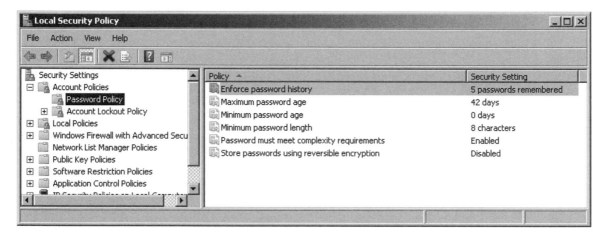

    A. The maximum password age is too low.

    B. The minimum password age is too low.

    C. The minimum password length is too low.

    D. Passwords should be stored using reversible encryption.

20. A Windows server has an inbound firewall rule allowing inbound RDP as shown here. Which term best describes this particular firewall rule?

    A. Explicit allow

    B. Explicit deny

    C. Implicit allow

    D. Implicit deny

21. A Microsoft SQL database administrator creates a service account for the SQL server agent with the following settings. What security problem exists with this configuration?

    A. The username does not follow a naming convention.

    B. The password is not long enough.

    C. Password never expires is enabled.

    D. Account is disabled is not enabled.

22. A Cisco router has the following ACL:

```
ip access-group 101 in
access-list 101 permit tcp any any eq 20
access-list 101 permit tcp any any eq 21
access-list 101 permit tcp any any eq 3389
```

Choose the correct description of the ACL configuration.

    A. SMTP, SNMP, and RDP are explicitly allowed; all else is implicitly denied.

    B. SMTP, SNMP, and RDP are implicitly allowed; all else is explicitly denied.

    C. FTP and RDP are explicitly allowed; all else is implicitly denied.

    D. FTP and RDP are implicitly allowed; all else is explicitly denied.

23. Which of the following is an example of physical access control?
   A. USB flash drive encryption
   B. Disabling USB ports on a computer
   C. Using cable locks to secure laptops
   D. Limiting who can back up sensitive data

24. A technician notices unauthorized computers accessing the local area network. What solutions should the technician consider?
   A. Stronger passwords
   B. Network encryption
   C. VPN
   D. NAC

25. A network administrator, Justin, must grant various departments read access to the Corp_Policies folder and other departments read and write access to the Current_Projects folder. What strategy should Justin employ?
   A. Add all departmental users to the shared folder ACLs with the appropriate permissions.
   B. Create one group, add members, and add the group to the folder ACLs with the appropriate permissions.
   C. Create a Users group and an Administrators group with the correct members. Add the groups to the folder ACLs with the appropriate permissions.
   D. Create a group for each department and add members to the groups. Add the groups to the folder ACLs with the appropriate permissions.

26. What provides secure access to corporate data in accordance with management policies?
   A. SSL
   B. Technical controls
   C. Integrity
   D. Administrative controls

27. Which of the following are considered administrative controls? (Choose two.)
   A. Personnel hiring policy
   B. VPN policy
   C. Disk encryption policy
   D. Separation of duties

28. What is the difference between security clearances and classification labels? (Choose two.)
   A. There is no difference.
   B. Classification labels identify data sensitivity.
   C. Security clearances identify data sensitivity.
   D. Security clearances are compared with classification labels.

QUICK ANSWER KEY

1.	B	**11.**	B	**21.**	C
2.	C	**12.**	A	**22.**	C
3.	B	**13.**	B	**23.**	C
4.	D	**14.**	C	**24.**	D
5.	A	**15.**	B	**25.**	D
6.	C	**16.**	A	**26.**	B
7.	B	**17.**	D	**27.**	A, D
8.	C	**18.**	C	**28.**	B, D
9.	B	**19.**	B		
10.	D	**20.**	A		

IN-DEPTH ANSWERS

1. A network administrator must grant the appropriate network permissions to a new employee. Which of the following is the best strategy?

    A. Give the new employee user account the necessary rights and permissions.

    B. Add the new employee user account to a group. Ensure the group has the necessary rights and permissions.

    C. Give the new employee administrative rights to the network.

    D. Ask the new employee what network rights they would like.

> ☑ **B.** The best strategy for assigning rights and permissions is to add users to groups. Working with rights and permissions for individual users becomes unmanageable beyond a small number of users. New employees can then simply be added to the appropriate group to acquire the needed access to network resources.
>
> ☒ **A, C,** and **D** are incorrect. **A** is incorrect because granting individual user rights and permissions becomes difficult to manage as the number of users grows. **C** is a violation of all network security best practices—only grant the rights needed. **D** is incorrect because users may not know what rights they need, or they may ask for rights they do not need to perform their job.

2. In securing your network, you enforce complex user passwords. Users express concern about forgetting their passwords. What should you configure to allay those concerns?

    A. Password expiration

    B. Periodic password change

    C. Password hints

    D. Maximum password length

> ☑ **C.** Password hints remind users what their password is without revealing the actual password.
>
> ☒ **A, B,** and **D** are incorrect. Password expiration, periodic password change, and password lengths should not be configured differently even if users have difficulty remembering passwords.

3. To quickly give a contractor network access, a network administrator adds the contractor account to the Windows Administrators group. Which security principle does this violate?

   A. Separation of duties

   B. Least privilege

   C. Job rotation

   D. Account lockout

   ☑ **B.** The least privilege principle states users should only be given the rights needed to perform the duties and nothing more. Adding a contractor to the Administrators group grants too much privilege to the contractor.

   ☒ **A, C,** and **D** are incorrect. **A** is incorrect because separation of duties requires multiple persons to perform a specific job. **C** is a strategy that exposes employees to various facets of a business and has nothing to do with security. **D** relates to security, but is not violated by giving a user too many permissions.

4. James is the branch network administrator for ABC, Inc. Recently the company headquarters requested a network security audit, so James performed an audit himself using freely available Linux tools. What is the problem with James' actions?

   A. ABC, Inc. should have sent a network administrator from headquarters to perform the audit.

   B. The Chief Security Officer should have conducted the audit.

   C. Freely available tools are not reliable and should not have been used.

   D. A third party should have been hired to conduct the audit.

   ☑ **D.** No one person should have control of implementing, maintaining, and auditing an IT infrastructure—this violates the separation of duties principle and presents a conflict of interest.

   ☒ **A, B,** and **C** are incorrect. **A** and **B** are incorrect because they still have a company employee conducting an audit. **C** is untrue; many freely available tools are robust and reliable.

5. A secure computing environment labels data with various security classifications. Authenticated users must have clearance to read this classified data. What type of access control model is this?

   A. Mandatory access control

   B. Discretionary access control

   C. Role-based access control

   D. Time of day access control

☑ **A.** Mandatory access control (MAC) models can use security labels to classify data. These labels are then compared to a user's sensitivity level to determine whether or not access is allowed.

☒ **B, C,** and **D** are incorrect. **B** does not match the scenario. Discretionary access control (DAC) models leave control of security to the data owner. Permissions are set at the individual object level as opposed to using data classification labels. **C** is not the best answer because role-based access control places users in roles where those roles have been granted groups of permissions to perform a job function; roles were not mentioned in the question. **D** does not apply, since dates or times of allowed access were not mentioned.

---

6. To ease giving access to network resources for employees, you decide there must be an easier way than to grant users individual access to files, printers, computers, and applications. What security model should you consider using?

   A. Mandatory access control

   B. Discretionary access control

   C. Role-based access control

   D. Time of day access control

☑ **C.** Role-based access control (RBAC) would allow you to group access privileges for files, printers, computers, and applications into a single entity (a role). Users needing these rights are then simply added as occupants of the appropriate role.

☒ **A, B,** and **D** are incorrect. **A** grants access based on security clearances given to users. **B** puts the control of giving access in the hands of the data owner (for example, a file owner can give permissions to others to that file). **D** controls access based on time of day and is therefore incorrect.

---

7. Linda creates a folder called Budget Projections in her home account and shares it with colleagues in her department. Which of the following best describes this type of access control system?

   A. Mandatory access control

   B. Discretionary access control

   C. Role-based access control

   D. Time of day access control

☑ **B.** Discretionary access control puts the ability to grant other people access in the hands of data owners, in this case, Linda.

☒ **A, C,** and **D** are incorrect. **A** is not applicable in this case; mandatory access control is security-policy driven, not user-driven. **C** is incorrect since a role grouping needed access rights is not required for access to a single folder. Finally, **D** is not applicable. Linda has given rights to the folder, and those rights are in effect at any time of the day.

8. You require that users not be logged on to the network after 6 P.M. while you analyze network traffic during non-business hours. What should you do?

   A. Unplug their stations from the network.

   B. Tell users to press CTRL-ALT-DEL to lock their stations.

   C. Configure time of day restrictions to ensure nobody can be logged in after 6 P.M.

   D. Disable user accounts at 6 P.M.

☑ **C.** Network operating systems (NOSs) have the ability to control when users can and cannot log on, as well as ending existing logon sessions based on time of day.

☒ **A, B,** and **D** are incorrect. **A** is not what you should do. It involves physically visiting each station; there are better ways. **B** will not work. Locking a workstation does not log the user out. **D** is an extreme solution and may not affect existing logon sessions immediately (for example, a Windows Active Directory Kerberos ticket would have to first expire).

9. One of your users, Matthias, is taking a three-month sabbatical due to a medical condition, after which he will return to work. What should you do with Matthias' user account?

   A. Delete the account and recreate it when he returns.

   B. Disable the account and enable it when he returns.

   C. Export his account properties to a text file for later import and then delete it.

   D. Ensure you have a backup of his account details and delete his account.

☑ **B.** Disabling his account will prevent anyone from logging on with the account, but will preserve all of the account settings. When he returns, simply enable the account.

☒ **A, C,** and **D** are incorrect. A user account should never be deleted when that user will be returning; instead, it should simply be disabled.

10. During an IT security meeting the topic of account lockout surfaces. When you suggest all user accounts be locked for thirty minutes after three incorrect logon attempts, your colleague Phil states this is a serious problem when applied to administrative accounts. What types of issues might Phil be referring to?

   A. Dictionary attacks could break into administrative accounts.

   B. Administrative accounts are much sought after by attackers.

   C. Administrative accounts are placed into administrative groups.

   D. DoS attacks could render administrative accounts unusable.

> ☑ **D.** DoS (denial of service) attacks render a legitimate network service unusable. Attempting three incorrect logon attempts every half hour to administrative accounts would effectively keep those accounts locked, thus preventing legitimate use of those accounts.
>
> ☒ **A**, **B**, and **C** are incorrect. Although these are all true, they are not issues resulting from account lockout settings.

11. Your VPN appliance is configured to disallow user authentication unless the user or group is listed as allowed. Regarding blocked users, what best describes this configuration?

   A. Implicit allow

   B. Implicit deny

   C. Explicit allow

   D. Explicit deny

> ☑ **B.** Implicit denial means all are denied unless specifically allowed; there are no specific listings of users or computers that are denied.
>
> ☒ **A**, **C**, and **D** are incorrect. **A** is incorrect because implicit allowance implies all are allowed unless specifically denied. **C** does apply to this configuration; the question asks about blocked users, not allowed users. **D** is incorrect because the configuration does not specify who (or what) is blocked.

12. Margaret is the head of Human Resources for Emrom, Inc. An employee does not wish to use his annual vacation allotment, but Margaret insists it is mandatory. What IT benefit is derived from mandatory vacations?

   A. Irregularities in job duties can be noticed when another employee fills that role.

   B. Users feel recharged after time off.

C. Emrom, Inc. will not be guilty of labor violations.

D. There is less security risk when fewer users are on the network.

☑ **A.** It is easy for an employee to spot inconsistencies or irregularities when someone is on vacation.

☒ **B, C,** and **D** are incorrect. **B** and **C** may both be true, but it is not the motivating factor in IT environments. **D** is incorrect. Less users on a network does not mean the network is more secure.

13. What type of attack is mitigated by strong, complex passwords?

A. DoS

B. Dictionary

C. Brute force

D. DNS poisoning

☑ **B.** Stronger passwords make it more difficult for dictionary password attacks to succeed. A stronger password is a minimum length of eight characters, where those characters might be a combination of uppercase letters, lowercase letters, symbols, and numerals.

☒ **A, C,** and **D** are incorrect. They are not directly impeded by stronger passwords, as are dictionary attacks.

14. A government contract requires your computers to adhere to mandatory access control methods and multilevel security. What should you do to remain compliant with this contract?

A. Patch your current operating system.

B. Purchase new network hardware.

C. Use a Trusted OS.

D. Purchase network encryption devices.

☑ **C.** A Trusted OS (operating system) uses a secured OS kernel that supports MAC, which applies security centrally to adhere with security policies. This type of OS is considered too strict for general use and is applicable in high-security environments.

☒ **A, B,** and **D** are incorrect. **A** in incorrect because the question does not state details about the operating system being patched, so patching in itself is not the best answer. **B** and **D** are incorrect because they refer to acquiring or replacing network hardware, not computer hardware.

15. Which term is best defined as an object's list of users, groups, processes, and their permissions?

    A. ACE

    B. ACL

    C. Active Directory

    D. Access log

    ☑ **B.** Access control lists (ACLs) detail which users, groups, or processes have permissions to an object, such as a file or folder.

    ☒ **A, C,** and **D** are incorrect. **A** is incorrect because an individual entry in an ACL is known as an ACE (access control entry). **C** describes Microsoft's replicated authentication database, Active Directory. Users and groups from Active Directory can appear in ACLs, but permissions themselves are not stored here; they are stored with the file system object. **D** is incorrect because an access log simply lists requests details (date, time, user, or computer) for a network resource such as a file.

16. Users complain that they must remember passwords for a multitude of user accounts to access software required for their jobs. How can this be solved?

    A. SSO

    B. ACL

    C. PKI

    D. Password complexity

    ☑ **A.** SSO (single sign-on) allows a user to authenticate once to multiple resources that would otherwise require separate logins.

    ☒ **B, C,** and **D** are incorrect. **B** is incorrect because ACL does not relate to passwords; an ACL controls who and what has access to a particular resource. Although a PKI (public key infrastructure) can be used to authenticate instead of or in addition to usernames and passwords, **C** is incorrect because it does not eliminate multiple password prompts; that is what SSO is for. **D** is incorrect because password complexity is liable to increase the burden that users are complaining about.

17. What security model uses data classifications and security clearances?

    A. RBAC

    B. DAC

    C. PKI

    D. MAC

☑ **D.** MAC is a security model that classifies data according to sensitivity that enables access to only those with proper clearance.

☒ **A, B,** and **C** are incorrect. **A** is incorrect because RBAC assigns rights and permissions to roles. Those persons occupying the role therefore acquire the role's access to resources. DAC allows the owner of a resource (for example, a file) to determine who else has access; therefore, answer **B** is incorrect. **C** does not apply; PKI (public key infrastructure) is a system of digital certificates used for authentication, data encryption, and digital signatures.

18. The permissions for a Windows folder are shown next. Permission inheritance has been disabled. User DLachance attempts to access the folder Jones_Vs_Cowell. What is the result?

A. JLachance is denied access due to explicit denial.

B. JLachance is allowed access due to being in the Everyone group.

C. JLachance is denied access due to implicit denial.

D. JLachance is allowed access due to implicit allowal.

☑ **C.** Because permission inheritance is disabled, the permissions listed are the only ones in effect. User JLachance is not listed with any privileges and is therefore blocked from the Jones_Vs_Cowell folder due to implicit denial.

☒ **A, B,** and **D** are incorrect. **A** is incorrect because JLachance is not explicitly denied any permission; JLachance is not even in the ACL. **B** is inapplicable; the Everyone group is not in the ACL. **D** is incorrect because JLachance will not have any access to the Jones_Vs_Cowell folder because she is not listed; this is an implicit denial.

19. What security problem exists with the password policy shown here?

A. The maximum password age is too low.

B. The minimum password age is too low.

C. The minimum password length is too low.

D. Passwords should be stored using reversible encryption.

☑ **B.** The minimum password age must be increased; otherwise, when a forced password change occurs every 42 days, users can immediately cycle through five passwords to eventually set their password to an old, easy-to-remember password.

☒ **A, C,** and **D** are incorrect. **A** is incorrect because increasing the maximum password age could be considered a security problem. **C** is incorrect because eight-character passwords are accepted throughout the industry as acceptable. **D** is incorrect because storing passwords using reversible encryption is a backward-compatible option that store passwords in what is comparable to plain text.

20. A Windows server has an inbound firewall rule allowing inbound RDP as shown here. Which term best describes this particular firewall rule?

A. Explicit allow

B. Explicit deny

C. Implicit allow

D. Implicit deny

☑ **A.** Computers with an IP address in the range of 172.17.82.90–172.17.82.99 are specifically allowed Remote Desktop access; this is explicit allowance.

☒ **B, C,** and **D** are incorrect. **B** is incorrect because explicit denial would mean the firewall rule would block, not allow, Remote Desktop access. **C** and **D** do not apply, since there is a specific direct firewall rule allowing access.

21. A Microsoft SQL database administrator creates a service account for the SQL server agent with the following settings. What security problem exists with this configuration?

A. The username does not follow a naming convention.

B. The password is not long enough.

C. Password never expires is enabled.

D. Account is disabled is not enabled.

☑ **C.** Administrators often enable the Password Never Expires option on service accounts so that they are exempt from regular user password policies that force periodic password change. This presents a security problem, since the service account password remains the same indefinitely. Changing the password on a service account means changing the password for each service using that account. Windows Server 2008 R2 has a Managed Accounts option that resets service account passwords automatically.

☒ **A, B,** and **D** are incorrect. We do not know whether or not a naming convention is being followed; **A** is incorrect. **B** is incorrect because the password is eight characters long, the minimum accepted length. **D** is incorrect because if the account is disabled, it cannot be used.

22. A Cisco router has the following ACL:

```
ip access-group 101 in
access-list 101 permit tcp any any eq 20
access-list 101 permit tcp any any eq 21
access-list 101 permit tcp any any eq 3389
```

Choose the correct description of the ACL configuration.

A. SMTP, SNMP, and RDP are explicitly allowed; all else is implicitly denied.

B. SMTP, SNMP, and RDP are implicitly allowed; all else is explicitly denied.

C. FTP and RDP are explicitly allowed; all else is implicitly denied.

D. FTP and RDP are implicitly allowed; all else is explicitly denied.

☑ **C.** FTP (File Transfer Protocol) uses TCP ports 20 and 21. RDP (Remote Desktop Protocol) uses TCP port 3398. The ACL on the Cisco router explicitly allows this traffic in; all other traffic is implicitly denied.

☒ **A, B,** and **D** are incorrect. **A** and **B** are incorrect because SMTP (Simple Mail Transfer Protocol) uses TCP port 25, SNMP (Simple Network Management Protocol) uses UDP port 161, and RDP uses TCP port 3389. **D** is incorrect; it is the opposite of C, the correct answer.

23. Which of the following is an example of physical access control?

A. USB flash drive encryption

B. Disabling USB ports on a computer

C. Using cable locks to secure laptops

D. Limiting who can back up sensitive data

☑ **C.** Locking laptops down with a cable lock physically prevents the theft of laptops.

☒ **A, B,** and **D** are incorrect. They are all examples of software access control, not physical access control.

24. A technician notices unauthorized computers accessing the local area network. What solutions should the technician consider?

A. Stronger passwords

B. Network encryption

C. VPN

D. NAC

☑ **D.** NAC (Network Access Control) is software or a network appliance that can verify that connecting computers are allowed to access the network. This can be done by checking PKI certificates, checking that antivirus software is installed and updated, and so on.

☒ **A, B,** and **C** are incorrect. **A** and **B** are incorrect because stronger passwords or network encryption protect user accounts and data transmissions, but they are applicable once a computer has gained access to the network, not before. **C** does not apply to a local area network. VPNs (virtual private networks) secure a data channel to a private network over an untrusted network.

25. A network administrator, Justin, must grant various departments read access to the Corp_ Policies folder and other departments read and write access to the Current_Projects folder. What strategy should Justin employ?

A. Add all departmental users to the shared folder ACLs with the appropriate permissions.

B. Create one group, add members, and add the group to the folder ACLs with the appropriate permissions.

C. Create a Users group and an Administrators group with the correct members. Add the groups to the folder ACLs with the appropriate permissions.

D. Create a group for each department and add members to the groups. Add the groups to the folder ACLs with the appropriate permissions.

☑ **D.** Each department should have its own group with department employees as members. This facilitates granting group members' access to the appropriate resources.

☒ **A, B,** and **C** are incorrect. **A** is not recommended, since managing individual user permissions becomes difficult as the network grows. **B** is incorrect because a single group will not work here, since different sets of users require different sets of permissions to different shared folders. **C** is also incorrect because a users group and an administrators group will not suffice; each department should have its own group.

26. What provides secure access to corporate data in accordance with management policies?

   A. SSL

   B. Technical controls

   C. Integrity

   D. Administrative controls

☑ **B.** Technical controls include any hardware or software solution utilizing access control in adherence with established security policies.

☒ **A, C,** and **D** are incorrect. **A** is incorrect because SSL (Secure Sockets Layer) provides application-specific transmission encryption to ensure data confidentiality. **C** assures data is authentic and has not been tampered with. **D** provide a foundation for how a business should be run.

27. Which of the following are considered administrative controls? (Choose two.)

   A. Personnel hiring policy

   B. VPN policy

   C. Disk encryption policy

   D. Separation of duties

☑ **A** and **D.** The hiring of correct personnel and ensuring no one employee has control of a business transaction (separation of duties) are part of creating a business management foundation; these are examples of administrative controls.

☒ **B** and **C** are incorrect. VPN and disk encryption policies deal with specific technologies and thus are considered technical controls.

28. What is the difference between security clearances and classification labels? (Choose two.)

   A. There is no difference.

   B. Classification labels identify data sensitivity.

   C. Security clearances identify data sensitivity.

   D. Security clearances are compared with classification labels.

   ☑ **B** and **D**. Data sensitivity is referred to with classification labels. Security clearances are compared against these labels to determine if access is granted or not.

   ☒ **A** and **C** are incorrect. **A** is incorrect because there is a difference between the two. **C** is incorrect because it is the definition for classification labeling.

12

Introduction to Cryptography

CERTIFICATION OBJECTIVES

❑   **1.4**   Implement and use common protocols

❑   **1.5**   Identify commonly used default network ports

❑   **6.1**   Summarize general cryptography concepts

❑   **6.2**   Use and apply appropriate cryptographic tools and products

QUESTIONS

Cryptography has been used in various forms for thousands of years. It is the act of scrambling data such that only intended persons can read it. Modern cryptography feeds plain text through encryption algorithms, resulting in cipher text. Symmetric encryption uses a single key for encryption and decryption, whereas asymmetric uses mathematically related keys to secure data. This section explores the differences between the most common encryption standards.

1. A network technician notices TCP port 80 traffic when users authenticate to their mail server. What should the technician configure to protect the confidentiality of these transmissions?
    A. MD5
    B. SHA-256
    C. SHA-512
    D. HTTPS

2. Which of the following allows secured remote access to a Unix host?
    A. SSH
    B. SSL
    C. SSO
    D. SHA

3. An IT manager asks you to recommend a LAN encryption solution. The solution must support current and future software that does not have encryption of its own. What should you recommend?
    A. SSL
    B. SSH
    C. IPSec
    D. VPN

4. Which protocol supersedes SSL?
    A. TLS
    B. SSO
    C. TKIP
    D. VPN

5. Which TCP port would a firewall administrator allow so that users can access SSL-enabled web sites?
    A. 443
    B. 80
    C. 3389
    D. 69

6. Data integrity is provided by which of the following?
- **A.** 3DES
- **B.** RC4
- **C.** AES
- **D.** MD5

7. You are configuring a network encryption device and must account for other devices that may not support newer and stronger algorithms. Which of the following lists encryption standards from weakest to strongest?
- **A.** DES, 3DES, RSA
- **B.** 3DES, DES, AES
- **C.** RSA, DES, Blowfish
- **D.** RSA, 3DES, DES

8. Which of the following uses two mathematically related keys to secure data transmissions?
- **A.** AES
- **B.** RSA
- **C.** 3DES
- **D.** Blowfish

9. Your company has implemented a PKI. You would like to encrypt e-mail messages you send to another employee, Amy. What do you require to encrypt messages to Amy?
- **A.** Amy's private key
- **B.** Amy's public key
- **C.** Your private key
- **D.** Your public key

10. You decide that your LAN computers will use asymmetric encryption with IPSec to secure LAN traffic. While evaluating how this can be done, you are presented with an array of encryption choices. Select the correct classification of crypto standards.
- **A.** Symmetric
     DES
     3DES
   Asymmetric
     RSA
     AES

B. Symmetric
  3DES
  DES

  Asymmetric
  Blowfish
  RSA

C. Symmetric
  3DES
  DES

  Asymmetric
  RC4
  RSA

D. Symmetric
  AES
  3DES

  Asymmetric
  RSA

11. Data confidentially is provided by which of the following?
  A. MD5
  B. Disk encryption
  C. E-mail digital signatures
  D. SHA

12. Which symmetric block cipher supersedes Blowfish?
  A. TwoFish
  B. ThreeFish
  C. RSA
  D. PKI

13. A user connects to a secured online banking web site. Which of the following statements is incorrect?
  A. The workstation public key is used to encrypt data transmitted to the web server. The web server private key performs the decryption.
  B. The workstation session key is encrypted with the server public key and transmitted to the web server. The web server private key performs the decryption.
  C. The workstation-generated session key is used to encrypt data sent to the web server.
  D. The workstation-generated session key is used to decrypt data received by the web server.

14. Which term describes the process of concealing messages within a file?
  A. Trojan
  B. Steganography

    C. Encryption

    D. Digital signature

15. Which term best describes the assurance that a message is authentic and neither party can dispute its transmission or receipt?

    A. Digital signature

    B. Encryption

    C. PKI

    D. Non-repudiation

16. You are a developer at a software development firm. Your latest software build must be made available on the corporate web site. Internet users require a method of ensuring they have downloaded an untampered version of the software. What should you do?

    A. Generate a file hash for the download file and make it available on the web site.

    B. Make sure Internet users have antivirus software installed.

    C. Configure the web site to use TLS.

    D. Make sure the web server has antivirus software installed.

17. Which cryptographic approach uses points on a curve to define public and private key pairs?

    A. RSA

    B. DES

    C. ECC

    D. PKI

18. Your company currently uses an FTP server and you have been asked to make FTP traffic secure using SSL. What should you configure?

    A. FTPS

    B. SFTP

    C. IPSec

    D. TLS

19. On which protocol is SCP built?

    A. FTP

    B. SSL

    C. SSH

    D. ICMP

20. Which of the following are true regarding ciphers? (Choose two.)

    A. Block ciphers analyze data patterns and block malicious data from being encrypted.

    B. Stream ciphers encrypt data one byte at a time.

    C. Block ciphers encrypt chunks of data.

    D. Stream ciphers encrypt streaming media traffic.

21. Which of the following are block ciphers? (Choose two.)
- A. DES
- B. RSA
- C. RC4
- D. AES

22. What type of encryption has been configured here?

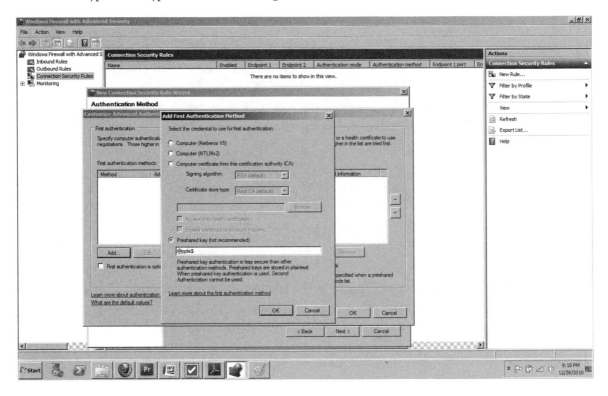

- A. Asymmetric
- B. Symmetric
- C. SSL
- D. RSA

23. Which of the following are message digest algorithms? (Choose two.)
- A. 3DES
- B. RIPEMD
- C. Blowfish
- D. HMAC

24. A military institution requires the utmost in security for transmitting messages during wartime. What provides the best security?

    A. AES

    B. 3DES

    C. One-time pad

    D. RSA

25. When hardening a VPN, what should you consider? (Choose two.)

    A. Enable PAP

    B. Disable PAP

    C. Disable EAP-TLS

    D. Enable EAP-TLS

26. Encrypting and digitally signing e-mail with public and private keys can be done with which technology?

    A. 3DES

    B. DES

    C. Blowfish

    D. PGP

27. Which of the following is considered the least secure?

    A. MS-CHAP v2

    B. NTLM v2

    C. EAP-TLS

    D. PAP

28. A user digitally signs a sent e-mail message. What security principle does this apply to?

    A. Least privilege

    B. Integrity

    C. Confidentiality

    D. Authorization

29. Which of the following are true regarding user private keys? (Choose two.)

    A. It is used to encrypt sent messages.

    B. It is used to decrypt received messages.

    C. It is used to create digital signatures.

    D. It is used to verify digital signatures.

30. You are the IT directory for a company with military contracts. An employee, Sandra, leaves the company and her user account is removed. A few weeks later somebody requires access to Sandra's old files but is denied access. After investigating the issue you determine that Sandra's files are encrypted with a key generated from a passphrase. What type of encryption is this?

A. WEP

B. Asymmetric

C. Symmetric

D. RSA

QUICK ANSWER KEY

1.	D	11.	B	21.	A, D
2.	A	12.	A	22.	B
3.	C	13.	A	23.	B, D
4.	A	14.	B	24.	C
5.	A	15.	D	25.	B, D
6.	D	16.	A	26.	D
7.	A	17.	C	27.	D
8.	B	18.	A	28.	B
9.	B	19.	C	29.	B, C
10.	D	20.	B, C	30.	C

IN-DEPTH ANSWERS

1. A network technician notices TCP port 80 traffic when users authenticate to their mail server. What should the technician configure to protect the confidentiality of these transmissions?

   A. MD5

   B. SHA-256

   C. SHA-512

   D. HTTPS

   ☑ **D.** TCP port 80 is HTTP (Hypertext Transfer Protocol) network traffic. Web browsers use HTTP to connect to web servers. In this case users are using web-based e-mail that is not encrypted. HTTPS (Hypertext Transfer Protocol Secure) uses either SSL (Secure Sockets Layer) or TLS (Transport Layer Security) to encrypt HTTP traffic. This requires the installation of a digital certificate on the server.

   ☒ **A, B,** and **C** are incorrect. These are cryptographic hashing algorithms which do not encrypt, or protect the confidentiality of, information. Data is fed to a hashing algorithm resulting in a "hash" (sometimes called a message digest) that represents the encoded data. Any change in the data will result in a different hash.

2. Which of the following allows secured remote access to a Unix host?

   A. SSH

   B. SSL

   C. SSO

   D. SHA

   ☑ **A.** Secure Shell (SSH) listens on TCP port 22 and is used commonly on Unix and Linux hosts to allow secure remote administration. An SSH daemon must be running on the server, and an SSH client (such as Putty) is required to make the connection. Unlike its predecessor, Telnet, SSH encrypts network traffic.

   ☒ **B, C,** and **D** are incorrect. **B** is incorrect because SSL is not used for remote admin access to Unix and Linux hosts. SSL encrypts higher-level protocols such or HTTP or SMTP (Simple Mail Transfer Protocol). **C** is incorrect because SSO (single sign-on) allows access to multiple applications without prompting to authenticate to each one. SHA (secure hash algorithm) is a specific hashing algorithm used to verify that data has not been tampered with. It is not tied to being used for remote admin access for Unix and Linux; thus, **D** is incorrect.

3. An IT manager asks you to recommend a LAN encryption solution. The solution must support current and future software that does not have encryption of its own. What should you recommend?

   A. SSL

   B. SSH

   C. IPSec

   D. VPN

   ☑ **C.** IPSec (IP Security) is not specific to an application; all network traffic is encrypted and authenticated. Both sides of the secured connection must be configured to use IPSec.

   ☒ **A, B,** and **D** are incorrect. **A** is application-specific encryption. SSL can be applied to higher-level protocols such as SMTP (Simple Mail Transfer Protocol) or HTTP. **B** is not an encryption solution. SSH is a secure remote administration mechanism. **D** does encrypt all traffic, including applications that don't support encryption, but a VPN (virtual private network) is not a LAN solution; it is a WAN solution.

4. Which protocol supersedes SSL?

   A. TLS

   B. SSO

   C. TKIP

   D. VPN

   ☑ **A.** TLS replaces SSL. For example, TLS offers more secure data authentication to ensure data has not been tampered with while in transit.

   ☒ **B, C,** and **D** are incorrect. **B** enables authenticating only once to allow access multiple applications. **C** is incorrect because TKIP (Temporal Key Integrity Protocol) is a wireless security enhancement to WEP (Wired Equivalent Privacy). **D** does not supersede SSL, although there are SSL VPN solutions available. VPNs allow secure remote access to a LAN across an untrusted network.

5. Which TCP port would a firewall administrator allow so that users can access SSL-enabled web sites?

   A. 443

   B. 80

    C. 3389

    D. 69

> ☑ **A.** SSL uses TCP port 443.
>
> ☒ **B, C,** and **D** are incorrect. HTTP uses port 80, Remote Desktop Protocol uses port 3389, and TFTP (Trivial File Transfer Protocol) uses UDP port 69, not TCP.

6. Data integrity is provided by which of the following?

    A. 3DES

    B. RC4

    C. AES

    D. MD5

> ☑ **D.** MD5 (Message Digest 5) is a hashing algorithm that computes a digest from provided data. Any change in the data will invalidate the digest, thus data integrity is attained.
>
> ☒ **A, B,** and **C** are incorrect. These are symmetric encryption algorithms providing confidentiality, not integrity. 3DES (Triple Digital Encryption Standard) is a 168-bit encryption standard. RC4 and AES (Advanced Encryption Standard) are symmetric ciphers whose bit strengths come in various lengths.

7. You are configuring a network encryption device and must account for other devices that may not support newer and stronger algorithms. Which of the following lists encryption standards from weakest to strongest?

    A. DES, 3DES, RSA

    B. 3DES, DES, AES

    C. RSA, DES, Blowfish

    D. RSA, 3DES, DES

> ☑ **A.** DES (Digital Encryption Standard) is a 56-bit cipher, and 3DES is a 168-bit cipher; both are symmetric encryption algorithms. RSA (Rivest, Shamir, Adleman) is a public and private key (asymmetric) encryption and digital signing standard whose bit strength varies. The bit length of a cipher is not the only factor influencing its strength; the specific implementation of the cryptographic functions also plays a role.

⊠ **B, C,** and **D** are incorrect. **B** is incorrect because 3DES is a stronger standard than DES. **C** is incorrect because RSA is stronger than DES. **D** is incorrect because RSA is considered more secure than 3DES or DES.

8. Which of the following uses two mathematically related keys to secure data transmissions?

- **A.** AES
- **B.** RSA
- **C.** 3DES
- **D.** Blowfish

☑ **B.** RSA is an asymmetric cryptographic algorithm that uses mathematically related public and private key pairs to digitally sign and encrypt data.

⊠ **A, C,** and **D** are incorrect. These are symmetric encryption standards. Symmetric encryption means the same key that encrypts a message is used to decrypt that message. The problem this presents is how to securely get the key to other parties.

9. Your company has implemented a PKI. You would like to encrypt e-mail messages you send to another employee, Amy. What do you require to encrypt messages to Amy?

- **A.** Amy's private key
- **B.** Amy's public key
- **C.** Your private key
- **D.** Your public key

☑ **B.** A PKI (public key infrastructure) implies the use of public and private key pairs. To encrypt messages for Amy, you must have her public key. This can be installed locally on a computer or published centrally on a directory server. The related private key, which only Amy should have access to, is used to decrypt the message.

⊠ **A, C,** and **D** are incorrect. **A** is incorrect because Amy's private key is used to decrypt received messages encrypted with her public key. **C** is incorrect because you need your private key to digitally sign messages, not to send encrypted messages. **D** is incorrect because your public key is used by others to encrypt data they send to you, or it can be used to verify items you digitally sign with your private key.

10. You decide that your LAN computers will use asymmetric encryption with IPSec to secure LAN traffic. While evaluating how this can be done, you are presented with an array of encryption choices. Select the correct classification of crypto standards.

A. Symmetric
   DES
   3DES

   Asymmetric
   RSA
   AES

B. Symmetric
   3DES
   DES

   Asymmetric
   Blowfish
   RSA

C. Symmetric
   3DES
   DES

   Asymmetric
   RC4
   RSA

D. Symmetric
   AES
   3DES

   Asymmetric
   RSA

☑ **D.** AES and 3DES are cryptographic standards using symmetric algorithms. This means a single key is used to both encrypt and decrypt. RSA (Rivest, Shamir, Adleman) is an asymmetric encryption algorithm. This means two mathematically related keys (public and private) are used to secure data; normally a public key encrypts data and a private key decrypts it.

☒ **A, B,** and **C** are incorrect. **A** and **B** are incorrect because AES is not asymmetric, and neither is Blowfish. **C** is incorrect because RC4 is symmetric, not asymmetric.

11. Data confidentially is provided by which of the following?

   A. MD5

   B. Disk encryption

   C. E-mail digital signatures

   D. SHA

   ☑ **B.** Encryption provides data confidentiality. Only authorized parties have the ability to decrypt disk contents.

   ☒ **A, C,** and **D** are incorrect. These provide data integrity. This assures a recipient that data is authentic and has not been tampered with.

12. Which symmetric block cipher supersedes Blowfish?

   A. TwoFish

   B. ThreeFish

   C. RSA

   D. PKI

   ☑ **A.** TwoFish is a symmetric block cipher that replaces Blowfish.

   ☒ **B, C,** and **D** are incorrect. **B** is incorrect because it does not exist. **C** is incorrect because RSA is an asymmetric standard. **D** is incorrect because PKI is a term referring to the use of public and private key pairs (asymmetric); it is not a symmetric block cipher.

13. A user connects to a secured online banking web site. Which of the following statements is incorrect?

   A. The workstation public key is used to encrypt data transmitted to the web server. The web server private key performs the decryption.

   B. The workstation session key is encrypted with the server public key and transmitted to the web server. The web server private key performs the decryption.

   C. The workstation-generated session key is used to encrypt data sent to the web server.

   D. The workstation-generated session key is used to decrypt data received by the web server.

☑ **A.** It is not the workstation public key that is used; it is the server's. The workstation-generated session key is encrypted with the server public key and transmitted to the web server, where a related private key decrypts the message to reveal the session key.

☒ **B, C,** and **D** are incorrect. These are incorrect answers because they are true. The question asks identification of the incorrect statement. Once the unique session key is known to the server, it is used to encrypt and decrypt data between the two hosts.

14. Which term describes the process of concealing messages within a file?

A. Trojan

B. Steganography

C. Encryption

D. Digital signature

☑ **B.** Steganography hides messages within files. For example, a message could be hidden within an inconspicuous JPG picture file.

☒ **A, C,** and **D** are incorrect. **A** is incorrect because a Trojan is malware masking itself as a useful file or software. **C** is not applicable. Encryption makes no attempt to hide the fact that data is encrypted. **D** is used to verify the untampered authenticity of data. No attempt is made to conceal a message.

15. Which term best describes the assurance that a message is authentic and neither party can dispute its transmission or receipt?

A. Digital signature

B. Encryption

C. PKI

D. Non-repudiation

☑ **D.** Non-repudiation means neither the sending nor the receiving party can dispute the fact that a transmission occurred. The recipient is assured of data authenticity and integrity via a digital signature applied with the sender's private key.

☒ **A, B,** and **C** are incorrect. Answer **A** does assure a recipient that a message is authentic, but non-repudiation is a better answer. **B** is incorrect because encryption ensures data confidentiality but does not ensure data is authentic. PKI (public key infrastructure) is a general term describing a security framework that does include message authentication and non-repudiation, but answer **C** is too ambiguous compared to answer **D**.

16. You are a developer at a software development firm. Your latest software build must be made available on the corporate web site. Internet users require a method of ensuring they have downloaded an untampered version of the software. What should you do?

    A. Generate a file hash for the download file and make it available on the web site.

    B. Make sure Internet users have antivirus software installed.

    C. Configure the web site to use TLS.

    D. Make sure the web server has antivirus software installed.

> ☑ **A.** File hashing performs a calculation on a file resulting in what is called a hash. Changing a file in some way and then performing the same calculation would result in a different hash. This is one way to verify that file is the correct version.
>
> ☒ **B, C,** and **D** are incorrect. While very valid points, **B** and **D** will not conclusively ensure users they are downloading an authentic version of a file. **C** is incorrect because, while TLS could be used to secure the Internet traffic to the web site, it cannot check for file tampering.

17. Which cryptographic approach uses points on a curve to define public and private key pairs?

    A. RSA

    B. DES

    C. ECC

    D. PKI

> ☑ **C.** Elliptic curve cryptography (ECC) is public key cryptography based on points on an elliptic curve.
>
> ☒ **A, B,** and **D** are incorrect. They are not based on elliptic curve points. **A** is incorrect because RSA is an asymmetric cryptographic standard. **B** is incorrect because DES is a symmetric standard. **D** is incorrect because although PKI does involve public and private key pairs, it has nothing specifically to do with elliptic curve points.

18. Your company currently uses an FTP server and you have been asked to make FTP traffic secure using SSL. What should you configure?

    A. FTPS

    B. SFTP

    C. IPSec

    D. TLS

☑ **A.** FTPS (File Transfer Protocol Secure) can use SSL to secure FTP traffic.

☒ **B, C,** and **D** are incorrect. **B** is incorrect because SFTP (Secure File Transfer Protocol) refers to tunneling FTP traffic through an SSH–encrypted session. **C** does not apply because IPSec (IP Security) cannot use SSL; it is an alternative to SSL. IPSec performs at a lower level in the OSI (Open Systems Interconnect) model, which means IPSec can secure network traffic for higher-level applications that do not encrypt. SSL is application specific. **D** is incorrect; TLS (Transport Layer Security) supersedes SSL.

19. On which protocol is SCP built?

A. FTP

B. SSL

C. SSH

D. ICMP

☑ **C.** SCP (Secure Copy) is a secure way of copying files between computers over an SSH session.

☒ **A, B,** and **D** are incorrect. **A** is incorrect because FTP (File Transfer Protocol) is not secured and is not related to SCP. SCP is not built on SSL; therefore, **B** is incorrect. **D** does not apply, since ICMP (Internet Control Message Protocol) has nothing to do with security. ICMP reports on network congestion and the reachability of network nodes.

20. Which of the following are true regarding ciphers? (Choose two.)

A. Block ciphers analyze data patterns and block malicious data from being encrypted.

B. Stream ciphers encrypt data one byte at a time.

C. Block ciphers encrypt chunks of data.

D. Stream ciphers encrypt streaming media traffic.

☑ **B** and **C.** Stream ciphers encrypt data a bit or a byte at a time, whereas block ciphers encrypt segments (blocks) of data at one time in various block sizes.

☒ **A** and **D** are incorrect. **A** is incorrect because bock ciphers do not block malicious data from being encrypted. **D** is incorrect because stream ciphers are not designed to encrypt only streaming media traffic.

21. Which of the following are block ciphers? (Choose two.)

   A. DES

   B. RSA

   C. RC4

   D. AES

☑ **A** and **D**. Block ciphers encrypt data a block at a time (rather than a bit or byte at a time). DES and AES are both block ciphers.

☒ **B** and **C** are incorrect. Both are stream ciphers; they encrypt data a bit or byte at a time.

22. What type of encryption has been configured here?

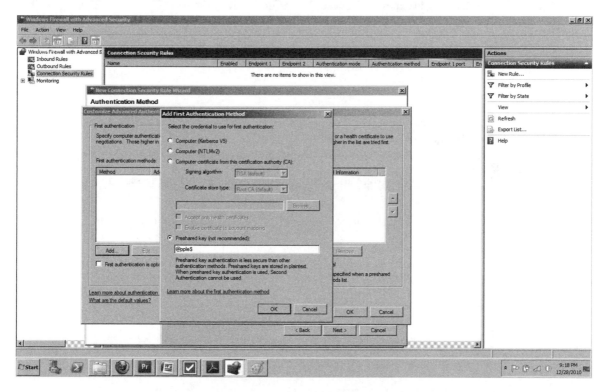

    A. Asymmetric

    B. Symmetric

    C. SSL

    D. RSA

> ☑ **B.** Configuring the same preshared key on both sides of a connection defines symmetric (same key) encryption.
>
> ☒ **A, C,** and **D** are incorrect. **A** is incorrect because different related keys (public and private) would be used for asymmetric encryption. **C** and **D** are incorrect because they are not configured with preshared keys.

23. Which of the following are message digest algorithms? (Choose two.)

    A. 3DES

    B. RIPEMD

    C. Blowfish

    D. HMAC

> ☑ **B** and **D.** RIPEMD (RACE Integrity Primitives Evaluation Message Digest) and HMAC (Hash-based Message Authentication Code) are both cryptographic hashing functions.
>
> ☒ **A** and **C** are incorrect. They are encryption functions, not hashing (message digest) functions.

24. A military institution requires the utmost in security for transmitting messages during wartime. What provides the best security?

    A. AES

    B. 3DES

    C. One-time pad

    D. RSA

> ☑ **C.** One-time pads are used to combine completely random keys with plaintext, resulting in ciphertext. Both communicating parties must have the same one-time pads, which presents a problem if communicating with a large number of entities. No amount of computing power or time can increase the likelihood of breaking this type of ciphertext.
>
> ☒ **A, B,** and **D** are incorrect. While considered secure, AES, 3DES, and RSA encryption do not provide the utmost in security compared to one-time pads.

25. When hardening a VPN, what should you consider? (Choose two.)

    A. Enable PAP

    B. Disable PAP

    C. Disable EAP-TLS

    D. Enable EAP-TLS

    ☑ **B** and **D.** PAP (Password Authentication Protocol) should be disabled. PAP sends unencrypted passwords across the network during authentication. EAP-TLS (Extensible Authentication Protocol–Transport Layer Security) should not be disabled when hardening VPNs; it is considered very secure due to its mutual authentication of both VPN client and VPN server.

    ☒ **A** and **C** are incorrect. **A** is incorrect because PAP should only be considered as a last resort; even then it may violate security policies in place. **C** is incorrect because EAP-TLS should not be disabled when hardening a VPN; it is considered very secure.

26. Encrypting and digitally signing e-mail with public and private keys can be done with which technology?

    A. 3DES

    B. DES

    C. Blowfish

    D. PGP

    ☑ **D.** PGP (Pretty Good Privacy) uses public and private key pairs to encrypt and digitally sign messages.

    ☒ **A, B,** and **C** are incorrect. These are symmetric algorithms. Symmetric algorithms use the same key to encrypt and decrypt data, not related public and private key pairs.

27. Which of the following is considered the least secure?

    A. MS-CHAP v2

    B. NTLM v2

    C. EAP-TLS

    D. PAP

☑ **D.** PAP (Password Authentication Protocol) is considered insecure because it does not encrypt transmitted credentials.

☒ **A, B,** and **C** are incorrect. **A** is incorrect because MS-CHAP v2 (Microsoft Challenge Handshake Authentication Protocol) does not send credentials, even in encrypted form, over the network at all because it hashes credentials on both sides of a connection. This, of course, requires both parties to have knowledge of a shared secret to compute the hash. **B** is incorrect because NTLM (New Technology LAN Manager) hashes data on both sides of a connection similarly to CHAP and is, therefore, more secure than PAP. **C** is incorrect because EAP-TLS (Extensible Authentication Protocol–Transport Layer Security) is the most secure of the presented choices. This is because it required both the client and the server to possess a certificate used for authentication.

28. A user digitally signs a sent e-mail message. What security principle does this apply to?

A. Least privilege

B. Integrity

C. Confidentiality

D. Authorization

☑ **B.** Message integrity is achieved when digitally signing an e-mail message. The sender's private key creates the unique signature, which is verified on the receiving end using the sender's related public key. If the message has not changed since it was sent, the signature will be considered valid.

☒ **A, C,** and **D** are incorrect. **A** is incorrect because the principle of least privilege ensures users have only the rights they need to complete a task. **C** would only apply if the user had encrypted the e-mail message. **D** is incorrect because authorization occurs when an authenticated entity is granted access to a particular network resource.

29. Which of the following are true regarding user private keys? (Choose two.)

A. It is used to encrypt sent messages.

B. It is used to decrypt received messages.

C. It is used to create digital signatures.

D. It is used to verify digital signatures.

☑ **B** and **C**. Decryption occurs using the receiver's private key. If their public key were used, anybody could decrypt received messages, since public keys are designed to be publicly available. Digitally signing a message must assure the recipient it came from who it says it came from. Because only the owner of a private key has access to it, the private key is used to create digital signatures. The related public key verifies the validity of that signature.

☒ **A** and **D** are incorrect. **A** is incorrect because the public key of the recipient(s) of the message is required to encrypt a message to them. They then decrypt the message using the related private key. **D** is incorrect because in modern systems this process is completely transparent. Verifying digital signatures is performed using the sender's public key.

30. You are the IT directory for a company with military contracts. An employee, Sandra, leaves the company and her user account is removed. A few weeks later somebody requires access to Sandra's old files but is denied access. After investigating the issue you determine that Sandra's files are encrypted with a key generated from a passphrase. What type of encryption is this?

A. WEP

B. Asymmetric

C. Symmetric

D. RSA

☑ **C**. Symmetric encryption uses the same key for encryption and decryption. In this case, if the same passphrase is used, the data can be decrypted.

☒ **A**, **B**, and **D** are incorrect. **A** is incorrect because WEP (Wired Equivalent Privacy) is for wireless networks, not file encryption. **B** and **D** are not applicable because only a single key is being used in this example. Asymmetric encryption (RSA is asymmetric) uses two related keys.

13

Managing a PKI Infrastructure

CERTIFICATION OBJECTIVES

❑   **1.4**   Implement and use common protocols

❑   **6.1**   Summarize general cryptography concepts

QUESTIONS

Any financial or sensitive data exchange on the Internet benefits from PKI. A public key infrastructure (PKI) provides security using digital certificates. Certificate authorities (CAs) issue certificates to valid parties for the purpose of confidentially (encryption), integrity (digital signatures and hashing), authentication (user or computer), and non-repudiation (no disputing of private key usage). Each certificate contains a unique related public and private key pair in addition to other data such as the certificate expiration date. Untrusted private keys can be revoked and published with a certificate revocation list (CRL).

1. After importing their user certificate file to an e-mail program, a user finds she cannot digitally sign sent e-mail messages. What are some possible reasons for this? (Choose two.)
    A. The public key is not in the certificate.
    B. The private key is not in the certificate.
    C. The certificate was not created for e-mail usage.
    D. The PKI is not in the certificate.

2. Which of the following would not be found in a digital certificate?
    A. Public key
    B. Private key
    C. Digital signature of issuing CA
    D. IP address of PKI server

3. You are providing consulting services to a legal firm that has a PKI. They would like to enable document workflow where documents are sent electronically to the appropriate employees within the firm. You are asked if there is a way to prove that documents were sent from the user listed in the From field. Of the following, what would you recommend?
    A. File encryption
    B. Digital signatures
    C. E-mail encryption
    D. Certificate revocation list

4. As a security auditor, you focus on hardening an existing PKI. Which of the following should you consider? (Choose two.)
    A. Take the CA offline.
    B. Do not make public keys publicly accessible.
    C. Configure a recovery agent.
    D. Encrypt all digital certificates.

5. Your colleagues report that there is a short time frame where a revoked certificate can still be used. Why is this?
   A. The CRL is only published periodically.
   B. The CRL is published immediately but must replicate to all hosts.
   C. The CRL only lists revoked certificates; it is not enforced.
   D. The CRL is dependent on network bandwidth.

6. Which of the following best describes the term "key escrow"?
   A. A trusted third party with decryption keys in case the original keys have expired
   B. A trusted third party with decryption keys in addition to existing original keys
   C. An account that can be used to encrypt private keys
   D. An account that can be used to encrypt data for any user

7. Which PKI component verifies the identity of certificate requestors before a certificate is issued?
   A. Public key
   B. RA
   C. PKI
   D. CRL

8. A user reports that they are unable to authenticate to the corporate VPN while traveling. You have configured the VPN to require X.509 user certificate authentication. After investigating the problem, you learn that the user certificate has expired. Which of the following presents the quickest secure solution?
   A. Recreate a new user certificate and configure it on the user computer.
   B. Disable X.509 certificate authentication for your VPN.
   C. Renew the expired user certificate.
   D. Set the date back on the VPN appliance to before the user certificate expired.

9. When users connect to an intranet server by typing https://intranet.acme.local, their web browser displays a warning message stating the site is not to be trusted. How can this warning message be removed while maintaining security?
   A. Use HTTP instead of HTTPS.
   B. Install the intranet server private key on all client workstations.
   C. Use TCP port 443 instead of TCP port 80.
   D. Install the trusted root certificate in the client web browser for the issuer of the intranet server certificate.

10. A web server's security is being configured as shown here. Identify the configuration error.

A. The physical web site path should not be on drive C:.

B. HTTPS web sites must use port 443.

C. Port 444 must be used for HTTP, not HTTPS.

D. An SSL certificate must be selected.

11. An HTTPS-secured web site requires the ability to restrict which workstations can make a connection. Which option is the most secure?

A. Configure the web site to only allow connections from the IP addresses of valid workstations.

B. Configure the web site to only allow connections from the MAC addresses of valid workstations.

C. Configure the web site to use user authentication.

D. Configure the web site to require client-side certificates.

12. Which of the following is untrue regarding certificates containing private keys?

A. They can be used to encrypt mail sent to others.

B. They can be used to encrypt hard disk contents.

C. They should be password protected.

D. They can be used to digitally sign mail sent to others.

13. Why would a digital certificate be used for a computer? (Choose the best answer.)
- **A.** NAC
- **B.** IPSec
- **C.** All of the above
- **D.** None of the above

14. You are responsible for enabling SSL on an e-commerce web site. What should you do first?
- **A.** Install the web server digital certificate.
- **B.** Enable SSL on the web server.
- **C.** Create a CSR and submit to a CA.
- **D.** Configure the web server to use port 443.

15. While generating a certificate signing request for a web site, you enter the information listed here. Users will connect to the web site by typing https://www.acme.com. Identify the configuration error.

Expiry: 12 months
Bit length: 2048
Common Name: 215.66.77.88
Organization: Acme, Inc.
OU: Sales
Country: US
State: TN
City: Memphis

- **A.** The expiry date is one year away.
- **B.** The bit length should be 128.
- **C.** The common name should be www.acme.com.
- **D.** The State field must not be abbreviated.

16. A national company with headquarters in Dallas, Texas, is implementing a PKI. There are corporate locations in 12 other major U.S. cities. Each of those locations has a senior network administrator. Which option presents the best secure solution?
- **A.** Install a Root CA in Dallas. Create subordinate CAs for each city and use these to issue certificates for users and computers in that city. Take the root CA offline.
- **B.** Install a Root CA in Dallas. Issue certificates for users and computers in all locations.
- **C.** Install a Root CA in Dallas. Issues certificates for users and computers in all locations. Take the Root CA offline.
- **D.** Install a Root CA in Dallas and each city. Issue certificates for users and computers using each city Root CA. Take the Root CAs offline.

17. A work colleague has sent you a digital certificate file to install on your computer so that you can encrypt e-mail messages to him. What error was made in this illustration when the file was generated?

A. There should not be a private key password.

B. A private key should never be shared with others.

C. The option Enable Strong Private Key Protection must be enabled.

D. The option Include All Extended Properties must be disabled.

Certificate Import Wizard ☒

Password
To maintain security, the private key was protected with a password.

Type the password for the private key.

Password:

☐ Enable strong private key protection. You will be prompted every time the private key is used by an application if you enable this option.

☐ Mark this key as exportable. This will allow you to back up or transport your keys at a later time.

☑ Include all extended properties.

Learn more about protecting private keys

< Back | Next > | Cancel

18. To secure your server, you would like to ensure server hard disk data cannot be accessed if the hard disks are stolen. What should you do?

A. Configure EFS.

B. Configure TPM with PKI encryption keys.

C. Configure NTFS security.

D. Configure a power-on password.

19. Which security objectives are met by PKI? (Choose two.)

A. Least privilege

B. Integrity

C. Non-repudiation

D. DMZ

20. Your company, Acme, Inc., conducts business with a supplier, Widgets, Inc. Both companies have an existing PKI with departmental subordinate CAs. Select Widgets, Inc. departments require access to specific secured Acme web servers that require client-side certificates before access is granted. What solution should you propose?

A. Acme, Inc. administrators should create a new root CA for Widgets, Inc. and issue certificates to those employees needing access to the Acme server.

B. Acme, Inc. administrators should create a new subordinate CA for Widgets, Inc. and issue certificates to those employees needing access to the Acme server.

C. The Acme web servers should be cross-certified with the appropriate Widgets subordinate CAs.

D. The appropriate Widgets, Inc. and Acme, Inc. departmental CAs should be cross-certified.

21. Which types of keys are commonly used for e-commerce web sites?

   A. Public, private, session

   B. Public and private

   C. Public, private, TPM

   D. Public, private, PKI

22. The CA signature exists in all digital certificates that it issues. Which key does the CA use to create its signature?

   A. Private

   B. Public

   C. Symmetric

   D. Asymmetric

23. In a PKI, what role does the CA play? (Choose two.)

   A. Revoke certificates

   B. Use its private key to digitally sign certificates

   C. Use its public key to digitally sign certificates

   D. Control access to the network using certificates

24. To which does the X.509 standard apply?

   A. LDAP

   B. PKI certificates

   C. Biometric authentication

   D. A type of network transport

QUICK ANSWER KEY

1.	B, C	**9.**	D	**17.**	B
2.	D	**10.**	D	**18.**	B
3.	B	**11.**	D	**19.**	B, C
4.	A, C	**12.**	A	**20.**	C
5.	A	**13.**	C	**21.**	A
6.	B	**14.**	C	**22.**	A
7.	B	**15.**	C	**23.**	A, B
8.	C	**16.**	A	**24.**	B

IN-DEPTH ANSWERS

1. After importing their user certificate file to an e-mail program, a user finds she cannot digitally sign sent e-mail messages. What are some possible reasons for this? (Choose two.)

A. The public key is not in the certificate.

B. The private key is not in the certificate.

C. The certificate was not created for e-mail usage.

D. The PKI is not in the certificate.

    ☑   **B** and **C**. A private key is used to create digital signatures, and the related public key verifies the authenticity of that signature. A certificate lacking a private key cannot be used to digitally sign e-mail messages. Depending on how the certificate file was created, the private key may have been omitted. This is sometimes done when you send your public key to another party so that they can encrypt messages to you. Certificates can be created for specific uses, such as e-mail.

    ☒   **A** and **D** are incorrect. **A** is incorrect because public keys do not create digital signatures, they verify them. **D** does not make sense. A public key infrastructure (PKI) is a collection of certificates generated from a certificate authority (CA) to establish a chain of trust. Each certificate contains data such as the issuer, the subject to whom the certificate was issued and expiration date, public keys, optionally private keys, and so on.

2. Which of the following would not be found in a digital certificate?

A. Public key

B. Private key

C. Digital signature of issuing CA

D. IP address of PKI server

    ☑   **D**. A PKI server does not write its IP address within certificates it issues; however, it does write its digital signature with a private key.

    ☒   **A**, **B**, and **C** are incorrect. A digital certificate would contain public and private keys as well as the signature of the issuing CA.

3. You are providing consulting services to a legal firm that has a PKI. They would like to enable document workflow where documents are sent electronically to the appropriate employees within the firm. You are asked if there is a way to prove that documents were sent from the user listed in the From field. Of the following, what would you recommend?

   A. File encryption

   B. Digital signatures

   C. E-mail encryption

   D. Certificate revocation list

   ☑ **B.** Digital signatures are created with the sender's private key (to which only they have access) and verified with the corresponding public key. This is the best solution for workflow documents in this scenario.

   ☒ **A, C,** and **D** are not valid solutions. **A** and **C** are incorrect because encrypting files or messages conceals the data from unauthorized parties, but does nothing to verify its authenticity. **D** is incorrect because the certificate revocation list (CRL) periodically publishes a list of invalidated certificates to ensure the PKI does not accept these revoked certificates for any use.

4. As a security auditor, you focus on hardening an existing PKI. Which of the following should you consider? (Choose two.)

   A. Take the CA offline.

   B. Do not make public keys publicly accessible.

   C. Configure a recovery agent.

   D. Encrypt all digital certificates.

   ☑ **A and C.** The CA is used to issue and renew X.509 certificates and should be taken offline when not in use for security purposes. Recovery agents have the ability to recover encrypted data when the original private key is unavailable. Failure to configure this could result in no access to important data.

   ☒ **B and D** are incorrect. Public keys are designed to be made publicly available, so **B** is incorrect. **D** should not be considered. Digital certificates are not normally themselves encrypted; this is not as strong an answer as **A** or **C**.

5. Your colleagues report that there is a short time frame where a revoked certificate can still be used. Why is this?

   A. The CRL is only published periodically.

   B. The CRL is published immediately, but must replicate to all hosts.

   C. The CRL only lists revoked certificates; it is not enforced.

   D. The CRL is dependent on network bandwidth.

> ☑ **A.** The CRL is not published immediately; it is published either manually or on a schedule, so there may be a small time frame where revoked certificates can still be used.
>
> ☒ **B, C,** and **D** are incorrect. **B** is untrue. Conversely, the Online Certificate Status Protocol (OCSP) does publish revoked certificates immediately. **C** is untrue. Once the CRL is published, it is enforced. **D** is incorrect because network bandwidth does not affect when the CRL is published.

6. Which of the following best describes the term "key escrow"?

   A. A trusted third party with decryption keys in case the original keys have expired

   B. A trusted third party with decryption keys in addition to existing original keys

   C. An account that can be used to encrypt private keys

   D. An account that can be used to encrypt data for any user

> ☑ **B.** Key escrow refers to a trusted third party with a copy of decryption keys. A court order may be necessary to use these keys under certain circumstances.
>
> ☒ **A, C,** and **D** are incorrect. **A** is incorrect because private keys that have expired are published in a CRL and any copy of those expired keys is thus unusable. **C** and **D** are incorrect because key escrow is not used to encrypt private keys. An account to encrypt data for any user is unnecessary; all public keys for all users are available to all other users to perform encryption.

7. Which PKI component verifies the identity of certificate requestors before a certificate is issued?

   A. Public key

   B. RA

   C. PKI

   D. CRL

☑ **B.** A registration authority (RA) is an optional PKI component that performs requestor verification before certificates are issued.

☒ **A, C, and D are incorrect. A** is incorrect because public keys verify digital signatures created with the corresponding private key; they do not verify the identity of a certificate requestor. **C** is not a PKI component. **D** is not involved with the issuance of digital certificates; instead, the CRL publishes a list of untrusted private keys.

8. A user reports that they are unable to authenticate to the corporate VPN while traveling. You have configured the VPN to require X.509 user certificate authentication. After investigating the problem, you learn that the user certificate has expired. Which of the following presents the quickest secure solution?

A. Recreate a new user certificate and configure it on the user computer.

B. Disable X.509 certificate authentication for your VPN.

C. Renew the expired user certificate.

D. Set the date back on the VPN appliance to before the user certificate expired.

☑ **C.** Expired X.509 certificates can be renewed by a CA if they have expired. This is quicker than having expired certificates deleted and re-issued.

☒ **A, B, and D are incorrect.** Recreating the user certificate simply because it has expired is not quicker than renewing their existing certificate, so **A** is incorrect. **B** would not be a secure solution. **D** is not a secure solution. VPN logs will have incorrect date and time stamps, and some VPN clients that could previously connect may no longer be able to connect.

9. When users connect to an intranet server by typing https://intranet.acme.local, their web browser displays a warning message stating the site is not to be trusted. How can this warning message be removed while maintaining security?

A. Use HTTP instead of HTTPS.

B. Install the intranet server private key on all client workstations.

C. Use TCP port 443 instead of TCP port 80.

D. Install the trusted root certificate in the client web browser for the issuer of the intranet server certificate.

☑ **D.** The web browser must trust the digital signature in the intranet web server certificate; this is the digital signature of the server certificate issuer. If a client trusts the signer, it then trusts all certificates signed by the signer.

☒ **A**, **B**, and **C** are incorrect. **A** is incorrect because using Hypertext Transfer Protocol (HTTP) instead of Hypertext Transfer Protocol Secure (HTTPS) would make the connection less secure. Client workstations do not need the server private key to trust the web site. Only the owner of a private key should have access to it, so **B** is incorrect. **C** is incorrect because HTTPS implies TCP port 443 is already being used.

10. A web server's security is being configured as shown here. Identify the configuration error.

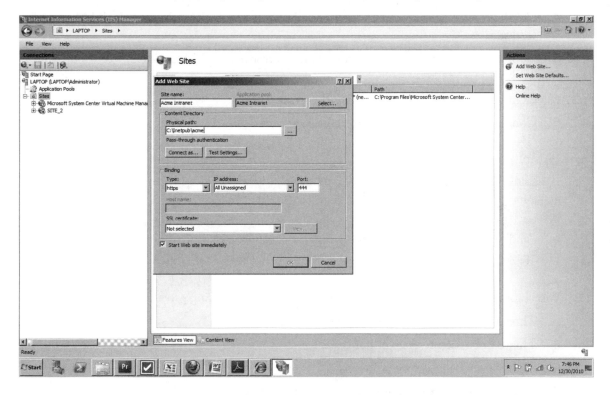

- **A.** The physical web site path should not be on drive C:.
- **B.** HTTPS web sites must use port 443.
- **C.** Port 444 must be used for HTTP, not HTTPS.
- **D.** An SSL certificate must be selected.

☑ **D.** To configure HTTPS, a digital certificate must be selected. The certificate (among other things) contains a public and private key pair used to secure HTTP traffic.

☒ **A, B,** and **C** are incorrect. While answer **A** is good advice, the web site residing on drive C: does not constitute a configuration error. **B** and **C** are incorrect because HTTP and HTTPS can use any unused port configured by the administrator; however, straying from the default port 80 for HTTP and port 443 for HTTPS requires users to enter the port number as part of the URL.

11. An HTTPS-secured web site requires the ability to restrict which workstations can make a connection. Which option is the most secure?

   A. Configure the web site to only allow connections from the IP addresses of valid workstations.

   B. Configure the web site to only allow connections from the MAC addresses of valid workstations.

   C. Configure the web site to use user authentication.

   D. Configure the web site to require client-side certificates.

☑ **D.** Client-side digital certificates must be installed on each workstation to access the web site. The web server must also be configured to allow access only from workstations with appropriate certificates installed.

☒ **A, B,** and **C** are incorrect. **A** and **B** are not the most secure solutions because IP addresses and MAC addresses are easy to spoof. **C** is not the most secure solution. Usernames and passwords can be learned much more easily than forging a digital certificate.

12. Which of the following is untrue regarding certificates containing private keys?

   A. They can be used to encrypt mail sent to others.

   B. They can be used to encrypt hard disk contents.

   C. They should be password protected.

   D. They can be used to digitally sign mail sent to others.

☑ **A.** Private keys are not used to encrypt message to others; for that you must have the recipient's public key.

☒ **B, C,** and **D** are incorrect. These are all true.

13. Why would a digital certificate be used for a computer? (Choose the best answer.)

   A. NAC

   B. IPSec

   C. All of the above

   D. None of the above

> ☑ **C.** Computer digital certificates are used to authenticate the computer to another host such as with Network Access Control (NAC) before network access is granted, or with IPSec before two hosts can communicate securely.
>
> ☒ **A, B**, and **D** are incorrect. **A** and **B** are true, so answer **C** is the best choice. **D** is incorrect.

14. You are responsible for enabling SSL on an e-commerce web site. What should you do first?

   A. Install the web server digital certificate.

   B. Enable SSL on the web server.

   C. Create a CSR and submit to a CA.

   D. Configure the web server to use port 443.

> ☑ **C.** Creating a Certificate Signing Request (CSR) and submitting it to a CA is the first step that must be completed. There are various Internet certificate authorities such as Verisign and Entrust with varying pricing structures. Then the CA digitally signed certificate must be installed on your web server. Finally, you must configure your web site to use the digital certificate.
>
> ☒ **A, B**, and **D** are incorrect. These cannot be done until a CA-approved CSR exists. Also, secured web sites do not have to use port 443.

15. While generating a certificate signing request for a web site, you enter the information listed here. Users will connect to the web site by typing https://www.acme.com. Identify the configuration error.

Expiry: 12 months
Bit length: 2048
Common Name: 215.66.77.88
Organization: Acme, Inc.
OU: Sales
Country: US
State: TN
City: Memphis

A. The expiry date is one year away.

B. The bit length should be 128.

C. The common name should be www.acme.com.

D. The State field must not be abbreviated.

☑ **C.** The common name in a web server certificate must match the name that will be typed in as the Uniform Resource Locator (URL) host name; otherwise, client web browsers will not trust the web site.

☒ **A, B,** and **D** are incorrect. **A** is not a configuration error; 12 months is normally how long web server certificates are valid. **B** is not a configuration error. 2048 is a valid bit strength selection for the public and private key pair. Web browsers use 128-bit session keys to secure transactions, but the client-generated session key will be transmitted to the server initially after having been encrypted with the web server's 2048 bit public key. **D** is not a problem. The state name can be abbreviated.

16. A national company with headquarters in Dallas, Texas, is implementing a PKI. There are corporate locations in 12 other major U.S. cities. Each of those locations has a senior network administrator. Which option presents the best secure solution?

A. Install a Root CA in Dallas. Create subordinate CAs for each city and use these to issue certificates for users and computers in that city. Take the root CA offline.

B. Install a Root CA in Dallas. Issue certificates for users and computers in all locations.

C. Install a Root CA in Dallas. Issues certificates for users and computers in all locations. Take the Root CA offline.

D. Install a Root CA in Dallas and each city. Issue certificates for users and computers using each city Root CA. Take the Root CAs offline.

☑ **A.** Because there is IT expertise in each city, create a subordinate CA for each city and issue certificates using these CAs for their respective cities. The root CA should be taken offline for security purposes. If a single subordinate CA is compromised, you should revoke that certificate. This will invalidate all certificates issued by this CA. The other subordinate city CAs and their issued certificates would still be valid.

☒ **B, C,** and **D** are incorrect. **B** and **C** are weak solutions. If the Root CA is compromised, all certificates must be revoked. Taking the Root CA offline is a step in the right direction, but in a large distributed environment you should consider using subordinate CAs. **D** is not a good solution. A PKI solution within a company normally should allow a chain of trust such that certificates in one part of the company trust certificates in another part of the company.

17. A work colleague has sent you a digital certificate file to install on your computer so that you can encrypt e-mail messages to him. What error was made in this illustration when the file was generated?

A. There should not be a private key password.

B. A private key should never be shared with others.

C. The option Enable Strong Private Key Protection must be enabled.

D. The option Include All Extended Properties must be disabled.

> ☑ **B.** Under no circumstances should you send others your private key; otherwise, they can decrypt messages sent to you and create digital signatures on your behalf.
>
> ☒ **A, C,** and **D** are incorrect. **A** is wrong. If a private key is exported to a digital certificate file, you must have a password. **C** and **D** are incorrect because they are optional; they are not errors.

18. To secure your server, you would like to ensure server hard disk data cannot be accessed if the hard disks are stolen. What should you do?

A. Configure EFS.

B. Configure TPM with PKI encryption keys.

C. Configure NTFS security.

D. Configure a power-on password.

☑ **B.** Trusted Platform Module (TPM) is a firmware security solution that can use PKI certificate keys to encrypt and decrypt hard disk contents. TPM-encrypted disks placed in a different computer (with or without a TPM chip) are unreadable.

☒ **A, C,** and **D** are incorrect. **A** will not secure hard disk data. If server hard disks are stolen, user accounts can easily be hacked, which allows access to Encrypting File System (EFS)–encrypted data. **C** is easily circumvented by taking ownership of files and folders. **D** is useless, since it only applies to a single computer.

19. Which security objectives are met by PKI? (Choose two.)

A. Least privilege

B. Integrity

C. Non-repudiation

D. DMZ

☑ **B** and **C.** Integrity proves data is authentic and came from who it says it came from. Non-repudiation means neither party can dispute a transmission occurred or who it came from because only the owner of a private key has access to it; the private key is used to create unique digital signatures used for data integrity. Both of these are met by a PKI.

☒ **A** and **D** are incorrect. **A** is incorrect because least privilege refers to granting only the rights needed to perform a specific duty. **D** is incorrect because a demilitarized zone (DMZ) is a network sitting between a private LAN and the Internet. Hosts in a DMZ are reachable from the Internet. Neither least privilege nor DMZ is directly related to PKI.

20. Your company, Acme, Inc., conducts business with a supplier, Widgets, Inc. Both companies have an existing PKI with departmental subordinate CAs. Select Widgets, Inc. departments require access to specific secured Acme web servers that require client-side certificates before access is granted. What solution should you propose?

A. Acme, Inc. administrators should create a new root CA for Widgets, Inc. and issue certificates to those employees needing access to the Acme server.

B. Acme, Inc. administrators should create a new subordinate CA for Widgets, Inc. and issue certificates to those employees needing access to the Acme server.

C. The Acme web servers should be cross-certified with the appropriate Widgets subordinate CAs.

D. The appropriate Widgets, Inc. and Acme, Inc. departmental CAs should be cross-certified.

☑ **C.** Cross-certifying the appropriate subordinate CAs with the correct Acme servers would allow only required Widgets departmental users to use their existing certificates to authenticate to the Acme servers.

☒ **A, B,** and **D** are incorrect. **A** and **B** are not a good solutions because they require much more initial and ongoing work than option **C**. **D** is incorrect because access is required to only specific Acme web servers, not all of them. Cross-certifying entire subordinate CAs does not allow you to control to which specific servers Widgets employees could be authenticated.

21. Which types of keys are commonly used for e-commerce web sites?

   A. Public, private, session

   B. Public and private

   C. Public, private, TPM

   D. Public, private, PKI

☑ **A.** The web server sends its public key to the client. The client encrypts its self-generated session key with the server public key. The server decrypts the message with its private key, thus exposing the session key to the server. The symmetric session key is then used for the remainder of the session to encrypt data.

☒ **B, C,** and **D** are incorrect. **B** is not complete. Public and private key pairs are used to securely transmit a session key, but answer **B** does not list the session key. **C** is incorrect because TPM is not involved with securing e-commerce data. **D** is incorrect because PKI is not a key; it is a system of using digital certificates for authentication, integrity, confidentiality, and non-repudiation.

22. The CA signature exists in all digital certificates that it issues. Which key does the CA use to create its signature?

   A. Private

   B. Public

   C. Symmetric

   D. Asymmetric

☑ **A.** The CA's private key creates the digital signature that exists in issued certificates.

☒ **B, C,** and **D** are incorrect. **B** is incorrect because the public key is used to verify a signature. **C** and **D** are too ambiguous compared to the other answers.

23. In a PKI, what role does the CA play? (Choose two.)

    A. Revoke certificates

    B. Use its private key to digitally sign certificates

    C. Use its public key to digitally sign certificates

    D. Control access to the network using certificates

☑   **A** and **B.** The CA can revoke certificates that are no longer trusted, and it uses its private key to digitally sign all certificates it issues—this establishes a chain of trust.

☒   **C** and **D** are incorrect. **C** is incorrect because signatures are verified with the public key. **D** is incorrect because the CA cannot directly control access to the network. Network appliance can use PKI certificates issued by CAs to accomplish this.

24. To which does the X.509 standard apply?

    A. LDAP

    B. PKI certificates

    C. Biometric authentication

    D. A type of network transport

☑   **B.** The X.509 standard stems from the 1980s. It defines a hierarchy of certificate authorities that issue, renew, and revoke certificates.

☒   **A, C,** and **D** are incorrect. **A** is incorrect because the Lightweight Directory Access Protocol (LDAP) is used to access a network database (directory), often for authentication purposes. **C** is a mechanism for authenticating a user based on a physical trait such as voice or fingerprint. **D** is untrue.

14

Physical Security

CERTIFICATION OBJECTIVES

☐ **2.6** Explain the impact and proper use of environmental controls

☐ **3.6** Analyze and differentiate among types of mitigation and deterrent techniques

☐ **4.3** Explain the importance of data security

QUESTIONS

Many IT professionals focus on sophisticated software-based security countermeasures. While these are very important, they are more effective with physical security measures put into place. Everything from tall fences surrounding the perimeter of a property to environmental factors in a locked server room can protect data. You must also consider the possibility of physical security breaches—disk encryption keeps data confidential even if disks are stolen.

1. Over the last month servers have been mysteriously shutting down for no apparent reason. The servers restart normally only to eventually shut down again. Servers are fully patched and virus scanners are up to date. Which of the following is the most likely reason for these failures?
   A. The server room temperature is too hot.
   B. The server room temperature is too cool.
   C. The servers are infected with a virus.
   D. The servers have operating system flaws.

2. You are consulting with a client regarding a new facility. Access to the building must be restricted to only those knowing an access code. What might you suggest?
   A. Cipher lock
   B. Deadbolt lock
   C. Smartcard
   D. Biometric authentication

3. A top-secret pharmaceutical research laboratory building uses CAT6 network cabling. They require no disruption or interception of Bluetooth, network, and video monitor transmissions. What should they consider?
   A. Wireless networking with WPA2 Enterprise
   B. EMI shielding for the building
   C. Fiber optic cabling
   D. IPSec

4. Which access control method electronically logs entry into a facility?
   A. Picture ID card
   B. Security guard and log book
   C. IPSec
   D. Proximity card

5. A data center administrator uses thermal imaging to identify hot spots in a large data center. She then arranges rows of rack-mounted servers such that cool air is directed to server fan inlets and hot air is exhausted into the room. Which of the following terms best define this scenario?

   A. HVAC

   B. Form factoring

   C. Hot and cold aisles

   D. Data center breathing

6. Your company has moved to a new location where a new server room is being built. The server room currently has a water sprinkler system in case of fire. Regarding fire suppression, what should you suggest?

   A. Keep the existing water sprinkler system.

   B. Purchase a smoke detection waterless fire suppression system.

   C. Keep the existing water sprinkler system and install a raised floor.

   D. Place a fire extinguisher in the server room.

7. You would like to minimize disruption to your IT infrastructure. Which of the following environmental factors should you monitor? (Choose three.)

   A. Air flow

   B. Tape backups

   C. Server hard disk encryption

   D. Humidity

   E. Power

8. Which of the following physical access control methods do not normally identify who has entered a secure area? (Choose two.)

   A. Mantrap

   B. Hardware locks

   C. Fingerprint scan

   D. Smartcard

9. A data center IT director requires the ability to analyze facility physical security breaches after they have occurred. Which present the best solutions? (Choose two.)

   A. Motion sensor logs

   B. Laser security system

   C. Mantrap

   D. Software video surveillance system

10. What advantages do human security guards have over video surveillance systems? (Choose two.)
    A. Human security guards have a more detailed memory than saved video surveillance.
    B. Human security guards can notice abnormal circumstances.
    C. Human security guards can detect smells.
    D. Human security guards can recall sounds more accurately than saved video surveillance.

11. While reviewing facility entry points, you decide to replace existing doors with ones that will stay locked during power outages. Which term best describes this feature?
    A. Fail secure
    B. Fault tolerant
    C. Fail safe
    D. UPS

12. Which of the following is the first step in preventing physical security breaches?
    A. Firewall
    B. IDS
    C. Perimeter fencing
    D. Door keypad lock

13. How can security guards verify whether or not somebody is authorized to access a facility? (Choose two.)
    A. Employee ID badge
    B. Username and password
    C. Access list
    D. Smartcard

14. What can limit the data emanation from electromagnetic radio frequencies?
    A. Faraday cage
    B. Antistatic wrist strap
    C. ESD mat
    D. ESD boots

15. In the event of a physical security breach, what can you do to secure data in your server room? (Choose three.)
    A. Install a UPS.
    B. Use TPM.
    C. Prevent booting from removal devices.
    D. Lock the server chassis.

16. You are configuring an uninterruptible power supply (UPS) for your three servers such that in the event of a power failure, the servers will shut down gracefully. Which term best describes this configuration?

    A. Fail open

    B. Fail safe

    C. False positive

    D. False negative

17. What can be used to effectively protect data on stolen USB flash drives?

    A. NTFS security

    B. Encryption

    C. Write protection

    D. Steganography

18. What potential security problem exists with fiber SAN disks?

    A. Various servers have access to the same disks.

    B. Users on the LAN can directly access SAN disks because they are on the same network.

    C. Stolen SAN disks could contain data from many servers.

    D. SAN traffic cannot be encrypted.

19. What can be done to physically secure switches and routers? (Choose two.)

    A. Configure ACLs.

    B. Use SSH instead of Telnet.

    C. Set a console port password.

    D. Disable unused ports.

20. Which of the following would not be a physical security concern?

    A. Printer

    B. USB flash drive

    C. Workstation

    D. USB mouse

21. Which user authentication method is considered the most secure?

    A. Fingerprint scan

    B. Retinal scan

    C. Voiceprint scan

    D. Smartcard

QUICK ANSWER KEY

1.	A	8.	A, B	15.	B, C, D
2.	A	9.	A, D	16.	B
3.	B	10.	B, C	17.	B
4.	D	11.	A	18.	C
5.	C	12.	C	19.	C, D
6.	B	13.	A, C	20.	D
7.	A, D, E	14.	A	21.	B

IN-DEPTH ANSWERS

1. Over the last month servers have been mysteriously shutting down for no apparent reason. The servers restart normally only to eventually shut down again. Servers are fully patched and virus scanners are up to date. Which of the following is the most likely reason for these failures?

- **A.** The server room temperature is too hot.
- **B.** The server room temperature is too cool.
- **C.** The servers are infected with a virus.
- **D.** The servers have operating system flaws.

☑ **A.** Heat is the most likely cause of the server failures, since the servers are fully patched and properly protected. An HVAC (Heating Ventilation Air Conditioning) technician should be consulted.

☒ **B, C,** and **D** are incorrect. **B** is possible, but not as likely as answer **A. C** and **D** are not as likely, since the servers are patched and protected.

2. You are consulting with a client regarding a new facility. Access to the building must be restricted to only those knowing an access code. What might you suggest?

- **A.** Cipher lock
- **B.** Deadbolt lock
- **C.** Smartcard
- **D.** Biometric authentication

☑ **A.** Cipher locks are electronic keypads whereby authorized persons enter an access code to gain access to a room or a building. All the user needs to know is an access code, no physical card is required.

☒ **B, C,** and **D** are incorrect. They do not meet the client requirement of users knowing an access code. **B** is incorrect because a deadbolt lock requires possession of a key, **C** is incorrect because a smartcard is a physical object a user must have, and **D** is incorrect because biometric authentication does not require knowledge of an access code.

3. A top-secret pharmaceutical research laboratory building uses CAT6 network cabling. They require no disruption or interception of Bluetooth, network, and video monitor transmissions. What should they consider?

   A. Wireless networking with WPA2 Enterprise

   B. EMI shielding for the building

   C. Fiber optic cabling

   D. IPSec

   ☑ **B.** EMI (electromagnetic interference) can disrupt network transmissions. CAT6 cabling consists of four twisted copper wire pairs. As such, CAT6 is susceptible to wiretap eavesdropping. Video screen emissions can be captured with the correct equipment. All of these factors put a top-secret facility at risk. The best solution is to shield the entire facility.

   ☒ **A, C, and D** are incorrect. **A** will not solve any problems and will make things worse. Wireless networking always presents more security risks than a wired network. **C** will keep network transmissions secure and free from interference, but Bluetooth and video monitor emissions would still be a security issue. **D** is incorrect because IPSec (IP Security) does nothing to quell electromagnet interference or prevent screen emissions. IPSec encrypts and authenticates network data.

4. Which access control method electronically logs entry into a facility?

   A. Picture ID card

   B. Security guard and log book

   C. IPSec

   D. Proximity card

   ☑ **D.** Proximity cards must only be within a few inches to read the card number and either allow or deny access to a facility. All access is logged electronically without the need of a physical log book or security guard.

   ☒ **A, B, and C** are incorrect. **A** and **B** do not control facility access logging electronically. **C** is incorrect because IPSec is a mechanism by which packets are authenticated and encrypted; there is no correlation to physical site security.

5. A data center administrator uses thermal imaging to identify hot spots in a large data center. She then arranges rows of rack-mounted servers such that cool air is directed to server fan inlets and hot air is exhausted into the room. Which of the following terms best define this scenario?

A. HVAC

B. Form factoring

C. Hot and cold aisles

D. Data center breathing

☑ **C.** Hot and cold aisles are an important consideration in data center cooling. Equipment layout and raised floors to distribute cold air are a few examples of the specifics involved.

☒ **A, B,** and **D** are incorrect. **A** is not as specific as answer **C**. HVAC generally refers to air flow and environmental control within a room or building. **B** and **D** are fictitious terms.

6. Your company has moved to a new location where a new server room is being built. The server room currently has a water sprinkler system in case of fire. Regarding fire suppression, what should you suggest?

A. Keep the existing water sprinkler system.

B. Purchase a smoke detection waterless fire suppression system.

C. Keep the existing water sprinkler system and install a raised floor.

D. Place a fire extinguisher in the server room.

☑ **B.** Assuming local building codes allow, you should suggest waterless fire suppression systems because they will not damage or corrode computer systems or components as water will.

☒ **A, C,** and **D** are incorrect. **A** and **C** are water options that will damage or destroy computer equipment and data and should be avoided when possible. While important, placing a fire extinguisher in the server room is not the only thing you should recommend; water damage devastates computer systems, so **D** is incorrect.

7. You would like to minimize disruption to your IT infrastructure. Which of the following environmental factors should you monitor? (Choose three.)

A. Air flow

B. Tape backups

C. Server hard disk encryption

D. Humidity

E. Power

   ☑ **A, D,** and **E.** Enterprise-class environmental monitoring solutions track a variety of items such as air flow, humidity, and power availability. Any of these variables could create unfavorable conditions in a server room, resulting in server downtime.

   ☒ **B** and **C** are incorrect. They are not classified as environmental factors, although they are critically important. Tape backups provide a copy of important data should server hard disks fail. Server hard disk encryption protects hard disk data should the server hard disks be physically stolen.

8. Which of the following physical access control methods do not normally identify who has entered a secure area? (Choose two.)

A. Mantrap

B. Hardware locks

C. Fingerprint scan

D. Smartcard

   ☑ **A** and **B.** Mantraps are designed to trap trespassers in a restricted area. Some mantrap variations use two sets of doors, one of which must close before the second one opens. Traditional mantraps do not require access cards. Hardware locks simply require possession of a key. Neither reveals the person's identity.

   ☒ **C** and **D** are incorrect. **C** identifies the user via biometric authentication. **D** identifies the user through a unique code or PKI certificate in a smartcard.

9. A data center IT director requires the ability to analyze facility physical security breaches after they have occurred. Which present the best solutions? (Choose two.)

A. Motion sensor logs

B. Laser security system

C. Mantrap

D. Software video surveillance system

☑ **A** and **D**. Motion sensor logs can track a perpetrator's position more accurately than most video systems; however, software video surveillance can be played back and used to physically identify unauthorized persons. To conserve disk space, most solutions only record when there is motion.

☒ **B** and **C** are incorrect. **B** is not the best solution compared to the others. Laser security systems rely on laser beams being interrupted and do not work well with detailed analysis after the fact. **C** is incorrect because mantraps trap perpetrators when the security breach occurs and offer little in terms of post analysis.

10. What advantages do human security guards have over video surveillance systems? (Choose two.)

   A. Human security guards have a more detailed memory than saved video surveillance.

   B. Human security guards can notice abnormal circumstances.

   C. Human security guards can detect smells.

   D. Human security guards can recall sounds more accurately than saved video surveillance.

☑ **B** and **C**. Video surveillance systems cannot detect smells or notice anything out of the ordinary as a human security guard could.

☒ **A** and **D** are incorrect. Video surveillance with sound can be analyzed frame by frame, resulting in a much more detailed analysis.

11. While reviewing facility entry points, you decide to replace existing doors with ones that will stay locked during power outages. Which term best describes this feature?

   A. Fail secure

   B. Fault tolerant

   C. Fail safe

   D. UPS

☑ **A**. Fail secure systems ensure that a component failure (such as a power source) will not compromise security as in this case (the doors will stay locked).

☒ **B**, **C**, and **D** are incorrect. **B** and **C** are incorrect because fault tolerance (sometimes referred to as fail-safe) ensures that a system can continue functioning despite a failure of some type. For example, a server may spread file and error recovery data across multiple disks. In the event of a disk failure, data can be reconstructed from the remaining disks. **D** is incorrect because a UPS (uninterruptible power supply) provides temporary power to devices when there is a power outage.

12. Which of the following is the first step in preventing physical security breaches?

    A. Firewall

    B. IDS

    C. Perimeter fencing

    D. Door keypad lock

> ☑ **C.** The first step in physical security involves perimeter fencing to prevent intruders from getting on the property.
>
> ☒ **A, B,** and **D** are incorrect. **A** and **B** are not physical security mechanisms. Firewalls allow or block network traffic based on configured rules. IDSs (intrusion detection systems) analyze network traffic for suspicious activity and either log or take action for this incident. Door keypad locks do apply to physical security, but one must first get on the property to get to a door, so **D** is incorrect.

13. How can security guards verify whether or not somebody is authorized to access a facility? (Choose two.)

    A. Employee ID badge

    B. Username and password

    C. Access list

    D. Smartcard

> ☑ **A and C.** An employee ID badge allows physical verification that somebody is allowed to access a building. An access list defines who is allowed to access a facility.
>
> ☒ **B and D** are incorrect. These elements cannot be verified by security guards. Usernames and passwords can authenticate a user to a computer system, as can a smartcard. Smartcards contain an embedded microchip. Users enter a PIN in conjunction with using their smartcard.

14. What can limit the data emanation from electromagnetic radio frequencies?

    A. Faraday cage

    B. Antistatic wrist strap

    C. ESD mat

    D. ESD boots

☑ **A.** Faraday cages enclose electronic equipment to prevent data emanation or to protect components from external static charges.

☒ **B, C,** and **D** are incorrect. These items are important when touching electrical components. Each of them is designed to put the user and the equipment and equal charge to prevent the flow of static electricity, but they do not prevent actual data emanation.

15. In the event of a physical security breach, what can you do to secure data in your server room? (Choose three.)

    A. Install a UPS.

    B. Use TPM.

    C. Prevent booting from removal devices.

    D. Lock the server chassis.

☑ **B, C,** and **D.** Trusted Platform Module (TPM) is a chip that encrypts hard disk contents. Data on disks taken from one TPM system and placed in another TPM or non-TPM machine will not be accessible. Preventing removable media boot is critical because there are many free tools that can reset administrative passwords this way. Physically locking the server chassis further deters an intruder from stealing physical hard disks.

☒ **A** is incorrect. A UPS provides power during an outage but does nothing to secure data.

16. You are configuring an uninterruptible power supply (UPS) for your three servers such that in the event of a power failure, the servers will shut down gracefully. Which term best describes this configuration?

    A. Fail open

    B. Fail safe

    C. False positive

    D. False negative

☑ **B.** Fail safe is a term meaning a response to a failure will result in the least amount of damage. For example, during a power outage servers connected to the UPS will have enough power to shut down properly.

☒ **A, C,** and **D** are incorrect. **A** is incorrect because fail open would mean if the firewall failed, instead of analyzing traffic to determine if it is allowed in or out, all network traffic would be free to flow. **C** and **D** are not applicable to this scenario. False positives and false negatives relate to IDSs or security systems. A false positive occurs when a system reports there is a problem when in fact there is none.

17. What can be used to effectively protect data on stolen USB flash drives?

   A. NTFS security

   B. Encryption

   C. Write protection

   D. Steganography

   ☑ **B.** When storage media are stolen, the best protection is file or disk encryption.

   ☒ **A, C,** and **D** are incorrect. NTFS (New Technology File System) permissions are useless when the disk is removed from the source machine, so **A** is incorrect. **C** and **D** are incorrect because write protection only prevents accidental writing of data, it is not a security deterrent. Steganography conceals messages within innocuous-looking files. This does potentially protect data, but not to the degree that encryption does.

18. What potential security problem exists with fiber SAN disks?

   A. Various servers have access to the same disks.

   B. Users on the LAN can directly access SAN disks because they are on the same network.

   C. Stolen SAN disks could contain data from many servers.

   D. SAN traffic cannot be encrypted.

   ☑ **C.** A SAN (storage area network) is a collection of high-speed and high-capacity disks shared among servers. The shared disk storage appears to each server as local storage. A fiber SAN requires each server to have a fiber channel card linked to a fiber channel switch, which in turn connects to the disk array. A compromise of SAN disks could mean the compromise of data from many servers.

   ☒ **A, B,** and **D** are incorrect. Answer **A** is not a security problem. Techniques such as LUN (logical unit number) masking restrict which servers can access which SAN disk partitions. **B** is not true. LAN (local area network) traffic is completely isolated from SAN traffic. **D** is incorrect because SAN traffic can be encrypted.

19. What can be done to physically secure switches and routers? (Choose two.)

   A. Configure ACLs.

   B. Use SSH instead of Telnet.

   C. Set a console port password.

   D. Disable unused ports.

☑ **C** and **D**. A console port allows a local user to plug a cable into the router or switch to locally administer the device. A strong password is recommended. Disabling unused switch ports and router interfaces prevents unauthorized persons from gaining access to the device or the network.

☒ **A** and **B** are incorrect. These are not physical security measures. **A** is incorrect because ACLs on routers determine what type of traffic is allowed or denied. **B** is incorrect because SSH (Secure Shell) is an encrypted remote command-line administrative tool; Telnet passes data across the network in clear text.

20. Which of the following would not be a physical security concern?

   A. Printer

   B. USB flash drive

   C. Workstation

   D. USB mouse

☑ **D**. A USB mouse does not store data and does not grant access to data, so it is not a security concern.

☒ **A**, **B**, and **C** incorrect. These are all valid security concerns. **A** is incorrect because printer can retain print job information and statistics in volatile or non-volatile memory. **B** is incorrect because USB flash drives are small and easily stolen or forgotten. **C** is incorrect because user workstations could have sensitive data on their disks, and they can give access to network resources. Each of these three items must be accounted for when considering physical security.

21. Which user authentication method is considered the most secure?

   A. Fingerprint scan

   B. Retinal scan

   C. Voiceprint scan

   D. Smartcard

☑ **B**. Retinal scans are considered to be the most secure because unique blood vessel patterns are very difficult to duplicate.

☒ **A**, **C**, and **D** are incorrect. **A** is incorrect because fingerprint scans are not the most secure but the next most secure. **C** is incorrect because voiceprints can be spoofed with the proper audio equipment. **D** is incorrect because smartcards are the least secure; they can be stolen and the smartcard PIN can be learned.

15

Risk Analysis

CERTIFICATION OBJECTIVES

❑   **2.1**   Explain risk-related concepts

❑   **2.2**   Carry out appropriate risk mitigation strategies

❑   **3.7**   Implement assessment tools and techniques to discover security threats and
vulnerabilities Questions

QUESTIONS

Risk analysis determines the possible threats a business could face and how to effectively minimize their impact. Quantitative risk analysis results in a prioritized list of risks by dollar amount, whereas qualitative risk analysis uses a relative prioritizing system to rate risks to one another. Failure to properly perform a risk analysis could result in violation of laws, customer trust, or even bankruptcy in the event of the realization of risks.

1. You are conducting a risk analysis for a stock brokerage firm in Miami, Florida. What factors should you consider? (Choose two.)
    A. Server downtime due to earthquakes
    B. Destruction of government regulation documentation due to fire
    C. Server downtime due to power outages
    D. Customer invoicing data destroyed due to fire

2. You are responsible for completing an IT asset report for your company. All IT-related equipment and data must be identified and given a value. What term best describes what you must next do?
    A. Asset identification
    B. Risk assessment
    C. Risk mitigation
    D. Threat analysis

3. You are identifying security threats to determine the likelihood of virus infection. Identify potential sources of infection. (Choose two.)
    A. USB flash drives
    B. USB keyboard
    C. Smartcard
    D. Downloaded documentation from a business partner web site

4. During a risk analysis meeting, you are asked to specify internal threats being considered. Which item is not considered an internal threat from the list that follows?
    A. Embezzlement
    B. Hackers breaking in through the firewall
    C. Employees using corporate assets for personal gain
    D. Users plugging in personal USB flash drives

5. A client conveys their concern to you regarding malicious Internet users gaining access to corporate resources. What type of assessment would you perform to determine this likelihood?

    A. Threat assessment

    B. Risk analysis

    C. Asset identification

    D. Total cost of ownership

6. You are an IT consultant performing a risk analysis for a seafood company. The client is concerned with specific cooking and packaging techniques the company uses being disclosed to competitors. What type of security concern is this?

    A. Integrity

    B. Confidentiality

    C. Availability

    D. Authorization

7. After identifying internal and external threats, you must determine how these potential risks will affect business operations. What is this called?

    A. Risk analysis

    B. Fault tolerance

    C. Availability

    D. Impact analysis

8. When determining how best to mitigate risk, which items should you consider? (Choose two.)

    A. Insurance coverage

    B. Number of server hard disks

    C. How fast CPUs in new computers will be

    D. Network bandwidth

9. You are listing preventive measures for potential risks. Which of the following would you document? (Choose three.)

    A. Larger flat-screen monitors

    B. Data backup

    C. Employee training

    D. Comparing reliability of network load-balancing appliances

10. An insurance company charges an additional $200 monthly premium for natural disaster coverage for your business site. What figure must you compare this against to determine whether or not to accept this additional coverage?

    A. ALE

    B. ROI

    C. Total cost of ownership

    D. Total monthly insurance premium

11. Which of the following is true regarding qualitative risk analysis?
    A. Only numerical data is considered.
    B. ALE must be calculated.
    C. Threats must be identified.
    D. ROI must be calculated.

12. Which values must be calculated to derive annual loss expectancy? (Choose two.)
    A. Single loss expectancy
    B. Annualized rate of occurrence
    C. Monthly loss expectancy
    D. Quarterly loss expectancy

13. You are the server expert for a cloud computing firm named Cloud Nine Computing. Management would like to set aside funds to respond to server downtime risks. Using historical data you determine the probability of server downtime is 17 percent. Past data suggests the server would be down for an average of one hour and that $3,000 of revenue can be earned in one hour. You must calculate the annual loss expectancy. Which is the correct ALE?
    A. $300
    B. $510
    C. $3,000
    D. $36,000

14. Your boss asks you to calculate how much money the company loses when critical servers required by employees are down for two hours. You have determined that the probability of this happening is 70 percent. The company has 25 employees each earning $18.50 per hour. Which is the correct value?
    A. $12.95
    B. $18.50
    C. $323.75
    D. $3,885

15. Your company is considering having the e-mail server hosted by Hosted Solutions, Inc. to reduce hardware and mail server technician costs at the local site. What type of document formally states the reliability and recourse if the reliability is not met?
    A. ALE
    B. SLE
    C. SLA
    D. IRQ

16. Which term best describes monies spent to minimize the impact that threats and unfavorable conditions have on a business?

    A. Risk management

    B. Security audit

    C. Budgetary constraints

    D. Impact analysis

17. Which risk analysis approach makes use of ALE?

    A. Best possible outcome

    B. Quantitative

    C. ROI

    D. Qualitative

18. You are presenting data at a risk analysis meeting. During your presentation you display a list of ALE values sorted ranked by dollar amount. Bob, a meeting participant, asks how reliable the numeracy used to calculate the ALE is. What can you tell Bob?

    A. The numbers are 100 percent reliable.

    B. The numbers are 50 percent reliable.

    C. ALEs are calculated using probability values that vary.

    D. ALEs are calculated using percentages and are very accurate.

19. Which of the following should be performed when conducting a qualitative risk assessment? (Choose two.)

    A. Asset valuation

    B. ARO

    C. SLE

    D. Ranking of potential threats

20. You are the IT security analyst for Big John's Gourmet Foods. Big John's plans to open a plant in Oranjestad, Aruba next year. You are meeting with a planning committee in the next week and must come up with questions to ask the committee about the new location so that you can prepare a risk analysis report. Which of the following would be the most relevant questions to ask? (Choose two.)

    A. How hot does it get in the summer?

    B. How reliable is the local power?

    C. What kind of physical premise security is in place?

    D. How close is the nearest highway?

21. Your corporate web site is being hosted by an Internet service provider. How does this apply to the concept of risk?
    A. Risk avoidance
    B. Risk transference
    C. Risk analysis
    D. Increase in ALE

22. Which of the following regarding risk management is true?
    A. Funds invested in risk management could have earned much more profit if spent elsewhere.
    B. ALEs are only estimates and are subject to being inaccurate.
    C. IT security risks are all handled by the corporate firewall.
    D. Qualitative risk analysis results are expressed in dollar amounts.

23. Your competitors are offering a new product that is predicted to sell well. After much careful study, your company has decided against launching a competing product due to the uncertainty of the market and the enormous investment required. Which term best describes your company's decision?
    A. Risk analysis
    B. Risk transfer
    C. Risk avoidance
    D. Product avoidance

24. How can management determine which risks should be given the most attention?
    A. IT risks are more important than physical facility risks.
    B. Rank risks by likelihood.
    C. Rank risks by probable date of occurrence.
    D. Rank risks by SLE.

25. Recently your data center was housed in Albuquerque, New Mexico. Due to corporate downsizing, the data center equipment was moved to an existing office in Santa Fe. The server room in Santa Fe was not designed to accommodate all the new servers arriving from Albuquerque and the server room temperature is very warm. Because this is a temporary solution until a new data center facility is built, management has decided not to pay for an updated air conditioning system. Which term best describes this scenario?
    A. Risk transfer
    B. Risk avoidance
    C. Risk acceptance
    D. Risk reduction

26. Which factors could influence your risk management strategy?
    A. Government regulations
    B. Moving operations to a new building
    C. The purchase of a newer firewall solution
    D. None of the above
    E. All of the above

27. You are a member of an IT project team. The team is performing an IT risk analysis and has identified assets and their values as well threats and threat mitigation solutions. What must be done next?
    A. Perform a cost-benefit analysis of proposed risk solutions.
    B. Calculate the ALE values.
    C. Decide which vulnerabilities exist.
    D. There is nothing more to do.

28. To reduce the likelihood of internal fraud, organization implements policies that ensure more than one person is responsible for a financial transaction from beginning to end. Which of the following best describes this scenario?
    A. Probability
    B. Mitigation solution
    C. Impact analysis
    D. Threat analysis

29. What is the difference between risk assessment and risk management?
    A. They are the same thing.
    B. Risk assessment identifies and prioritizes risks; risk management is the governing of risks to minimize their impact.
    C. Risk management identifies and prioritizes risks; risk assessment is the governing of risks to minimize their impact.
    D. Risk assessment identifies threat; risk management controls those threats.

30. What are the two drawbacks to quantitative risk analysis compared to qualitative risk analysis?
    A. Complex calculations.
    B. Risks are not prioritized by monetary value.
    C. Quantitative analysis is more time consuming than qualitative.
    D. It is difficult to determine how much money to allocate to reduce a risk.

QUICK ANSWER KEY

1.	C, D	11.	C	21.	B
2.	A	12.	A, B	22.	B
3.	A, D	13.	B	23.	C
4.	B	14.	C	24.	B
5.	A	15.	C	25.	C
6.	B	16.	A	26.	E
7.	D	17.	B	27.	B
8.	A, B	18.	C	28.	B
9.	B, C, D	19.	A, D	29.	B
10.	A	20.	B, C	30.	A, C

IN-DEPTH ANSWERS

1. You are conducting a risk analysis for a stock brokerage firm in Miami, Florida. What factors should you consider? (Choose two.)

   A. Server downtime due to earthquakes

   B. Destruction of government regulation documentation due to fire

   C. Server downtime due to power outages

   D. Customer invoicing data destroyed due to fire

   ☑ **C** and **D**. Risk analysis includes calculating plausible risks such as server downtime due to power outage and loss of equipment and data due to fire.

   ☒ **A** and **B** are incorrect. **A** is incorrect because the likelihood of earthquakes in this part of the world is minimal. **B** is incorrect because government regulations documentation can be easily re-acquired, so there is no risk in losing it.

2. You are responsible for completing an IT asset report for your company. All IT-related equipment and data must be identified and given a value. What term best describes what you must next do?

   A. Asset identification

   B. Risk assessment

   C. Risk mitigation

   D. Threat analysis

   ☑ **A**. Asset identification involves identifying assets (including data) and associating a value with them. This can then be used to justify expenditures to protect these assets.

   ☒ **B**, **C**, and **D** are incorrect. **B** is incorrect because risk assessment is the identification of threats, but the next step in this case is asset identification. **C** is incorrect because risk mitigation minimizes the impact of perceived risks. **D** is incorrect because threat analysis does not involve identifying IT hardware with a cost.

3. You are identifying security threats to determine the likelihood of virus infection. Identify potential sources of infection. (Choose two.)

   A. USB flash drives

   B. USB keyboard

   C. Smartcard

   D. Downloaded documentation from a business partner web site

> ☑ **A and D.** USB flash drives could have files downloaded from the Internet or copied from less secure machines that could infect your network. Business partner documentation downloaded from the Internet could potentially be infected.
>
> ☒ **B and C** are incorrect. USB keyboards and smartcards are not likely sources of malware.

4. During a risk analysis meeting, you are asked to specify internal threats being considered. Which item is not considered an internal threat from the list that follows?

   A. Embezzlement

   B. Hackers breaking in through the firewall

   C. Employees using corporate assets for personal gain

   D. Users plugging in personal USB flash drives

> ☑ **B.** Hackers breaking in through a firewall would be considered an external threat.
>
> ☒ **A, C, and D** are incorrect. These are all considered internal threats. Anything involving employees and security would be considered a potential internal threat.

5. A client conveys their concern to you regarding malicious Internet users gaining access to corporate resources. What type of assessment would you perform to determine this likelihood?

   A. Threat assessment

   B. Risk analysis

   C. Asset identification

   D. Total cost of ownership

> ☑ **A.** Determining how an entity can gain access to corporate resources would require a threat assessment.
>
> ☒ **B, C, and D** are incorrect. **B** is incorrect because risk analysis is a general term that includes conducting a threat assessment, but threat assessment is a more specific and applicable answer. Asset identification involves determining what items (tangible and non-tangible) are of value, and associating a dollar value with those items, so **C** is not correct. **D** is incorrect because cost of ownership allows consumers to determine the true cost of a product or service.

6. You are an IT consultant performing a risk analysis for a seafood company. The client is concerned with specific cooking and packaging techniques the company uses being disclosed to competitors. What type of security concern is this?

A. Integrity

B. Confidentiality

C. Availability

D. Authorization

☑ **B.** Confidentiality means keeping data hidden from those that should not see it, such as competitors.

☒ **A, C,** and **D** are incorrect. **A** does not apply here—integrity verifies the authenticity of data; it does not conceal it. **C** is incorrect because availability ensures a resource is available as often as possible, for example, clustering a database server. Authorization (**D**) grants access to a resource once the identity of an entity has been verified through authentication.

7. After identifying internal and external threats, you must determine how these potential risks will affect business operations. What is this called?

A. Risk analysis

B. Fault tolerance

C. Availability

D. Impact analysis

☑ **D.** Determining the effect that materialized risks have on the operation of a business is called impact analysis. It is often used to determine whether or not expenditure against these risks is justified.

☒ **A, B,** and **C** are incorrect. **A** is not the best answer because it is too general; D is a much better answer. **B,** fault tolerance, can reduce the impact if a disk fails, but it is very specific; the question refers to more than a single risk. **C,** availability, ensures resources are available as often as possible to minimize risks, but it does not determine how risks affect a business.

8. When determining how best to mitigate risk, which items should you consider? (Choose two.)

   A. Insurance coverage

   B. Number of server hard disks

   C. How fast CPUs in new computers will be

   D. Network bandwidth

> ☑ **A and B.** Assessing risk includes determining what is and is not covered by various types of insurance coverage, and whether or not the cost of those insurance premiums is justified. The number of server hard disks is definitely risk related. The likelihood of hard disk data loss is minimized when there are multiple hard disks configured properly, such as RAID 1 (disk mirroring).
>
> ☒ **C and D** are incorrect. **C**, CPU speed, and **D**, network bandwidth, are not directly related to risk assessment; they are related to performance.

9. You are listing preventive measures for potential risks. Which of the following would you document? (Choose three.)

   A. Larger flat-screen monitors

   B. Data backup

   C. Employee training

   D. Comparing reliability of network load-balancing appliances

> ☑ **B, C, and D.** Backing up data minimizes the risk of losing data. Employee training reduces the likelihood of errors or disclosure of confidential information. Choosing the most reliable network load balancing appliance can reduce the risk of network traffic congestion.
>
> ☒ **A** is incorrect. Larger flat-screen monitors are not related to risk prevention.

10. An insurance company charges an additional $200 monthly premium for natural disaster coverage for your business site. What figure must you compare this against to determine whether or not to accept this additional coverage?

   A. ALE

   B. ROI

   C. Total cost of ownership

   D. Total monthly insurance premium

☑ **A.** The annual loss expectancy (ALE) value is used with quantitative risk analysis approaches to prioritize and justify expenditures that protect from potential risks. For example, an ALE value of $1,000 might justify a $200 annual expense to protect against that risk.

☒ **B, C, and D are incorrect. B** is incorrect because the return on investment (ROI) calculates how efficient an investment is (does the benefit of a product or service outweigh the cost?). **C** is incorrect because the total cost of ownership exposes all direct and indirect dollar figures associated with a product or service. **D** is incorrect because using the total monthly premium value to determine whether or not to accept the additional insurance coverage would be meaningless; it must be compared against the probability of natural disasters in your area.

11. Which of the following is true regarding qualitative risk analysis?

    A. Only numerical data is considered.

    B. ALE must be calculated.

    C. Threats must be identified.

    D. ROI must be calculated.

☑ **C.** Qualitative risk analysis is categorizes risks (threats) with general (not hard numerical) terms and numerical ranges; for example, a risk falling between 1 (small risk) and 10 (big risk). For this to happen, threats must first be identified.

☒ **A, B, and D are incorrect. A** is incorrect because, although numerical data is very important in both quantitative and qualitative risk assessments, it is not only numerical data that is considered; the scale of the risks and their effects, as well as how responses to risks are handled, are also considered. ALE is a specific dollar figure used in quantitative analysis. Qualitative analysis uses a relative measurement scale to rank risks; therefore, **B** is incorrect. **D** does not apply. ROI cannot be determined until a risk analysis has been done.

12. Which values must be calculated to derive annual loss expectancy? (Choose two.)

    A. Single loss expectancy

    B. Annualized rate of occurrence

    C. Monthly loss expectancy

    D. Quarterly loss expectancy

☑   **A** and **B**. ALE is derived by multiplying the ARO (annual rate of occurrence) by the SLE (single loss expectancy).

☒   **C** and **D** are incorrect. These are not used to calculate the ALE.

13. You are the server expert for a cloud computing firm named Cloud Nine Computing. Management would like to set aside funds to respond to server downtime risks. Using historical data you determine the probability of server downtime is 17 percent. Past data suggests the server would be down for an average of one hour and that $3,000 of revenue can be earned in one hour. You must calculate the annual loss expectancy. Which is the correct ALE?

A. $300

B. $510

C. $3,000

D. $36,000

☑   **B**. ALE is calculated by multiplying the ARO (ARO – 0.17) by the SLE (SLE – 3,000). So 0.17 multiplied by 3,000 equals 510.

☒   **A, C**, and **D** are incorrect. ALE = ARO multiplied by SLE.

14. Your boss asks you to calculate how much money the company loses when critical servers required by employees are down for two hours. You have determined that the probability of this happening is 70 percent. The company has 25 employees each earning $18.50 per hour. Which is the correct value?

A. $12.95

B. $18.50

C. $323.75

D. $3,885

☑   **C**. This question is asking you to calculate the ALE. Multiple the probability ARO by the dollar amount associated with a single failure (SLE), so 0.7 multiplied by (25 * 18.5) equals 323.75.

☒   **A, B**, and **D** are incorrect. ALE = ARO multiplied by SLE.

15. Your company is considering having the e-mail server hosted by Hosted Solutions, Inc. to reduce hardware and mail server technician costs at the local site. What type of document formally states the reliability and recourse if the reliability is not met?

   A. ALE

   B. SLE

   C. SLA

   D. IRQ

> ☑ **C.** A service level agreement (SLA) formally defines what type of service a customer can expect and what type of recourse is available should that level of service not be provided.
>
> ☒ **A, B,** and **D** are incorrect. **A** is incorrect because ALE is used in a quantitative risk analysis to set aside funds to deal with probable risks. It does not deal directly with the level of service provided by a third party. **B** is incorrect because SLE is used to calculate the ALE; it is the monetary value associated with a single failure occurrence. **D** is incorrect because IRQ is a fictitious risk analysis acronym.

16. Which term best describes monies spent to minimize the impact that threats and unfavorable conditions have on a business?

   A. Risk management

   B. Security audit

   C. Budgetary constraints

   D. Impact analysis

> ☑ **A.** Risk assessment means determining the impact that threats and less than optimal conditions can have on a business or agency. Risk management involves setting aside the funds to account for these eventualities. Determining the amount of money to set aside may involve many detailed calculations.
>
> ☒ **B, C,** and **D** are incorrect. **B** is not the best answer. A security audit may be one factor influencing how monies are to be spent to protect a business, but a risk analysis is used to determine how a reasonable amount of funds must be set aside to deal with risks after all factors (perhaps including a security audit) have been considered. **C**, budgetary constraints, does not describe the definition presented in the question. **D**, an impact analysis, specifically determines the effect threats and unfavorable circumstances have on the operation of a business, but, like a security audit, it would be one of many factors influencing what the appropriate amount of dollars to mitigate these issues would be.

17. Which risk analysis approach makes use of ALE?

A. Best possible outcome

B. Quantitative

C. ROI

D. Qualitative

> ☑ **B.** The ALE is a specific figure derived from the probability of a loss and the cost of one occurrence of this loss. Because specific dollar values (quantities) are used to prioritize risks, this falls into the category of quantitative risk analysis.
>
> ☒ **A, C,** and **D** are incorrect. **A** is not a risk analysis approach. **C**, return on investment, cannot be calculated prior to a risk analysis being completed. **D**, qualitative, is a risk analysis approach that uses a relative ranking scale to rate risks instead of using specific figures.

18. You are presenting data at a risk analysis meeting. During your presentation you display a list of ALE values sorted ranked by dollar amount. Bob, a meeting participant, asks how reliable the numeracy used to calculate the ALE is. What can you tell Bob?

A. The numbers are 100 percent reliable.

B. The numbers are 50 percent reliable.

C. ALEs are calculated using probability values that vary.

D. ALEs are calculated using percentages and are very accurate.

> ☑ **C.** ALE values use the probability of a loss in conjunction with the cost of a single incident. Probability values are rarely accurate, but because the future cannot be predicted, they are acceptable.
>
> ☒ **A, B,** and **D** are incorrect. **A** and **B** are false. When dealing with probabilities, we cannot state a definite percentage of accuracy. **D** is incorrect because, although the ALE is calculated using a percentage (probability of annual rate of occurrence), you cannot tell Bob that the ALE is very accurate.

19. Which of the following should be performed when conducting a qualitative risk assessment? (Choose two.)

A. Asset valuation

B. ARO

C. SLE

D. Ranking of potential threats

☑ **A** and **D.** Qualitative risk analysis assesses the likelihood of risks that will impede normal business operations and prioritizes (ranks) them relative to one another. Assets that must be protected from identified risks must have an assigned value to determine if the cost of risk mitigation is justified.

☒ **B** and **C** are incorrect. They use specific dollar figures (quantitative) to calculate the ALE. ALE = ARO multiplied by SLE.

20. You are the IT security analyst for Big John's Gourmet Foods. Big John's plans to open a plant in Oranjestad, Aruba next year. You are meeting with a planning committee in the next week and must come up with questions to ask the committee about the new location so that you can prepare a risk analysis report. Which of the following would be the most relevant questions to ask? (Choose two.)

A. How hot does it get in the summer?

B. How reliable is the local power?

C. What kind of physical premise security is in place?

D. How close is the nearest highway?

☑ **B** and **C.** A reliable power source is critical for IT systems. Unreliable power would mean a different plant location or the use of UPS (uninterruptible power supply) and power generators. Physical security should always be considered during risk analysis. Robbery or break-ins could adversely impact Big John's.

☒ **A** and **D** are incorrect. Answer **A** might be a relevant question to ask, but power reliability (answer B) will deal with this, since reliable power means reliable HVAC (Heating Ventilation Air Conditioning). Unless toxic waste or something similar is being transported on the nearest highway, **D** is not as relevant a question to ask the planning committee as are answers B and C.

21. Your corporate web site is being hosted by an Internet service provider. How does this apply to the concept of risk?

A. Risk avoidance

B. Risk transference

C. Risk analysis

D. Increase in ALE

☑ **B.** Risk transference shifts some or all of the burden of risk to a third party.

☒ **A, C,** and **D** are incorrect. **A** is not applicable in this case; risk avoidance removes threats. Risk analysis is the practice of identifying and ranking threats jeopardizing business goals in order to allocate funds to mitigate these threats, so **C** is incorrect. **D** is incorrect because the ALE is a dollar value associated with the probability of a failure.

22. Which of the following regarding risk management is true?

   A. Funds invested in risk management could have earned much more profit if spent elsewhere.

   B. ALEs are only estimates and are subject to being inaccurate.

   C. IT security risks are all handled by the corporate firewall.

   D. Qualitative risk analysis results are expressed in dollar amounts.

☑ **B.** ALE figures are considered inaccurate because part of their calculation is based on probabilities.

☒ **A, C,** and **D** are incorrect. **A** is incorrect because assuming risk analysis was conducted properly, the allocated funds to minimize the impact of risk are probably better invested where they are than in other endeavors. **C** is incorrect because firewalls do not handle all IT security risks. **D** is incorrect because qualitative risk analysis reports do not express results in dollar values; instead risks are weighed against each other and ranked.

23. Your competitors are offering a new product that is predicted to sell well. After much careful study, your company has decided against launching a competing product due to the uncertainty of the market and the enormous investment required. Which term best describes your company's decision?

   A. Risk analysis

   B. Risk transfer

   C. Risk avoidance

   D. Product avoidance

☑ **C.** Deciding to invest heavily in a new product for an uncertain market is a gamble. Deciding against it would be classified as risk avoidance.

☒ **A, B,** and **D** are incorrect. Risk analysis is not as specific an answer as risk avoidance, so **A** is not the best answer. **B** is incorrect because risk transfer would imply some or all risk is assumed by another party. **D** is a fictitious risk management term.

24. How can management determine which risks should be given the most attention?

    A. IT risks are more important than physical facility risks.

    B. Rank risks by likelihood.

    C. Rank risks by probable date of occurrence.

    D. Rank risks by SLE.

    ☑ **B.** Whether qualitative or quantitative risk analysis is done, once data have been properly considered, risks should be ranked by likelihood.

    ☒ **A, C,** and **D** are incorrect. **A** is untrue. Physical risks such as floods could devastate an IT infrastructure. In some cases ranking threats by date can be beneficial, but this is usually factored in when ranking by priority, so **C** is not the best answer. **D** is incorrect because the SLE is a dollar value associated with a single failure. The ALE uses the SLE as well as a probability of the incident occurring resulting in a dollar figure. ALE figures can be sorted by dollar value to determine which threats should be given the most attention, but the SLE by itself is not enough.

25. Recently your data center was housed in Albuquerque, New Mexico. Due to corporate downsizing, the data center equipment was moved to an existing office in Santa Fe. The server room in Santa Fe was not designed to accommodate all the new servers arriving from Albuquerque and the server room temperature is very warm. Because this is a temporary solution until a new data center facility is built, management has decided not to pay for an updated air conditioning system. Which term best describes this scenario?

    A. Risk transfer

    B. Risk avoidance

    C. Risk acceptance

    D. Risk reduction

    ☑ **C.** Accepting the potential consequences of a threat is referred to as risk acceptance. The amount of money to minimize the risk is not warranted, as was the case of a temporary data center in Santa Fe.

    ☒ **A, B,** and **D** are incorrect. **A** is incorrect because risk transfer shifts risk consequence responsibility to another party. **B** is incorrect because risk avoidance refers to the disregard of an opportunity due to the risk involved. **D** is incorrect because risk reduction is the application of mitigation techniques to minimize the occurrence of threats.

26. Which factors could influence your risk management strategy?

A. Government regulations

B. Moving operations to a new building

C. The purchase of a newer firewall solution

D. None of the above

E. All of the above

> ☑ **E.** Government regulations (**A**) might involve the privacy of client information which could mean a new or more prevalent security risk. A new building (**B**) might have better security than an old one, which may reduce the physical security risks. Newer firewall solutions (**C**) generally have better protection than older solutions (if configured and maintained properly), which again could reduce risk.
>
> ☒ **D** is incorrect. All listed items could influence your risk management strategy.

27. You are a member of an IT project team. The team is performing an IT risk analysis and has identified assets and their values as well threats and threat mitigation solutions. What must be done next?

A. Perform a cost-benefit analysis of proposed risk solutions.

B. Calculate the ALE values.

C. Decide which vulnerabilities exist.

D. There is nothing more to do.

> ☑ **B.** The ALE values must be calculated now that threats have been identified and assets have been valued.
>
> ☒ **A, C,** and **D** are incorrect. **A** is not the next step. A cost-benefit analysis can only be done once ALE values have been calculated. ALE values give you something to compare threat mitigation costs against to determine whether expenditures are warranted. **C** has already been done at this stage. **D** is untrue; there is much more to be done (ALE, cost-benefit analysis, and so on).

28. To reduce the likelihood of internal fraud, organization implements policies that ensure more than one person is responsible for a financial transaction from beginning to end. Which of the following best describes this scenario?

A. Probability

B. Mitigation solution

C. Impact analysis

D. Threat analysis

   ☑   **B.** Implementation of policies for internal control of transactions encompasses mitigation solutions. The threat is identified and a solution is put into place.

   ☒   **A, C,** and **D** are incorrect. These choices do not describe the scenario. **A** is incorrect because probability is a factor used to calculate the ALE. **C** is incorrect because an impact analysis determines the effect various threats can have on business operations. **D** is incorrect because a threat analysis defines threats and possible solutions.

29. What is the difference between risk assessment and risk management?

A. They are the same thing.

B. Risk assessment identifies and prioritizes risks; risk management is the governing of risks to minimize their impact.

C. Risk management identifies and prioritizes risks; risk assessment is the governing of risks to minimize their impact.

D. Risk assessment identifies threat; risk management controls those threats.

   ☑   **B.** Risk assessment requires identification and prioritization of risks either using a relative ranking scale or objective numeric data. Management of those risks involves minimizing their impact on the business.

   ☒   **A, C,** and **D** are incorrect. **A** is untrue. **C** is incorrect because the definitions are reversed. **D** describes threat analysis, not risk assessment or risk management.

30. What are the two drawbacks to quantitative risk analysis compared to qualitative risk analysis?

A. Complex calculations.

B. Risks are not prioritized by monetary value.

C. Quantitative analysis is more time consuming than qualitative.

D. It is difficult to determine how much money to allocate to reduce a risk.

☑ **A** and **C**. Quantitative risk analysis involves complex time consuming calculations. Results are expressed in specific percentages or monetary values despite the fact that probability figures are used to arrive at these results.

☒ **B** and **D** are incorrect. **B** applies to qualitative risk analysis where risks are ranked relative to each other, not necessarily by dollar value. **D** also applies to qualitative risk analysis, quantitative risk analysis strives to provide specific dollar amounts to facilitate allocating funds.

16

Disaster Recovery

CERTIFICATION OBJECTIVES

❑   2.5   Compare and contrast aspects of business continuity

❑   2.7   Execute disaster recovery plans and procedures

QUESTIONS

Unfavorable circumstances can temporarily or permanently cripple a business. A disaster recovery plan attempts to minimize the impact these circumstances, whether caused by nature or by humans, have on a business. The plan should include incident assessment, and it should specify who performs which tasks under specific circumstances.

1. In the event of a server hard disk failure, you have been asked to configure server hard disks as depicted here. What type of disk configuration is this?

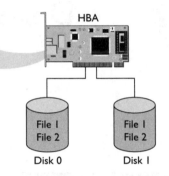

A. RAID 0

B. RAID 1

C. RAID 5

D. RAID 5+1

2. A team leader assigns Ron, a server administrator, the task of determining the business and financial effect a failed e-mail server would have if it was down for two hours. What type of analysis must Ron perform?

A. Risk analysis

B. Business impact analysis

C. Security audit

D. Disk surface scan

3. An urban law enforcement agency leases a new space in another part of town complete with a functioning computer network mirroring the current live site. A high-speed network link constantly synchronizes data between the two sites. What type of site is the new leased location?

A. Frost site

B. Cold site

C. Warm site

D. Hot site

4. An urban law enforcement agency leases a new space in another part of town complete with functioning computer network mirroring the current live site. Data backups from the primary site are copied to the new leased location every two days. What type of site is the new leased location?

    A. Frost site

    B. Cold site

    C. Warm site

    D. Hot site

5. Turtle Airlines has hired you to ensure their customer reservation system is always online. The software runs and stores data locally on the Linux operating system. What should you do?

    A. Install two Linux servers in a cluster. Cluster the airline software with its data being written to shared storage.

    B. Install a new Linux server. Ensure the airline software runs from the first server. Schedule airline data to replicate to the new Linux server nightly.

    C. Configure the Linux server with RAID 5.

    D. Configure the Linux server with RAID 1.

6. A busy clustered web site regularly experiences congested network traffic. You must improve the web site response time. What should you implement?

    A. Ethernet switch

    B. Network load balancer

    C. Fiber channel switch

    D. Proxy server

7. Your primary e-mail server uses three hot-swappable hard disks in a RAID 5 configuration. When one disk fails, you have other disks readily available in the server room that you simply plug in while the server is still running. Which term best describes this scenario?

    A. Disk clustering

    B. Hardware fault tolerance

    C. Disk striping

    D. Disk mirroring

8. Your server backup routine consists of a full backup each Friday night and a nightly backup of all data changed since Friday's backup. What type of backup schedule is this?

    A. Full

    B. Full and incremental

    C. Full and differential

    D. Fully incremental

9. The Chief Security Officer at a national bank chain will be retiring next year, and an IT security employee must be groomed to fill that position. What term encompasses this procedure?

   A. Retirement

   B. Job rotation

   C. Succession planning

   D. Disaster recovery

10. You are a network engineer for a San Francisco–based law firm. After the 1989 earthquake, an emphasis on continued business operation after future earthquakes dominated the San Francisco business community. What type of plan focuses on ensuring that personnel, customers, and IT systems are minimally affected after a disaster?

   A. Risk management

   B. Fault tolerant

   C. Disaster recovery

   D. Business continuity

11. A server is configured with three hard disks as shown here. What type of configuration is this?

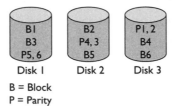

Disk 1   Disk 2   Disk 3

B = Block
P = Parity

   A. RAID 0

   B. RAID 1

   C. RAID 5

   D. RAID 5+1

12. Windows Server 2008 backups are scheduled as follows: Saturday 3 A.M. – Full Backup, Weeknights 9 P.M. – Incremental Backup. Write verification has been enabled. Backup tapes are stored offsite at a third-party location. Which two things should be done to ensure the integrity and confidentially of the backups?

   A. Have a different person than the backup operator analyze each day's backup logs.

   B. Ensure the user performing the backup is a member of the Windows Administrator group.

   C. Encrypt the backup media.

   D. Use SSL to encrypt backup media.

13. You are an IT network architect. Your firm has been hired to perform a network security audit for Acme Shipping, Inc. One of Acme's warehouses has a server room containing one Windows server and two Linux servers. After interviewing the server administrators, you learn they have no idea what to do if the Linux servers cease to function. What is needed here?

    A. Disaster recovery plan

    B. Risk analysis

    C. Windows servers

    D. Server clustering

14. Which two items should be considered when ensuring high availability for an ecommerce web site?

    A. Using TPM to encrypt server hard disks

    B. Redundant Internet links

    C. Network load balancing

    D. Upgrading the server CMOS to the latest version

15. Which three items should be considered when creating a DRP?

    A. Consider which class of IP addresses are in use.

    B. Rank risks.

    C. Disable unused switch ports.

    D. Assign recovery tasks to personnel.

    E. Establish an alternate location to continue business operations.

16. As part of your disaster recovery planning, you create a prioritized list of professionals that can be contacted in the event of a flood. Which items should you include? (Choose three.)

    A. Property restoration specialist

    B. Document restoration specialist

    C. Server backup specialist

    D. Server restoration specialist

17. What should be used to make informed decisions regarding your specific DRP?

    A. DRP template freely downloaded from a web site

    B. ROI analysis

    C. TCO analysis

    D. Business impact analysis

18. Identify the two least desirable DRP practices:

   A. Perform a business impact analysis first.

   B. Base your DRP on a downloaded template.

   C. Data backups are never tested; it costs the company too much money.

   D. Keep existing backup solutions in place even though the software is two versions out of date.

19. You are creating a DRP for a small independent car dealership. There are four employees who each use a desktop computer; there are no servers. All company data is stored on the four computers. A single high-speed DSL link is shared by all users. Choose the two best DRP solutions:

   A. Store data with an online data storage service.

   B. Ensure employees know exactly what to in the event of a disaster.

   C. Purchase faster desktops.

   D. Purchase a file server.

20. Mark is the server specialist for Big Game Hunting, Inc. While installing a new server data hard disk, Mark spills his cup of coffee on the old server data hard disk. What should Mark do?

   A. Use a blow dryer to dry the hard disk.

   B. Immerse the hard disk in warm water to remove the corrosive coffee.

   C. Place the hard disk in an air-sealed container.

   D. Contact a network specialist.

21. You are working with management to justify the cost of a warm site versus a cold site. What factors can help justify the cost of a warm site? (Choose two.)

   A. Large revenue loss during downtime

   B. Small revenue loss during downtime

   C. Customer contracts tolerating no more than 8 hours downtime

   D. Customer contracts tolerating no more than 72 hours downtime

22. Your senior network administrator has decided that the five physical servers at your location will be virtualized and run on a single physical host. The five virtual guests will use the physical hard disks in the physical host. The physical host has the hard disks configured with RAID 1. What is the flaw in this plan?

   A. The physical server should be using RAID 5.

   B. The physical hard disks must not reside in the physical host.

   C. You cannot run five virtual machines on a physical host simultaneously.

   D. The physical host is a single point of failure.

23. Your company is virtualizing DNS, DHCP, web, and e-mail servers at your location. Each of the four virtual machines will be spread out across two physical hosts. Virtual machines are using virtual hard disks, and these files exist on a SAN. What is the best virtual machine backup strategy that will allow the quickest granular restore?
    A. Back up the virtual machine hard disks at the SAN level.
    B. Install a backup agent in each virtual machine and perform backups normally.
    C. Duplicate your SAN disk array so that backups are not necessary.
    D. All four virtual machines must run on the same physical host to be backed up.

24. What should you do when storing server backup tapes offsite?
    A. Encrypt backed-up data.
    B. Generate file hashes for each backed-up file.
    C. Place backup tapes in static shielding bags.
    D. It is a security violation to store backup tapes offsite.

25. You are the administrator for a virtual Windows server running Active Directory Domain Services (ADDS). Abnormal server behavior and finally a server freeze lead you to believe that the server has a virus infection. What should you do?
    A. Revert to an earlier virtual machine snapshot prior to the virus infection.
    B. Format the hard disk, reinstall the server, restore from tape.
    C. Refer to your DRP.
    D. Refer to your ARP.

26. What is the purpose of a DRP? (Choose the best two answers.)
    A. Minimize economic loss.
    B. Premeditate a reaction to public relations blunders.
    C. Install confidence in shareholders.
    D. Earn a high rate of return annually.

27. Which of the following would appear on a DRP?
    A. Prioritized list of critical computer systems
    B. Single points of failure
    C. Employee birthdates
    D. Dollar value associated with one hour of downtime

28. You are the network administrator for a small IT consulting firm. All servers are located at the single site. After testing the DRP and receiving management approval, you e-mail a copy to all employees for their reference in the event of a disaster. Identify the problem.

    A. The e-mail should have been encrypted.

    B. The e-mail should have been digitally signed.

    C. Only executives should have received the message.

    D. The mail server might not be available in the event of a disaster.

29. You are the network administrator for a small IT consulting firm. All servers are hosted externally. After analyzing threats, creating a DRP, and receiving management approval, you e-mail a copy to all employees for their reference in the event of a disaster. What is the problem?

    A. The e-mail should have been encrypted.

    B. The DRP plan was not tested.

    C. The e-mail should have been digitally signed.

    D. Only executives should have received the message.

30. Which of the following regarding disaster recovery are true? (Choose two.)

    A. Once the plan is complete, it need never be revisited.

    B. Once the plan is complete, it must have management approval.

    C. The plan must evolve with the business.

    D. The plan should include only IT systems.

QUICK ANSWER KEY

1.	B	11.	C	21.	A, C
2.	B	12.	A, C	22.	D
3.	D	13.	A	23.	B
4.	C	14.	B, C	24.	A
5.	A	15.	B, D, E	25.	C
6.	B	16.	A, B, D	26.	A, C
7.	B	17.	D	27.	A
8.	C	18.	B, C	28.	D
9.	C	19.	A, B	29.	B
10.	D	20.	C	30.	B, C

IN-DEPTH ANSWERS

1. In the event of a server hard disk failure, you have been asked to configure server hard disks as depicted here. What type of disk configuration is this?

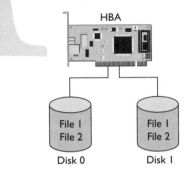

   A. RAID 0
   B. RAID 1
   C. RAID 5
   D. RAID 5+1

   ☑ **B.** RAID (redundant array of inexpensive disks) level 1 refers to disk mirroring. When data is written to one disk, it is duplicated on the second disk. In the event of a single disk failure, the second disk can take over.

   ☒ **A, C,** and **D** are incorrect. **A** is incorrect because RAID 0 involves striping data across multiple disks to increase performance, but there is no fault tolerance. **C** is incorrect because RAID 5 stripes data across disks, but distributes parity (recovery) data on disks so that a single disk failure means data can still be reconstructed. **D** is incorrect because RAID 5+1 is a mirrored RAID 5 array.

2. A team leader assigns Ron, a server administrator, the task of determining the business and financial effect a failed e-mail server would have if it was down for two hours. What type of analysis must Ron perform?
   A. Risk analysis
   B. Business impact analysis
   C. Security audit
   D. Disk surface scan

> ☑ **B.** A business impact analysis identifies the effect unwanted events have on the operation of a business.
>
> ☒ **A, C, and D are incorrect. A** is incorrect because a risk analysis identifies, evaluates, and prioritizes assets and threats that could jeopardize a business and is conducted before a business impact analysis. **C** is incorrect because a security audit tests how effective security policy implementation is for safeguarding corporate assets. **D** is incorrect because a disk surface scan tests for bad sectors. Neither of the last two answers deal with calculating financial loss.

3. An urban law enforcement agency leases a new space in another part of town complete with a functioning computer network mirroring the current live site. A high-speed network link constantly synchronizes data between the two sites. What type of site is the new leased location?

   A. Frost site
   B. Cold site
   C. Warm site
   D. Hot site

> ☑ **D.** Hot sites offer the least downtime, but at the most cost.
>
> ☒ **A, B, and C are incorrect. A** is a fictitious term. **B** and **C** are incorrect because cold sites are backup sites that are not immediately functional but are cheaper to maintain than hot sites. Warm sites require little time to be fully operational. In the question, data is being constantly synchronized between the sites, so the backup site is immediately functional.

4. An urban law enforcement agency leases a new space in another part of town complete with functioning computer network mirroring the current live site. Data backups from the primary site are copied to the new leased location every two days. What type of site is the new leased location?

   A. Frost site
   B. Cold site
   C. Warm site
   D. Hot site

☑ **C.** Warm sites are only functional once critical data is available.

☒ **A, B,** and **D** are incorrect. **A** is a fictitious term. **B** and **D** are incorrect because cold sites are not equipped with a functional computer network mirroring the original site; they are often nothing more than leased space. Because the data is copied only every two days, this does not constitute a hot site.

5. Turtle Airlines has hired you to ensure their customer reservation system is always online. The software runs and stores data locally on the Linux operating system. What should you do?

   A. Install two Linux servers in a cluster. Cluster the airline software with its data being written to shared storage.

   B. Install a new Linux server. Ensure the airline software runs from the first server. Schedule airline data to replicate to the new Linux server nightly.

   C. Configure the Linux server with RAID 5.

   D. Configure the Linux server with RAID 1.

☑ **A.** Clustering software between two servers will allow the customer reservation system to function even if one server fails, because the data is not stored within a single server; it exists on shared storage that both cluster nodes can access.

☒ **B, C,** and **D** are incorrect. **B** is incorrect because scheduling nightly data replication does not ensure the airline software is always online. **C** and **D** are not as fault tolerant as answer **A**; RAID 1 (mirroring) and RAID 5 (striping with distributed parity) are useless if the server fails.

6. A busy clustered web site regularly experiences congested network traffic. You must improve the web site response time. What should you implement?

   A. Ethernet switch

   B. Network load balancer

   C. Fiber channel switch

   D. Proxy server

☑ **B.** Network load balancers (NLBs) can distribute network traffic to multiple servers hosting the same content to improve performance.

☒ **A, C,** and **D** are incorrect. **A** is incorrect because most networks already use Ethernet switches. **C** is incorrect because fiber channel switches are used in a SAN (storage area network) environment, not LANs (local area networks) or WANs (wide area networks). **D** is incorrect because a proxy server retrieves Internet content for clients and then optionally caches it for later requests; it would not improve performance here.

7. Your primary e-mail server uses three hot-swappable hard disks in a RAID 5 configuration. When one disk fails, you have other disks readily available in the server room that you simply plug in while the server is still running. Which term best describes this scenario?
  A. Disk clustering
  B. Hardware fault tolerance
  C. Disk striping
  D. Disk mirroring

  ☑ **B.** Hardware fault tolerance allows a hardware component to fail while not completely impeding data access. A single disk failure in a RAID 5 configuration means the failed disk can be hot-swapped with a functional disk. Because RAID 5 stripes data across disks in the array and parity is distributed across disks, user requests for data can be reconstructed dynamically in RAM until the data is reconstructed on the replaced disk.

  ☒ **A, C, and D** are incorrect. **A** is incorrect because disk clustering is not a proper term. **C** is incorrect because disk striping offers no fault tolerance, only performance increases. **D** is incorrect because disk mirroring is not applicable, since the question states RAID 5 is in use.

8. Your server backup routine consists of a full backup each Friday night and a nightly backup of all data changed since Friday's backup. What type of backup schedule is this?
  A. Full
  B. Full and incremental
  C. Full and differential
  D. Fully incremental

  ☑ **C.** Differential backups will archive data that has changed since the last full backup. Restoring data means first restoring the full backup and then the latest differential.

  ☒ **A, B, and D** are incorrect. **A** is only partially correct. **B** is incorrect because incremental backups archive data changed since the last incremental backup. **D** is a fictitious term.

9. The Chief Security Officer at a national bank chain will be retiring next year, and an IT security employee must be groomed to fill that position. What term encompasses this procedure?
  A. Retirement
  B. Job rotation
  C. Succession planning
  D. Disaster recovery

> ☑ **C.** Succession planning involves identifying and preparing individuals to fill specific job roles.
>
> ☒ **A, B,** and **D** are incorrect. **A** is not the correct term for this procedure. **B** and **D** are not applicable. Job rotation could help prepare an individual to fill a key role, but letter **C** is a much better answer. Disaster recovery involves business continuity in the event of unfavorable circumstances; it has nothing to do with preparing an employee to fill a key role.

10. You are a network engineer for a San Francisco–based law firm. After the 1989 earthquake, an emphasis on continued business operation after future earthquakes dominated the San Francisco business community. What type of plan focuses on ensuring that personnel, customers, and IT systems are minimally affected after a disaster?

   A. Risk management
   B. Fault tolerant
   C. Disaster recovery
   D. Business continuity

> ☑ **D.** Business continuity is considered the key goal to which disaster recovery plays a part. DR (disaster recovery) normally involves implementing steps taken to get the business operational. Business continuity ensures business operation after successful implementation of the DR.
>
> ☒ **A, B,** and **C** are incorrect. **A** is incorrect because risk management refers to minimizing the impact potential risks could have on the primary goal of a business. **B** is incorrect because fault tolerance is not a type of plan; fault tolerance falls under the umbrella of risk management. **C** is not the best answer. Disaster recovery involves methodically returning the business to normal operation and is a component of a BC (business continuity) plan.

11. A server is configured with three hard disks as shown here. What type of configuration is this?

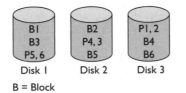

B1 B3 P5, 6	B2 P4, 3 B5	P1, 2 B4 B6
Disk 1	Disk 2	Disk 3

B = Block
P = Parity

A. RAID 0
B. RAID 1
C. RAID 5
D. RAID 5+1

☑ **C.** Distributing data and parity information across disks is referred to as RAID level 5.

☒ **A, B,** and **D** are incorrect. **A** is incorrect because RAID 0 (striping) writes data across disks without parity, so there is a performance benefit but no fault tolerance. **B** is incorrect because RAID 1 (mirroring) duplicates data written the first disk to the second disk in case one disk fails. **D** is incorrect because RAID 5+1 mirrors a RAID 5 configuration for additional fault tolerance.

12. Windows Server 2008 backups are scheduled as follows: Saturday 3 A.M. – Full Backup, Weeknights 9 P.M. – Incremental Backup. Write verification has been enabled. Backup tapes are stored offsite at a third-party location. Which two things should be done to ensure the integrity and confidentially of the backups?
A. Have a different person than the backup operator analyze each day's backup logs.
B. Ensure the user performing the backup is a member of the Windows Administrator group.
C. Encrypt the backup media.
D. Use SSL to encrypt backup media.

☑ **A** and **C.** To reduce the likelihood of tampering, a different person should review backup logs. For confidentiality, backup tapes stored offsite should be encrypted.

☒ **B** and **D** are incorrect. **B** is incorrect because there is no need to be a member of the Administrators group, but there is a need to be in the Backup Operators group. **D** is incorrect because SSL (Secure Sockets Layer) encrypts network traffic, not stored data.

13. You are an IT network architect. Your firm has been hired to perform a network security audit for Acme Shipping, Inc. One of Acme's warehouses has a server room containing one Windows server and two Linux servers. After interviewing the server administrators, you learn they have no idea what to do if the Linux servers cease to function. What is needed here?
A. Disaster recovery plan
B. Risk analysis
C. Windows servers
D. Server clustering

☑ **A.** Disaster recovery plans outline exactly who must do what in case unfavorable events occur.

☒ **B, C,** and **D** are incorrect. **B** is incorrect because risk analysis identifies threats to assets and prioritizes those threats, but actions taken in a disaster are included in a disaster recovery plan. **C** is incorrect because windows servers are not needed here; a DRP (disaster recovery plan) is. **D** is incorrect because clustering the Linux servers would only make matters worse if they ceased functioning because clustering introduces more complexity. The administrators should get Linux training, and a DRP addressing the Linux servers should be crafted.

14. Which two items should be considered when ensuring high availability for an ecommerce web site?

  A. Using TPM to encrypt server hard disks
  B. Redundant Internet links
  C. Network load balancing
  D. Upgrading the server CMOS to the latest version

☑ **B** and **C.** High availability makes a resource available as often as is possible. Redundant Internet links allow access to the web site even if one Internet link fails. Network load balancing (which could use the redundant Internet links) distributes traffic evenly either to server cluster nodes or through redundant network links.

☒ **A** and **D** are incorrect. These choices do not apply. **A** is incorrect because TPM (trusted platform module) encrypts hard disk contents. While this addresses confidentiality, it does not address high availability. **D** is incorrect because CMOS upgrades may improve or give new hardware capabilities to the web server, but this does not directly address high availability. If the CMOS update corrects a problem with RAID configurations, then it would address high availability, but the possible answers do not list this.

15. Which three items should be considered when creating a DRP?

  A. Consider which class of IP addresses are in use.
  B. Rank risks.
  C. Disable unused switch ports.
  D. Assign recovery tasks to personnel.
  E. Establish an alternate location to continue business operations.

☑ **B, D,** and **E.** Risks should be ranked to determine which are the most probable. Most attention should be given to the most likely threats. Personnel must be assigned tasks according to the DRP to minimize confusion and downtime. An alternate site (cold, warm, or hot) should at least be considered. Larger businesses or agencies may be able to justify the cost of maintaining an alternate site.

☒ **A** and **C** are incorrect. **A** is incorrect because IP address classes have no impact on creating DRPs. **C** is incorrect because, although unused switch ports should always be disabled, this would not be considered when crafting a DRP.

16. As part of your disaster recovery planning, you create a prioritized list of professionals that can be contacted in the event of a flood. Which items should you include? (Choose three.)
   A. Property restoration specialist
   B. Document restoration specialist
   C. Server backup specialist
   D. Server restoration specialist

☑ **A, B,** and **D.** Property restoration specialists efficiently restore the state of a facility so that a business can continue to operate. Their responsibilities include HVAC, electricity, water, lighting, and so on. Document restoration specialists have expertise in retrieving damaged data, whether it is physical (paper documents) or digital. Server restoration specialists are trained in quickly getting servers up and running to their previous state. A disaster recovery plan is required for server restoration specialists to efficiently perform their duties.

☒ **C** is incorrect. Server backup is not a consideration after a disaster has occurred, but server restoration is.

17. What should be used to make informed decisions regarding your specific DRP?
   A. DRP template freely downloaded from a web site
   B. ROI analysis
   C. TCO analysis
   D. Business impact analysis

☑ **D.** A business impact analysis identifies which risks will affect business operations more than others. This is valuable in determining how to recover from a disaster.

☒ **A, B,** and **C** are incorrect. **A** is incorrect because freely downloadable DRP templates are generic and will not address your specific business or IT configuration. **B** and **C** are incorrect because ROI (return on investment) determines the efficiency of an investment (is the cost justified?). TCO (total cost of ownership) identifies the true cost of a product or service. Neither the ROI or TCO are tied directly to your DRP as a business impact analysis is.

18. Identify the two least desirable DRP practices:
   A. Perform a business impact analysis first.
   B. Base your DRP on a downloaded template.
   C. Data backups are never tested; it costs the company too much money.
   D. Keep existing backup solutions in place even though the software is two versions out of date.

☑ **B** and **C.** Your DRP should be much more specific than what a downloaded template can provide. DRPs are not worth their investment if their success has not been proven through testing.

☒ **A** and **D** are incorrect. **A** is incorrect because a DRP takes the business impact analysis into account. **D** is incorrect because backup software two versions out of date might still function correctly; often there are risks involved with immediately using the newest software.

19. You are creating a DRP for a small independent car dealership. There are four employees who each use a desktop computer; there are no servers. All company data is stored on the four computers. A single high-speed DSL link is shared by all users. Choose the two best DRP solutions:
   A. Store data with an online data storage service.
   B. Ensure employees know exactly what to in the event of a disaster.
   C. Purchase faster desktops.
   D. Purchase a file server.

☑ **A** and **B.** Online data storage would be an affordable solution to safeguard business data. Users must know what to do in the event of a catastrophe to ensure the timely resumption of business.

☒ **C** and **D** are incorrect. **C** is incorrect because faster computers will not have an impact on a DRP for a small business. **D** is incorrect because purchasing a file server is not justified given the small number of employees and a single site; online data storage could be justified.

20. Mark is the server specialist for Big Game Hunting, Inc. While installing a new server data hard disk, Mark spills his cup of coffee on the old server data hard disk. What should Mark do?

   A. Use a blow dryer to dry the hard disk.
   B. Immerse the hard disk in warm water to remove the corrosive coffee.
   C. Place the hard disk in an air-sealed container.
   D. Contact a network specialist.

   ☑ **C.** Mark must ensure the coffee does not dry onto any electrical components. An air-sealed container is a good solution, followed by immediately contacting a data recovery specialist.

   ☒ **A, B,** and **D** are incorrect. **A** is incorrect because a blow dryer will dry the coffee onto electrical components and disk surfaces and could damage the hard disk. **B** is incorrect because you should never immerse hard disks in water. Instead of contacting a network specialist, a data recovery specialist should be contacted, and therefore **D** is incorrect.

21. You are working with management to justify the cost of a warm site versus a cold site. What factors can help justify the cost of a warm site? (Choose two.)

   A. Large revenue loss during downtime
   B. Small revenue loss during downtime
   C. Customer contracts tolerating no more than 8 hours downtime
   D. Customer contracts tolerating no more than 72 hours downtime

   ☑ **A** and **C.** Calculating these figures enables intelligent decisions to be made regarding justification of the cost of an alternate site. Your business may have customer contracts requiring minimal downtime in the event of a disaster. The cost of the loss of this business could be factored into justifying the cost of an alternate (warm) site.

   ☒ **B** and **D** are incorrect. **B** is incorrect because losing a small amount of money even if long downtime is experienced cannot justify requiring a warm alternate site. **D** is incorrect becuase 72 hours is enough time to bring a cold site online to resume business services.

22. Your senior network administrator has decided that the five physical servers at your location will be virtualized and run on a single physical host. The five virtual guests will use the physical hard disks in the physical host. The physical host has the hard disks configured with RAID 1. What is the flaw in this plan?

    A. The physical server should be using RAID 5.

    B. The physical hard disks must not reside in the physical host.

    C. You cannot run five virtual machines on a physical host simultaneously.

    D. The physical host is a single point of failure.

> ☑   **D.** If the single physical host experiences a failure, all five virtual machine will be unavailable. A second server should be clustered with the first, and virtual guests should use shared disk storage versus local disk storage.
>
> ☒   **A, B,** and **C** are incorrect. **A** is not the best answer. RAID 5 would not solve the problem of the disks being in a single server. Regarding answer **B**, even if shared storage were used, the physical server would still be a single point of failure. Answer **C** is untrue. Given enough hardware resources, many more than five virtual guests can run simultaneously on a virtualization server.

23. Your company is virtualizing DNS, DHCP, web, and e-mail servers at your location. Each of the four virtual machines will be spread out across two physical hosts. Virtual machines are using virtual hard disks, and these files exist on a SAN. What is the best virtual machine backup strategy that will allow the quickest granular restore?

    A. Back up the virtual machine hard disks at the SAN level.

    B. Install a backup agent in each virtual machine and perform backups normally.

    C. Duplicate your SAN disk array so that backups are not necessary.

    D. All four virtual machines must run on the same physical host to be backed up.

> ☑   **B.** If granular restores are required, backing up each virtual machine using a backup agent installed in each virtual machine is the best choice.
>
> ☒   **A, C,** and **D** are incorrect. Backing up the SAN means backing up virtual hard disks used by the virtual machines. This presents some difficulty if you must restore specific (granular) files compared to answer **B.** Answer **C** is wrong—backups are always necessary no matter what. **D** is untrue. If virtual hard disks are on a SAN, all four virtual machines do not have to be running on the same physical host.

24. What should you do when storing server backup tapes offsite?
   A. Encrypt backed-up data.
   B. Generate file hashes for each backed-up file.
   C. Place backup tapes in static shielding bags.
   D. It is a security violation to store backup tapes offsite.

   ☑ **A.** Backup tapes stored offsite must be encrypted to ensure data confidentiality.

   ☒ **B, C,** and **D** are incorrect. **B** is incorrect because generating file hashes for every backed-up file would take a long time. The benefit of file hashing is to ensure the file has not changed (been tampered with), which is not as useful as encryption—encrypted files cannot be altered without the proper decryption key. **C** is incorrect because static shielding bags protect electrical components from electrostatic discharge; they do nothing for backup tapes. **D** is untrue. Offsite backup tape storage is a critical component in a disaster recovery plan.

25. You are the administrator for a virtual Windows server running Active Directory Domain Services (ADDS). Abnormal server behavior and finally a server freeze lead you to believe that the server has a virus infection. What should you do?
   A. Revert to an earlier virtual machine snapshot prior to the virus infection.
   B. Format the hard disk, reinstall the server, restore from tape.
   C. Refer to your DRP.
   D. Refer to your ARP.

   ☑ **C.** A DRP specifies who should do what in case of a disaster, such as in the case of an infected server.

   ☒ **A, B,** and **D** are incorrect. **A** is incorrect because snapshots should not be used on servers that rely on date and time stamps for their operation (as Active Directory does). **B** may be what the DRP requires be done, but the best answer is to refer to your DRP. **D** does not exist. ARP does not apply to the disaster recovery realm.

26. What is the purpose of a DRP? (Choose the best two answers.)
   A. Minimize economic loss.
   B. Premeditate a reaction to public relations blunders.
   C. Install confidence in shareholders.
   D. Earn a high rate of return annually.

☑ **A and C.** Minimizing downtime, customer disruption, and economic loss is the reason for a disaster recovery plan. Shareholder confidence is solidified when an efficient, well-thought-out disaster recovery plan is in place.

☒ **B and D** are incorrect. **B** is incorrect in that a better term for this situation might be damage control. **D** defines an ideal investment, not the purpose of a disaster recovery plan.

27. Which of the following would appear on a DRP?
   A. Prioritized list of critical computer systems
   B. Single points of failure
   C. Employee birthdates
   D. Dollar value associated with one hour of downtime

☑ **A.** Prioritized lists of critical computer systems allow minimal downtime.

☒ **B, C, and D** are incorrect. **B** is incorrect because single points of failure would be identified in a risk analysis. **C** is incorrect because employee birthdates have nothing to do with a DRP. **D** is incorrect because downtime and dollar values are calculated during risk analysis.

28. You are the network administrator for a small IT consulting firm. All servers are located at the single site. After testing the DRP and receiving management approval, you e-mail a copy to all employees for their reference in the event of a disaster. Identify the problem.
   A. The e-mail should have been encrypted.
   B. The e-mail should have been digitally signed.
   C. Only executives should have received the message.
   D. The mail server might not be available in the event of a disaster.

☑ **D.** The only copy of the DRP exists on a mail server that users may not have access to when they need it most.

☒ **A, B, and C** are incorrect. Although good advice, encrypted and signed e-mail is not a problem in this scenario, so **A** and **B** do not apply. **C** is incorrect because a comprehensive DRP must be made known to applicable employees.

29. You are the network administrator for a small IT consulting firm. All servers are hosted externally. After analyzing threats, creating a DRP, and receiving management approval, you e-mail a copy to all employees for their reference in the event of a disaster. What is the problem?

   A. The e-mail should have been encrypted.

   B. The DRP plan was not tested.

   C. The e-mail should have been digitally signed.

   D. Only executives should have received the message.

> ☑ **B.** A DRP changes with the business and must be tested to ensure its success.
>
> ☒ **A, C,** and **D** are incorrect. **A** and **C** are good advice, but are not problems here. **D** is incorrect because, for example, an IT DRP must be known by all IT employees.

30. Which of the following regarding disaster recovery are true? (Choose two.)

   A. Once the plan is complete, it need never be revisited.

   B. Once the plan is complete, it must have management approval.

   C. The plan must evolve with the business.

   D. The plan should include only IT systems.

> ☑ **B** and **C.** Without management support and approval, a disaster recovery plan will not succeed. The plan must be revisited periodically to ensure it is in step with changes in the business.
>
> ☒ **A** and **D** are incorrect. **A** is untrue; disaster recovery plans must be periodically revisited. **D** is incorrect because, besides IT systems, disaster recovery can also include facility restoration and employee relocation.

17

Introduction to Computer Forensics

CERTIFICATION OBJECTIVES

❑   1.1   Explain the security function and purpose of network devices and technologies

❑   1.4   Implement and use common protocols

❑   2.1   Explain risk-related concepts

❑   2.3   Execute appropriate incident response procedures

❑   6.1   Summarize general cryptography concepts

QUESTIONS

Digital footprints are left with all electronic devices we use daily from our cars to cell phones to personal computers. Computer forensics refers to the documentation, acquisition, and preservation of this digital data for use as evidence. Care must be taken to ensure that the proper steps are taken to legally perform data acquisition.

1. What must be determined by the first responder to an incident?

  A. The severity of the event

  B. Which other personnel must be called in

  C. The dollar amount associated with the incident

  D. Who is at fault

2. After seizing computer equipment alleged to have been involved in a crime, it is left in a corridor unattended for ten minutes while officers subdue a violent suspect. The seized equipment is no longer admissible as evidence because of what violation?

  A. Order of volatility

  B. Damage control

  C. Chain of custody

  D. Time offset

3. A warrant has been issued to investigate a server believed to be used to swap credit card information by organized crime. Following the order of volatility, which data should you collect first?

  A. Electronic memory (RAM)

  B. Hard disk

  C. USB flash drive

  D. CMOS

4. A server configured with a RAID-5 array must be properly imaged to preserve the original state of the data. You decide against imaging each physical hard disk in the array. Which two tasks must you perform?

  A. Change the server CMOS boot order.

  B. Image the array as a single logical disk.

  C. Ensure your imaging solution supports RAID.

  D. Update the firmware for the RAID controller.

5. While capturing network traffic, you notice an abnormally excessive amount of outbound SMTP packets. To determine if this is an incident that requires escalation, what else should you consult?

  A. The contents of your inbox

  B. The mail server log

    C. The mail server documentation

    D. The web server log

6. You decide to work late on a Saturday night to replace wiring in your server room. Upon arriving, you realize there has been a break-in and server backup tapes appear to be missing. What should you do as law enforcement officials arrive?

    A. Clean up the server room.

    B. Sketch a picture of the broken-into premises on a notepad.

    C. Alert officials that the premise has surveillance video.

    D. Check the surrounding area for the perpetrator.

7. Which of the following best visually illustrates the state of a computer at the time it was seized by law enforcement?

    A. Digital photograph of the motherboard

    B. Screenshot

    C. Visio network diagram

    D. Steganography

8. Which is the correct OOV (order of volatility) when collecting digital evidence?

    A. Hard disk, DVD-R, RAM, swap file

    B. Swap file, RAM, DVD-R, hard disk

    C. RAM, DVD-R, swap file, hard disk

    D. RAM, swap file, hard disk, DVD-R

9. What can a forensic analyst do to reduce the amount of files that must be analyzed on a seized disk?

    A. Write a Visual Basic script.

    B. Delete files thought to be operating system files.

    C. Ensure the original disk is pristine; use a hash table on a copy of the files.

    D. Ensure the original disk is pristine; use a script to process a copy of the files.

10. A professional that is present at the time of evidence gathering can be summoned to appear in court or to prepare a report on their findings for use in court. What is this person referred to as?

    A. Plaintiff

    B. Defendant

    C. Auditor

    D. Forensic expert witness

11. Which of the following best describes chain of custody?
   A. Delegating evidence collection to your superior
   B. Preserving, protecting, and documenting evidence
   C. Capturing a system image to another disk
   D. Capture memory contents before hard disk contents

12. In working on an insider trading case, you are asked to prove that an e-mail message is authentic and was sent to another employee. Which two items should you consider?
   A. Was the message encrypted?
   B. Was the message digitally signed?
   C. Are user public keys properly protected?
   D. Are user private keys properly protected?

13. What type of evidence would be the most difficult for a perpetrator to forge?
   A. IP address
   B. MAC address
   C. Cell phone SIM card
   D. Documents on a USB flash drive

14. What is the purpose of disk forensic software? (Choose two.)
   A. Use file encryption to ensure copied data mirrors original data.
   B. Use file hashes to ensure copied data mirrors original data.
   C. Protect data on the original disks.
   D. Create file hashes on the original disks.

15. You are preparing to gather evidence from a cell phone. Which of the following is false?
   A. CDMA mobile devices do not use SIM cards.
   B. CDMA mobile devices store user data on the mobile device.
   C. GSM mobile devices do not use SIM cards.
   D. GSM mobile devices use SIM cards.

16. You must analyze data on a digital camera's internal memory. You plan to connect your forensic computer to the camera using a USB cable. What should you do to ensure you do not modify data on the camera?
   A. Ensure the camera is turned off.
   B. Flag all files on the camera as read-only.
   C. Log in with a non-administrative account on the forensic computer.
   D. Use a USB write-blocking device.

17. What can be used to ensure seized mobile wireless devices do not communicate with other devices?

    A. SIM card

    B. Faraday bag

    C. Antistatic bag

    D. GPS jammer

18. Robin works as a network technician at a stock brokerage firm. To test network forensic capturing software, she plugs her laptop into an Ethernet switch and begins capturing network traffic. During later analysis, she notices some broadcast and multicast packets as well as only her own computer's network traffic. Why was she unable to capture all network traffic on the switch?

    A. She must enable promiscuous mode on her NIC.

    B. She must disable promiscuous mode on her NIC.

    C. Each switch port is an isolated collision domain.

    D. Each switch port is an isolated broadcast domain.

19. A NID (network intrusion detection) device captures network traffic during the commission of a crime on a network. You notice NTP and TCP packets from all network hosts in the capture. You must find a way to correlate captured packets to a date and time to ensure the packet captures will be considered as admissible as evidence. What should you do? (Choose two.)

    A. Nothing. NTP keeps time in sync on a network.

    B. Nothing. Packet captures are time stamped.

    C. Without digital signatures, date and time cannot be authenticated.

    D. Without encryption, date and time cannot be authenticated.

20. You arrive at a scene where a computer must be seized as evidence. The computer is powered off and has an external USB hard drive plugged in. What should you do?

    A. Turn on the computer.

    B. Unplug the external USB hard drive.

    C. Thoroughly document the state of the equipment.

    D. Place the computer in a faraday bag.

21. You are asked to examine a hard disk for fragments of instant messaging conversations as well as deleted files. How should you do this?

    A. Use bit stream copying tools.

    B. Log in to the computer and copy the original hard drive contents to an external USB hard drive.

    C. Map a drive across the network to the original hard drive and copy the contents to an external USB hard drive.

    D. View log files.

22. Which type of file is most likely to contain incriminating data?

    A. Password-protected Microsoft Word file

    B. Encrypted Microsoft Word file

    C. Digitally signed Microsoft Word file

    D. File hash of Microsoft Word file

23. How can a forensic analyst benefit from analyzing metadata? (Choose three.)

    A. JPEG metadata can reveal specific camera settings.

    B. Microsoft Word metadata can reveal the author name.

    C. Microsoft Excel metadata can reveal your MAC address.

    D. PDF metadata can reveal the registered company name.

24. Which of the following rules must be followed when performing forensic analysis? (Choose two.)

    A. Work only with the original authentic data.

    B. Work only with a copy of data.

    C. Seek legal permission to conduct an analysis.

    D. Seek your manager's permission to conduct an analysis.

25. Refer to the accompanying illustration. You must determine if network traffic captured on interface E0 on Router A appears authentic or spoofed. You are analyzing a packet destined for Server A. The source MAC address in the packet is 0034D69B088C, and the source IP address is 200.0.0.55. For a legitimate packet, which of the following statements is correct?

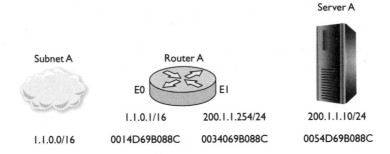

    A. The source MAC address should be 0014D69B088C.

    B. The source IP address cannot be from the 200.1.1.0/24 network.

    C. The source IP address should be 200.1.1.254.

    D. The source IP address should be 1.1.0.1.

26. The IT director is creating the following year's budget. You are asked to submit forensic dollar figures for your IT forensic team. Which one item should you not submit?

    A. Travel expenses

    B. Man hour expenses

    C. Training expenses

    D. ALE amounts

27. Users report at 9:30 A.M. severely degraded network performance since the work day began at 8:00 A.M. After network analysis and a quick discussion with your IT security team, you conclude a worm virus has infected your network. What should you do to control the damage?

    A. Determine the severity of the security breach.

    B. Unplug SAN devices.

    C. Shut down all servers.

    D. Shut down Ethernet switches.

28. A suspect deletes incriminating files and empties the Windows Recycle Bin. Which two of the following statements are true regarding the deletion?

    A. The files cannot be recovered.

    B. The files can be recovered.

    C. Deleted files contain all of their original data until the hard disk is filled with other data.

    D. Deleted files contain all of their original data until the hard disk is defragmented.

29. The local police suspect a woman is using her computer to commit online fraud, but she encrypts her hard disk with a strong passphrase. Law enforcement would like to access the data on the encrypted disk to obtain forensic evidence. What two tasks should be done?

    A. Harness the processing power of thousands of Internet computers and attempt to crack the encryption passphrase.

    B. Obtain a warrant.

    C. Install a packet sniffer on the suspect's network.

    D. Install a keylogger to capture the passphrase.

30. A seized USB flash drive contains only natural scenic pictures. Law enforcement were convinced incriminating data was stored on the USB flash drive. What else should be done?

    A. Decrypt the USB flash drive.

    B. Format the USB flash drive.

    C. Check for steganographic hidden data.

    D. Analyze the USB flash drive log.

QUICK ANSWER KEY

1. B	11. B	21. A
2. C	12. B, D	22. B
3. A	13. C	23. A, B, D
4. B, C	14. B, C	24. B, C
5. B	15. C	25. B
6. C	16. D	26. D
7. B	17. B	27. D
8. D	18. C	28. B, C
9. C	19. A, B	29. B, D
10. D	20. C	30. C

IN-DEPTH ANSWERS

1. What must be determined by the first responder to an incident?
   A. The severity of the event
   B. Which other personnel must be called in
   C. The dollar amount associated with the incident
   D. Who is at fault

   ☑ **B.** The first responder will determine who needs to be called or what should be done next, based on the Incident Response policy.

   ☒ **A, C,** and **D** are incorrect. **A** is incorrect because the first responder may not be qualified to determine the severity of the event. **C** is incorrect because calculating financial loss can be done once the situation is under control—this is not the first thing that should be done; neither is pointing fingers, and therefore **D** is incorrect.

2. After seizing computer equipment alleged to have been involved in a crime, it is left in a corridor unattended for ten minutes while officers subdue a violent suspect. The seized equipment is no longer admissible as evidence because of what violation?
   A. Order of volatility
   B. Damage control
   C. Chain of custody
   D. Time offset

   ☑ **C.** Chain of custody has been violated. Chain of custody involves documenting evidence being collected thoroughly and legally while ensuring the evidence cannot be tampered with.

   ☒ **A, B,** and **D** are incorrect. **A** is incorrect because order of volatility determines what type of data is most easily lost, for example, data in electronic memory (RAM) versus data stored on a DVD. **B** is incorrect because damage control involves minimizing further damage in the event of an unfavorable event. **D** is incorrect because time offset is used to validate the date and time stamps of digital forensic evidence.

3. A warrant has been issued to investigate a server believed to be used to swap credit card information by organized crime. Following the order of volatility, which data should you collect first?

   A. Electronic memory (RAM)

   B. Hard disk

   C. USB flash drive

   D. CMOS

> ☑ **A.** The order of volatility determines which data is most at risk of loss. RAM data is lost when a device is powered off; therefore, it must be properly collected first.
>
> ☒ **B, C,** and **D** are incorrect. **B, C,** and **D** exist even without power. CMOS chips on the motherboard require a small battery to retain their configurations (boot sequence, date/time, and so on).

4. A server configured with a RAID-5 array must be properly imaged to preserve the original state of the data. You decide against imaging each physical hard disk in the array. Which two tasks must you perform?

   A. Change the server CMOS boot order.

   B. Image the array as a single logical disk.

   C. Ensure your imaging solution supports RAID.

   D. Update the firmware for the RAID controller.

> ☑ **B** and **C.** You should ensure your forensic imaging tool supports the RAID controller on the system you must image, and then you should image the disks as a single logical disk.
>
> ☒ **A** and **D** are incorrect. These things are not as likely to be done. **A** is incorrect because ideally, your forensic imaging tool is a separate device, so you shouldn't have to modify the CMOS boot order. **D** is incorrect because unless there are problems with the RAID controller, you should not have to update the firmware to image the logical disk.

5. While capturing network traffic, you notice an abnormally excessive amount of outbound SMTP packets. To determine if this is an incident that requires escalation, what else should you consult?

   A. The contents of your inbox

   B. The mail server log

   C. The mail server documentation

   D. The web server log

☑ **B.** The mail server log will reveal SMTP activity such as excessive outbound SMTP traffic.

☒ **A, C,** and **D** are incorrect. **A** is incorrect because your inbox is not related to general outbound SMTP traffic, unless you have configured your mail server to notify you. **C** is incorrect because, although mail server documentation will detail what to do to have the server function properly, it will not specifically address this issue. **D** is incorrect because the web server log will not contain SMTP outbound traffic details.

6. You decide to work late on a Saturday night to replace wiring in your server room. Upon arriving, you realize there has been a break-in and server backup tapes appear to be missing. What should you do as law enforcement officials arrive?

   A. Clean up the server room.

   B. Sketch a picture of the broken-into premises on a notepad.

   C. Alert officials that the premise has surveillance video.

   D. Check the surrounding area for the perpetrator.

☑ **C.** Video surveillance provides important evidence that could be used to solve this crime.

☒ **A, B,** and **D** are incorrect. **A** is incorrect because you must not disturb the crime scene. **B** is not as good an answer as letter **C**. **D** is incorrect because you must never seek those that have committed a crime—leave that to law enforcement.

7. Which of the following best visually illustrates the state of a computer at the time it was seized by law enforcement?

   A. Digital photograph of the motherboard

   B. Screenshot

   C. Visio network diagram

   D. Steganography

☑ **B.** A screenshot can be acquired in many ways and can prove relevant to the particular crime, since it may reveal what was happening on the system at the time.

☒ **A, C,** and **D** are incorrect. **A** is incorrect because a picture of the motherboard would generally be useless—user data is not exposed when viewing a motherboard. **C** is incorrect because a Visio network diagram is not as valuable as a screenshot. **D** is incorrect because steganography is the art of concealing data within other data (for example, messages hidden within pictures). This would not apply in this case.

8. Which is the correct OOV (order of volatility) when collecting digital evidence?

    A. Hard disk, DVD-R, RAM, swap file

    B. Swap file, RAM, DVD-R, hard disk

    C. RAM, DVD-R, swap file, hard disk

    D. RAM, swap file, hard disk, DVD-R

    ☑ **D.** Digital forensic evidence must first be collected from the most fragile (power-dependent) locations such as RAM and the swap file. Swap files contain data from physical RAM that were paged to disk to make room for something else in physical RAM. Hard disks are the next most vulnerable, since hard disk data can simply be deleted and the hard disk can be filled with useless data to make data recovery very difficult. A DVD-R is less susceptible to data loss than hard disks, since it is read-only.

    ☒ **A, B,** and **C** are incorrect. **A** and **B** are incorrect because RAM is much more volatile (power-dependent) than hard disks and swap files. **C** is incorrect because swap files are more volatile than DVD-Rs.

9. What can a forensic analyst do to reduce the amount of files that must be analyzed on a seized disk?

    A. Write a Visual Basic script.

    B. Delete files thought to be operating system files.

    C. Ensure the original disk is pristine; use a hash table on a copy of the files.

    D. Ensure the original disk is pristine; use a script to process a copy of the files.

    ☑ **C.** A hash table calculates file hashes for each file. Known standard operating system file hashes can be compared to your file hashes to quickly exclude known authentic files that have not been modified.

    ☒ **A, B,** and **D** are incorrect. **A** is incorrect because writing a Visual Basic script is too generic—we would have to know how the script was written for this answer to be considered. **B** is incorrect because deleting files that are thought to belong to the operating system is not a thorough method of reducing files that must be analyzed. Answer **D** is similar to answer **A**; it is too ambiguous to simply state writing a script will solve our problems.

10. A professional that is present at the time of evidence gathering can be summoned to appear in court or to prepare a report on their findings for use in court. What is this person referred to as?

A. Plaintiff

B. Defendant

C. Auditor

D. Forensic expert witness

☑ **D.** A forensic expert witness has specialized knowledge and experience in a field beyond that of the average person, and thus such a person's testimony is deemed authentic.

☒ **A, B**, and **C** are incorrect. **A** is incorrect because the plaintiff is the party that initiates a lawsuit, **B** is incorrect because the defendant is the party against which charges are alleged. **C** is incorrect because an auditor examines records of some type to ensure their thoroughness and authenticity.

11. Which of the following best describes chain of custody?

A. Delegating evidence collection to your superior

B. Preserving, protecting, and documenting evidence

C. Capturing a system image to another disk

D. Capture memory contents before hard disk contents

☑ **B.** Capturing, documenting, and safeguarding evidence is referred to as chain of custody.

☒ **A, C**, and **D** are incorrect. These are tasks that could be performed when gathering forensic evidence, but they do not describe the entire chain of custody.

12. In working on an insider trading case, you are asked to prove that an e-mail message is authentic and was sent to another employee. Which two items should you consider?

A. Was the message encrypted?

B. Was the message digitally signed?

C. Are user public keys properly protected?

D. Are user private keys properly protected?

☑ **B** and **D.** Digitally signing an e-mail message requires a user's unique private key to which only she has access, which means she had to have sent the message. One factor used to arrive at this conclusion is how well protected user private keys are. If user private keys are simply stored on a hard disk without a password, anybody could have digitally signed the message.

☒ **A** and **C** are incorrect. These are not factors you would consider in this case. **A** is incorrect because encryption is separate from verifying message sender authenticity; it scrambles data to ensure confidentiality. **C** is incorrect because public keys need not be protected; that is why they are called public keys. Their mathematically-related counterpart (private keys) must be safeguarded.

13. What type of evidence would be the most difficult for a perpetrator to forge?

   A. IP address

   B. MAC address

   C. Cell phone SIM card

   D. Documents on a USB flash drive

☑ **C.** Cell phone SIM (Subscriber Identity Module) cards contain unique data such as a serial number, the user's contacts, text messages and other relevant mobile subscriber data. This is used in GSM (Global System for Mobility Communication) mobile devices and allows the user to use any GSM mobile device as long as his SIM card is inserted.

☒ **A, B,** and **D** are incorrect. These are all easily forged (spoofed) with freely available tools.

14. What is the purpose of disk forensic software? (Choose two.)

   A. Use file encryption to ensure copied data mirrors original data.

   B. Use file hashes to ensure copied data mirrors original data.

   C. Protect data on the original disks.

   D. Create file hashes on the original disks.

☑ **B** and **C.** A generated file hash is unique to the file on which it was based. Any change to the file invalidates the file hash. This is a method to digitally ensure the correct version of a file is being analyzed. Data on a seized hard disk must be left intact. Forensic disk software runs on a separate device or boots using its own operating system and uses bit stream copying to copy entire hard disk contents. File hashes should never be generated on the source hard disk; it is imperative that the hard disk remain undisturbed.

☒ **A** and **D** are incorrect. **A** is incorrect because file encryption does not ensure copied data is the same as the source; instead, it scrambles the data so that only authorized persons with the correct decryption key can view it. **D** is incorrect because you should never create file hashes on the original disk; its state at the time of seizure must be preserved.

15. You are preparing to gather evidence from a cell phone. Which of the following is false?

    A. CDMA mobile devices do not use SIM cards.

    B. CDMA mobile devices store user data on the mobile device.

    C. GSM mobile devices do not use SIM cards.

    D. GSM mobile devices use SIM cards.

    ☑ **C.** GSM devices use SIM cards. CDMA (Code Division Multiple Access) mobile devices do not. SIM cards contain personal user information as well as mobile account subscription information. This means you could purchase a new GSM mobile device and simply insert your SIM card without having to contact your mobile wireless service provider

    ☒ **A, B,** and **D** are incorrect. These are all true. The question is asking for which statement is false.

16. You must analyze data on a digital camera's internal memory. You plan to connect your forensic computer to the camera using a USB cable. What should you do to ensure you do not modify data on the camera?

    A. Ensure the camera is turned off.

    B. Flag all files on the camera as read-only.

    C. Log in with a non-administrative account on the forensic computer.

    D. Use a USB write-blocking device.

    ☑ **D.** USB write-blocking devices ensure that data can only travel in one direction when collecting digital evidence from storage media, such as a digital camera's internal memory. The fact that this tool was used must be documented to adhere to chain of custody procedures.

    ☒ **A, B,** and **C** are incorrect. **A** is incorrect because the camera should be left in its seizure state, so you should not power it on if it is powered off. Do not flag anything on the camera as read-only; you must not disturb the state of the camera, therefore **B** is incorrect. **C** is incorrect because simply logging on to a forensic computer using an administrative account has nothing to do with not modifying data on the camera.

17. What can be used to ensure seized mobile wireless devices do not communicate with other devices?

    A. SIM card

    B. Faraday bag

C. Antistatic bag

D. GPS jammer

☑ **B.** A faraday bag is a mobile device shield that prevents wireless signals to or from the mobile device. This must be used immediately upon seizure of a wireless mobile device to ensure data on it is not modified through wireless remote communications.

☒ **A, C,** and **D** are incorrect. SIM cards contain user mobile data, but answer **A** is incorrect because it does not state whether we are inserting or removing the SIM card. **B** is incorrect because antistatic bags shield sensitive electronic components from ESD (electrostatic discharge), but do nothing to prevent wireless signals. **D** is incorrect because GPS (Global Positioning System) jammers prevent unwanted GPS tracking but do not prevent normal wireless communication.

---

18. Robin works as a network technician at a stock brokerage firm. To test network forensic capturing software, she plugs her laptop into an Ethernet switch and begins capturing network traffic. During later analysis, she notices some broadcast and multicast packets as well as only her own computer's network traffic. Why was she unable to capture all network traffic on the switch?

A. She must enable promiscuous mode on her NIC.

B. She must disable promiscuous mode on her NIC.

C. Each switch port is an isolated collision domain.

D. Each switch port is an isolated broadcast domain.

☑ **C.** Ethernet switches isolate each port into its own collision domain. When capturing network traffic, you will not see traffic to or from other computers plugged into other switch ports, other than broadcast and multicast packets. Some switches allow you to copy all switch traffic to a monitoring port, but the scenario did not mention this.

☒ **A, B,** and **D** are incorrect. **A** is required to capture network traffic, but it is not the problem in this case. **B** is untrue. **D** is untrue. Each switch port is a collision domain, but all switch ports can be grouped into VLANs (virtual local area networks); each VLAN is a broadcast domain.

---

19. A NID (network intrusion detection) device captures network traffic during the commission of a crime on a network. You notice NTP and TCP packets from all network hosts in the capture. You must find a way to correlate captured packets to a date and time to ensure the packet captures will be considered as admissible as evidence. What should you do? (Choose two.)

A. Nothing. NTP keeps time in sync on a network.

B. Nothing. Packet captures are time stamped.

    C. Without digital signatures, date and time cannot be authenticated.

    D. Without encryption, date and time cannot be authenticated.

> ☑ **A** and **B**. NTP (Network Time Protocol) keeps computers synchronized to a reliable time source. Captured network traffic is time stamped and includes offset time stamps from when the capture was started.
>
> ☒ **C** and **D** are incorrect. **C** is incorrect because digital signatures ensure the authenticity of the message as well as the sender, but their time stamps are not guaranteed. **D** is incorrect because encryption secures data, but has nothing to do with ensuring date and time stamps are authentic.

20. You arrive at a scene where a computer must be seized as evidence. The computer is powered off and has an external USB hard drive plugged in. What should you do?

    A. Turn on the computer.

    B. Unplug the external USB hard drive.

    C. Thoroughly document the state of the equipment.

    D. Place the computer in a faraday bag.

> ☑ **C**. Thoroughly documenting the state of seized equipment is critical to adhere to chain of custody procedures. Failure to do so will render collected evidence inadmissible.
>
> ☒ **A**, **B**, and **D** are incorrect. Never turn on a computer that was turned off. Turning it on could destroy valuable data, therefore **A** is incorrect. Do not unplug the USB hard drive. **B** is incorrect because you must not disturb the state of the equipment until it has been documented. **D** is incorrect because placing the computer in a faraday bag might be appropriate if it has a wireless interface, but the scene must be documented first.

21. You are asked to examine a hard disk for fragments of instant messaging conversations as well as deleted files. How should you do this?

    A. Use bit stream copying tools.

    B. Log in to the computer and copy the original hard drive contents to an external USB hard drive.

    C. Map a drive across the network to the original hard drive and copy the contents to an external USB hard drive.

    D. View log files.

☑ **A.** Bit stream forensic copying tools copy hard disk data at the bit level, not at the file level. When a file is deleted, it may disappear from the file system, but the file data in its entirety is intact on the hard disk until the hard disk is filled with new data. Deleted files are not copied with file-level copying, but they are with bit stream copying.

☒ **B, C,** and **D** are incorrect. Never log in to a seized computer to copy disk contents. Use an external forensic tool instead; therefore, **B** is incorrect. Do not copy data from a seized computer across the network; this will affect log entries on the target computer and will disturb the original state of the data; therefore, **C** is incorrect. **D** is incorrect because viewing log files could revel data regarding e-mail and instant messaging, but they will not reveal deleted data.

22. Which type of file is most likely to contain incriminating data?

    A. Password-protected Microsoft Word file

    B. Encrypted Microsoft Word file

    C. Digitally signed Microsoft Word file

    D. File hash of Microsoft Word file

☑ **B.** Encrypted files imply somebody sought to protect confidential or incriminating data. The required key (file, passphrase, or physical device) must be used to decrypt the data.

☒ **A, C,** and **D** are incorrect. Compared to an encrypted file, they are not as likely to contain incriminating data.

23. How can a forensic analyst benefit from analyzing metadata? (Choose three.)

    A. JPEG metadata can reveal specific camera settings.

    B. Microsoft Word metadata can reveal the author name.

    C. Microsoft Excel metadata can reveal your MAC address.

    D. PDF metadata can reveal the registered company name.

☑ **A, B,** and **D.** Metadata is information that describes data. For example, a JPEG (Joint Photographic Experts Group) picture taken with a digital camera could also contain hidden data, including camera settings, date and time, and so on. Microsoft Word and PDF (Portable Document Format) documents contain metadata such as the document author name, registered company name, and so on.

☒ **C** is incorrect. This choice is untrue. Excel documents do not record your computer's network card hardware address (MAC address).

24. Which of the following rules must be followed when performing forensic analysis? (Choose two.)

    A. Work only with the original authentic data.

    B. Work only with a copy of data.

    C. Seek legal permission to conduct an analysis.

    D. Seek your manager's permission to conduct an analysis.

    ☑ **B** and **C.** You must obtain proper legal permission to seize and analyze data. Perform analysis on a forensic copy of data; never work on the original data, because this will render evidence inadmissible.

    ☒ **A** and **D** are incorrect. You should never work with the original digital data—this disturbs the data original state. Only work on a forensic copy of the data. Your manager may not have the authority to grant permission for you to examine data; ensure proper legal permission is obtained.

25. Refer to the accompanying illustration. You must determine if network traffic captured on interface E0 on Router A appears authentic or spoofed. You are analyzing a packet destined for Server A. The source MAC address in the packet is 0034D69B088C, and the source IP address is 200.0.0.55. For a legitimate packet, which of the following statements is correct?

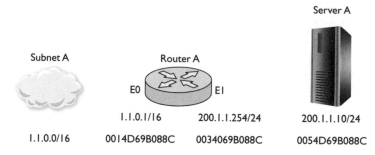

    A. The source MAC address should be 0014D69B088C.

    B. The source IP address cannot be from the 200.1.1.0/24 network.

    C. The source IP address should be 200.1.1.254.

    D. The source IP address should be 1.1.0.1.

    ☑ **B.** A packet entering interface E0 on Router A cannot have a source IP address of 200.0.0.55. A packet from 200.0.0.55 would not pass through the router; it would go directly to Server A because it is on the same subnet. A packet with 200.0.0.55 as an IP address entering from another network has been spoofed.

> ☒ **A, C,** and **D** are incorrect. **A** is incorrect because on a destination network the source MAC address should be that of the last router on the destination network; in this case, 0034D69B088C. **C** and **D** are incorrect because unless NAT or proxy servers are used, the source IP address does not change as packets travel through networks. The MAC address does, however.

26. The IT director is creating the following year's budget. You are asked to submit forensic dollar figures for your IT forensic team. Which one item should you not submit?

    A. Travel expenses

    B. Man hour expenses

    C. Training expenses

    D. ALE amounts

> ☑ **D.** ALE (annual loss expectancy) is used to calculate the probability of asset failure over a year. It is used when performing a risk assessment.
>
> ☒ **A, B,** and **C** are incorrect. These are valid IT forensic budget items.

27. Users report at 9:30 A.M. severely degraded network performance since the work day began at 8:00 A.M. After network analysis and a quick discussion with your IT security team, you conclude a worm virus has infected your network. What should you do to control the damage?

    A. Determine the severity of the security breach.

    B. Unplug SAN devices.

    C. Shut down all servers.

    D. Shut down Ethernet switches.

> ☑ **D.** The quickest way to control the spread of a worm virus is to eliminate network connectivity.
>
> ☒ **A, B,** and **C** are incorrect. **A** is incorrect because the severity would have already been discussed when talking with your IT security team. **B** is incorrect because unplugging SAN (storage area network) devices might protect data on SAN disks from infected servers, but the worm could still spread to other devices. **C** is incorrect because shutting down all servers takes longer than simply powering down network switches.

28. A suspect deletes incriminating files and empties the Windows Recycle Bin. Which two of the following statements are true regarding the deletion?

 A. The files cannot be recovered.

 B. The files can be recovered.

 C. Deleted files contain all of their original data until the hard disk is filled with other data.

 D. Deleted files contain all of their original data until the hard disk is defragmented.

☑ **B** and **C**. Emptying the Windows Recycle Bin makes deleted files inaccessible to Windows users; however, the entire file contents are still on the disk until the disk is filled with other data. A third-party tool must be used to recover the deleted items in this case.

☒ **A** and **D** are incorrect. **A** is incorrect because files emptied from the recycle bin are easily recovered using third-party tools. **D** is incorrect because defragmentation has no impact on whether deleted files can be recovered.

29. The local police suspect a woman is using her computer to commit online fraud, but she encrypts her hard disk with a strong passphrase. Law enforcement would like to access the data on the encrypted disk to obtain forensic evidence. What two tasks should be done?

 A. Harness the processing power of thousands of Internet computers and attempt to crack the encryption passphrase.

 B. Obtain a warrant.

 C. Install a packet sniffer on the suspect's network.

 D. Install a keylogger to capture the passphrase.

☑ **B** and **D**. A warrant should be obtained to install a keylogger on the suspect's computer. A keylogger captures everything typed in, including passphrases used to decrypt hard disks.

☒ **A** and **C** are incorrect. **A** is incorrect because although many computers working together could eventually determine the encryption passphrase, this is not the best option. **C** is incorrect because captured network traffic would not help in determining a hard disk encryption passphrase.

30. A seized USB flash drive contains only natural scenic pictures. Law enforcement were convinced incriminating data was stored on the USB flash drive. What else should be done?

A. Decrypt the USB flash drive.

B. Format the USB flash drive.

C. Check for steganographic hidden data.

D. Analyze the USB flash drive log.

☑ **C.** Steganography is the art of concealing data within other data, such as hiding messages within pictures. There are tools that can identify if this is the case.

☒ **A, B,** and **D** are incorrect. **A** is incorrect because decrypting the USB flash drive would first be required to get to the files, but the question doesn't state that this is the case. **B** is incorrect because formatting the USB drive would be counterproductive. **D** is incorrect because USB flash drives do not have logs, although the operating system might log data activity to and from the USB device.

18

Security Assessments and Audits

CERTIFICATION OBJECTIVES

- ❑ 1.4 Implement and use common protocols

- ❑ 2.1 Explain risk-related concepts

- ❑ 3.6 Analyze and differentiate among types of mitigation and deterrent techniques

- ❑ 3.7 Implement assessment tools and techniques to discover security threats and vulnerabilities

- ❑ 3.8 Within the realm of vulnerability assessments, explain the proper use of penetration testing versus vulnerability scanning

- ❑ 5.1 Explain the function and purpose of authentication services

- ❑ 5.3 Implement appropriate security controls when performing account management

- ❑ 6.1 Summarize general cryptography concepts

QUESTIONS

Periodic testing of computer systems and networks over time identifies security weaknesses. Security assessments are best conducted by a third party, and may be required by government regulation or to acquire business contracts. As a Security + professional, you must know when to use various tools and how to interpret their results.

1. As part of your security audit, you would like to see what type of network traffic is being transmitted on the network. Which tool should you use?
   A. Protocol analyzer
   B. Port scanner
   C. Vulnerability scanner
   D. Password cracker

2. A network consists of 250 computers. You must determine which machines are secure and which are not. Which tool should you use?
   A. Protocol analyzer
   B. Port scanner
   C. Vulnerability scanner
   D. Password cracker

3. You would like to focus and track malicious activity to a particular host in your DMZ. What should you configure?
   A. Honeynet
   B. Honeypot
   C. DMZ tracker
   D. Web server

4. Which tool would you employ to determine which TCP and UDP ports on a host are open?
   A. Vulnerability scanner
   B. Packet sniffer
   C. Performance monitor
   D. Port scanner

5. Which procedure identifies assets, threats, risks, and determines methods to minimize the impact of these threats?
   A. Risk analysis
   B. Vulnerability assessment
   C. Port scanning
   D. Network mapper

6. A technician must identify deviations from normal network activity. Which task must she first perform?

   A. Trend analysis

   B. Baseline analysis

   C. Performance monitor

   D. Risk analysis

7. A developer analyzes source code to ensure there are no errors or potential security risks. Which term best identifies this activity?

   A. Risk assessment

   B. Patch management

   C. Debugging

   D. Code review

8. A Windows computer has not been patched, nor have unnecessary services been disabled. Which of the following statements is true regarding security?

   A. The computer will perform faster.

   B. The computer has a large attack surface.

   C. The computer has a small attack surface.

   D. The computer will perform slower.

9. A network security auditor simulates various network attacks against a corporate network. Which term best defines this procedure?

   A. Vulnerability analysis

   B. Network mapping

   C. Penetration testing

   D. Risk assessment

10. Your manager asks you to configure a collection of purposely vulnerable hosts in a DMZ for the purpose of tracking hacking attempts. What term best describes what you are configuring?

   A. Honeynet

   B. Honeypot

   C. Firewall

   D. Proxy server

11. You run a vulnerability scan on subnet 192.168.1.0/24. The results state TCP ports 135 through 139 are open on most hosts. What does this refer to?

   A. File and Print Sharing

   B. Web server

   C. Mail server

   D. Remote Desktop Protocol

12. You are a network consultant in charge of creating a wireless network infrastructure for a hotel. Toward the end of the implementation your team evaluates the project to ensure it meets the original stated requirements. What is this called?

    A. Penetration testing

    B. Risk assessment

    C. Design review

    D. Code review

13. After careful log examination you realize somebody has hacked into your WEP-secured home wireless network. What can you do to further secure wireless traffic?

    A. Use WPA2 Enterprise.

    B. Use WPA2 PSK.

    C. Disable SSID broadcasting.

    D. Change the SSID name.

14. What should be done to ensure your network security is effective?

    A. Patch all operating systems.

    B. Update the BIOS on all systems.

    C. Periodically test network security controls.

    D. Upgrade to the latest version of Microsoft Office.

15. Which of the following is considered passive security testing?

    A. Capturing network traffic

    B. Brute-force password attack

    C. Dictionary-based disk decryption

    D. OS fingerprinting

16. From the following list, identify the security misconfiguration:

    A. A domain administrative account is used as a service account.

    B. An Active Directory account is used as a service account.

    C. Windows stations receive updates from a WSUS server instead of the Internet.

    D. The Windows Guest account is disabled.

17. A security auditing team has been hired to conduct network penetration tests against a network. The team has not been given any data related to the network or its layout. What type of testing will the team perform?

    A. Black box

    B. White box

    C. Gray box

    D. Blue box

18. Refer to the following illustration. Which of the following two statements are true?

A. The web server IP address is 66.220.151.75.

B. The web server IP address is 192.168.2.12.

C. The web site is not using SSL.

D. Packet 24 is going to the web site.

19. You are having trouble pinging host 192.168.17.45; there are no replies. One of your users must use RDP (Remote Desktop Protocol) against the host to run an application. You cannot test RDP for them because you are currently logged on locally to a Linux server with only a command line. What can you use to quickly determine if RDP is running on 192.168.17.45?

A. Packet sniffer

B. Virus scanner

C. Wireless scanner

D. Port scanner

20. After conducting a security audit, you inform the network owner that you discovered two unencrypted wireless networks. Your client asks how to best secure wireless traffic. Which of the following is the most secure wireless network encryption?

A. WEP

B. WPA

C. WPA2

D. WPA3

21. Refer to the illustration. What configuration error would a security audit find?

A. The Administrator account should be deleted.

B. The Administrator account is enabled and has not been renamed.

C. The Guest account is enabled.

D. The Guest account should be deleted.

22. A security auditor must determine what types of servers are running on a network. Which tool should be used?

A. Network mapper

B. Protocol analyzer

C. Port scanner

D. Virus scanner

23. A security auditor discovers open wireless networks. She must recommend a secure solution. Which of the following is the most secure wireless solution?

A. 802.1x

B. WEP

C. WPA PSK

D. Disable SSID broadcast

24. Which of the following would *not* be considered during a security audit?

A. Locked server rooms

B. Wireless encryption in use

C. Patch status of all hosts

D. Price of server licensing

25. While auditing a Windows Active Directory environment, you discover that administrative accounts do not have configured account lockout policies. Which of the following are security concerns? (Choose two.)

    A. If account lockout is enabled, administrative accounts could be locked out as a result of repeated password attempts.

    B. If account lockout is not enabled, administrative accounts could be subjected to password attacks.

    C. If account lockout is enabled, administrative accounts could be subjected to password attacks.

    D. If account lockout is not enabled, administrative accounts could be locked out as a result of repeated password attempts.

26. You are reviewing password policies during a security audit. Refer to the illustration and identify two security problems.

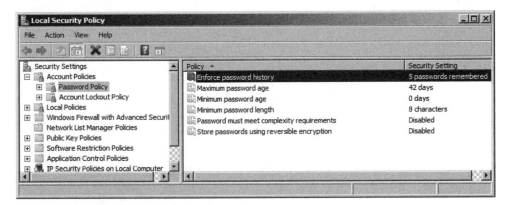

    A. Minimum password age is 0 days.

    B. Password history is set only to 5.

    C. Store passwords using reversible encryption is disabled.

    D. Passwords do not meet complexity requirements.

27. Which type of security testing provides network configuration information to testers?

    A. White box

    B. Black box

    C. Gray box

    D. Blue box

28. Which tool scans for known security threats on a group of computers?
   A. Packet sniffer
   B. Vulnerability scanner
   C. Risk scanner
   D. Port scanner

29. You would like an unused host to log zero-day exploit activity. What should you configure?
   A. Patch server
   B. Honeynet
   C. Honeypot
   D. Virus scanner

30. A large wireless network currently uses WPA PSK. As part of your network audit findings, you recommend a centralized wireless authentication option. What should you recommend?
   A. RADIUS
   B. WEP
   C. WPA2 PSK
   D. TKIP

QUICK ANSWER KEY

1.	A	11.	A	21.	B
2.	C	12.	C	22.	A
3.	B	13.	B	23.	A
4.	D	14.	C	24.	D
5.	A	15.	A	25.	A, B
6.	B	16.	A	26.	A, D
7.	D	17.	A	27.	A
8.	B	18.	A, C	28.	B
9.	C	19.	D	29.	C
10.	A	20.	C	30.	A

IN-DEPTH ANSWERS

1. As part of your security audit, you would like to see what type of network traffic is being transmitted on the network. Which tool should you use?
   A. Protocol analyzer
   B. Port scanner
   C. Vulnerability scanner
   D. Password cracker

   ☑ **A.** Protocol analyzers use a promiscuous-mode network card driver that allows the capture of all network traffic. Each switch port is a collision domain that prevents capturing unicast traffic related to other hosts; however, some switches allow mirroring of all switch traffic to a specific port.

   ☒ **B, C, and D** are incorrect. **B** is incorrect because port scanners identify running services on a host. For example, a running web server might show TCP port 80 as being open. **C** is incorrect because vulnerability scanners assess computers for weaknesses and will often generate reports. **D** is incorrect because password cracking refers to repeated attempts to guess a password and is often automated.

2. A network consists of 250 computers. You must determine which machines are secure and which are not. Which tool should you use?
   A. Protocol analyzer
   B. Port scanner
   C. Vulnerability scanner
   D. Password cracker

   ☑ **C.** Vulnerability scanners scan computers for known security violations and weaknesses.

   ☒ **A, B, and D** are incorrect. **A** is incorrect because protocol analyzers capture network traffic. **B** is incorrect because port scanners list some or all open ports on one or more hosts. **D** is incorrect because password crackers repeatedly attempt to determine a password. Although port scanners and password cracking could be utilized to test system security, a vulnerability scanner provides much more data about computer security, including open ports and vulnerable password settings.

3. You would like to focus and track malicious activity to a particular host in your DMZ. What should you configure?

   A. Honeynet

   B. Honeypot

   C. DMZ tracker

   D. Web server

   ☑ **B.** A honeypot is an intentionally vulnerable host used to attract and track malicious activity.

   ☒ **A, C,** and **D** are incorrect. **A** is incorrect because the question stated activity tracking on a single host, not a network of hosts. **C** is fictitious. **D** is not a tool to track malicious activity; web sites deliver content to web browsers.

4. Which tool would you employ to determine which TCP and UDP ports on a host are open?

   A. Vulnerability scanner

   B. Packet sniffer

   C. Performance monitor

   D. Port scanner

   ☑ **D.** Port scanners identify open ports on hosts. Personal firewall software may impede the success of port scanners. It should also be noted that port scanning can be detected.

   ☒ **A, B,** and **C** are incorrect. **A** is incorrect because vulnerability scanners can detect open ports as well as many more items; if all that is required is a list of open TCP and UDP ports, a port scanner is a better (and faster) choice. **B** is incorrect because packet sniffers capture network traffic, and from that captured traffic you can see port numbers in the TCP and UDP packet headers, but you cannot identify exactly which ports are open on a host. **C** is incorrect because performance monitor is a Windows tool used to measure and monitor performance metrics of a Windows computer; it does not scan for open ports.

5. Which procedure identifies assets, threats, risks, and determines methods to minimize the impact of these threats?

   A. Risk analysis

   B. Vulnerability assessment

   C. Port scanning

   D. Network mapper

☑ **A.** Risk analysis identifies and prioritizes threats while determining how to minimize their effect on business operations.

☒ **B, C, and D are incorrect. B** is incorrect because vulnerability assessment identifies and prioritizes potential threats and are performed during a risk analysis. **C** is incorrect because port scanning identifies open TCP and UDP port; the impact of the open ports is not determined. **D** is incorrect because network mapping refers to the process of creating a map of the network layout, its configuration, and its computer systems. Threats are not identified.

6. A technician must identify deviations from normal network activity. Which task must she first perform?
   A. Trend analysis
   B. Baseline analysis
   C. Performance Monitor
   D. Risk analysis

☑ **B.** A baseline analysis establishes what is normal on a given network. Without this data, it is difficult to determine deviations from the norm.

☒ **A, C, and D are incorrect. A** is incorrect because trend analysis refers to the collection of data in hopes of identifying a pattern. **C** is incorrect because performance monitor is a tool for Windows computers that measures performance metrics such as CPU and memory utilization. **D** is incorrect because risk analysis identifies assets and related risks along with methods to minimize business disruption.

7. A developer analyzes source code to ensure there are no errors or potential security risks. Which term best identifies this activity?
   A. Risk assessment
   B. Patch management
   C. Debugging
   D. Code review

☑ **D.** Code review is an examination of source code in order to uncover errors or security risks.

☒ **A, B, and C are incorrect. A** is incorrect because, although risk assessment might involve code review, risk management also includes identifying assets and threat mitigation. Patch management involves the orderly application of software updates to hosts, so **B** is incorrect. **C** is also incorrect because debugging implies the developer is aware of a specific problem with the code— analyzing code for errors would occur before debugging.

8. A Windows computer has not been patched, nor have unnecessary services been disabled. Which of the following statements is true regarding security?
    A. The computer will perform faster.
    B. The computer has a large attack surface.
    C. The computer has a small attack surface.
    D. The computer will perform slower.

    ☑ **B.** Computers with many potential vulnerabilities (software, physical) are said to have a larger attack surface than patched machines that only run software that is required. A larger attack surface means a higher degree of possibility of a machine becoming compromised.

    ☒ **A, C,** and **D** are incorrect. **A** is incorrect and deals more with performance than with security. Computers generally run faster with patches applied and less services running. **C** is incorrect because the opposite is true. **D** is incorrect because the question refers to security, not performance; the computer might very well be performing slower, since extra unnecessary services may be running.

9. A network security auditor simulates various network attacks against a corporate network. Which term best defines this procedure?
    A. Vulnerability analysis
    B. Network mapping
    C. Penetration testing
    D. Risk assessment

    ☑ **C.** Penetration testing ("pen testing") involves simulating malicious activity against hosts or entire networks in order to assess how secure they are. Proper written consent must be obtained prior to performing this type of testing.

    ☒ **A, B,** and **D** are incorrect. **A** is incorrect because vulnerability analysis identifies and classifies potential threats. **B** is incorrect because network mapping plots the network layout using a discovery tool. **D** is incorrect because risk assessment does not simulate network attacks; it is used to identify business threats and how to mitigate them.

10. Your manager asks you to configure a collection of purposely vulnerable hosts in a DMZ for the purpose of tracking hacking attempts. What term best describes what you are configuring?

    A. Honeynet

    B. Honeypot

    C. Firewall

    D. Proxy server

> ☑ **A.** A honeynet is composed of two or more honeypots. These are intentionally vulnerable hosts used to track malicious activity.
>
> ☒ **B, C,** and **D** are incorrect. **B** is incorrect because the question stated a collection of hosts, not a single (honeypot) host. **C** and **D** are incorrect because firewalls and proxy servers should never be left intentionally vulnerable.

11. You run a vulnerability scan on subnet 192.168.1.0/24. The results state TCP ports 135 through 139 are open on most hosts. What does this refer to?

    A. File and Print Sharing

    B. Web server

    C. Mail server

    D. Remote Desktop Protocol

> ☑ **A.** Windows File and Print Sharing generally use TCP ports 135–139.
>
> ☒ **B, C,** and **D** are incorrect. Web servers typically use TCP port 80 (clear text) or 443 (SSL). Mail servers use a variety of ports, depending on their type and role. For example, SMTP (Simple Mail Transfer Protocol) servers listen on TCP port 25. The Remote Desktop Protocol uses TCP port 3389.

12. You are a network consultant in charge of creating a wireless network infrastructure for a hotel. Toward the end of the implementation your team evaluates the project to ensure it meets the original stated requirements. What is this called?

    A. Penetration testing

    B. Risk assessment

    C. Design review

    D. Code review

> ☑ **C.** Design review is a process whereby the original project objectives are compared against current progress to ensure the objectives are being met.

☒ **A, B**, and **D** are incorrect. **A** is incorrect because penetration testing simulates attacks against hosts or networks to test their security. **B** is incorrect because risk asseseement determines which assets need protection from risks and how to minimize the threat impact. **D** is incorrect because a code review refers to the analysis of computer source code to ensure it functions as intended and does not contain errors or security holes.

13. After careful log examination you realize somebody has hacked into your WEP-secured home wireless network. What can you do to further secure wireless traffic?
    A. Use WPA2 Enterprise.
    B. Use WPA2 PSK.
    C. Disable SSID broadcasting.
    D. Change the SSID name.

☑ **B.** WPA2 (Wi-Fi Protected Access) PSK (Pre-Shared Key) is considered more secure than WEP (Wired Equivalent Privacy).

☒ **A, C**, and **D** are incorrect. **A** is incorrect because WPA2 Enterprise requires a central authentication server; the average user will not have one at home. **C** is incorrect because disabling SSID (station set identifier) suppresses the WLAN name from appearing in Wi-Fi beacon packets, but this is easily circumvented with freely available tools. **D** is incorrect because changing the SSID name may make it difficult for a hacker to identify what he is breaking into, but WPA2 is a much more secure solution.

14. What should be done to ensure your network security is effective?
    A. Patch all operating systems.
    B. Update the BIOS on all systems.
    C. Periodically test network security controls.
    D. Upgrade to the latest version of Microsoft Office.

☑ **C.** Period network testing, perhaps even penetration testing, is valuable to ensure your network security controls remain valid over time.

☒ **A, B**, and **D** are incorrect. **A, B**, and **D** are all important for a single host's security, but the question asks about network security; therefore, answer C is the best answer.

15. Which of the following is considered passive security testing?
   A. Capturing network traffic
   B. Brute-force password attack
   C. Dictionary-based disk decryption
   D. OS fingerprinting

> ☑ **A.** Passive security testing techniques do not interfere with the normal operation of a computer system or network. Capturing network traffic simply takes a copy of network packets already being transmitted.
>
> ☒ **B, C,** and **D** are incorrect. These are not passive testing techniques. Brute-force password attacks, disk decryption, and OS fingerprinting all must interact directly with a computer system and might affect the performance or normal operation of that host.

16. From the following list, identify the security misconfiguration:
   A. A domain administrative account is used as a service account.
   B. An Active Directory account is used as a service account.
   C. Windows stations receive updates from a WSUS server instead of the Internet.
   D. The Windows Guest account is disabled.

> ☑ **A.** Windows services (and Unix and Linux daemons) must run under the context of a user account. Assigning a powerful domain administrative account presents a major threat in the event that the service is compromised—the hacker would then have domain administrative privileges. Service accounts should only have the rights and permissions required to function, nothing more. Many administrators do not force periodic password changes for service accounts, which presents yet another security risk.
>
> ☒ **B, C,** and **D** are incorrect. **B** is incorrect because some services run on Windows Domain Controller computers and must use an Active Directory account. **C** is incorrect because using WSUS (Windows Server Update Services) to update client workstations is considered ideal; this is not a security misconfiguration. **D** is incorrect because the Windows guest account is disabled by default in newer Windows versions. It should not be enabled in the interest of security and user auditing.

17. A security auditing team has been hired to conduct network penetration tests against a network. The team has not been given any data related to the network or its layout. What type of testing will the team perform?
   A. Black box
   B. White box

C. Gray box

D. Blue box

☑ **A.** Black box testing refers to the process by which computer software or networks are tested where the testers have no information on how the software or networks are designed.

☒ **B, C,** and **D** are incorrect. **B** is incorrect because white box testing means the testers have been given details regarding the item they are testing, for example, software source code, or network diagrams. **C** is incorrect because testers have a minimal knowledge of the internals of software or network configuration when conducting gray box testing. This allows testers to make better-informed testing decisions. **D** is incorrect because blue box testing does not exist; in the past a blue box was a device used to make free long-distance telephone calls.

---

18. Refer to the following illustration. Which of the following two statements are true?

A. The web server IP address is 66.220.151.75.

B. The web server IP address is 192.168.2.12.

C. The web site is not using SSL.

D. Packet 24 is going to the web site.

☑ **A and C.** Packet 24 shows the packet coming from 66.220.151.75 with a source port of 80 (look at the middle of the figure at the "Transmission Control Protocol, Src Port" area). Since web servers use port 80, we now know the IP address of the web server. Because the packet payload (bottom-right panel) contains readable text, we know the packet is not encrypted with SSL (Secure Sockets Layer). We could determine this another way as well; SSL web servers normally use TCP port 443, not 80.

☒ **B and D** are incorrect. **B** is incorrect because the client station IP address is 192.168.2.12 (look at the "Transmission Control Protocol" destination port of 3837 in Packet 24). **D** is incorrect because if this were the web server, traffic would be going to either port 80 or port 443. Web browsing clients are assigned a dynamic port value above 1024 (such as 3837) that is used when receiving data from the web server.

19. You are having trouble pinging host 192.168.17.45; there are no replies. One of your users must use RDP (Remote Desktop Protocol) against the host to run an application. You cannot test RDP for them because you are currently logged on locally to a Linux server with only a command line. What can you use to quickly determine if RDP is running on 192.168.17.45?
    A. Packet sniffer
    B. Virus scanner
    C. Wireless scanner
    D. Port scanner

☑ **D.** A port scanner is a quick simple way to determine which ports are open on a host. Even though ping packets may be blocked, RDP packets may not be.

☒ **A, B,** and **C** are incorrect. **A** is incorrect because a packet sniffer captures transmitted network traffic, but it cannot determine if RDP is available on 192.168.17.45. **B** is incorrect because a virus scanner looks for malicious code; they do not test for open ports on remote hosts. **C** is incorrect because a wireless scanner lists wireless networks within range; they do not perform port scans.

20. After conducting a security audit, you inform the network owner that you discovered two unencrypted wireless networks. Your client asks how to best secure wireless traffic. Which of the following is the most secure wireless network encryption?
    A. WEP
    B. WPA
    C. WPA2
    D. WPA3

☑ **C.** WPA2 is the most secure option from the presented list. Unlike WPA, WPA2 must be tested and certified by the Wi-Fi Alliance. WPA2 also uses a stronger encryption implementation.

☒ **A, B,** and **D** are incorrect. **A** is incorrect because WEP (Wired Equivalent Privacy) encryption is easily broken, sometimes within seconds, with freely available tools. **B** is incorrect because WPA addresses weaknesses with WEP, but WPA2 is superior to WPA. **D** is incorrect because WPA3 does not exist (yet).

21. Refer to the illustration. What configuration error would a security audit find?

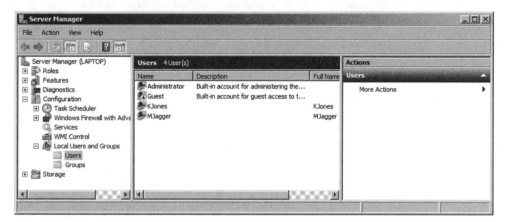

A. The Administrator account should be deleted.

B. The Administrator account is enabled and has not been renamed.

C. The Guest account is enabled.

D. The Guest account should be deleted.

☑ **B.** Default administrative accounts must be renamed and/or disabled. Malicious users will try default admin accounts before moving on. Consider renaming the default admin account and creating a new "administrator" named account (as a regular user) with no rights or permissions. Always have more than one inconspicuous administrative account.

☒ **A, C,** and **D** are incorrect. **A, C,** and **D** are incorrect because the Windows Administrator and Guest accounts cannot be deleted because they are built-in accounts, but they can be renamed and/or disabled.

22. A security auditor must determine what types of servers are running on a network. Which tool should be used?

    A. Network mapper

    B. Protocol analyzer

    C. Port scanner

    D. Virus scanner

    ☑ **A.** Network mapping utilities such as the open-source Cheops tool can map out a network's layout and identify operating systems running on hosts.

    ☒ **B, C,** and **D** are incorrect. **B** is incorrect because protocol analyzer only captures transmitted network traffic; they do not scan for network hosts or network configuration. **C** is incorrect because a port scanner identifies listening ports. **D** is incorrect because a virus scanner protects against malicious software on a host; they do not scan entire networks.

23. A security auditor discovers open wireless networks. She must recommend a secure solution. Which of the following is the most secure wireless solution?

    A. 802.1x

    B. WEP

    C. WPA PSK

    D. Disable SSID broadcast

    ☑ **A.** 802.1x requires that connecting hosts and/or users first authenticate with a central authentication server before even gaining access to the network. This is considered the most secure of the listed choices, since WEP and WPA PSK do not require authentication to get on the network; only a passphrase is required. Neither of the two uses a centralized authentication server.

    ☒ **B, C,** and **D** are incorrect. **B** is incorrect because WEP encryption is easily defeated with freely available tools, so it is not a secure choice. **C** is incorrect because WPA PSK is more secure than WEP, but WPA2 PSK would be a more secure choice if it were listed. **D** is incorrect because disabling the SSID broadcast will only stop the very inexperienced wireless hackers. 802.1x is the most secure option from the presented list.

24. Which of the following would not be considered during a security audit?

    A. Locked server rooms

    B. Wireless encryption in use

    C. Patch status of all hosts

    D. Price of server licensing

☑ **D.** The cost of licensing software is not considered during a security audit. Ensuring license compliance might be considered, but not the cost of the licenses.

☒ **A, B,** and **C** are incorrect. **A, B,** and **C** are incorrect because these are all valid considerations during a security audit because they directly impact how secure data systems are.

25. While auditing a Windows Active Directory environment, you discover that administrative accounts do not have configured account lockout policies. Which of the following are security concerns? (Choose two.)

   A. If account lockout is enabled, administrative accounts could be locked out as a result of repeated password attempts.

   B. If account lockout is not enabled, administrative accounts could be subjected to password attacks.

   C. If account lockout is enabled, administrative accounts could be subjected to password attacks.

   D. If account lockout is not enabled, administrative accounts could be locked out as a result of repeated password attempts.

☑ **A** and **B.** These answers present a catch 22 scenario. The best solution is to authenticate admin accounts with a smartcard. This would eliminate remote attacks on admin accounts due to the requirement of possessing a physical smartcard.

☒ **C** and **D** are incorrect. **C** is incorrect because account lockout impedes the success of password attacks by locking the account for a time after a small number of successive incorrect passwords. **D** is incorrect because not configuring account lockout means password attacks could run against admin accounts incessantly.

26. You are reviewing password policies during a security audit. Refer to the illustration and identify two security problems.

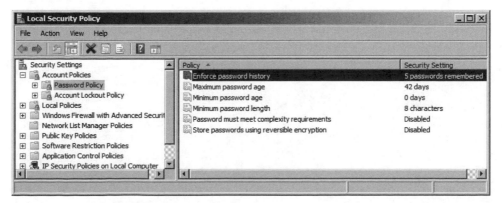

A. Minimum password age is 0 days.
B. Password history is set only to 5.
C. Store passwords using reversible encryption is disabled.
D. Passwords do not meet complexity requirements.

> ☑ **A and D.** The minimum password age prevents users from immediately changing their password a number of times (password history) to return to one they have already used that is easy to remember. Complexity requirements on Windows systems means the password cannot contain any variation of the username, it must be at least six characters long, it must contain an uppercase/lowercase character and number, and so on.
>
> ☒ **B and C** are incorrect. Compared to answers A and D, **B** is not a security issue. **C** is incorrect because storing passwords using reversible encryption is meant to be used by specific software needing the user password. Enabling this option does not store the passwords in a secure manner.

27. Which type of security testing provides network configuration information to testers?
    A. White box
    B. Black box
    C. Gray box
    D. Blue box

> ☑ **A.** A white box test provides testers with detailed configuration information regarding the software or network they are testing.
>
> ☒ **B, C, and D** are incorrect. **B** is incorrect because black box testing provides no information at all to system testers. **C** is incorrect because gray box testing provides some, but not detailed, information to testers, which allows a more informed testing environment. **D** is incorrect because blue box testing does not exist in this context.

28. Which tool scans for known security threats on a group of computers?
    A. Packet sniffer
    B. Vulnerability scanner
    C. Risk scanner
    D. Port scanner

☑ **B.** Vulnerability scanners normally use an updated database of known security vulnerabilities and misconfigurations for various operating systems and network devices. This database is compared against a single host or a network scan to determine if any hosts or devices are vulnerable. Reports can then be generated from the scan.

☒ **A, C, and D are incorrect. A** is incorrect because packet sniffers are not designed to look for vulnerabilities; they simply capture transmitted network packets. **C** does not exist. **D** does not identify security threats; port scanners list open TCP and UDP ports.

29. You would like an unused host to log zero-day exploit activity. What should you configure?
    A. Patch server
    B. Honeynet
    C. Honeypot
    D. Virus scanner

☑ **C.** Honeypots are intentionally exposed systems used to attract the attention of hackers or malicious code for further study.

☒ **A, B, and D are incorrect. A** is incorrect because patch server ensures software on network hosts is kept up to date. **B** is incorrect because honeynet is a collection of two or more honeypots; the question specifically states a single host. **D** is incorrect because a virus scanner would not detect zero-day exploits. A zero-day exploit is a vulnerability that has not yet been made known to the software author or virus scanner.

30. A large wireless network currently uses WPA PSK. As part of your network audit findings, you recommend a centralized wireless authentication option. What should you recommend?
    A. RADIUS
    B. WEP
    C. WPA2 PSK
    D. TKIP

☑ **A.** RADIUS (Remote Authentication Dial In User Service) is a central server that authenticates users connecting to a network. Failure to authenticate to the RADIUS server means access to the network is denied.

☒ **B, C, and D are incorrect. B** is incorrect because WEP is not a centralized authentication mechanism; it must be configured on each access point and client station. **C** is incorrect because WPA2 PSK must also be configured on each access point and client. **D** is incorrect because TKIP (Temporal Key Integrity Protocol) uses key mixing and packets sequence counters to enhance security. It is used with WPA to address the lack of security offered by WEP.

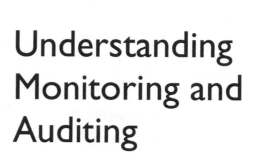

19

Understanding Monitoring and Auditing

CERTIFICATION OBJECTIVES

❑   1.2   Apply and implement secure network administration principles

❑   3.6   Analyze and differentiate among different types of mitigation and deterrent techniques

QUESTIONS

Monitoring networks and host computers proactively can detect or even prevent successful attacks. Network intrusion detection systems detect and report suspicious network activity. Host intrusion detection systems detect and report suspicious host-based activity. Prevention systems have the ability to stop attacks once they have begun. Log files present a method of tracing activity that has already occurred. Today's networks include logs in many places—you must know which log to consult under specific circumstances.

1. Which tool can stop in-progress attacks to your network?
   A. NIDS
   B. NIPS
   C. Proxy server
   D. Packet filtering firewall

2. Which of the following could an administrator use to determine if there has been unauthorized use of a wireless LAN?
   A. Protocol analyzer
   B. Proxy server
   C. Performance monitor
   D. Wireless access point log

3. You are responsible for managing an internal FTP server. A user reports that files available on the server yesterday are no longer available. Where can you look to determine what happened to the missing files?
   A. Firewall log
   B. FTP access log
   C. FTP download log
   D. FTP upload log

4. As a Windows server administrator for server ALPHA, you configure auditing so that you can track who deletes files on file share SALES. Where will you view the audit results?
   A. Security log
   B. Audit log
   C. Application log
   D. Deletion log

5. Your manager asks you to configure a honeypot to track malicious user activity. You install the host in the DMZ without any patches and configure a web site and an SMTP server on it. You have configured nothing else on the host. Identify a problem with this configuration.

    A. Patch the honeypot.

    B. Honeypots should not run a web site.

    C. Forward honeypot logs to another, secured host.

    D. Honeypots should not run SMTP services.

6. Which two of the following are true regarding behavior-based network monitoring?

    A. A baseline of normal behavior must be established.

    B. Deviations from acceptable activity cannot be monitored.

    C. New threats can be blocked.

    D. A database of known attack patterns is consulted.

7. You have configured a NIPS appliance to prevent web server directory traversal attacks. What type of configuration is this?

    A. Behavior-based

    B. Signature-based

    C. Anomaly-based

    D. Web-based

8. An administrator reports that a Windows file server is performing much more slowly than it normally does. The server is fully patched and has an up-to-date virus scanner. You open an RDP connection to the server to investigate the problem. Which tool should you first use?

    A. Virus scanner

    B. Port scanner

    C. System restore point

    D. Performance Monitor

9. You have inherited the responsibility of managing an office network for which there is no documentation. As you perform desktop support duties over time, you notice many users seem to have more privileges on the network than they need. What should you do?

    A. Delete and recreate all user accounts.

    B. Conduct a user access and rights review.

    C. Check server audit logs.

    D. Enforce stronger user passwords.

10. To adhere to new corporate security guidelines, your branch offices must track details regarding visited web sites. What should you install?

    A. VPN

    B. Proxy server

    C. Packet filtering firewall

    D. NIDS

11. You would like to know when user accounts are modified in any way. What should you configure?

    A. Keyloggers on all user stations

    B. Firewall auditing

    C. User account auditing

    D. Personal firewall on all user stations

12. Which of the following are true regarding NIDSs? (Choose two.)

    A. Network traffic is analyzed for malicious packets.

    B. Alerts and notifications can be configured.

    C. Malicious packets are dropped.

    D. Laptops are protected when disconnected from the LAN.

13. Which of the following is true regarding HIDSs (host intrusion detection systems)?

    A. Suspicious traffic entering the network can be blocked.

    B. Encrypted transmissions cannot be monitored.

    C. It must be installed on each system where needed.

    D. HIDSs can attempt to stop attacks in progress.

14. Your company would like to standardize how long various types of documents are kept and deleted. What is needed to do this?

    A. Storage retention policy

    B. RAID 0

    C. Disaster recovery policy

    D. RAID 1

15. You are asked to analyze events in a firewall log that occurred six months ago. When you analyze the log file, you notice events only go back two months. What is the problem?

    A. You must have administrative access to the logs.

    B. The log file size is too small.

    C. Firewalls cannot keep logs for more than two months.

    D. The firewall is not patched.

16. A Windows administrator must track key performance metrics for a group of seven Windows servers. What should she do?

A. Run Performance Monitor on each host.

B. RDP into each host and run Performance Monitor.

C. RDP into each host and check Event Viewer logs.

D. Run Performance Monitor on her machine and add counters from the other seven servers.

17. You are a firewall appliance administrator for your company. Previously restricted outbound RDP packets are now successfully reaching external hosts, and you did not configure this firewall allowance. Where should you look to see who made the firewall change and when?

A. Security log

B. Firewall log

C. Audit log

D. Event Viewer logs

18. In reviewing your firewall log, you notice a large number of your stations connecting to http://www.freetripsforyou.com and downloading an .EXE file, sometimes in the middle of the night. Your users state they did not visit the web site. Your firewall does not allow any inbound packets initiated from the Internet. What does this indicate?

A. User stations are connecting to Windows Update to apply patches.

B. User stations have been hijacked and are downloading malware.

C. User stations are infected with a password cracking program.

D. User stations are being controlled from the Internet through RDP.

19. A corporate network baseline has been established over the course of two weeks. Using this baseline data, you configure your intrusion prevention systems to notify you of abnormal network activity. A new sales initiative requires sales employees to run high-bandwidth usage applications across the Internet. As a result, you begin receiving security alerts regarding abnormal network activity. What are these type of alerts referred to as?

A. False positives

B. False negatives

C. True positives

D. True negatives

20. What can be done to prevent malicious users from tampering with log files? (Choose three.)

A. Store log files on a secured centralized logging host.

B. Encrypt archived log files.

C. Run Windows Update.

D. Generate file hashes for log files.

21. You have been asked to identify any irregularities from the following sequential lines from a web server log:

```
199.0.14.202, -, 03/15/09, 8:33:12, W3SVC2, SERVER, 192.168.1.1, 4502
12.168.12.79, -, 03/15/09, 8:34:09, W3SVC2, SERVER, 192.168.1.1, 3455
12.168.12.79, -, 03/15/09, 17:02:26, W3SVC2, SERVER, 192.168.1.1, 4302
192.16.255.202, -, 03/15/09, 17:03:11, W3SVC2, SERVER, 192.168.1.1, 4111
```

    A. 199.0.14.202 is not a valid IP address.

    B. 192.16.255.202 is not a valid IP address.

    C. Web servers cannot use 192.168.1.1.

    D. The log is missing entries for a long period of time.

22. You are the Windows server administrator for a clothing outlet in Manhattan, New York. There are six Windows Server 2008 Active Directory computers used regularly. Files are being modified on servers during non-business hours. You would like to audit who makes the changes and when. What is the quickest method of deploying your audit settings?

    A. Configure audit settings using Group Policy.

    B. Configure each server with the appropriate audit settings.

    C. Configure one server appropriately, export the settings, import to the other five.

    D. Delegate the audit configuration task to six other administrators.

23. What is the difference between a packet sniffer and a NIDS?

    A. There is no difference.

    B. Packet sniffers put the network card in promiscuous mode.

    C. A NIDS puts the network card(s) in promiscuous mode.

    D. Packet sniffers do not analyze captured traffic.

24. Your manager has asked you to identify which internal client computers have been controlled using RDP (Remote Desktop Protocol) from the Internet. What should you do?

    A. Check the logs on each computer.

    B. Check the logs on your RDP servers.

    C. Check your firewall log.

    D. Contact your ISP and have them check their logs.

25. What is a potential problem with enabling detailed verbose logging on hosts for long periods of time?

    A. There is no problem.

    B. Performance degrades.

    C. Network bandwidth is consumed.

    D. Verbose logging consumes a user license.

26. A user, Jeff, reports his client Windows XP station has been slow and unstable since last Tuesday. What should you first do?

  A. Use System Restore to revert the computer state to last Monday.

  B. Check log entries for Monday and Tuesday on Jeff's computer.

  C. Run Windows Update.

  D. Re-image Jeff's computer.

27. User workstations on your network connect through NAT (Network Address Translation) to a DMZ (demilitarized zone), where your Internet perimeter firewall exists. On Friday night a user connects to an inappropriate web site. You happened to have been capturing all network traffic on the DMZ at the time. How can you track which user workstation visited the web site? (Choose two.)

  A. View logs on the NAT router.

  B. View logs on the perimeter firewall.

  C. View your packet capture.

  D. View all workstation web browser histories.

28. An administrator is scheduling backup for Windows servers. She chooses to back up system state as well as user data folders on drive D:. What else should she have included in the backup?

  A. Drive C:

  B. Log files

  C. Wallpaper images

  D. Registry

29. You are monitoring the performance on a Unix server called Alpha. Alpha is used to host concurrent remote sessions for users. You notice that long periods of intense server disk activity on Alpha coincide with remote users working with large documents stored on a separate Unix server called Bravo. What might be causing the degraded performance on Alpha?

  A. Too much network traffic.

  B. The CPU is too slow.

  C. The disks are too slow.

  D. There is not enough RAM.

30. A server, Charlie, runs a mission-critical database application. The application encrypts all data from connected client workstations. You would like to monitor Charlie for suspicious activity and prevent any potential attacks. What should you deploy?

  A. Honeypot

  B. HIPS

  C. NIDS

  D. PKI

QUICK ANSWER KEY

1.	B	11.	C	21.	D
2.	D	12.	A, B	22.	A
3.	B	13.	C	23.	D
4.	A	14.	A	24.	C
5.	C	15.	B	25.	B
6.	A, C	16.	D	26.	B
7.	B	17.	C	27.	A
8.	D	18.	B	28.	B
9.	B	19.	A	29.	D
10.	B	20.	A, B, D	30.	B

IN-DEPTH ANSWERS

1. Which tool can stop in-progress attacks to your network?
  A. NIDS
  B. NIPS
  C. Proxy server
  D. Packet filtering firewall

    ☑   **B.** NIPSs (network intrusion prevention systems) analyze network traffic patterns. Some implementations have a database of known attack patterns, while others can take notice of abnormal traffic for a specific network. Measures can then be taken to stop the attack, for example, by simply dropping the offending packets.

    ☒   **A, C,** and **D** are incorrect. **A** is incorrect because NIDSs (network intrusion detection systems) can detect network anomalies, but they don't stop them; instead they raise an alert or notify an administrator. **C** is incorrect because proxy servers retrieve Internet content on behalf of users; they do not analyze network traffic at all. **D** is incorrect because packet filtering firewalls only analyze packet headers to determine if traffic should be allowed or denied; they are not designed to stop in-progress network attacks; NIPSs are.

2. Which of the following could an administrator use to determine if there has been unauthorized use of a wireless LAN?
  A. Protocol analyzer
  B. Proxy server
  C. Performance monitor
  D. Wireless access point log

    ☑   **D.** A wireless access point log can reveal all wireless LAN activity. Some access points may require you to enable logging.

    ☒   **A, B,** and **C** are incorrect. **A** is incorrect because protocol analyzers capture network traffic; the question asks if unauthorized WLAN usage in the past can be determined. **B** is incorrect because proxy servers have nothing to do with wireless LANs. **C** is incorrect because performance monitors measure various metrics of a computer system.

3. You are responsible for managing an internal FTP server. A user reports that files available on the server yesterday are no longer available. Where can you look to determine what happened to the missing files?

A. Firewall log

B. FTP access log

C. FTP download log

D. FTP upload log

> ☑ **B.** FTP (File Transfer Protocol) access logs list file activity on FTP servers, including file deletions or renames.
>
> ☒ **A, C,** and **D** are incorrect. **A** is incorrect because firewall logs can list traffic to or from an FTP site, but unless the firewall logs all packet payloads (this is rare for performance and space reasons), it cannot reveal who deleted or renamed files on the FTP site. **C** and **D** are incorrect because FTP download and upload logs are just that: records of who downloaded files from the FTP server and who uploaded files to the FTP server, respectively.

4. As a Windows server administrator for server ALPHA, you configure auditing so that you can track who deletes files on file share SALES. Where will you view the audit results?

A. Security log

B. Audit log

C. Application log

D. Deletion log

> ☑ **A.** Windows machines write audit data to the event viewer security log.
>
> ☒ **B, C,** and **D** are incorrect. **B** and **D** are incorrect because Windows machines do not have audit or application log. **C** is incorrect because an application log lists events related to specific applications, not audit data.

5. Your manager asks you to configure a honeypot to track malicious user activity. You install the host in the DMZ without any patches and configure a web site and an SMTP server on it. You have configured nothing else on the host. Identify a problem with this configuration.

A. Patch the honeypot.

B. Honeypots should not run a web site.

C. Forward honeypot logs to another, secured host.

D. Honeypots should not run SMTP services.

☑ **C.** The honeypot host is unpatched and is therefore vulnerable. Storing the only copy of log files on a honeypot is self-defeating.

☒ **A, B,** and **D** are incorrect. **A** is incorrect because the honeypot does not need to be patched; this creates an easy target for malicious users and/or malicious code. **B** and **D** are incorrect because honeypots can run web or SMTP mail services if you want to track related malicious activity.

6. Which two of the following are true regarding behavior-based network monitoring?
   A. A baseline of normal behavior must be established.
   B. Deviations from acceptable activity cannot be monitored.
   C. New threats can be blocked.
   D. A database of known attack patterns is consulted.

☑ **A** and **C.** Behavior-based monitoring detects activity that deviates from the norm. A baseline is required to establish what normal is. Because of this, new attacks could potentially be stopped if they do not conform to normal network usage patterns.

☒ **B** and **D** are incorrect. **B** is incorrect—the opposite is true. **D** is incorrect; signature-based monitoring uses a database of known attack patterns to compare against current network activity.

7. You have configured a NIPS appliance to prevent web server directory traversal attacks. What type of configuration is this?
   A. Behavior-based
   B. Signature-based
   C. Anomaly-based
   D. Web-based

☑ **B.** Comparing known attacks against current activity is called signature-based detection.

☒ **A, C,** and **D** are incorrect. **A** and **C** generally mean the same thing. A deviation from normal behavior is referred to as an anomaly. **D** is a fictitious detection method in this context.

8. An administrator reports that a Windows file server is performing much more slowly than it normally does. The server is fully patched and has an up-to-date virus scanner. You open an RDP connection to the server to investigate the problem. Which tool should you first use?

   A. Virus scanner

   B. Port scanner

   C. System restore point

   D. Performance Monitor

   ☑ **D.** Windows machines include Performance Monitor to measure which aspect of the software or hardware is not performing as well as it should.

   ☒ **A, B,** and **C** are incorrect. None of these is the first thing to do when a machine performs slowly. **A** is incorrect because the question states the virus scanner is up to date, so running a virus scan is pointless, since modern virus scanners watch all activity in real time. **B** is incorrect because port scanners only show open ports; they cannot identify why a system is slowing down. **C** is incorrect because system restore points can sometimes revert the computer to a previous (and faster) state to solve these types of problems, but Windows servers do not support system restore points.

9. You have inherited the responsibility of managing an office network for which there is no documentation. As you perform desktop support duties over time, you notice many users seem to have more privileges on the network than they need. What should you do?

   A. Delete and recreate all user accounts.

   B. Conduct a user access and rights review.

   C. Check server audit logs.

   D. Enforce stronger user passwords.

   ☑ **B.** A user access and rights review identifies the rights and permissions users must have compared against what they have been given. In this case, the review would reveal what needs to be changed so that users only have the rights needed to do their jobs.

   ☒ **A, C,** and **D** are incorrect. **A** is incorrect because there is no reason to delete and recreate user accounts; existing account permissions and rights could be configured properly instead. **C** and **D** are incorrect because server audit logs could reveal how and when users got so many rights, but this will not help you solve the problem; nor will stronger user passwords.

10. To adhere to new corporate security guidelines, your branch offices must track details regarding visited web sites. What should you install?

A. VPN

B. Proxy server

C. Packet filtering firewall

D. NIDS

☑ **B.** Proxy servers can track detailed web surfing activity, including site visited, time of day, user account name, and so on.

☒ **A, C,** and **D** are incorrect. **A** is incorrect because VPNs (virtual private networks) allow secure connection to a private LAN across an untrusted network, but they do not track web surfing activity. **C** is incorrect because packet filtering firewalls cannot track details, although they can log general network traffic allowed to pass through the firewall. **D** is incorrect because NIDSs do not track visited web sites; they instead analyze network traffic for irregularities and then trigger alarms or notifications.

11. You would like to know when user accounts are modified in any way. What should you configure?

A. Keyloggers on all user stations

B. Firewall auditing

C. User account auditing

D. Personal firewall on all user stations

☑ **C.** Enabling auditing of user account administrative activities will log any modifications made to user accounts.

☒ **A, B,** and **D** are incorrect. Keyloggers capture all keystrokes on a given host; this is not what is required in this case, so **A** is incorrect. Firewall auditing would apply to firewall activity, not specifically to user account modifications. Some firewalls do have their own user account capabilities, but answer **C** is a better one, so **B** is incorrect. **D** is incorrect because personal firewalls do not track changes to user accounts.

12. Which of the following are true regarding NIDSs? (Choose two.)

A. Network traffic is analyzed for malicious packets.

B. Alerts and notifications can be configured.

C. Malicious packets are dropped.

D. Laptops are protected when disconnected from the LAN.

☑ **A and B.** NIDSs do analyze network traffic for malicious packets, and they then trigger an alarm or notification.

☒ **C and D are incorrect. C** is incorrect because NIPSs have the ability to drop malicious packets; NIDSs do not. **D** is incorrect because a NIDS does absolutely nothing to protect laptops disconnected from the LAN. A HIDS could, though.

13. Which of the following is true regarding HIDSs (host intrusion detection systems)?
    A. Suspicious traffic entering the network can be blocked.
    B. Encrypted transmissions cannot be monitored.
    C. It must be installed on each system where needed.
    D. HIDSs can attempt to stop attacks in progress.

☑ **C.** A HIDS is a host-based solution and thus must be installed on hosts where you would like this protection. HIDSs have the benefit of being very application specific.

☒ **A, B,** and **D are incorrect. A** is incorrect because a HIDS cannot block suspicious traffic entering the network; this is the job of a NIPS. **B** is incorrect because a HIDS resides on a host, encrypted network traffic is no longer encrypted by the time the HIDS analyzes it (if it does at all). **D** is incorrect because a HIDS does not attempt to stop attacks in progress as a HIPS can.

14. Your company would like to standardize how long various types of documents are kept and deleted. What is needed to do this?
    A. Storage retention policy
    B. RAID 0
    C. Disaster recovery policy
    D. RAID 1

☑ **A.** Storage retention policies are sometime mandated by government regulation. Even if they are not, this type of policy states how and where data is stored, how it is backed up, how long it must be kept, and how it is to be disposed of.

☒ **B, C,** and **D are incorrect.** These choices are simply inapplicable. **B** is incorrect because RAID (redundant array of inexpensive disks) 0 increases disk performance by striping data writes across multiple physical disks. **D** is incorrect because RAID 1 provides fault tolerance (disk mirroring); data written to one disk is automatically immediately written to the second disk. **C** is incorrect because disaster recovery policy outlines what is done by whom in the event of a catastrophe.

15. You are asked to analyze events in a firewall log that occurred six months ago. When you analyze the log file, you notice events only go back two months. What is the problem?

A. You must have administrative access to the logs.

B. The log file size is too small.

C. Firewalls cannot keep logs for more than two months.

D. The firewall is not patched.

☑ **B. The firewall is probably configured to overwrite oldest log entries first once the maximum log size has been reached. Even if this is the case, there are normally log archival options available for configuration.**

☒ **A, C, and D are incorrect. A** is incorrect because administrative rights are definitely required to access firewall logs, but you wouldn't be able to see any entries if you did not have this privilege. **C** is in correct because most firewalls can keep logs as long as you configure them to (log archiving). **D** is incorrect because failure to patch a firewall (software or firmware) would not be the cause of the problem stated in the question.

16. A Windows administrator must track key performance metrics for a group of seven Windows servers. What should she do?

A. Run Performance Monitor on each host.

B. RDP into each host and run Performance Monitor.

C. RDP into each host and check Event Viewer logs.

D. Run Performance Monitor on her machine and add counters from the other seven servers.

☑ **D. Like many Microsoft administrative tools, Performance Monitor can run locally, but display data (performance counters) added from remote hosts.**

☒ **A, B, and C are incorrect. Although A and B would work, they require much more effort. C** is incorrect because you cannot monitor system performance with event view log data.

17. You are a firewall appliance administrator for your company. Previously restricted outbound RDP packets are now successfully reaching external hosts, and you did not configure this firewall allowance. Where should you look to see who made the firewall change and when?

A. Security log

B. Firewall log

C. Audit log

D. Event Viewer logs

> ☑ **C.** Audit logs differ from regular activity logs in that they record administrative configuration activities, such as modifying firewall rules.
>
> ☒ **A, B,** and **D** are incorrect. **A** is incorrect because on Windows machines, the Security log shows security events, including Windows auditing events. Firewall logs display normal usage firewall activity, not administrative configuration activity, so **B** is incorrect. **D** is incorrect because Windows event viewer logs would not display anything related to firewall appliance configurations.

18. In reviewing your firewall log, you notice a large number of your stations connecting to http://www.freetripsforyou.com and downloading an .EXE file, sometimes in the middle of the night. Your users state they did not visit the web site. Your firewall does not allow any inbound packets initiated from the Internet. What does this indicate?

    A. User stations are connecting to Windows Update to apply patches.

    B. User stations have been hijacked and are downloading malware.

    C. User stations are infected with a password cracking program.

    D. User stations are being controlled from the Internet through RDP.

> ☑ **B.** If a computer is visiting a web site and downloading an .EXE file without the user's knowledge, the machine is under malicious control. It would appear the malware is trying to download a Trojan of some kind.
>
> ☒ **A, C,** and **D** are incorrect. **A** is incorrect because Windows Update does not use the listed URL. **C** is incorrect because password cracking programs try to guess passwords; they do not download .EXE files without user consent. **D** is unlikely since the firewall blocks connections initiated from the Internet.

19. A corporate network baseline has been established over the course of two weeks. Using this baseline data, you configure your intrusion prevention systems to notify you of abnormal network activity. A new sales initiative requires sales employees to run high-bandwidth usage applications across the Internet. As a result, you begin receiving security alerts regarding abnormal network activity. What are these type of alerts referred to as?

    A. False positives

    B. False negatives

    C. True positives

    D. True negatives

    ☑   **A.** False positives report there is a problem when in fact there is none, such as in this case. The alert should still be checked to ensure an attack is not coinciding with this new network activity.

    ☒   **B, C,** and **D** are incorrect. **B** is not so—the opposite is true. **C** and **D** are fictitious terms.

20. What can be done to prevent malicious users from tampering with log files? (Choose three.)

    A. Store log files on a secured centralized logging host.

    B. Encrypt archived log files.

    C. Run Windows Update.

    D. Generate file hashes for log files.

    ☑   **A, B,** and **D.** Log files should be encrypted and stored on secured centralized hosts so that if a machine is compromised there is still a copy of the log. File hashes ensure files have not been tampered with in any way; a modified file generates a different hash.

    ☒   **C** is incorrect. Windows Update would not prevent log file tampering.

21. You have been asked to identify any irregularities from the following sequential lines from a web server log:

```
199.0.14.202, -, 03/15/09, 8:33:12, W3SVC2, SERVER, 192.168.1.1, 4502
12.168.12.79, -, 03/15/09, 8:34:09, W3SVC2, SERVER, 192.168.1.1, 3455
12.168.12.79, -, 03/15/09, 17:02:26, W3SVC2, SERVER, 192.168.1.1, 4302
192.16.255.202, -, 03/15/09, 17:03:11, W3SVC2, SERVER, 192.168.1.1, 4111
```

    A. 199.0.14.202 is not a valid IP address.

    B. 192.16.255.202 is not a valid IP address.

    C. Web servers cannot use 192.168.1.1.

    D. The log is missing entries for a long period of time.

    ☑   **D.** There is a long time discrepancy between lines 23 and 24. Almost nine hours of log activity are unaccounted for. This could mean somebody cleared incriminating log entries.

    ☒   **A, B,** and **C** are incorrect. **A** and **B** are incorrect because the IP addresses are valid. **C** is untrue. Web servers can use 192.168.1.1.

22. You are the Windows server administrator for a clothing outlet in Manhattan, New York. There are six Windows Server 2008 Active Directory computers used regularly. Files are being modified on servers during non-business hours. You would like to audit who makes the changes and when. What is the quickest method of deploying your audit settings?

    A. Configure audit settings using Group Policy.

    B. Configure each server with the appropriate audit settings.

    C. Configure one server appropriately, export the settings, import to the other five.

    D. Delegate the audit configuration task to six other administrators.

    ☑ **A.** In Active Directory environment Group Policy can be used to deliver settings to domain computers, such as audit settings for servers.

    ☒ **B, C,** and **D** are incorrect. These will work, but they take much more time than Group Policy.

23. What is the difference between a packet sniffer and a NIDS?

    A. There is no difference.

    B. Packet sniffers put the network card in promiscuous mode.

    C. A NIDS puts the network card(s) in promiscuous mode.

    D. Packet sniffers do not analyze captured traffic.

    ☑ **D.** Packet sniffers (protocol analyzers) capture network traffic, but they do not analyze it in any way.

    ☒ **A, B,** and **C** are incorrect. **A** is untrue—there is a difference. **B** and **C** are true, but the question asks what the difference is.

24. Your manager has asked you to identify which internal client computers have been controlled using RDP (Remote Desktop Protocol) from the Internet. What should you do?

    A. Check the logs on each computer.

    B. Check the logs on your RDP servers.

    C. Check your firewall log.

    D. Contact your ISP and have them check their logs.

☑ **C.** Since RDP connections from the Internet would go through the firewall, it would be quickest and easiest to consult your firewall log.

☒ **A, B,** and **D** are incorrect. **A** would work, but it is much more time consuming. **B** is incorrect because your RDP servers would not be involved with somebody from the Internet RDPing to one of your internal client stations. **D** is not practical, since your own firewall would have this information.

25. What is a potential problem with enabling detailed verbose logging on hosts for long periods of time?
  A. There is no problem.
  B. Performance degrades.
  C. Network bandwidth is consumed.
  D. Verbose logging consumes a user license.

☑ **B.** Detailed verbose logging presents much more log data than normal logging, therefore performance is affected. Depending on what is being logged and how much activity there is will determine how much of a performance degradation there will be.

☒ **A, C,** and **D** are incorrect. **A** would be correct for a short period of time, but the questions states long periods of time. **C** is incorrect; if you were sending log data to a centralized host across the network bandwidth could be affected, but the question does not state this. Changing logging levels does not consume a user license, so **D** is incorrect.

26. A user, Jeff, reports his client Windows XP station has been slow and unstable since last Tuesday. What should you first do?
  A. Use System Restore to revert the computer state to last Monday.
  B. Check log entries for Monday and Tuesday on Jeff's computer.
  C. Run Windows Update.
  D. Re-image Jeff's computer.

☑ **B.** Before jumping the gun and re-imaging or applying a restore point, first check the log files for any indication of what changed before the machine became slow and unstable.

☒ **A, C,** and **D** are incorrect. **A** and **D** are knee-jerk reactions and should normally not be performed immediately (unless your corporate policy states to). Windows Update would most likely not make a difference on Jeff's computer, so **C** is incorrect.

27. User workstations on your network connect through NAT (Network Address Translation) to a DMZ (demilitarized zone), where your Internet perimeter firewall exists. On Friday night a user connects to an inappropriate web site. You happened to have been capturing all network traffic on the DMZ at the time. How can you track which user workstation visited the web site? (Choose two.)

A. View logs on the NAT router.

B. View logs on the perimeter firewall.

C. View your packet capture.

D. View all workstation web browser histories.

☑ **A** and **C**. NAT router logs will list which internal address were translated and at what time. This could be used in correlation with captured packet time stamps to establish who visited the web site.

☒ **B** and **D** are incorrect. **B** will not help by itself—the IP address will simply be that of the NAT router's public interface—all outbound packets assume this IP address. **D** is an option, but it would take much longer than answers **A** and **C**.

28. An administrator is scheduling backup for Windows servers. She chooses to back up system state as well as user data folders on drive D:. What else should she have included in the backup?

A. Drive C:

B. Log files

C. Wallpaper images

D. Registry

☑ **B**. Log files must be backed up along with user data and system configuration data.

☒ **A**, **C**, and **D** are incorrect. **A** is incorrect because Drive C: normally contains the operating system files and these are replaceable. **C** is not critical data that must be backed up. **D** is relevant, but backing up system state already includes the registry.

29. You are monitoring the performance on a Unix server called Alpha. Alpha is used to host concurrent remote sessions for users. You notice that long periods of intense server disk activity on Alpha coincide with remote users working with large documents stored on a separate Unix server called Bravo. What might be causing the degraded performance on Alpha?

A. Too much network traffic.

B. The CPU is too slow.

C. The disks are too slow.

D. There is not enough RAM.

☑   **D.** Lack of RAM causes the oldest used data in RAM to be swapped to disk to make room for what must now be placed in RAM (many large documents). This sometimes makes it appear as if the disk is the problem.

☒   **A, B,** and **C** are incorrect. The reason is they are unlikely. The server network connection, CPU, and disks seem fine other than when remote users work with large documents.

30. A server, Charlie, runs a mission-critical database application. The application encrypts all data from connected client workstations. You would like to monitor Charlie for suspicious activity and prevent any potential attacks. What should you deploy?

A. Honeypot

B. HIPS

C. NIDS

D. PKI

☑   **B.** To monitor specific apps running on host computers and prevent potential attacks, you should deploy a HIPS.

☒   **A, C,** and **D** are incorrect. **A** is incorrect. Honeypots are hosts left intentionally vulnerable for the purpose of tracking or studying malicious code. **C** is incorrect. NIDSs analyze network packets looking for suspicious traffic. PKI (Public Key Infrastructure) is a hierarchy of certificates containing public and private keys for securing data, so **D** is incorrect.

20

Practice Exam

QUESTIONS

1. A technician has captured network traffic using a protocol analyzer. When she views the captured packets, she only sees her own transmissions. What might the problem be?

   A. The technician was plugged into a switch.

   B. The technician was plugged into a hub.

   C. The technician enabled a TCP traffic filter.

   D. The technician enabled a UDP traffic filter.

2. You must distribute the network traffic among a collection of mirrored servers. Which device should you use?

   A. Proxy server

   B. Load mirror

   C. Load balancer

   D. NAT

3. Refer to the illustration. Workstation A cannot connect to Server A. What is the problem?

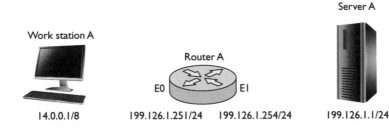

   A. Workstation A has an invalid IP address.

   B. Server A has an invalid IP address.

   C. Interface E1 on Router A has an incorrect subnet mask.

   D. Interface E0 on Router A has an incorrect IP address and subnet mask.

4. An Ethernet switch at a private school has been configured with two VLANs called Classroom A and Classroom B. Stations on the Classroom A VLAN cannot contact stations on the Classroom B VLAN. Refer to the following configuration from a computer on the Classroom A VLAN to identify the problem.

```
Connection-specific DNS Suffix  . :
IPv4 Address. . . . . . . . . . . : 10.0.0.72
Subnet Mask . . . . . . . . . . . : 255.255.255.0
Default Gateway . . . . . . . . . :
```

    A. A DNS Suffix must be configured.
    B. The IP address is invalid.
    C. The subnet mask is invalid.
    D. The default gateway must be configured.

5. You must filter an existing packet capture to show only DNS traffic. What port should you filter on?
    A. 80
    B. 53
    C. 443
    D. 25

6. Your Internet mail server resides in your DMZ. You must create one inbound perimeter firewall rule for your mail server to receive Internet mail. Which TCP port will your rule specify?
    A. 25
    B. 80
    C. 161
    D. 110

7. Which network device separates a large network into smaller broadcast domains?
    A. Hub
    B. Bridge
    C. Switch
    D. Router

8. An administrator uses SSH to remotely administer a network device. She then issues the command "show mac-address-table." What type of network device is she administering?
    A. Hub
    B. VPN appliance
    C. Switch
    D. Router

9. As the network specialist, you must ensure only authenticated users can access the Internet from your LAN. What should you implement?
   A. Packet filtering firewall
   B. Proxy server
   C. NAT
   D. Hub

10. A company requires that traveling users have secure access to the corporate LAN across the Internet. Which technology provides this solution?
   A. NAT
   B. Packet filtering firewall
   C. Proxy server
   D. VPN

11. Marcel, a security specialist, configures a network appliance to detect and impede suspicious network activity. What has Marcel configured?
   A. Signature-based NIDS
   B. Anomaly-based NIPS
   C. Signature-based NIPS
   D. Anomaly-based NIDS

12. How can a wireless network be made more secure? (Choose two.)
   A. Use high-gain antennae.
   B. Disable SSID broadcasting.
   C. Use PKI.
   D. Enable MAC address filtering.

13. You would like to decrease the amount of network traffic to and from the Internet. Which solution should you use?
   A. Proxy server
   B. NAT
   C. Packet filtering firewall
   D. VPN

14. You must ensure user network traffic is protected when users are connected to public networks. What should you use?
   A. Antivirus software
   B. HIDS
   C. HIPS
   D. VPN

15. Which of the following centrally authenticates connecting wireless LAN users?

    A. IPSec

    B. SSL

    C. RADIUS

    D. PKI

16. Scheduled packet capturing occurs on your network daily from 15:00 to 17:00. You have been asked to open yesterday's capture and filter out any PING packets. What protocol should you filter by?

    A. IGMP

    B. TCP

    C. ICMP

    D. UDP

17. Your company has decided to purchase six new computers with Windows 7 preinstalled. Shortly after the first new machine connects to the network, your NIDS reports unusual network traffic coming from fe80::2422:8c14:1e45:7ee8. What is the problem?

    A. There is no problem.

    B. This is a known worm source address.

    C. An ARP poisoning attack is occurring.

    D. This is a malformed multicast broadcast.

18. Which of the following can be used to secure all internal LAN traffic?

    A. IPSec

    B. SSL

    C. HTTPS

    D. Antivirus

19. Which of the following is untrue regarding server virtualization?

    A. Running virtualized servers cannot be moved to other physical hosts.

    B. A compromised virtual machine does not translate to a compromised physical host.

    C. Virtual machines can read and write directly to raw disk partitions instead of virtual hard disks.

    D. Virtualized environments do not require a SAN.

20. Which of the following are true regarding remote network appliance administration? (Choose two.)

    A. SSH encrypts traffic but can only restrict connections by username and password.

    B. SSH encrypts traffic and can restrict connections using public keys.

    C. SSH uses UDP port 22.

    D. SSH uses TCP port 22.

21. Which of the following statements are correct?
   A. SSL supersedes TLS.
   B. TLS supersedes SSL.
   C. SSL encrypts data using a private key.
   D. SSL uses TCP port 80.

22. Computers on your LAN are configured with PKI certificates. The certificates are used to establish proof of computer identify. Which security term does this apply to?
   A. Availability
   B. Authentication
   C. Confidentiality
   D. Encryption

23. File hashing addresses which security concern?
   A. Integrity
   B. Encryption
   C. Confidentiality
   D. Authentication

24. Which security role addresses who decides on and controls access to data?
   A. Custodian
   B. Server administrator
   C. Data owner
   D. End user

25. Your server hard disks are configured with RAID 1. To which security principle does this apply?
   A. Least privilege
   B. Availability
   C. Confidentiality
   D. Authentication

26. Chris, a network technician, identifies a way to remotely gain administrative access to a Linux host without knowing administrative credentials. What has Chris discovered?
   A. Virus
   B. Exploit
   C. Vulnerability
   D. Worm

27. An employee signs a document stating that company e-mail may only be used to conduct business; personal messages are forbidden. What type of policy is this?
   - **A.** Disaster recovery
   - **B.** E-mail retention
   - **C.** Storage retention
   - **D.** Acceptable use

28. What is malicious code that is discovered before a solution exists called?
   - **A.** Worm
   - **B.** Trojan
   - **C.** Zero-day exploit
   - **D.** Virus

29. Which of the following are ways to mask PII (personally identifiable information)? (Choose two.)
   - **A.** Anonymous proxy server
   - **B.** Tattoo
   - **C.** Gloves
   - **D.** Fingerprint

30. Your company is donating old Windows 2000 computers to a local school. A junior technician has deleted company data from these computers and emptied the recycle bins. What is the problem with this situation? (Choose two.)
   - **A.** You cannot let others use your Windows 2000 product keys.
   - **B.** The hard disks should have been formatted.
   - **C.** The hard disks should have been repartitioned.
   - **D.** The hard disks should have been completely filled with random data.

31. A retail sales clerk does not have the ability to maintain related bookkeeping records for accounting purposes. Which security principle does this apply to?
   - **A.** Due diligence
   - **B.** Separation of duties
   - **C.** Least privilege
   - **D.** Job rotation

32. Your boss asks you to calculate the ALE value related to database server downtime. Which two numeric values do you need?
   - **A.** Annual rate of occurrence
   - **B.** Return on investment
   - **C.** Single loss expectancy
   - **D.** Total cost of ownership

33. Which of the following will remove single points of failure? (Choose two.)

   A. Server clustering

   B. RAID 0

   C. NAT

   D. RAID 1

34. A technician is researching new rack mount servers to determine the maximum BTU value of all servers in the server room. Which related item should the technician consider?

   A. Required server processing speed

   B. Network bandwidth requirements

   C. Fire suppression

   D. HVAC

35. Your disaster recovery plan requires the quickest possible data restoration from backup tape. Which strategy should you employ?

   A. Weekly full backup, daily incremental backup

   B. Daily full backup, weekly incremental backup

   C. Daily full backup

   D. Daily differential backup

36. While discussing incident response policies during a meeting, your boss requests a dollar figure and the amount of downtime the company would suffer if a worm infected the corporate LAN. What type of study should you conduct?

   A. Business impact analysis

   B. Risk analysis

   C. Packet analysis

   D. Vulnerability analysis

37. Which procedure ensures evidence is collected and protected properly?

   A. Due diligence

   B. Order of volatility

   C. Incident response

   D. Chain of custody

38. Your behavior-based network intrusion detection system (NIDS) reports a potential network attack. After investigation, you conclude that there was no problem. What term describes what the NIDS reported?

   A. False negative

   B. Behavior-based alarm

   C. False positive

   D. Anomaly exception

39. Which type of risk analysis weighs potential threats based on dollar figures?
   A. ALE
   B. Qualitative
   C. ARO
   D. Quantitative

40. What will prevent users from immediately cycling through passwords in an attempt to reuse an old password?
   A. Minimum password length
   B. Maximum password length
   C. Minimum password age
   D. Maximum password age

41. Which type of attack attempts to trick users into providing their legitimate web site credentials to malicious web sites?
   A. Spam
   B. Phishing
   C. Cross-site scripting
   D. Social engineering

42. An attacker gains access to your network. She then broadcasts a transmission to all hosts with her MAC addresses as the physical address of the default gateway. What type of attack is this?
   A. MAC attack
   B. Broadcast attack
   C. Trojan
   D. ARP poisoning

43. In the past your company has experienced malware unleashed on your LAN through users clicking malicious web site links in e-mail messages. What can you do to prevent this occurrence?
   A. Provide malware training to users.
   B. Encrypt the contents of hard disks.
   C. Enable e-mail digital signatures.
   D. Install a personal firewall on all computers.

44. An attacker telephones the front desk of a branch office and tells the receptionist he is the senior network engineer. He then asks the receptionist for her e-mail password due to an approaching e-mail server upgrade. What type of attack is this?
   A. E-mail
   B. Man-in-the-middle
   C. Social engineering
   D. Telephone

45. What danger is prevalent for companies that do not shred corporate documents before disposing of them?

    A. Whaling

    B. Dumpster diving

    C. Phishing

    D. Tailgating

46. What term is used to identify e-mail message attempts to trick users out of account or login information?

    A. Spam

    B. Phishing

    C. Whaling

    D. Spoofing

47. You are configuring a group of laptops for traveling executives. What should you do to prevent operating system passwords from being locally hacked? (Choose two.)

    A. Use strong user account passwords.

    B. Encrypt the hard disk.

    C. Disable booting from removable media and set a CMOS password.

    D. Enable the password protection feature.

48. While visiting your neighbor, he mentions his computer constantly displays the latest tropical vacation sales. You learn he has been visiting related web sites while planning the next family vacation. What is causing this nuisance?

    A. Adware

    B. Spyware

    C. Botnet

    D. Logic bomb

49. What type of malware is self-replicating?

    A. Trojan

    B. Worm

    C. Clone

    D. Spam

50. An unsuspecting user downloads a free hard disk optimization program. A few days later her bank notifies her that her credit card has been used in another country. Which type of malware is most likely responsible for this security breach?

    A. Zombie

    B. Worm

    C. Spam

    D. Trojan

51. What name is given to unsolicited e-mail messages?

A. SMTP

B. POP

C. Adware

D. Spam

52. Refer to the illustration. What two tasks should be performed to further secure the system?

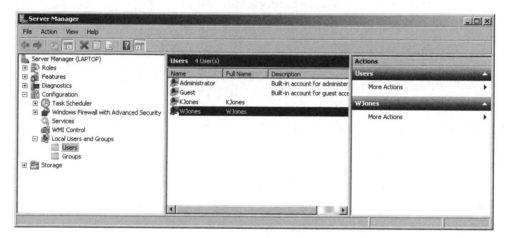

A. Disable the Guest account.

B. Rename the Administrator account.

C. Delete the Guest account.

D. Delete the Administrator account.

53. While working over the telephone with a network technician, you mention that your wireless network is using Layer 2 filtering. What type of filtering is this?

A. IP addresses

B. Computer name

C. PKI certificate

D. MAC address

54. What can be done to prevent man-in-the-middle attacks?

A. Authentication

B. Availability

C. Authorization

D. Fault tolerance

55. An attacker enters an office building and plugs his laptop into an unused network jack behind a plant in the reception area. He is then connected to the LAN, where he initiates an ARP poisoning attack. How could this have been prevented? (Choose two.)

    A. Update all virus scanners.

    B. Use a strict IPSec policy for all LAN computers.

    C. Disable unused switch ports.

    D. Use a strict firewall policy on the perimeter firewall.

56. How can a user eavesdrop on Wi-Fi communications?

    A. Use a vulnerability scanner.

    B. Use a port scanner.

    C. Configure an evil twin.

    D. Configure an HTTP server.

57. Which measure should be in place to prevent cross-site scripting attacks?

    A. Enable personal host-based firewalls.

    B. Update virus scanners.

    C. Disable registry editing tools to prevent cookie theft.

    D. Web sites should validate user input before allowing submissions.

58. Which of the following apply to physical port security? (Choose two.)

    A. TCP filtering

    B. MAC filtering

    C. UDP filtering

    D. 802.1x

59. You would like a network security solution that can detect and prevent the success of network attacks. What should you deploy?

    A. NIDS

    B. HIDS

    C. NIPS

    D. HIPS

60. Which tool can detect security misconfigurations?

    A. Protocol analyzer

    B. Vulnerability scanner

    C. Port scanner

    D. Virus scanner

61. Your traveling users all have smart phones. To protect data on these devices in case they are lost or stolen, what should you configure?

    A. Virus scanner

    B. Cable lock

    C. Password

    D. Remote wipe

62. Which of the following is true regarding virtualized server security?

    A. A compromised host operating system means all guest virtual machines are compromised.

    B. A compromised host operating system could render all guest virtual machines unavailable.

    C. A compromised virtual guest operating system means the host operating system is compromised.

    D. A compromised virtual guest operating system means all other virtual guest operating systems are compromised.

63. Users store company files on USB flash drives so that they can work from various computers outside of the corporate network. What should you do to secure this data?

    A. Generate file hashes for USB flash drive content.

    B. Scan USB flash drives for viruses.

    C. Encrypt USB flash drives.

    D. Digitally sign files on USB flash drives.

64. You are responsible for two servers, Apollo and Zeus. Both Apollo and Zeus have TPM (Trusted Platform Module) chips that are fully configured for all server hard disks. The power supplies in Apollo fail, so you remove the hard disk and place it in Zeus. How can you access this replaced hard disk?

    A. You cannot because it was encrypted with Apollo's TPM chip.

    B. You must place Apollo's TPM chip in Zeus.

    C. You must place Zeus' TPM chip in Apollo.

    D. You must supply a separate recovery key.

65. You must ensure that server hard disk data is always protected. What should you do?

    A. Encrypt the entire hard disk.

    B. Configure a CMOS power-on password.

    C. Encrypt files and folders.

    D. Disable booting from removable media.

66. A military division uses portable computing units to aid in flight take-off and landings at ad hoc landing strips. How can the military track the position of these portable units?

   A. SSL

   B. GPS

   C. TPM

   D. Bluetooth

67. A junior developer creates a custom database application. During testing, she discovers that unexpected conditions cause her application to crash. What did she forget to implement?

   A. Error trapping

   B. Function parameters

   C. Input validation

   D. Variable declarations

68. You notice excessive network traffic when client stations connect to Windows Update to download patches and hotfixes. You would like to minimize network utilization. What should you do?

   A. Use full duplex.

   B. Disable SSL.

   C. Configure an internal patch update server.

   D. Disable Windows Update on all client stations.

69. The web site administrator for your company would like an external device to handle all encryption and decryption processing to enhance server performance. What should you recommend?

   A. Trusted root certificate

   B. HSM

   C. TPM

   D. SSL

70. What can be done to harden a public web server? (Choose two.)

   A. Patch the operating system.

   B. Configure the web server to use TCP port 4634.

   C. Implement input validation for web forms.

   D. Name web pages with .HTML instead of .HTM.

71. You must harden six Linux computers on a small departmental network. What should you check for? (Choose three.)

A. Enabled unneeded daemons

B. Apache daemon

C. SSH daemon

D. Linux patches

72. What types of attacks cannot be mitigated by virus scanners? (Choose two.)

A. DNS poisoning

B. ARP cache poisoning

C. Trojan

D. Keylogging

73. Which of the following best describes security fuzzing?

A. Providing random data to test application security

B. Conducting a quick overview security audit

C. Jamming Wi-Fi radio frequencies to prevent rogue access points

D. Injecting spoofed packets on a network

74. Which type of attack exploits the trust that a web site has for a user session?

A. Cross-site scripting

B. Smurf

C. DoS

D. Cross-site request forgery

75. Identify two benefits of server virtualization:

A. Cheaper software licensing

B. More secure than a physical server

C. Less hardware costs

D. Less space required in server room

76. A Windows domain administrator has identified a number of settings that must be enabled to harden client operating systems. What is the best way to deploy these settings to more than one computer?

A. Send an e-mail message to each user with the appropriate instructions.

B. Use Group Policy.

C. Configure one computer, export the settings to a file, and use that file to import settings on the other computers.

D. Configure one computer, export the settings to a file, and attach the file to an e-mail message.

77. What can be done to secure smart phones? (Choose three.)
- A. Configure a strong password.
- B. Enable Bluetooth
- C. Enable screen lock.
- D. Install a virus scanner.

78. What function does a RADIUS server provide?
- A. Internal server that distributes operating system updates to client stations
- B. Software that detects rogue access points
- C. Centralized authentication for network access
- D. File encryption

79. Which protocol uses a ticket-granting service to prove user identity when accessing network resources?
- A. TACACS
- B. RADIUS
- C. IPSec
- D. Kerberos

80. Your NIDS notifies you of excessive traffic destined for TCP port 389 on one of your servers. What type of traffic is this?
- A. LDAP
- B. HTTP
- C. RDP
- D. RADIUS

81. You are ordering new laptops for your law enforcement division. In the past, productivity has been hampered because of strict password requirements. You would like to continue with a secure computing environment while eliminating password problems. Which of the following are possible solutions? (Choose two.)
- A. Reducing password length to six characters
- B. Smart card authentication
- C. Biometric authentication
- D. Security clearances

82. A router is configured to allow outbound TCP ports 80, 443, and 25. You would like to use the Remote Desktop Protocol to access a server at another location. Which of the following statements is correct?

   A. You will be able to RDP to the external server.

   B. You will not be able to RDP the external server because the router is explicitly denying RDP packets.

   C. You will not be able to RDP the external server because the router is implicitly denying RDP packets.

   D. You will not be able to RDP the external server because the router is implicitly allowing RDP packets.

83. Which concept exposes employees to varying job roles to increase their overall knowledge of the business?

   A. Mandatory vacations

   B. Least privilege

   C. Separation of duties

   D. Job rotation

84. You are configuring an enterprise wireless router. A wizard allows you to select user accounts from Microsoft Active Directory that should have administrative access to the wireless router. What type of security model is this?

   A. DAC

   B. RBAC

   C. MAC

   D. Least privilege

85. Which two of the following are related to computing security access control?

   A. Authentication

   B. Encryption

   C. Job rotation

   D. PII

86. A shared folder on server Bruno is configured as shown here. A database file named HfxClients .mdb in the shared folder lists Authenticated Users with Full Control. Which UNC path will allow the appropriate users to write changes to the database file?

- **A.** \\Bruno\CorpData\HfxClients.mdb
- **B.** //Bruno/CorpData/HfxClients.mdb
- **C.** \\HfxClients.mdb\CorpData\Bruno
- **D.** Users will not have write access to the file across the network.

87. A user logs on to her station in the morning and supplies her username and password. During the day she accesses e-mail, databases, and corporate Intranet web sites without having to specify credentials. What is allowing this seamless access of network resources?
- **A.** LDAP
- **B.** Multifactor authentication
- **C.** PKI
- **D.** Single sign-on

88. Your assistant, Claire, must have access to create Microsoft Active Directory user accounts in the path "ou=Toronto,dc=Acme,dc=Ca" while you are on vacation in Hawaii. You add Claire to the built-in Domain Admins group. What security principle have you violated?

- A. Separation of duties
- B. Least privilege
- C. Job rotation
- D. Mandatory vacations

89. You are a new sales agent for Acme Floor Store, Inc. When traveling on the road for business, you sign in to the company VPN using a PIN and a hardware device–generated unique code. What is this code generating device called?

- A. Code-generating device
- B. PIN aggregator
- C. Token
- D. PIN aggravator

90. You have hired three summer students who will be in your employment from July 11, 2011, to August 26, 2011. What can you do to ensure their user accounts are only valid until August 26, 2011?

- A. Delete the user accounts after work hours on August 26, 2011.
- B. Force a password change on August 26, 2011, after work hours.
- C. Set the account expiration date to August 26, 2011, after work hours.
- D. Set a calendar entry for August 26, 2011, reminding you to delete the user accounts.

91. Which key does a secured web server use to decrypt a client session key? (Choose the best answer.)

- A. Public key
- B. Private key
- C. Symmetric key
- D. Asymmetric key

92. Which key is used when you send an encrypted e-mail message?

- A. Your public key
- B. Recipient's public key
- C. Your private key
- D. Recipient's private key

93. Which are the two symmetric encryption algorithms in the list?

    A. Blowfish

    B. RC4

    C. RSA

    D. MD5

94. While configuring IPSec to secure internal LAN traffic, you must specify an integrity algorithm. Which of the following would be valid choices? (Choose two.)

    A. SHA-1

    B. 3DES

    C. RSA

    D. MD5

95. Which of the following encryption algorithms are block ciphers?

    A. RC4

    B. IPSec

    C. AES

    D. RSA

96. SSL implies the use of what?

    A. PKI

    B. TLS

    C. IPSec

    D. VPN

97. A network technician has configured a wireless router such that stations must be authenticated before allowing network access. What did he configure?

    A. WEP

    B. WPA PSK

    C. 802.1x

    D. WPA2 PSK

98. What type of cryptographic function is used to detect changes to data?

    A. Block

    B. Stream

    C. Blowfish

    D. Hashing

99. Where are the serial numbers of revoked certificates posted?

    A. PKI

    B. CRL

    C. Trusted root web site

    D. CAL

100. A CA (Certificate Authority) is established and directly issues user and computer certificates that expire in ten years. The CA is then immediately brought offline. Which of the following statements are true? (Choose two.)

    A. Issued user and computer certificates can no longer be used despite the expiration date.

    B. Issued user and computer certificates can continue to be used until the expiration date.

    C. New user certificates cannot be issued.

    D. Expired user certificates can be renewed.

QUICK ANSWER KEY

1. A	21. B	41. B	61. D	81. B, C
2. C	22. B	42. D	62. B	82. C
3. D	23. A	43. A	63. C	83. D
4. D	24. C	44. C	64. D	84. B
5. B	25. B	45. B	65. C	85. A, B
6. A	26. B	46. B	66. B	86. D
7. D	27. D	47. B, C	67. A	87. D
8. C	28. C	48. A	68. C	88. B
9. B	29. A, C	49. B	69. B	89. C
10. D	30. A, D	50. D	70. A, C	90. C
11. B	31. B	51. D	71. A, D	91. B
12. B, D	32. A, C	52. A, B	72. A, B	92. B
13. A	33. A, D	53. D	73. A	93. A, B
14. D	34. D	54. A	74. D	94. A, D
15. C	35. C	55. B, C	75. C, D	95. D
16. C	36. A	56. C	76. B	96. A
17. A	37. D	57. D	77. A, C, D	97. C
18. A	38. C	58. B, D	78. C	98. D
19. A	39. D	59. C	79. D	99. B
20. B, D	40. C	60. B	80. A	100. B, C

IN-DEPTH ANSWERS

1. A technician has captured network traffic using a protocol analyzer. When she views the captured packets, she only sees her own transmissions. What might the problem be?
   A. The technician was plugged into a switch.
   B. The technician was plugged into a hub.
   C. The technician enabled a TCP traffic filter.
   D. The technician enabled a UDP traffic filter.

   ☑ **A.** Each switch port is a collision domain, which means protocol analyzers will only see traffic sent from or going to the machine plugged into that switch port.

   ☒ **B, C,** and **D** are incorrect. **B** is incorrect because being plugged into a hub would have allowed the packet capture to include all traffic for all stations plugged into the hub. **C** and **D** are incorrect because protocol analyzers allow capture or view filtering based on many variables, including TCP and UDP protocols.

2. You must distribute the network traffic among a collection of mirrored servers. Which device should you use?
   A. Proxy server
   B. Load mirror
   C. Load balancer
   D. NAT

   ☑ **C.** Load balancers attempt to evenly distribute network traffic to a collection of hosts. Unlike DNS round robin configurations to distribute network traffic, load balancers can detect unavailable hosts and prevent traffic from being sent to them.

   ☒ **A, B,** and **D** are incorrect. **A** is incorrect because proxy server retrieves Internet content on behalf of users, but they cannot balance network traffic workloads. **B** is incorrect because load mirror is a fictitious term. **D** is incorrect because NAT (Network Address Translation) does not control network traffic; it allows a single public IP address to be used for many internal computers connecting externally.

3. Refer to the illustration. Workstation A cannot connect to Server A. What is the problem?

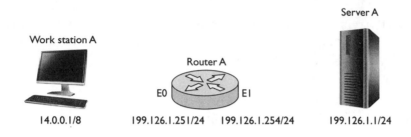

A. Workstation A has an invalid IP address.

B. Server A has an invalid IP address.

C. Interface E1 on Router A has an incorrect subnet mask.

D. Interface E0 on Router A has an incorrect IP address and subnet mask.

☑ **D.** Interface E0 on Router A is incorrect because interface E1 has an IP address in the same range (199.126.1) as E0 does. Since Server A uses an IP address in the range 199.126.1, we can assume Interface E1 on Router A is configured correctly. Interface E0 on Router A should have an IP address on the same subnet as Workstation A, for example 14.0.0.2/8.

☒ **A, B,** and **C** are incorrect. These are untrue—all referenced IP addresses and subnet masks are indeed correct.

4. An Ethernet switch at a private school has been configured with two VLANs called Classroom A and Classroom B. Stations on the Classroom A VLAN cannot contact stations on the Classroom B VLAN. Refer to the following configuration from a computer on the Classroom A VLAN to identify the problem.

```
Connection-specific DNS Suffix  . :
IPv4 Address. . . . . . . . . . . : 10.0.0.72
Subnet Mask . . . . . . . . . . . : 255.255.255.0
Default Gateway . . . . . . . . . :
```

A. A DNS Suffix must be configured.

B. The IP address is invalid.

C. The subnet mask is invalid.

D. The default gateway must be configured.

☑ **D.** A TCP/IP VLAN (virtual local area network) must have a default gateway (IP address of router) configured to contact other VLANs.

☒ **A, B,** and **C** are incorrect. **A** is incorrect because DNS suffixes are not required to interconnect VLANs. **B** is incorrect because the IP address is valid. Zeros are allowed for host IP addresses as long as all the host bits (binary) are not set to binary zeros or ones. **C** is incorrect because the subnet mask is valid even though the IP address is a Class A address usually having a subnet mask of 255.0.0.0.

5. You must filter an existing packet capture to show only DNS traffic. What port should you filter on?
   A. 80
   B. 53
   C. 443
   D. 25

☑ **B.** DNS (Domain Name Service) clients to DNS server transmissions have a destination UDP port of 53.

☒ **A, C,** and **D** are incorrect. **A** and **C** are incorrect because HTTP (Hypertext Transfer Protocol) web servers listen on TCP port 80 for clear text transmissions and TCP port 443 for encrypted connections. SMTP (Simple Mail Transfer Protocol) uses TCP port 25 to transfer mail to other SMTP hosts, therefore **D** is incorrect.

6. Your Internet mail server resides in your DMZ. You must create one inbound perimeter firewall rule for your mail server to receive Internet mail. Which TCP port will your rule specify?
   A. 25
   B. 80
   C. 161
   D. 110

☑ **A.** Internet mail servers receive mail from other Internet mail server using the SMTP protocol, which uses TCP port 25.

☒ **B, C,** and **D** are incorrect. **B** is incorrect because web servers use port 80. **C** is incorrect because SNMP (Simple Network Management Protocol) uses UDP port 161 to query network devices. **D** is incorrect because TCP port 110 is used by POP3 (Post Office Protocol) clients retrieving mail from POP3 servers.

7. Which network device separates a large network into smaller broadcast domains?
   A. Hub
   B. Bridge
   C. Switch
   D. Router

   ☑ **D.** Routers have more than one network interface and do not forward broadcast network traffic to other networks; thus, routers separate connected networks into smaller broadcast domains. Broadcast traffic is not an address to a particular host, instead it is addresses to all hosts.

   ☒ **A, B,** and **C** are incorrect. **A** is incorrect because a hub floods any network activity, including unicasts to all other hub ports. Linking multiple hubs together still results in a single broadcast and single collision domain. **B** is incorrect because a bridge has multiple network interfaces and are used to separate larger networks into smaller collision domains to increase network throughput, but a single broadcast domain would still remain. **C** is incorrect because each switch port is a collision domain. Unless VLANs are configured within a switch, all switch ports are in the same broadcast domain.

8. An administrator uses SSH to remotely administer a network device. She then issues the command "show mac-address-table." What type of network device is she administering?
   A. Hub
   B. VPN appliance
   C. Switch
   D. Router

   ☑ **C.** Switches retain machine MAC addresses to physical switch port mappings in memory so that traffic destined to a particular host (MAC address) is sent to a single switch port. Viewing the switch MAC address table is done with the "show mac-address-table" command.

   ☒ **A, B,** and **D** are incorrect. **A** is incorrect because most hubs cannot be administered, and they do not retain which MAC address is plugged into which hub port; network traffic is always flooded to all hub ports. **B** is incorrect because VPN (virtual private network) appliances do not retain MAC address information in a memory table, nor do routers, and therefore **D** is incorrect.

9. As the network specialist, you must ensure only authenticated users can access the Internet from your LAN. What should you implement?

A. Packet filtering firewall

B. Proxy server

C. NAT

D. Hub

☑ **B.** Proxy servers can work at all upper OSI layers, which means they can perform deep packet inspection and require authentication during certain times of day, they can check whether a URL is appropriate or not, and so on.

☒ **A, C, and D** are incorrect. **A** and **C** are incorrect because packet filtering firewalls and NAT routers can only analyze addressing information (IP address, TCP/UDP port address), which maps to OSI layers 3 and 4, but they cannot look into the packet payload where user authentication messages exist. **D** is incorrect because hubs cannot analyze any addressing or authentication data in packets.

10. A company requires that traveling users have secure access to the corporate LAN across the Internet. Which technology provides this solution?

A. NAT

B. Packet filtering firewall

C. Proxy server

D. VPN

☑ **D.** VPN technology establishes an encrypted tunnel between a traveling user computer and a VPN concentrator on a corporate network over an untrusted network, such as the Internet. Any data transmitted through the encrypted tunnel is secure and is decrypted by the other endpoint device.

☒ **A, B, and C** are incorrect. These do not provide secure access to a LAN for traveling external users. **A** is incorrect because NAT allows multiple computers to gain public network access using a single public IP address. **B** is incorrect because packet filtering firewall allows or restricts packets based on packet address and protocol information. **C** is incorrect because proxy server controls outbound network connections.

11. Marcel, a security specialist, configures a network appliance to detect and impede suspicious network activity. What has Marcel configured?

A. Signature-based NIDS

B. Anomaly-based NIPS

C. Signature-based NIPS

D. Anomaly-based NIDS

☑   **B.** Suspicious network activity is activity that does not resemble a normal baseline of activity. This network deviation is referred to as an anomaly. NIPSs (network intrusion prevention systems) prevent the suspicious activity from continuing.

☒   **A, C,** and **D** are incorrect. **A** and **C** are incorrect because signature-based analysis compares network activity against known existing network attacks, whereas anomaly-based analysis compares network activity against a known normal baseline, which is unique for each network. It is important to note that NIDSs (network intrusion detection systems) detect and report suspicious activity, but do nothing to prevent it from continuing, therefore **D** is incorrect.

12. How can a wireless network be made more secure? (Choose two.)
- **A.** Use high-gain antennae.
- **B.** Disable SSID broadcasting.
- **C.** Use PKI.
- **D.** Enable MAC address filtering.

☑   **B** and **D.** Disabling SSID broadcasting prevents users within range from seeing the network name. There are freely available tools that will show wireless networks even if the SSID name has been suppressed. Windows 7 clients will still show these wireless networks with a name of "Other." MAC address filtering requires a list of either allowed or restricted MAC addresses to control access to the wireless network.

☒   **A** and **C** are incorrect. **A** is incorrect because high-gain antennae will allow WLAN connectivity over longer distances, which would decrease security. **C** is incorrect because PKI in itself does nothing to secure a wireless network, although PKI certificates can be used to authenticate stations to 802.1x-compliant networks.

13. You would like to decrease the amount of network traffic to and from the Internet. Which solution should you use?
- **A.** Proxy server
- **B.** NAT
- **C.** Packet filtering firewall
- **D.** VPN

☑ **A.** Not only does a proxy server retrieve Internet content on behalf of users, but it can also cache requested content so that subsequent requests can be satisfied locally from cache rather than from the Internet, thus reducing Internet traffic.

☒ **B, C,** and **D** are incorrect. NAT, packet filtering firewalls, and VPNs are not designed to decrease the amount of network traffic. **B** is incorrect because NAT is designed to allow outbound access using a single IP address. **C** is incorrect because packet filter allows or denies traffic based on protocol or address information. **D** is incorrect because VPN allows secure access to a LAN across the Internet.

14. You must ensure user network traffic is protected when users are connected to public networks. What should you use?
    A. Antivirus software
    B. HIDS
    C. HIPS
    D. VPN

☑ **D.** VPNs encrypt all network traffic from the user device to the VPN appliance even if the user is connected to a public network with Internet access.

☒ **A, B,** and **C** are incorrect. **A** is incorrect because antivirus software protects a computing device and its file system, but it does nothing to secure network traffic. **B** and **C** are incorrect because HIDSs (host intrusion detection systems) and HIPSs (host intrusion prevention systems) prevent malicious activity on the host itself by monitoring applications and logs, but they cannot protect network traffic.

15. Which of the following centrally authenticates connecting wireless LAN users?
    A. IPSec
    B. SSL
    C. RADIUS
    D. PKI

☑ **C.** RADIUS (Remote Authentication Dial In User Service) uses a server to authenticate user credentials centrally; various endpoint network devices can forward authentication requests from supplications to this central host.

☒ **A, B,** and **D** are incorrect. **A** is incorrect because IPSec encrypts and digitally signs network traffic but cannot centrally authenticate users, nor can SSL or PKI, therefore **B** and **D** are incorrect. SSL (Secure Sockets Layer) uses one or more PKI certificates to encrypt and/or sign network data. A PKI is a hierarchy of related X.509 certificates.

16. Scheduled packet capturing occurs on your network daily from 15:00 to 17:00. You have been asked to open yesterday's capture and filter out any PING packets. What protocol should you filter by?

A. IGMP

B. TCP

C. ICMP

D. UDP

☑ **C.** ICMP (Internet Control Message Protocol) reports on network congestion and reachability. Utilities such as PING and Tracert use ICMP as their transport.

☒ **A, B** and **D** are incorrect. These would not work. **A** is incorrect because IGMP (Internet Group Message Protocol) uses multicasting to transmit data to groups of stations that are registered with the correct multicast IP address. **B** and **D** are incorrect because TCP (Transmission Control Protocol) and UDP (User Datagram Protocol) are OSI layer 4 transport protocols. PING uses ICMP, not TCP or UDP, as its transport protocol.

17. Your company has decided to purchase six new computers with Windows 7 preinstalled. Shortly after the first new machine connects to the network, your NIDS reports unusual network traffic coming from fe80::2422:8c14:1e45:7ee8. What is the problem?

A. There is no problem.

B. This is a known worm source address.

C. An ARP poisoning attack is occurring.

D. This is a malformed multicast broadcast.

☑ **A.** Indeed there is no problem. fe80::2422:8c14:1e45:7ee8 is a self-assigned IPv6 address. Windows 7 has IPv6 automatically enabled; all Windows 7 machines will have an address starting with fe80, which is the equivalent of an IPv4 self-assigned APIPA (Automatic Private IP Addressing) address starting with 169.254.

☒ **B, C**, and **D** are incorrect. These choices are untrue. It is simply a self-assigned IPv6 address.

18. Which of the following can be used to secure all internal LAN traffic?

A. IPSec

B. SSL

C. HTTPS

D. Antivirus

☑ **A.** IPSec (Internet Protocol Security) can encrypt and digitally sign network traffic at OSI layer 4 (the Transport Layer), which means it is not application specific (unlike SSL). All network traffic can be encrypted with a single IPSec policy.

☒ **B, C,** and **D** are incorrect. **B** is incorrect because SSL must be configured for each application requiring network encryption. **C** is incorrect because HTTPS (Hypertext Transfer Protocol Secure) is HTTP traffic secured with SSL. **D** is incorrect because antivirus software does not encrypt network traffic.

19. Which of the following is untrue regarding server virtualization?
   A. Running virtualized servers cannot be moved to other physical hosts.
   B. A compromised virtual machine does not translate to a compromised physical host.
   C. Virtual machines can read and write directly to raw disk partitions instead of virtual hard disks.
   D. Virtualized environments do not require a SAN.

☑ **A.** Virtualized servers running on a physical host can be moved to another physical host. This can happen with zero downtime if both physical hosts are clustered and are using shared storage. VMWare calls this "VMotion," and Microsoft Hyper-V calls this "Live Migration."

☒ **B, C,** and **D** are incorrect. These are all true.

20. Which of the following are true regarding remote network appliance administration? (Choose two.)
   A. SSH encrypts traffic, but can only restrict connections by username and password.
   B. SSH encrypts traffic and can restrict connections using public keys.
   C. SSH uses UDP port 22.
   D. SSH uses TCP port 22.

☑ **B** and **D.** SSH is not limited to restricting connections only by username and password. Public key authentication can be configured, which requires connecting users to possess a valid public and private key pair along with a passphrase. SSH uses TCP port 22.

☒ **A** and **C** are incorrect. They are untrue.

21. Which of the following statements are correct?
   A. SSL supersedes TLS.
   B. TLS supersedes SSL.
   C. SSL encrypts data using a private key.
   D. SSL uses TCP port 80.

☑ **B.** TLS (Transport Layer Security) supersedes SSL and is considered more secure. TLS requires the use of at least one x.509 certificate.

☒ **A, C,** and **D** are incorrect.

22. Computers on your LAN are configured with PKI certificates. The certificates are used to establish proof of computer identify. Which security term does this apply to?
   A. Availability
   B. Authentication
   C. Confidentiality
   D. Encryption

☑ **B.** Authentication requires proof of identity (in this case for computers and not users). PKI computer certificates are digitally signed by a CA (Certificate Authority) as is the PKI certificate on the authenticating device. If both parties trust the CA digital signature and the certificates are valid (not revoked or expired), then authentication is successful.

☒ **A, C,** and **D** are incorrect. **A** is incorrect because availability refers to the assurance that a resource will always be available. **C** (confidentiality) ensures that data can only be read by authorized parties. **D** (encryption) is an implementation of confidentiality.

23. File hashing addresses which security concern?
   A. Integrity
   B. Encryption
   C. Confidentiality
   D. Authentication

☑ **A.** File hashing generates a unique value (message digest) that is unique to a file. Any change to the file will result in a different unique message digest. This can be used to determine if files have changed.

⊠ **B, C,** and **D** are incorrect. **B** is incorrect because encryption addresses the confidentiality security concern. **C** is incorrect because confidentiality is addressed by encryption. **D** is incorrect because authentication requires proof of identity—none of these are related to the integrity provided by file hashing.

24. Which security role addresses who decides on and controls access to data?

  A. Custodian
  B. Server administrator
  C. Data owner
  D. End user

☑ **C.** Data owners determine which access rights certain parties have to information.

⊠ **A, B,** and **D** are incorrect. Custodians are responsible for maintaining and protecting data, much as a server administrator would, so **A** and **B** are incorrect. End users simply use data they have been given access to, so **D** is incorrect.

25. Your server hard disks are configured with RAID 1. To which security principle does this apply?

  A. Least privilege
  B. Availability
  C. Confidentiality
  D. Authentication

☑ **B.** RAID (redundant array of inexpensive disks) level 1 mirrors data written on one disk to a second disk. In the event of a single disk failure, the other disk is available with up-to-date data, thus making the data highly available.

⊠ **A, C,** and **D** are incorrect. **A** is incorrect because least privilege grants only rights needed to perform a task, **C** is incorrect because confidentiality ensures only authorized parties can access data, and **D** is incorrect because authentication involves proving one's identity—none of these are related to RAID 1.

26. Chris, a network technician, identifies a way to remotely gain administrative access to a Linux host without knowing administrative credentials. What has Chris discovered?

  A. Virus
  B. Exploit
  C. Vulnerability
  D. Worm

   ☑   **B.** An exploit takes advantage of a vulnerability.

   ☒   **A, C,** and **D** are incorrect. A virus may contain an exploit, but it is not necessarily an exploit itself, so **A** is incorrect. Vulnerabilities are weaknesses, exploits take advantage of those weaknesses, so **C** is incorrect. **D** is also not the answer—worms are pieces of self-replicating malicious code that may or may not be acting as a vehicle to deliver an exploit.

27. An employee signs a document stating that company e-mail may only be used to conduct business; personal messages are forbidden. What type of policy is this?

   A. Disaster recovery

   B. E-mail retention

   C. Storage retention

   D. Acceptable use

   ☑   **D.** A document stating how company assets can and cannot be used is an Acceptable use policy.

   ☒   **A, B,** and **C** are incorrect. **A** is incorrect because disaster recovery policy outlines which parties should perform which tasks in the event of a disaster. **B** is incorrect because e-mail retention policy determines how long e-mail messages must be kept and how they are to be kept. **C** is incorrect because storage retention policy determines how any data stored digitally is to be kept and for how long.

28. What is malicious code that is discovered before a solution exists called?

   A. Worm

   B. Trojan

   C. Zero-day exploit

   D. Virus

   ☑   **C.** Zero-day exploits are not yet known to the hardware or software vendor; thus, there is no fix for the vulnerability.

   ☒   **A, B,** and **D** are incorrect. **A** is incorrect because malicious code that is self-propagating is called a worm. **B** is incorrect because Trojans are malicious code hidden in what appears to be benign software. **D** is incorrect because viruses are malicious code that can copy themselves.

29. Which of the following are ways to mask PII (personally identifiable information)? (Choose two.)

A. Anonymous proxy server

B. Tattoo

C. Gloves

D. Fingerprint

> ☑ **A and C.** Personally identifiable information uniquely identifies a person and includes items such as a credit card number, e-mail address, signature and so on. Anonymous proxy servers mask your IP address and gloves prevent fingerprints being left behind— these both mask PII.
>
> ☒ **B and D** are incorrect. Tattoos and fingerprints are personally identifiable information.

30. Your company is donating old Windows 2000 computers to a local school. A junior technician has deleted company data from these computers and emptied the recycle bins. What is the problem with this situation? (Choose two.)

A. You cannot let others use your Windows 2000 product keys.

B. The hard disks should have been formatted.

C. The hard disks should have been repartitioned.

D. The hard disks should have been completely filled with random data.

> ☑ **A and D.** Licensed software should not be transferred to others. Deleted files are removed from file system indexes, but the data remains on disk and can be easily recovered with the correct tools. Formatted and partitioned hard disk data can also be recovered as long as the disk has not been filled with other data. There are tools designed to fill hard disks with random data over many passes to ensure the original data is not recoverable.
>
> ☒ **B and C** are incorrect. Formatting and partitioning hard disks does not securely remove data.

31. A retail sales clerk does not have the ability to maintain related bookkeeping records for accounting purposes. Which security principle does this apply to?

A. Due diligence

B. Separation of duties

C. Least privilege

D. Job rotation

☑ **B.** To reduce the possibility of fraud, no single business task and its bookkeeping should be performed by a single person.

☒ **A, C,** and **D** are incorrect. These do not involve separating business tasks. **A** is incorrect because due diligence involves analyzing documentation prior to committing to a business or legal relationship. **C** is incorrect because least privilege ensures employees only have rights needed to perform their job duties. **D** is incorrect because job rotation exposes employees to different facets of the business.

32. Your boss asks you to calculate the ALE value related to database server downtime. Which two numeric values do you need?
   A. Annual rate of occurrence
   B. Return on investment
   C. Single loss expectancy
   D. Total cost of ownership

☑ **A** and **C.** ALE (annual loss expectancy) is used for quantitative risk analysis to assign a cost to a probable risk. The ARO (annual rate of occurrence) is a derived figure multiplied by the SLE (single loss expectancy) dollar value, resulting in the ALE. The ALE is then used to budget funds for dealing with the risk.

☒ **B** and **D** are incorrect. These are not used to calculate the ALE value.

33. Which of the following will remove single points of failure? (Choose two.)
   A. Server clustering
   B. RAID 0
   C. NAT
   D. RAID 1

☑ **A** and **D.** Server clusters include two or more servers working together to offer services. A failure of single server should have minimal (if any) impact; any services hosted on the computer are simply taken over by another cluster node. RAID 1 (disk mirroring) can tolerate a single disk failure because every disk write is duplicated onto a separate disk.

☒ **B** and **C** are incorrect. These choices introduce single points of failure; they do not remove them. **B** is incorrect because RAID 0 writes data blocks across disks for a performance improvement, but a loss of even a single disk renders the data unavailable. **C** is incorrect because NAT allows internal hosts to access a public network using the NAT router's public IP address. Clients use NAT simply by having the NAT router's internal interface listed as their default gateway. Unless more than a single NAT router is available on the network, it is a single point of failure.

34. A technician is researching new rack mount servers to determine the maximum BTU value of all servers in the server room. Which related item should the technician consider?
- **A.** Required server processing speed
- **B.** Network bandwidth requirements
- **C.** Fire suppression
- **D.** HVAC

☑ **D.** HVAC (heating, ventilation, air conditioning) must be considered when discussing server BTUs (British thermal units). BTUs measure thermal energy (heat), and your server room air conditioning must be able to displace the BTUs generated by your computing equipment; otherwise, the server room will much too warm for your equipment.

☒ **A, B,** and **C** are incorrect. **A** is incorrect because BTUs are not related to the network or server processing speed. **B** and **C** are incorrect because fire suppression systems are critical to minimize fire and smoke damage, but BTUs are directly related to climate control (HVAC).

35. Your disaster recovery plan requires the quickest possible data restoration from backup tape. Which strategy should you employ?
- **A.** Weekly full backup, daily incremental backup
- **B.** Daily full backup, weekly incremental backup
- **C.** Daily full backup
- **D.** Daily differential backup

☑ **C.** Daily full backups archive all data, even if has not changed since the last full backup. This requires more storage capacity and time to perform the backup, but restoration is the quickest, since it is a single backup set.

☒ **A, B,** and **D** are incorrect. Incremental backups only archive data changed since the last full or incremental backup, so backup time and storage space are minimized.

36. While discussing incident response policies during a meeting, your boss requests a dollar figure and the amount of downtime the company would suffer if a worm infected the corporate LAN. What type of study should you conduct?
- **A.** Business impact analysis
- **B.** Risk analysis
- **C.** Packet analysis
- **D.** Vulnerability analysis

> ☑ **A.** Studying the effect of unfavorable events (such as a computer worm) upon business operations is referred to as a business impact analysis.
>
> ☒ **B, C,** and **D** are incorrect. **B** is incorrect because a risk analysis identifies objects that must be protected from risks and then prioritizes those items. **C** is incorrect because packet analysis involves studying network traffic and is not tied to corporate downtime due to worms. **D** is incorrect because a vulnerability analysis identifies security risks, but not their impact on business operations.

37. Which procedure ensures evidence is collected and protected properly?
   A. Due diligence
   B. Order of volatility
   C. Incident response
   D. Chain of custody

> ☑ **D.** Evidence must be collected in a strict and orderly manner from initial acquisition to storage and analysis. This is referred to as chain of custody and serves to ensure evidence is authentic and legitimate.
>
> ☒ **A, B,** and **C** are incorrect. **A** is incorrect because the study of relevant data before committing to a business or legal contract is referred to as due diligence, but there is no correlation to the collection of evidence. **B** is incorrect because order of volatility requires the most volatile evidence to be gathered first, for example, the contents of electronic memory (RAM) versus hard disk data. **C** is incorrect because the orderly management of security breaches is referred to as incident response. This does not imply the gathering of evidence.

38. Your behavior-based network intrusion detection system (NIDS) reports a potential network attack. After investigation, you conclude that there was no problem. What term describes what the NIDS reported?
   A. False negative
   B. Behavior-based alarm
   C. False positive
   D. Anomaly exception

> ☑ **C.** Raising an alarm to a problem when there in fact is no problem is called a false positive.
>
> ☒ **A, B** and **D** are incorrect. **A** is incorrect because false negative reports no problem when in fact one exists. **B** is incorrect because behavior-based network analysis compares a baseline with current network activity to identify anomalies. This was used in this case to generate the alarm, but it is not the correct answer. **D** is incorrect because it is a fictitious term.

39. Which type of risk analysis weighs potential threats based on dollar figures?
   A. ALE
   B. Qualitative
   C. ARO
   D. Quantitative

   ☑ **D.** Quantitative risk analysis identifies assets and risks and uses calculations such as ALE (annual loss expectancy) to prioritize and budget funds to manage these risks.

   ☒ **A, B,** and **C** are incorrect. **A** and **C** are incorrect because ALE is a dollar amount derived from multiplying the ARO (annual rate of occurrence) by the SLE (single loss expectancy) and is used in quantitative risk analysis. **B** is incorrect because qualitative risk analysis does not rank risks strictly by dollar amount; for example, a relative ranking in terms of the effect on the business might be used.

40. What will prevent users from immediately cycling through passwords in an attempt to reuse an old password?
   A. Minimum password length
   B. Maximum password length
   C. Minimum password age
   D. Maximum password age

   ☑ **C.** Setting a minimum password age to three days, for example, will prevent users from, upon password change, immediately cycling through the number of passwords remembered to re-use a familiar password they have used before.

   ☒ **A, B,** and **D** are incorrect. **A** and **B** are incorrect because minimum and maximum password lengths relate to password strength, not reuse of old passwords. **D** is incorrect because the maximum password age determines when users must change their current password.

41. Which type of attack attempts to trick users into providing their legitimate web site credentials to malicious web sites?
   A. Spam
   B. Phishing
   C. Cross-site scripting
   D. Social engineering

☑ **B.** Phishing scams often manifest themselves as web site links within official looking e-mail messages asking a user to confirm their account information or something similar. The unsuspecting user is then redirected to a malicious web site that captures the credentials they enter.

☒ **A, C,** and **D** are incorrect. **A** is incorrect because spam is junk e-mail, which could be unsolicited legitimate advertising. **C** is incorrect because cross-site scripting is a type of attack whereby an attacker injects malicious code into a web page that will be run by others, thus running the code on their computers. **D** is incorrect because social engineering involves tricking people into divulging some kind of private information such as passwords.

42. An attacker gains access to your network. She then broadcasts a transmission to all hosts with her MAC addresses as the physical address of the default gateway. What type of attack is this?

   A. MAC attack
   B. Broadcast attack
   C. Trojan
   D. ARP poisoning

☑ **D.** ARP (Address Resolution Protocol) poisoning is an attack that updates the ARP cache on targeted hosts with a legitimate IP address (in this case, the default gateway's) paired with an attackers MAC (Media Access Control) hardware address. Victimized computers directing network traffic through the default gateway will really be sending the data to the attacker's MAC address (the attacker's machine).

☒ **A, B,** and **C** are incorrect. **A** is not an attack type. **B** is an ambiguous term. Network broadcasts are used for many types of attacks, but this does not specifically apply to the described attack as ARP poisoning does. **C** is not applicable. Trojans appear innocent but really carry malicious code. Users downloading pirated software will often infect their systems with a Trojan.

43. In the past your company has experienced malware unleashed on your LAN through users clicking malicious web site links in e-mail messages. What can you do to prevent this occurrence?

   A. Provide malware training to users.
   B. Encrypt the contents of hard disks.
   C. Enable e-mail digital signatures.
   D. Install a personal firewall on all computers.

☑   **A.** User education and awareness goes a long way to protecting your network. Demonstrating examples of phishing attacks will enable users to make informed decisions about suspicious e-mail messages.

☒   **B, C,** and **D** are incorrect. All of these are extremely important, but they cannot stop a user from willfully clicking links and infecting computers and networks. Some personal firewall software can identify suspicious e-mail messages, but ultimately the user decides what to click on.

44. An attacker telephones the front desk of a branch office and tells the receptionist he is the senior network engineer. He then asks the receptionist for her e-mail password due to an approaching e-mail server upgrade. What type of attack is this?

A. E-mail
B. Man-in-the-middle
C. Social engineering
D. Telephone

☑   **C.** Social engineering refers to human trickery and is a big problem. Attackers will often study the business, its processes, and its employees so that they can convince victims of their authenticity.

☒   **A, B,** and **D** are incorrect. These do not match the attack described in the question. **A** and **D** are incorrect because e-mail and telephone attacks are ambiguous terms; they encompass a large array of specific e-mail and telephone attacks. **B** is incorrect because man-in-the-middle attacks are perpetrated by a third party who captures and modifies network traffic between two communicating hosts when they think they are communicating directly to each other.

45. What danger is prevalent for companies that do not shred corporate documents before disposing of them?

A. Whaling
B. Dumpster diving
C. Phishing
D. Tailgating

☑   **B.** Much can be learned about an individual or a business by rifling through their garbage. Often documentation, bills, contact lists, and so on can provide valuable information to malicious users, especially for social engineering attacks. Shredding documents eliminates this risk.

☒ **A, C,** and **D** are incorrect. These are not dangers resulting in unshredded documents. **A** and **C** are incorrect because whaling is similar to phishing (tricking people into providing credentials, usually through a legitimate-looking e-mail message), except the message is addressed to people with some prominence (whale versus phish), for example, a corporate executive. **D** is incorrect because tailgating refers to unauthorized persons following authorized persons into secured areas.

46. What term is used to identify e-mail message attempts to trick users out of account or login information?
  A. Spam
  B. Phishing
  C. Whaling
  D. Spoofing

☑ **B.** Users can sometimes be tricked into trusting official-looking e-mail messages asking them to provide some kind of sensitive information such as usernames, passwords, or account numbers, to name just a few.

☒ **A, C,** and **D** are incorrect. **A** is incorrect because spam is unsolicited junk mail. **C** is similar to phishing except the attack is targeted to individuals of higher prominence. **D** does not apply—to spoof something means to forge or fake it, such as spoofing a MAC address to gain access to a wireless network secured with MAC address filtering.

47. You are configuring a group of laptops for traveling executives. What should you do to prevent operating system passwords from being locally hacked? (Choose two.)
  A. Use strong user account passwords.
  B. Encrypt the hard disk.
  C. Disable booting from removable media and set a CMOS password.
  D. Enable the password protection feature.

☑ **B** and **C.** Given local physical access, an attacker can boot from removable media and use freely available tools to reset passwords if he can defeat the CMOS password. In case this happens, encrypting the hard disk will further protect its contents, including user account and password information.

☒ **A** and **D** are incorrect. **A** is incorrect because even strong passwords can be locally hacked by booting locally from removable media; however, strong passwords should always be used. **D** is incorrect because there is no named "password protection feature."

48. While visiting your neighbor, he mentions his computer constantly displays the latest tropical vacation sales. You learn he has been visiting related web sites while planning the next family vacation. What is causing this nuisance?
- A. Adware
- B. Spyware
- C. Botnet
- D. Logic bomb

☑ **A.** Adware identifies user interests and displays related advertisements.

☒ **B, C,** and **D** are incorrect. **B** is incorrect because spyware collects user information without their knowledge. **C** is incorrect because a botnet is a collection of infected computers under hacker control. **D** is incorrect because logic bomb is a malicious code triggered by a specific condition, such as a date.

49. What type of malware is self-replicating?
- A. Trojan
- B. Worm
- C. Clone
- D. Spam

☑ **B.** Worms are self-replicating malicious code that do not have to attach themselves to files as conventional viruses do.

☒ **A, C,** and **D** are incorrect. **A** is incorrect because Trojans are not self-replicating; they are malicious code posing as innocent software. **C** is incorrect because clone is not a type of malware. **D** is incorrect because spam is not malware, it is unsolicited junk mail.

50. An unsuspecting user downloads a free hard disk optimization program. A few days later her bank notifies her that her credit card has been used in another country. Which type of malware is most likely responsible for this security breach?
- A. Zombie
- B. Worm
- C. Spam
- D. Trojan

☑ **D.** Trojans present themselves as useful benign software when in fact they are malicious code. A downloaded disk optimization program could contain a keylogger that captures credit card information that users type in.

☒ **A, B,** and **C** are incorrect. **A** is incorrect because zombie is an infected computer under hacker control that could, for example, send spam messages. **B** is incorrect because worms are self-propagating malware. **C** is incorrect because spam is unsolicited e-mail.

51. What name is given to unsolicited e-mail messages?
   A. SMTP
   B. POP
   C. Adware
   D. Spam

☑ **D.** Spam is unsolicited electronic junk mail. Spammers will often hijack machines to send their spam messages.

☒ **A, B,** and **C** are incorrect. SMTP transfers Internet mail between SMTP servers, so **A** is incorrect. POP allows mail clients to retrieve their e-mail from a POP server, so **B** is incorrect. **C** is not directly related to e-mail—adware displays advertisements based on user computer activity without the user's consent.

52. Refer to the illustration. What two tasks should be performed to further secure the system?

A. Disable the Guest account.

B. Rename the Administrator account.

C. Delete the Guest account.

D. Delete the Administrator account.

☑ **A** and **B**. To harden a Windows system, the Guest account should be disabled so that any activity can be traced to a specific user account. The Administrator account should be renamed, since attackers will attempt to crack the password associated with this account. If the Administrator account is renamed, a new regular user account named Administrator should be created with restricted permissions.

☒ **C** and **D** are incorrect. These are not possible—you cannot delete built-in Windows user accounts.

53. While working over the telephone with a network technician, you mention that your wireless network is using Layer 2 filtering. What type of filtering is this?

A. IP addresses

B. Computer name

C. PKI certificate

D. MAC address

☑ **D**. Network cards have a built-in physical hardware hexadecimal address composed of 48 bits, for example, 00-24-D6-9B-08-8C. This address applies to layer 2 (Data Link Layer) of the international OSI (Open Systems Interconnect) model. When technicians refer to layer 2 filtering, they are talking about filtering access based on MAC addresses.

☒ **A**, **B**, and **C** are incorrect. **A** is incorrect because IP addresses apply to layer 3 (Network Layer) of the OSI model, and **B** is incorrect because computer names apply to layer 5 (Session Layer). **C** is incorrect because PKI certificate is not a type of filtering.

54. What can be done to prevent man-in-the-middle attacks?

A. Authentication

B. Availability

C. Authorization

D. Fault tolerance

☑   **A.** Because an attacker computer sits between two conversing hosts, authenticating the two conversing computers with each other will prevent man-in-the-middle attacks. For example, authentication might require each host to prove its identify via a trusted PKI certificate.

☒   **B, C,** and **D** are incorrect. They cannot prevent this type of attack. **B** is incorrect because availability ensures a resource is always available. **C** is incorrect because authorization verifies an entity has access to a resource. **D** is incorrect because fault tolerance removes single points of failure.

55. An attacker enters an office building and plugs his laptop into an unused network jack behind a plant in the reception area. He is then connected to the LAN, where he initiates an ARP poisoning attack. How could this have been prevented? (Choose two.)

   A.   Update all virus scanners.
   B.   Use a strict IPSec policy for all LAN computers.
   C.   Disable unused switch ports.
   D.   Use a strict firewall policy on the perimeter firewall.

☑   **B** and **C.** IPSec can be used to ensure network traffic is accepted only from appropriate computers. For example, a LAN could use PKI certificates with IPSec—traffic from computers without a trusted PKI certificate would simply be dropped.

☒   **A** and **D** are incorrect. **A** is incorrect because virus scanners will not prevent ARP poisoning attacks. ARP poisoning exploits the nature of how IP addresses are resolved to MAC addresses. **D** is incorrect because perimeter firewall policies will do nothing to prevent this type of attack, since the attacker is directly connected to the internal LAN.

56. How can a user eavesdrop on Wi-Fi communications?

   A.   Use a vulnerability scanner.
   B.   Use a port scanner.
   C.   Configure an evil twin.
   D.   Configure an HTTP server.

☑   **C.** An evil twin is a rogue wireless access point configured to look like a legitimate wireless access point. Unsuspecting users then connect to this "evil twin" unknowingly, thus allowing an attacker to capture network traffic.

☒   **A, B,** and **D** are incorrect. They do not allow eavesdropping on Wi-Fi traffic. **A** is incorrect because vulnerability scanners identify security weaknesses. **B** is incorrect because port scanners identify open TCP or UDP ports. **D** is incorrect because HTTP servers are simply web servers and cannot capture Wi-Fi traffic.

57. Which measure should be in place to prevent cross-site scripting attacks?
  A. Enable personal host-based firewalls.
  B. Update virus scanners.
  C. Disable registry editing tools to prevent cookie theft.
  D. Web sites should validate user input before allowing submissions.

☑ **D.** Cross-site scripting attacks involve an attacker injecting malicious code to a web site that others then visit. The malicious code could then possible run on the viewer's computer. Web site developers must validate submitted user data to ensure malicious code is not being uploaded to the web site.

☒ **A, B,** and **C** are incorrect. Host-based firewalls, virus scanners, and registry tools will not mitigate cross-site scripting attacks.

58. Which of the following apply to physical port security? (Choose two.)
  A. TCP filtering
  B. MAC filtering
  C. UDP filtering
  D. 802.1x

☑ **B** and **D.** Switches can utilize MAC address filtering to restrict which computers can plug into specific switch ports. 802.1x-compliant switches can authenticate connecting computers before allowing network access.

☒ **A** and **C** are incorrect. They do not apply to physical port security; they are software transport protocols.

59. You would like a network security solution that can detect and prevent the success of network attacks. What should you deploy?
  A. NIDS
  B. HIDS
  C. NIPS
  D. HIPS

☑ **C.** NIPSs analyze network traffic to identify and shut down suspicious activity.

☒ **A, B,** and **D** are incorrect. **A** is incorrect because NIDS analyzes network traffic and alert administrators of suspicious activity, but nothing is done to stop the activity. **B** and **D** are incorrect because HIDS and HIPS are host-based intrusion detection and prevention systems that protect hosts and their applications, not networks.

60. Which tool can detect security misconfigurations?
- A. Protocol analyzer
- B. Vulnerability scanner
- C. Port scanner
- D. Virus scanner

> ☑ **B.** Vulnerability scanners scan one or more network devices for security weaknesses. This is normally done by comparing a database of known vulnerabilities against a machine's configuration.
>
> ☒ **A, C,** and **D** are incorrect. Protocol analyzers simply capture network traffic without analyzing it, so **A** is incorrect. Port scanners detect open TCP and UDP ports, not vulnerabilities, so **C** is incorrect. Virus scanners attempt to detect the presence of computer viruses, they do not identify security misconfigurations, so **D** is incorrect.

61. Your traveling users all have smart phones. To protect data on these devices in case they are lost or stolen, what should you configure?
- A. Virus scanner
- B. Cable lock
- C. Password
- D. Remote wipe

> ☑ **D.** Remote wipe capability mechanisms differ depending on the type of smart phone in question. Assuming the smart phone battery has not run out or its data has not already been hacked, an administrator might send a command or special e-mail or SMS message over the wireless network instructing the device to wipe its data.
>
> ☒ **A, B,** and **C** are incorrect. **A** is incorrect because virus scanners protect the mobile device whether it is stolen or not. **C** is incorrect because passwords can protect the mobile device, but could be hacked; the safest solution is to remotely wipe the phone data. **B** is incorrect because cable locks secure laptop devices, not smart phones.

62. Which of the following is true regarding virtualized server security?
- A. A compromised host operating system means all guest virtual machines are compromised.
- B. A compromised host operating system could render all guest virtual machines unavailable.
- C. A compromised virtual guest operating system means the host operating system is compromised.
- D. A compromised virtual guest operating system means all other virtual guest operating systems are compromised.

☑ **B.** A compromised physical host means the attacker would have control of the machine and could turn off virtual machines, or even crash the host operating system, thus making the virtual machines unavailable.

☒ **A, C,** and **D** are incorrect. They are untrue.

63. Users store company files on USB flash drives so that they can work from various computers outside of the corporate network. What should you do to secure this data?
A. Generate file hashes for USB flash drive content.
B. Scan USB flash drives for viruses.
C. Encrypt USB flash drives.
D. Digitally sign files on USB flash drives.

☑ **C.** Encryption ensures only authorized parties can decrypt USB flash drive contents.

☒ **A, B,** and **D** are incorrect. They do not fully secure data. **A** is incorrect because file hashing ensures files have not changed. **B** is incorrect because virus scanning ensures files are not infected. **D** is incorrect because digital signatures establish trust as to the file's origin.

64. You are responsible for two servers, Apollo and Zeus. Both Apollo and Zeus have TPM (Trusted Platform Module) chips that are fully configured for all server hard disks. The power supplies in Apollo fail, so you remove the hard disk and place it in Zeus. How can you access this replaced hard disk?
A. You cannot because it was encrypted with Apollo's TPM chip.
B. You must place Apollo's TPM chip in Zeus.
C. You must place Zeus' TPM chip in Apollo.
D. You must supply a separate recovery key.

☑ **D.** TPM is a motherboard chip that stores keys to encrypt and decrypt hard disks. Diligent administrators will have a recovery key stored elsewhere in case the motherboard or some other aspect of the machine fails.

☒ **A, B,** and **C** are incorrect. **A** is untrue; a recovery key can be used. **B** and **C** are incorrect because TPM chips are embedded on the motherboard.

65. You must ensure that server hard disk data is always protected. What should you do?
A. Encrypt the entire hard disk.
B. Configure a CMOS power-on password.
C. Encrypt files and folders.
D. Disable booting from removable media.

☑ C. Encrypting files and folders ensures data is protected whether the server is on or off, and even if the hard disk is removed from the server.

☒ A, B, and D are incorrect. Encrypting the entire hard disk protects the data when the server is powered off; however, once the server is powered on and the disk is decrypted, the data is no longer protected by encryption, so A is incorrect. CMOS passwords and disabling removable media boot are useless if a hard disk is physically removed from the machine—B and D will not ensure data is always protected.

66. A military division uses portable computing units to aid in flight take-off and landings at ad hoc landing strips. How can the military track the position of these portable units?
A. SSL
B. GPS
C. TPM
D. Bluetooth

☑ B. GPS (Global Positioning System) uses satellites to track longitude and latitude coordinates of a GPS device.

☒ A, C, and D are incorrect. A is incorrect because SSL is an application-specific transmission encryption solution. C is incorrect because TPM is a chip used to store keys for encrypting and decrypting hard disk contents. D is incorrect because bluetooth is a short-range wireless technology and would not be suitable beyond ten meters.

67. A junior developer creates a custom database application. During testing, she discovers that unexpected conditions cause her application to crash. What did she forget to implement?
A. Error trapping
B. Function parameters
C. Input validation
D. Variable declarations

☑ **A.** Application developers employ error trapping to capture unanticipated behavior to prevent the application from crashing.

☒ **B, C,** and **D** are incorrect. Error trapping would capture the incorrect use of function parameters, input validation, or problems with variable declarations.

68. You notice excessive network traffic when client stations connect to Windows Update to download patches and hotfixes. You would like to minimize network utilization. What should you do?
- **A.** Use full duplex.
- **B.** Disable SSL.
- **C.** Configure an internal patch update server.
- **D.** Disable Windows Update on all client stations.

☑ **C.** Internal patch update servers (such as Microsoft WSUS—Windows Server Update Services) deploy software updates to internal stations instead of their each downloading the updates, thus minimizing network utilization.

☒ **A, B,** and **D** are incorrect. **A** is incorrect because full duplex allows the simultaneous sending and receiving of data, but it will not help minimize network utilization in this case. **B** is incorrect because disabling SSL would render an application less secure and is not related to reducing windows update traffic. **D** is incorrect because disabling Windows Update on all stations would prevent them from receiving updates—this would certainly minimize network utilization, but would leave hosts vulnerable, so it is not an acceptable solution.

69. The web site administrator for your company would like an external device to handle all encryption and decryption processing to enhance server performance. What should you recommend?
- **A.** Trusted root certificate
- **B.** HSM
- **C.** TPM
- **D.** SSL

> ☑ **B.** HSMs (hardware security modules) are cryptoprocessor devices that offload processing work from hosts.
>
> ☒ **A, C, and D are incorrect. A** is incorrect because trusted root certificates are used to establish a chain of trust with PKI certificates, but they are not external crypto-devices. **C** is incorrect because TPM chips store keys for encrypting and decrypting hard disks, but they are embedded on motherboards; they are not external devices. **D** is incorrect because SSL is a cryptographic function handled by HSM, but SSL is not an external device.

70. What can be done to harden a public web server? (Choose two.)
  A. Patch the operating system.
  B. Configure the web server to use TCP port 4634.
  C. Implement input validation for web forms.
  D. Name web pages with .HTML instead of .HTM.

> ☑ **A and C.** A hardened web server begins with a hardened (patched) operating system. Validating user-submitted data is a critical application developer responsibility—user-submitted data can compromise a web server or client web browsers visiting the web site.
>
> ☒ **B and D are incorrect.** A public web server should always use standard TCP ports such as 80 and 443. .HTML files are no more secure than .HTM.

71. You must harden six Linux computers on a small departmental network. What should you check for? (Choose two.)
  A. Enabled unneeded daemons
  B. Apache daemon
  C. SSH daemon
  D. Linux patches

> ☑ **A and D.** Linux operating systems must be patched to ensure they are secure. Running unnecessary daemons (services) increase the attack surface.
>
> ☒ **B and C are incorrect. B and C** are incorrect because Apache (web server) and SSH remote administration may be required daemons and therefore may not have to be disabled.

72. What types of attacks cannot be mitigated by virus scanners? (Choose two.)
- A. DNS poisoning
- B. ARP cache poisoning
- C. Trojan
- D. Keylogging

☑ **A** and **B**. DNS and ARP poisoning are network-based attacks and not viruses.

☒ **C** and **D** are incorrect. They are both viruses and can be mitigated by virus scanners.

73. Which of the following best describes security fuzzing?
- A. Providing random data to test application security
- B. Conducting a quick overview security audit
- C. Jamming Wi-Fi radio frequencies to prevent rogue access points
- D. Injecting spoofed packets on a network

☑ **A**. Application fuzzing refers to the process of submitting sample data to test software.

☒ **B**, **C**, and **D** are incorrect. They have nothing to do with security fuzzing.

74. Which type of attack exploits the trust that a web site has for a user session?
- A. Cross-site scripting
- B. Smurf
- C. DoS
- D. Cross-site request forgery

☑ **D**. Cross-site request forgery attacks exploit trusted user sessions to web servers. For example, victims might click an innocent-looking link in an e-mail message that sends unauthorized commands to a web site the victim is authenticated to.

☒ **A**, **B**, and **C** are incorrect. These are not attack types exploiting trusted user connections to web sites.

75. Identify two benefits of server virtualization:
- A. Cheaper software licensing
- B. More secure than a physical server
- C. Less hardware costs
- D. Less space required in server room

☑ **C and D.** Less hardware and physical space is required to host virtual servers than if they were all physical.

☒ **A and B** are incorrect. Neither are true.

76. A Windows domain administrator has identified a number of settings that must be enabled to harden client operating systems. What is the best way to deploy these settings to more than one computer?

A. Send an e-mail message to each user with the appropriate instructions.

B. Use Group Policy.

C. Configure one computer, export the settings to a file, and use that file to import settings on the other computers.

D. Configure one computer, export the settings to a file, and attach the file to an e-mail message.

☑ **B.** Group policy should be used in Microsoft Active Directory environment to deliver operating system settings to groups of computers with a single central configuration.

☒ **A, C, and D** are incorrect. They are valid options, but none is the best option.

77. What can be done to secure smart phones? (Choose three.)

A. Configure a strong password.

B. Enable Bluetooth

C. Enable screen lock.

D. Install a virus scanner.

☑ **A, C, and D.** Strong passwords will frustrate many malicious hacking attempts if the device is stolen. Screen lock will prompt the user for a passcode or PIN before allowing access. With the proliferation of smart phone apps and Internet connectivity, virus scanners are more important than ever.

☒ **B** is incorrect. Bluetooth should only be enabled if required and available Bluetooth security mechanisms have been considered

78. What function does a RADIUS server provide?

A. Internal server that distributes operating system updates to client stations

B. Software that detects rogue access points

C. Centralized authentication for network access

D. File encryption

  ☑   **C.** RADIUS (Remote Access Dial In User Service) is a service that centrally authenticates connecting network clients whether the network is wired or wireless.

  ☒   **A, B**, and **D** are incorrect. They have nothing to do with the functionality of a RADIUS server.

79. Which protocol uses a ticket-granting service to prove user identity when accessing network resources?
- **A.** TACACS
- **B.** RADIUS
- **C.** IPSec
- **D.** Kerberos

  ☑   **D.** Kerberos grants authenticated users "tickets." which are used to prove identity and acquire access to network services.

  ☒   **A, B**, and **C** are incorrect. These do not use a ticket granting service. **A** is incorrect because TACACS (Terminal Access Controller Access Control System) provides central user authentication services in Unix environments much as RADIUS does beyond Unix environments, so **B** is also incorrect. **C** is incorrect because IPSec is TCP/IP application-independent packet encryption/integrity mechanism.

80. Your NIDS notifies you of excessive traffic destined for TCP port 389 on one of your servers. What type of traffic is this?
- **A.** LDAP
- **B.** HTTP
- **C.** RDP
- **D.** RADIUS

  ☑   **A.** LDAP (Lightweight Directory Access Protocol) can provide clear-text read and write access over TCP port 389 to a central network directory that could include e-mail addresses, user account information, and so on.

  ☒   **B, C**, and **D** are incorrect. HTTP uses TCP port 80, RDP uses TCP port 3389, and RADIUS uses ports 1812 and 1813.

81. You are ordering new laptops for your law enforcement division. In the past, productivity has been hampered because of strict password requirements. You would like to continue with a secure computing environment while eliminating password problems. Which of the following are possible solutions? (Choose two.)

A. Reducing password length to six characters

B. Smart card authentication

C. Biometric authentication

D. Security clearances

☑ **B** and **C.** Smart card authentication requires a PIN to be entered along with inserting a card in a card reader. Biometric authentication for laptops normally means fingerprint authentication. Both of these are secure solutions that are easier to use than username and complex passwords.

☒ **A** and **D** are incorrect. **A** is definitely incorrect—decreasing password length reduces security. Security clearances are used to allow access to specifically labeled data, but they do not specify how users authenticate; therefore, **D** is incorrect.

82. A router is configured to allow outbound TCP ports 80, 443, and 25. You would like to use the Remote Desktop Protocol to access a server at another location. Which of the following statements is correct?

A. You will be able to RDP to the external server.

B. You will not be able to RDP the external server because the router is explicitly denying RDP packets.

C. You will not be able to RDP the external server because the router is implicitly denying RDP packets.

D. You will not be able to RDP the external server because the router is implicitly allowing RDP packets.

☑ **C.** RDP (Remote Desktop Protocol) uses TCP port 3389, and this is implicitly denied because only ports 80, 443, and 25 allow traffic out.

☒ **A, B,** and **D** are incorrect. **A** is incorrect because it is untrue. **B** is incorrect because there is no explicit denial of RDP traffic; the denial is implicit in this example. **D** is incorrect because RDP traffic is not allowed.

83. Which concept exposes employees to varying job roles to increase their overall knowledge of the business?
   A. Mandatory vacations
   B. Least privilege
   C. Separation of duties
   D. Job rotation

> ☑ **D.** Job rotation allows employees to learn about various business roles, which is beneficial to the organization.
>
> ☒ **A, B,** and **C** are incorrect. **A** is incorrect because mandatory vacations allow different employees to fill a job role, which will expose any improper activity in the job role if any exists. **B** is incorrect because least privilege only grants needed rights and permissions to perform a task. **C** is incorrect because separation of duties requires the involvement of more than one person in a business transaction end to end to reduce the likelihood of fraud or embezzlement.

84. You are configuring an enterprise wireless router. A wizard allows you to select user accounts from Microsoft Active Directory that should have administrative access to the wireless router. What type of security model is this?
   A. DAC
   B. RBAC
   C. MAC
   D. Least privilege

> ☑ **B.** Role-based access control (RBAC) assigned users to roles, thus granting them access to perform certain tasks such as wireless router administration.
>
> ☒ **A, C,** and **D** do not apply. **A** is incorrect because discretionary access control (DAC) allows a resource owner (such as a file owner) to grant others access to that resource at her discretion. Operating system control of security allowances in accordance with company policies is referred to as mandatory access control (MAC), therefore **C** is incorrect. **D** is incorrect because least privilege ensures users only have the rights needed to do their jobs.

85. Which two of the following are related to computing security access control?
   A. Authentication
   B. Encryption
   C. Job rotation
   D. PII

☑ **A** and **B**. Authentication requires proof of identity before allowing access to resources. Encryption scrambles data such that only authorized parties can decrypt that data. Both of these relate to computer security access control.

☒ **C** and **D** are incorrect. These are security concepts, but they are not related to computing security access control.

86. A shared folder on server Bruno is configured as shown here. A database file named HfxClients .mdb in the shared folder lists Authenticated Users with Full Control. Which UNC path will allow the appropriate users to write changes to the database file?

A. \\Bruno\CorpData\HfxClients.mdb

B. //Bruno/CorpData/HfxClients.mdb

C. \\HfxClients.mdb\CorpData\Bruno

D. Users will not have write access to the file across the network.

☑ **D.** When NTFS and share permissions are combined, the most restrictive permissions (read in this case) apply.

☒ **A, B,** and **C** are incorrect. **A** is a properly formed UNC for this scenario, but write access is not allowed. **B** is incorrect; UNC paths use backslashes, not forward slashes. **C** is improperly formed; the host name or IP address is the first item listed in a UNC path as per answer **D**.

87. A user logs on to her station in the morning and supplies her username and password. During the day she accesses e-mail, databases, and corporate Intranet web sites without having to specify credentials. What is allowing this seamless access of network resources?

A. LDAP

B. Multifactor authentication

C. PKI

D. Single sign-on

☑ **D.** Single sign-on solutions require involved authentication once. Further requirements for user authentication are transparently presented when needed.

☒ **A, B,** and **C** are incorrect. **A** is incorrect because LDAP can be an authentication source, but it does not behave as directed in the scenario. **B** is incorrect because multifactor authentication involves authenticating with something you have and something you know—this might be used in single-sign on solutions, but it does not define single sign-on. **C** is incorrect because PKI is a hierarchy of trusted x.509 certificates used to secure communications.

88. Your assistant, Claire, must have access to create Microsoft Active Directory user accounts in the path "ou=Toronto,dc=Acme,dc=Ca" while you are on vacation in Hawaii. You add Claire to the built-in Domain Admins group. What security principle have you violated?

A. Separation of duties

B. Least privilege

C. Job rotation

D. Mandatory vacations

☑ **B.** Claire should be been delegated user creation rights to only the Toronto OU. By adding her to the Domain Admins group, you have given her much more privilege than she needed.

☒ **A, C,** and **D** are incorrect. These security principles have not been violated.

89. You are a new sales agent for Acme Floor Store, Inc. When traveling on the road for business, you sign in to the company VPN using a PIN and a hardware device–generated unique code. What is this code generating device called?

    A. Code-generating device
    B. PIN aggregator
    C. Token
    D. PIN aggravator

    ☑ **C.** Hardware tokens provide a time-sensitive code used in conjunction with a PIN to authenticate to a computer system, or in this case, a VPN.

    ☒ **A, B,** and **D** are incorrect. Code-generating device, PIN aggregator, and PIN aggravator are not industry standard terms.

90. You have hired three summer students who will be in your employment from July 11, 2011, to August 26, 2011. What can you do to ensure their user accounts are only valid until August 26, 2011?

    A. Delete the user accounts after work hours on August 26, 2011.
    B. Force a password change on August 26, 2011, after work hours.
    C. Set the account expiration date to August 26, 2011, after work hours.
    D. Set a calendar entry for August 26, 2011, reminding you to delete the user accounts.

    ☑ **C.** Set the summer student accounts to expire immediately after they complete their terms.

    ☒ **A, B,** and **D** are incorrect. **A** is incorrect because deleting unnecessary accounts is a good idea, but requires the administrator to remember—answer C is a better answer. **B** is incorrect because forcing password changes would still allow access to the network. **D** is incorrect because a calendar reminder is also a good idea, but it could be ignored or missed.

91. Which key does a secured web server use to decrypt a client session key? (Choose the best answer.)

    A. Public key
    B. Private key
    C. Symmetric key
    D. Asymmetric key

    ☑   **B.** Web browsers generate a unique session key that is encrypted with the web server's public key and sent across the network. The web server then uses its mathematically related private key to decrypt the message to expose the session key.

    ☒   **A, C,** and **D** are incorrect. **A** is incorrect because the opposite key is used for decryption. **C** and **D** are generic terms and do not provide as good an answer as **B**.

92. Which key is used when you send an encrypted e-mail message?
   A. Your public key
   B. Recipient's public key
   C. Your private key
   D. Recipient's private key

    ☑   **B.** You must possess the recipient's public key to encrypt messages to him. He decrypts the message with his related private key.

    ☒   **A, C,** and **D** are incorrect. **A** is incorrect because your public key would be needed by a sender to encrypt messages sent to you. **C** is incorrect becasue your private key is used to digitally sign outgoing messages or to decrypt encrypted messages sent to you. **D** is incorrect because only the recipient should have access to his private key.

93. Which are the two symmetric encryption algorithms in the list?
   A. Blowfish
   B. RC4
   C. RSA
   D. MD5

    ☑   **A** and **B.** Blowfish and RC4 are both symmetric algorithms. Symmetric algorithms use the same key for encryption and decryption.

    ☒   **C** and **D** are incorrect. RSA is an asymmetric encryption algorithm. MD5 is a hashing integrity algorithm, not an encryption algorithm.

94. While configuring IPSec to secure internal LAN traffic, you must specify an integrity algorithm. Which of the following would be valid choices? (Choose two.)
A. SHA-1
B. 3DES
C. RSA
D. MD5

☑ **A** and **D**. Integrity algorithms are used to ensure message came from who they say they came from and have not been tampered with.

☒ **B** and **C** are incorrect. They are both encryption algorithms.

95. Which of the following encryption algorithms are block ciphers?
A. RC4
B. IPSec
C. AES
D. RSA

☑ **D**. RSA (Rivest, Shamir, Adelman) is a block cipher. Block ciphers encrypt blocks of data as opposed to incoming bits or bytes (stream cipher).

☒ **A, B**, and **C** are incorrect They are not block ciphers. **A** is incorrect because RC4 is a stream cipher. **B** is incorrect because IPSec is not an algorithm and is therefore neither a block nor a stream cipher, but it can use a wide variety of encryption and integrity algorithms. **C** is incorrect because AES (Advanced Encryption Standard) is a symmetric encryption stream cipher.

96. SSL implies the use of what?
A. PKI
B. TLS
C. IPSec
D. VPN

☑ **A**. A PKI is a collection of trusted x.509 certificates containing public and private keys (among other data) used to encrypt and decrypt network communications. SSL is application-specific encryption using one or more PKI certificates to secure communications.

☒ **B, C,** and **D** are incorrect. They are not directly related to SSL. **B** is incorrect because TLS supersedes SSL but still implies the use of a PKI. **C** is incorrect because IPSec can use PKI certificates but is not related to SSL; IPSec is not application-specific security as SSL is. **D** is incorrect because VPNs can also use PKI certificates to establish an encrypted tunnel, but VPNs are not tied to SSL as the only solution.

97. A network technician has configured a wireless router such that stations must be authenticated before allowing network access. What did he configure?
   A. WEP
   B. WPA PSK
   C. 802.1x
   D. WPA2 PSK

☑ **C.** 802.1x requires authentication to a central authentication server before allowing network access. The client network connection, whether wireless or through a physical switch port, is not fully functional until successful authentication is achieved.

☒ **A, B,** and **D** are incorrect. WEP and WPA variants encrypt wireless network traffic, but do not enforce network level authentication.

98. What type of cryptographic function is used to detect changes to data?
   A. Block
   B. Stream
   C. Blowfish
   D. Hashing

☑ **D.** A hash is a uniquely generated result from a piece of data such as a file or a packet. Any changes to that data will result in a different hash.

☒ **A, B,** and **C** are incorrect. **A** and **B** are incorrect because block and stream refer to encryption ciphers, not hashing to provide data integrity. **C** is incorrect because blowfish is a symmetric algorithm used to encrypt data, not verify its authenticity.

99. Where are the serial numbers of revoked certificates posted?

A. PKI

B. CRL

C. Trusted root web site

D. CAL

☑ **B.** Certificate revocation lists (CRLs) revoked certificate serial numbers. Certificates may be revoked because of fraudulent use or certificate theft or compromise. Applications can refer to a CRL to ensure certificates in use are valid.

☒ **A, C,** and **D** are incorrect. PKI describes the overall collection of related certificates used for integrity and confidentiality, so **A** is incorrect. **C** is a fictitious term. **D** is incorrect because a CAL is a client access license used to license certain types of software.

100. A CA (Certificate Authority) is established and directly issues user and computer certificates that expire in ten years. The CA is then immediately brought offline. Which of the following statements are true? (Choose two.)

A. Issued user and computer certificates can no longer be used despite the expiration date.

B. Issued user and computer certificates can continue to be used until the expiration date.

C. New user certificates cannot be issued.

D. Expired user certificates can be renewed.

☑ **B** and **C.** The CA is required to create and manage issued certificates, but it is not required for normal certificate use. Existing certificates can continue to be used, but new certificates cannot be issued.

☒ **A** and **D** are incorrect. They are untrue.

A

About the CD-ROM

T he CD-ROM included with this book comes complete with MasterExam and the electronic version of the book. The software is easy to install on any Windows 2000/ XP/Vista/Windows 7 computer and must be installed to access the MasterExam feature. You may, however, browse the electronic book directly from the CD without installation. To register for the bonus MasterExam, simply click the Bonus MasterExam link on the main launch page and follow the directions to the free online registration.

System Requirements

Software requires Windows 2000 or higher and Internet Explorer 6.0 or above and 20MB of hard disk space for full installation. The electronic book requires Adobe Acrobat Reader.

Installing And Running Masterexam

If your computer CD-ROM drive is configured to autorun, the CD-ROM will automatically start up upon inserting the disk. From the opening screen you may install MasterExam by clicking the MasterExam link. This will begin the installation process and create a program group named LearnKey. To run MasterExam, use Start | All Programs | LearnKey | MasterExam. If the autorun feature did not launch your CD, browse to the CD and click the LaunchTraining.exe icon.

MasterExam

MasterExam provides you with a simulation of the actual exam. The number of questions, the type of questions, and the time allowed are intended to be an accurate representation of the exam environment. You have the option to take an open-book exam, including hints, references, and answers, a closed-book exam, or the timed MasterExam simulation.

When you launch MasterExam, a digital clock display will appear in the bottom right-hand corner of your screen. The clock will continue to count down to zero unless you choose to end the exam before the time expires.

Electronic Book

The entire contents of this Practice Exam book are provided in PDF. Adobe's Acrobat Reader has been included on the CD.

Help

A help file is provided through the help button on the main page in the lower left-hand corner. An individual help feature is also available through MasterExam.

Removing Installation(s)

MasterExam is installed to your hard drive. For best results removing this program, use the Start | All Programs | LearnKey | Uninstall option.

Technical Support

For questions regarding the content of the electronic book or MasterExam, please visit www.mhprofessional.com/techsupport/. For customers outside the United States, e-mail international_cs@mcgraw-hill.com.

LearnKey Technical Support

For technical problems with the software (installation, operation, removing installation), please visit www.learnkey.com, e-mail techsupport@learnkey.com, or call toll free at 1-800-482-8244.

INDEX

NUMBERS

802.11a standard, 174
802.11b standard, 174
802.11g network
    correcting unstable connectivity,
        169–170
    microwave oven interference
        with, 172
    shared bandwidth on, 173–174
802.11n standard, 99, 108
802.1x standard
    authentication prior to gaining
        network access, 107–108,
        147–148, 174, 457
    defined, 99–100, 150
    for physical port security, 441
    preventing ARP cache poisoning
        with, 105
    securing open wireless networks, 368
    troubleshooting user access to
        wireless networks, 193
802.3 standard, 169, 174

A

abnormal activity
    analyzing network traffic with
        NIPSs, 381
    false positives reporting, 388–389
    handling infected server with
        DRP, 323
    human security guards noticing, 275
    IPS detecting and stopping, 141
    mail server log revealing SMTP
        excessive traffic, 337
    performance baselines gauging,
        45, 127
acceptable use policies
    clean desk policy vs., 52
    defined, 428
    example, 44
    password policies vs., 45
access codes, for cipher locks, 271

access control
    account lockout for, 210
    ACLs for, 212, 216
    adding new users to groups, 206
    administrative controls, 218
    auditing IT infrastructure for, 207
    authentication and encryption for,
        451–452
    disabling user accounts temporarily
        for, 209
    discretionary, 208–209, 213, 451
    explicit allowance firewall rule, 215
    granting to groups, 217–218
    implicit denial, 210, 213–214
    mandatory. see MAC (mandatory
        access control)
    mandatory vacations. see mandatory
        vacations
    overview of, 198
    password hints for complex
        passwords, 206
    password issues for service accounts,
        215–216
    password policies. see password
        policies
    physical, 216–217
    preventing unauthorized
        access, 217
    security clearances vs. classification
        labels, 219
    strong passwords, 211
    technical controls for, 218
    time of day, 209
    Trusted OS for, 211
    violating least privilege, 207
    violating separation of
        duties, 207
access control entry (ACE), 212
access control lists. see ACLs (access
    control lists)
access list, defining access to
    facility, 276
access logs, 212, 382
account lockout
    on administrative accounts, 210, 369
    least privilege vs., 207

mitigating brute-force password
    attacks, 70
mitigating user account password
    attacks, 108
accountability
    defined, 26
    implementing on server with
        auditing, 35
Accounting department, adding financial
    software to, 105
ACE (access control entry), 212
ACLs (access control lists)
    allowing/denying network traffic,
        144–145
    configuring Cisco router, 216
    controlling access to particular
        resource, 212
    defined, 212
Active Directory
    defined, 212
    deploying audit settings quickly
        in, 390
    using accounts as service
        accounts, 364
Address Resolution Protocol (ARP), 18
address translation, and NAT, 153
administrative activities
    audit log recording, 387–388
    RBAC granting users access to, 451
    tracking changes to user
        accounts, 385
administrative controls, 218
administrative passwords, disk
    encryption vs., 118
Administrator account
    account lockout on, 210, 369
    renaming or disabling for security, 367
    renaming to harden Windows
        system, 438–439
Advanced Encryption Standard. see AES
    (Advanced Encryption Standard)
adware
    changing web browser home page, 87
    defined, 437, 438
    example of, 78–79
    spyware vs., 123

AES (Advanced Encryption Standard)
  as block cipher, 239
  securing LANs with IPSec, 234
  as stream cipher, 456
  as symmetric encryption algorithm, 232
air conditioning. *see* HVAC (Heating
  Ventilation Air Conditioning)
air flow, monitoring, 273–274
air-sealed containers, for hard disks with
  spilled liquid, 321
alarms
  in behavior-based detection, 432
  mitigating security threats with, 102
ALE (annual loss expectancy) value
  calculating after identifying threats
    and valuing assets, 300
  calculating for server downtime,
    294, 430
  calculating overview, 293–294
  calculating using probability values
    that vary, 296
  defined, 295
  quantitative risk analysis using,
    292–293, 296, 433
  risk management example, 298
alerts
  alarms vs., 102
  configuring with NIDS, 385–386
  false positives as, 388–389
annual loss expectancy. *see* ALE (annual
  loss expectancy) value
annual rate of occurrence (ARO),
  calculating ALE, 293–294, 430
anomaly-based configuration, 383, 421
anonymous proxy servers, 429
antennas
  decreasing wireless security with
    hi-gain, 422
  placing wireless router with
    omnidirectional, 168
antispam software filtering, 123, 153
antistatic bags, 342
antistatic wrist strap, 276–277
antivirus software
  file hashing vs., 237
  for financial software, 105
  not encrypting network traffic,
    423, 425
  not preventing ARP poisoning, 64
  not related to laptop theft, 124
  not related to operating system
    defects, 123
  spyware vs., 123
  for USB devices on laptops, 104
APIPA (Automatic IP Address), 147
application pools, mitigating threats,
  109–110

applications
  financial software security, 105
  hosting with cloud computing, 120
  IPSec not applicable for specific, 125
  monitoring usage of, 127
  monitoring with HIDS, 125
  protecting from SQL injection
    attacks, 67
  protecting with error handling
    coding, 103
ARO (annual rate of occurrence),
  calculating ALE, 293–294, 430
ARP (Address Resolution Protocol), 18
ARP poisoning
  addressing with Network Access
    Control, 193–194
  countermeasures, 63–64
  cross-site scripting vs., 67
  DNS poisoning vs., 107
  example of, 60
  man-in-the-middle attacks with, 68
  preventing, 105–106, 440
  understanding, 434
  when attacker gains network
    access, 171
asset identification
  in risk analysis, 289, 359–360
  threat assessment vs., 290
asset valuation
  before calculating ALE, 300
  in qualitative risk analysis, 296–297
asymmetric encryption
  defined, 222
  RSA algorithm as, 232–235, 243, 455
attack types
  ARP poisoning. *see* ARP poisoning
  brute-force. *see* brute-force attacks
  certification objectives, 53
  cross-site scripting. *see* XSS (cross-site
    scripting) attack
  DDoS, 66
  dictionary. *see* dictionary attacks
  DNS poisoning, 60, 67, 106–107
  DNS redirection, 63, 65
  domain kiting, 65
  DoS. *see* DoS (denial of service)
    attacks
  dumpster diving, 66, 435–436
  eavesdrop, 63, 66
  hybrid password, 69
  man-in-the-middle, 68, 435, 439–440
  overview of, 54
  password. *see* password attacks
  phishing. *see* phishing scams
  session hijacking, 69
  smurf, 65–66
  social engineering, 65

spoof, 62, 436
SQL injection. *see* SQL injection
  attacks
zero-day. *see* zero-day exploits
audit logs, 384, 387–388
auditing
  configuring file system for file
    access, 126
  defined, 30
  implementing accountability with, 35
  monitoring and. *see* monitoring and
    auditing
  security assessments and. *see* security
    assessments and audits
  violating separation of duties
    example, 207
auditor, defined, 339
authentication. *see also* biometric
  authentication; smartcards; SSO (single
  sign-on) authentication
  802.1x standard for, 100, 107–108,
    193, 368
  access control related to, 451–452
  authorization vs., 27
  availability vs., 36
  CAs issuing certificates for, 246
  CHAP protocol, 192
  configuring computers with PKI
    certificates for, 426
  defined, 20, 178
  description of, 34
  examples of, 30, 193
  hardware tokens, 190–191
  identification before, 29, 30, 189
  iris scanning, 190
  Kerberos, 187, 449
  LDAP, 188, 195
  multifactor, 184, 190
  Network Access Control, 185,
    193–194
  PEAP using server-side PKI for, 166
  preventing man-in-the-middle
    attacks, 439–440
  preventing multiple logons with
    SSO, 191
  prior to gaining network access, 457
  proof of identity required for, 427
  proxy servers for user, 140, 421
  RADIUS. *see* RADIUS (Remote
    Authentication Dial In User
    Service) server
  reducing costs with VoIP, 185
  same username/password for internal
    web sites with SSO, 194
  single-factor, 189
  TACAS+, 187, 188
  VPN for remote access to servers, 184

Windows 7 workstations, 147–148
WPA2 using local computer
certificates, 192
authorization
authentication before, 29
confidentiality vs., 291
example of, 27
methods verified by security
guards, 276
Automatic IP Address (APIPA), 147
availability
authentication vs., 30
confidentiality vs., 28, 291
configuring hard disks with RAID 1
for, 427
defined, 26
ensuring by clustering e-mail
servers, 29
example of, 33
impact analysis vs., 291
of shielded computer rooms, 29
tasks helping with, 35–36

B

backdoors
botnets vs., 86
created by Trojans, 87
overview of, 80–81
backups
availability with, 35–36
differential, 315
as least desirable DRP practice, 320
of log files in server, 392
quickest restoration with daily full, 431
reducing risk using, 292
storage retention policies for, 386
storing financial data in safe, 124
tape, 274
TPM key, 128–129
baseline analysis
in behavior-based network
monitoring, 383
identifying deviations with, 360
Basic Service Set Identifiers (BSSIDs),
detecting rogue access points, 174
behavior-based detection
alarms, 432
network monitoring, 383
biometric authentication
defined, 184
fingerprint scanners, 44
iris scanning, 190
for laptops, 450

PII applied to personal traits
and, 47–48
retinal scans as most secure, 279
BIOS updates, 363
bit stream forensic copying tools, 343–344
black box testing, 364–365, 370
block cipher
defined, 238–239
DES and AES as, 239
RSA as, 456
Blowfish
as hot hashing function, 240
as symmetric algorithm, 455
TwoFish superseding, 235
blue box, 365
Bluejacking, 170, 175–176
Bluesnarfing, 171
Bluetooth
defined, 158
disabling discovery mode to harden
mobile devices, 120
not a threat to cell phones, 82
not necessarily using for smart
phones, 448
boot order, changing, 81, 82
boot sector virus, 27
booting from removable media, disabling
on laptops, 436
botnets
defined, 79, 437
dispatching DDoS attacks with, 84
example of, 80, 85–86
bridges
examining only MAC addresses
within packets, 17
single broadcast domains of, 420
using MAC addresses, 5, 15
British thermal units (BTUs), 431
broadcast domains
routers separating networks into
smaller, 420
VLANs and, 342
brute-force attacks
buffer overflow attacks vs., 63
defined, 60
hybrid password attacks vs., 69
passive security testing vs., 364
preventing with account lockout, 70
spoof attacks vs., 62
SQL injection attacks vs., 61
BSSIDs (Basic Service Set Identifiers),
detecting rogue access points, 174
BTUs (British thermal units), 431
budgets, valid IT forensic items for, 346
buffer overflow attacks
countermeasures, 64

defined, 60
example of, 61, 63
building access card, insecurity of, 190
buildings, new
establishing alternate location for
business in DRP, 319
risk analysis of, 297
risk management strategy for, 300
business continuity, goal of disaster
recovery, 316
business impact analysis
for disaster recovery, 312–313, 319–320
incident response policies, 431–432

C

cable locks, 124, 216–217
cabling
choosing most secure, 2, 9
EMI shielding for facility with
CAT6, 272
joining RJ-45 connectors to UTP or
STP using crimper, 11
cache
poisoning. see ARP poisoning
reducing Internet traffic using proxy
server, 423
calendar entry, user account deletion, 454
CAs (certificate authorities)
configuring PKI certificates for
authentication, 426
cross-certifying departmental,
262–263
digitally signing certificates with
private key, 263, 264
enabling SSL on e-commerce site, 259
installing root, 260
issuing certificates, 246
issuing certificates with expiration
date, 458
renewing expired X.509
certificates, 256
role in PKI, 264
taking offline to harden PKI, 254
CAT6 cabling, 272
CCMP (Counter Mode with Cipher Block
Chaining Message Authentication
Code Protocol), 167–168
CDMA mobile devices, 341
CD-ROM accompanying this
book, 459–461
cell phones
Bluejacking, 170, 175–176
Bluesnarfing, 171

cell phones (*Cont.*)
  difficulty of forging SIM cards, 340
  frequency range of, 172
  gathering evidence from, 341
  threats to, 82
  voice encryption software for, 127
cell towers, hackers posing as, 82
centralized authentication, RADIUS, 371, 448–449
certificate authorities. *see* CAs (certificate authorities)
certificate revocation lists (CRLs)
  defined, 246
  publishing list of untrusted private keys, 255–256
  revoked certificate serial numbers, 458
  time frame for revoked certificates, 255
Certificate Signing Request (CSR), 259–260
chain of custody
  for collection of evidence, 432
  in computer forensics, 335
  describing, 339
  documenting state of seized equipment in, 343
Challenge Handshake Authentication Protocol (CHAP), 168, 192
CHAP (Challenge Handshake Authentication Protocol), 168, 192
Cheops tool, 368
CIA (Confidentiality, Integrity, and Availability), 20
cipher locks, accessing building with, 271
ciphertext, one-time pads for wartime, 240
Cisco network authentication, TACAS+ for, 188
classification labels, 219
clean desk policy, 51–52
client-side certificates, restricting workstation access, 258
client-side script, hacker inserting into web page, 66–67
clones, 437
cloud computing, 120, 126
clustering, server
  creating disaster recovery plan vs., 317–318
  as due diligence, 29
  for e-mail service availability, 29
  removing single points of failure, 430
  software between two servers, 314
CMOS
  collecting data in order of volatility from, 336
  hardening for physical server room security, 81
  setting password for laptops, 436

code review, 360, 363
coding guidelines
  error handling, 103
  input validation. *see* input validation
cold and hot aisles, 273
cold sites, 313–314
collision domains, 342, 420
complex passwords. *see* strong passwords
computer digital certificates, 259
computer forensics
  admission of packet captures as evidence, 342–343
  analyzing network traffic, 345–346
  capturing network traffic, 342
  certification objectives, 327
  chain of custody in, 335, 339, 432
  collecting data following order of volatility, 336
  controlling spread of worm virus, 346
  documenting state of seized equipment, 343
  evidence from cell phones, 341
  evidence on digital cameras, 341
  examining hard disk with bit stream forensic copying tools, 343–344
  faraday bags for seized mobile wireless devices, 341–342
  forensic expert witnesses, 339
  forging cell phone SIM card, 340
  function of first responder, 335
  imaging RAID 5 arrays, 336
  incriminating data in encrypted files, 344
  IT budget items in, 346
  mail server log showing excessive SMTP outbound traffic, 336–337
  metadata analysis, 344
  obtaining encrypted disk in online fraud, 347
  overview of, 328
  proving authenticity of e-mail, 339–340
  purpose of disk forensic software, 340
  recovering deleted files from emptied Recycle Bin, 347
  reducing files to be analyzed, 338
  rules for, 345
  screenshots, 337
  video surveillance for, 337
confidentiality
  CAs issuing certificates for, 246
  concealing data in risk analysis, 291
  defined, 26
  enabling WPA on WLAN for, 164
  ensuring for backups stored offsite, 317

ensuring on USB flash drives, 121
  example of, 31
  implementing with EFS encryption, 28
  implementing with encryption, 35, 235, 427
  privacy policies protecting, 44
  protocol analyzers violating, 31
  of shielded computer rooms, 29
  violating, 34
connectivity, network
  alternative method for remote, 6, 17–18
  devices using MAC addresses for, 5, 15
  identifying transmission problems with TRACERT, 5, 16
console port passwords, 278–279
content filtering, with web security gateways, 142
continuous security monitoring, 101
cookies
  cross-site request forgeries using, 101–102
  storing preferences for specific web sites, 68
cooling data centers, with hot and cold aisles, 273
copies of data
  with bit stream forensic tools, 344
  performing forensic analysis only on, 345
corporate assets, using for personal gain, 290
cost-benefit analysis, 300
Counter Mode with Cipher Block Chaining Message Authentication Code Protocol (CCMP), 167–168
credit card numbers, 48
crime, computer. *see* computer forensics
crime scene, not disturbing, 337
criminals, never seeking out, 337
crimpers, 11
CRLs (certificate revocation lists)
  defined, 246
  publishing list of untrusted private keys, 255–256
  revoked certificate serial numbers, 458
  time frame for revoked certificates, 255
cross-certifying departmental CAs, 262–263
cross-site request forgeries, 101–102, 447
cross-site scripting. *see* XSS (cross-site scripting) attack
cryptography. *see also* EFS (Encrypting File System); encryption
  accessing SSL-enabled web sites, 231–232
  block ciphers, 239

connecting to online banking web site, 235–236
elliptic curve cryptography (ECC), 237
encryption strength of standards, 232–233
FTPS using SSL to secure FTP traffic, 238
hardening VPNs, 241
identifying message digest algorithms, 240
insecurity of PAP, 241–242
IPSec encryption, 231, 234
MD5 providing data integrity, 232
non-repudiation, 236
of one-time pads for wartime, 240
overview of, 222
PKI requirements, 233
Pretty Good Privacy, 241
private keys, 242–243
protecting e-mail confidentiality with HTTPS, 230
providing data confidentiality, 235
RSA using two mathematically related keys, 233
SCP, 238
SSH allowing secured remote access to Unix host, 230
steganography, 236
stream and block ciphers, 238
symmetric encryption, 239–240, 243
TLS superseding SSL, 231
TwoFish superseding Blowfish, 235
using digital signatures, 242
using file hashing, 237
CSR (Certificate Signing Request), 259–260
Custodian security role, 26–27, 32
customer contracts, justifying cost of warm sites, 321

D

DAC (discretionary access control)
defined, 208, 451
example of, 208–209
MAC vs., 213
daemons, hardening Linux computers, 445–446
daily full backups, 431
damage control, computer forensics, 335
data classifications, MAC, 212–213
data handling, USB flash drive encryption, 50

data labeling, 47–48
Data Link Layer (Layer 2) filtering, based on MAC addresses, 439
data loss prevention (DLP), 122, 128
Data Owner security role, 28, 427
data recovery specialist, 321
data sensitivity, classification labels for, 219
Data User, 28
Database Administrator, 28
DDoS (distributed denial of service) attack
facilitating with botnets, 80, 84
IV attacks in WEP vs., 171
smurf attack as, 66
deadbolt locks, 271
debugging
conducting code review before, 360
fuzzing and hardening vs., 97
operating systems, 123
decimal values, IPv4, 4, 12
decryption
key escrow as trusted third party with keys for, 255
private keys used for, 243
default configurations, insecure wireless routers using, 107
default gateways
not causing unlit link light on network card, 147
troubleshooting TCP/IP settings on workstation, 4, 13
VLANs interconnecting with other VLANs, 418–419
deleted files, examining forensic data, 343–344
demilitarized zone (DMZ)
mail servers using SMTP on TCP port 25 in, 419
not detecting or preventing attacks, 141
placing VPN concentrator for traveling users in, 147
plugging wireless router into, 140
tracking malicious activity to host in, 359, 362
using sniffers and NIDS in, 145
viewing network between two firewalls, 146
denial of service (DoS) attacks
DDoS attack vs., 66
example of, 65
not applying account lockouts to administrative accounts, 210
rendering system as unusable, 27
SYN flood protection preventing, 148
departmental CAs, cross-certifying, 262–263

Dependencies tab, hardening Windows server, 109
DES (Digital Encryption Standard), 232–233, 239
design review, example of, 362–363
detailed verbose logging, and performance, 391
DHCP (Dynamic Host Configuration Protocol)
getting IP address from, 6, 16
not authenticating connections, 140
not preventing wireless connectivity by disabling, 164
Diameter protocol, adding to RADIUS, 191
dictionary attacks
creating botnets, 85–86
defined, 61
hybrid password attack vs., 69
mitigating with complex passwords, 98, 211
phishing vs., 62
differential backups, 315
digital cameras, not modifying digital evidence on, 341
digital certificates
CAs issuing, 246, 263
computer, 258
enabling SSL for e-commerce, 259
HTTPS requiring, 230
installing root CAs in different cities, 260
not encrypting, 254
with private keys, 258
renewing expired X.509, 256
restricting workstation access with client-side, 258
for specific uses, 253
time frame for revoked, 255
verifying identity of requestor, 255–256
warning that web site not be trusted, 256–257
web server security with, 257–258
Digital Encryption Standard (DES), 232–233, 239
digital footprints. see computer forensics
digital signatures
CA using private key for, 263, 264
creating with private keys, 243
document workflow using, 254
error handling vs., 103
establishing trust with, 443
files not likely to contain incriminating forensic data, 344

digital signatures (*Cont.*)
    non-repudiation vs., 236
    with Pretty Good Privacy, 241
    preventing ARP cache poisoning
        with, 105
    providing data integrity with, 235, 242
    releasing servers from, 128
    verifying message sender authenticity
        in forensics, 339–340
    warning that web site not be trusted,
        256–257
disaster recovery
    best DRP solutions, 320
    business continuity in, 316
    business impact analysis in, 312–313,
        319–320
    certification objectives, 303
    clustering software between two
        servers for, 314
    configuring RAID 1 disk mirroring
        for, 312
    creating list of professionals in case of
        floods, 319
    differential backups for, 315
    ensuring high availability, 318
    ensuring integrity and confidentiality
        of backups stored offsite, 317
    hardware fault tolerance, 315
    hot sites, 313
    improving web site response time, 314
    least desirable DRP practices, 320
    overview of, 304
    RAID 5 example, 316–317
    spilling liquid on old server data hard
        disk, 321
    succession planning, 315–316
    warm sites, 313–314, 321
disaster recovery plans (DRPs)
    best solutions, 320
    business impact analysis in, 319–320
    creating list of professionals in case of
        flood, 319
    example of, 317–318
    items to be considered, 318–319
    least desirable practices, 320
    quick data restoration from backup
        tape, 431
disaster recovery policies, 386, 428
discretionary access control. *see* DAC
    (discretionary access control)
disk surface scan, 312–313
disks. *see* hard disks
distributed denial of service (DDoS) attack
    facilitating with botnets, 80, 84
    IV attacks in WEP vs., 171
    smurf attack as, 66

DLP (data loss prevention), 122, 128
DMZ (demilitarized zone)
    mail servers using SMTP on TCP
        port 25 in, 419
    not detecting or preventing attacks, 141
    placing VPN concentrator for
        traveling users in, 147
    plugging wireless router into, 140
    tracking malicious activity to host in,
        359, 362
    using sniffers and NIDS in, 145
    viewing network between two
        firewalls, 146
DNS (Domain Name Service)
    domain kiting vulnerability in, 65
    resolving FQDNs to IP addresses, 4, 12
    returning FQDNs to IP addresses, 4
    reverse lookups, 12
    troubleshooting TCP/IP settings on
        workstation, 4, 13
    UDP port 53, 419
DNS forwarding, 150
DNS poisoning, 60, 106–107
DNS redirection attacks, 63, 65
DNS round robin, 417
document restoration specialist, DRP, 319
documentation
    downloaded with virus from business
        partner site, 289–290
    of evidence in chain of custody, 339
    of SLAs, 46
    use of USB write-blocking devices, 341
    user access and rights reviews, 384
documents, paper
    clean desk policy for, 52
    mitigating physical threats by
        shredding, 66, 78, 435–436
domain administrative accounts, 364
Domain Controller, AD database
    replication, 186
domain kiting, 65
Domain Name Service. *see* DNS (Domain
    Name Service)
domain poisoning, 65
door keypad locks, 276
DoS (denial of service) attacks
    DDoS attack vs., 66
    example of, 65
    not applying account lockouts to
        administrative accounts, 210
    rendering system as unusable, 27
    SYN flood protection
        preventing, 148
downtime, server
    calculating ALE for, 294, 430
    justifying cost of warm sites, 321

drive encryption, TPM for, 121–122
DRPs (disaster recovery plans)
    best solutions, 320
    business impact analysis in, 319–320
    creating list of professionals in case of
        flood, 319
    example of, 317–318
    items to be considered, 318–319
    least desirable practices, 320
    quick data restoration from backup
        tape, 431
dual-factor authentication, 189
due care
    correcting security problems in, 26, 45
    due diligence vs., 33
    example of violating, 32
due diligence
    defined, 26, 432
    due care vs., 32–34
    using web server cluster for, 33
due process
    defined, 26
    due care vs., 32–34
    due diligence vs., 33
dumpster diving
    dangers of unshredded documents,
        435–436
    security policy to prevent, 66
DVD-R, as forensic evidence in order of
    volatility, 338
Dynamic Host Configuration Protocol. *see*
    DHCP (Dynamic Host Configuration
    Protocol)

EAP (Extensible Authentication
    Protocol), 166–167
EAP-TLS (Extensible Authentication
    Protocol-Transport Layer Security)
    enabling on wireless network, 173
    enabling when hardening VPNs, 241
    PEAP vs., 167
    security of, 242
eavesdrop attacks
    DDoS attack vs., 66
    defined, 63
    DoS attack vs., 65
ECC (elliptic curve cryptography), 237
EFS (Encrypting File System)
    ensuring confidentiality with, 28, 31
    hardening operating system with,
        103–104
    recovering encrypted files from old
        accounts, 118

requiring NTFS, 129
TPM chips vs., 122
electromagnetic interference (EMI)
shielding, for entire facility, 272
electromagnetic radio frequencies, Faraday
cage limiting, 276–277
electronic book, on CD-ROM
accompanying this book, 460–461
elliptic curve cryptography (ECC), 237
e-mail. *see also* spam
acceptable use policies, 428
antispam software incorrectly
identifying as spam, 153
clustering servers for availability, 29
encrypting with recipient's public
key, 455
mail server log revealing excessive
SMTP outbound traffic, 336–337
mail servers using SMTP on TCP
port 25, 419
phishing, 62
phishing, mitigating, 47
preventing information leakage,
127–128
providing valid addresses for
spammers, 119
retention policies, 428
stating identity during login, 28–29
training users in malware, 434–435
tricking users for account/login
information, 436
verifying message sender authenticity
in forensics, 339–340
embezzlement, as internal threat, 290
EMI (electromagnetic interference)
shielding, for entire facility, 272
employees
administrative control of hiring
policy for, 218
assigning tasks to in disaster recovery
plan, 319
authorized access with ID badges, 276
internal threats from, 290
training in disaster recovery plan, 320
training in security awareness, 47
training to reduce risk, 292
Encrypting File System. *see* EFS
(Encrypting File System)
encryption. *see also* cryptography; EFS
(Encrypting File System)
access control related to, 451–452
archived log file, 389
cell phone voice, 127
confidentiality of backup tapes stored
offsite with, 317
confidentiality with, 31, 35, 427

e-mail, using recipient's public key, 455
file hashes vs., 340
forensic data in files with, 344
hard disk contents protected by, 118,
124, 444
packet, 103, 155
PEAP using server-side PKI, 166
releasing servers from, 128
securing network traffic using
VPNs, 423
security audit of wireless, 368–369
SSH network traffic, 425
TCP/IP protocols for, 5
TPM chips for drive, 121–122
USB flash drive contents protected
by, 50, 121, 278
verifying message sender authenticity
vs., 340
WPA using TKIP for, 173
equipment, not disturbing in computer
forensics, 343
equipment disposal policies, 47
error handling, mitigating threats, 103
error trapping, for application developers,
444–445
ESD boots, 276–277
ESD mat, 276–277
/etc/passwd file, 63
event viewer logs, 382, 387–388
events
analyzing event viewer logs, 102–103
monitoring with HIDS, 125
evidence. *see* computer forensics
evil twin
configuring with rogue access
point, 170
eavesdropping on Wi-Fi
communications, 440
.EXE file, 388
expiration dates
certificates with, 458
Password Never Expires option for
service accounts, 256
renewing expired X.509
certificates, 256
setting for user accounts, 454
explicit allowance firewall rule, 215
exploits
botnets vs., 86
defined, 27
honeypots vs., 151
taking advantage of
vulnerabilities, 34
zero-day. *see* zero-day exploits
Extensible Authentication Protocol
(EAP), 166–167

Extensible Authentication Protocol-
Transport Layer Security. *see* EAP-TLS
(Extensible Authentication Protocol-
Transport Layer Security)
external threats, risk analysis, 290–291

fail open, 277
fail secure systems, 275
fail-safe. *see* fault tolerance
false negatives
defined, 152
false positives vs., 432
in IDS or security systems, 277
false positives
defined, 152
example of, 388–389
fail-safe vs., 277
faraday bags, for seized mobile wireless
devices, 341–343
faraday cage, 276–277
fault tolerance
business continuity vs., 316
configuring UPS for, 277
defined, 275
hardware, 315
impact analysis vs., 291
RAID 1 providing. *see* RAID 1 disk
mirroring
removing single points of failure with,
439–440
fiber channel switches, 314
fiber optics, 2, 9
File and Print Sharing, TCP ports for, 359
file hashes
detecting changes to data with,
443, 457
disk forensic software using, 340
file system auditing vs., 126
generating for log files, 389
for integrity, 426
never creating on original disk, 340
not likely to contain incriminating
forensic data, 344
overview of, 237
file servers, RADIUS vs., 186
file storage, using TFTP server, 4, 13
File Transfer Protocol. *see* FTP (File
Transfer Protocol)
File Transfer Protocol Secure. *see* FTPS
(File Transfer Protocol Secure)
filtering network traffic, web security
gateways, 142

fingerprint scanner
    defeating using valid lifted
        fingerprints, 190
    identifying users, 274
    logging into secured laptop using,
        44, 450
    as second most secure
        authentication, 279
fingerprints, as personally identifiable
    information, 429
fire suppression system, 273
Firefox on Linux, 87
firewall auditing, 385
firewall log
    audit log vs., 387–388
    FTP access log vs., 382
    identifying client computers
        controlled by RDP from Internet,
        390–391
    monitoring events from months
        ago, 387
    revealing machine under malicious
        control, 388
firewalls
    controlling inbound and outbound
        network traffic, 104, 276
    host-based. see host-based firewalls
    modifying logs using separation of
        duties, 45
    never leaving intentionally
        vulnerable, 362
    not preventing ARP poisoning, 64
    not preventing laptop theft, 124
    not preventing phishing scams, 47
    packet filtering. see packet filtering
        firewalls
    personal laptop, 121
    risk management strategy for, 300
    threat of hackers breaking into, 290
    viewing network between two
        DMZs, 146
    Web application, 149
first responder, function of, 335
floods, disaster recovery planning for, 319
footprints, digital. see computer forensics
forensic expert witnesses, 339
forensics. see computer forensics
FQDNs (fully qualified domain names)
    directing to malicious sites. see DNS
        poisoning
    resolving to IP addresses, 12
    resolving with DNS, 4
FTP (File Transfer Protocol)
    access log listing log activity, 382
    configuring ACLs on Cisco router, 216

download log, 382
FTPS securing traffic on, 238
upload log, 382
FTPS (File Transfer Protocol Secure)
    encrypting data transmissions, 15
    using SSL to secure FTP traffic, 238
    using TCP ports 989 and 990, 12
full backups
    differential and, 315
    ensuring integrity and confidentiality
        of, 317
    quickest restoration with daily, 431
full duplex
    defined, 445
    not configuring enabled ports for, 17
fully qualified domain names. see FQDNs
    (fully qualified domain names)
fuzzing, security
    describing, 447
    example of, 97
    hardening vs., 97

Global System for Mobility
    Communication (GSM) mobile
    devices, 340–341
gloves, masking PII with, 429
government regulations, and risk
    management strategy, 300
GPS (Global Positioning System)
    jammers not preventing wireless
        communications, 342
    not related to preventing laptop
        theft, 124
    tracking mobile device location, 122
    tracking portable units in
        military, 444
gray box testing, 365, 370
Group Policy
    deploying audit settings quickly in
        AD, 390
    financial software using, 105
    hardening client operating
        systems, 448
    security templates applied with, 108
groups
    adding new users to, 206
    granting access to resources in,
        217–218
GSM (Global System for Mobility
    Communication) mobile devices,
    340–341

Guest accounts
    disabling to harden Windows system,
        438–439
    renaming or disabling, 367

H

hard disks
    analyzing risk by number of server, 292
    capturing system image to another
        disk, 339
    collecting as forensic evidence in
        order of volatility, 336, 338
    configuring with RAID 1 for
        availability, 427
    encrypting and decrypting with TPM
        chips, 128–129
    encrypting to protect OS passwords
        on laptops, 436
    encryption of server, 274
    examining with bit stream forensic
        copying tools, 343–344
    filling with random data when
        donating computers, 429
    never creating file hashes on
        original, 340
    protecting contents with
        encryption, 118
    protecting financial data by
        encrypting server, 124
    protecting with file and folder
        encryption, 444
    purpose of disk forensic software, 340
    recovering deleted files from emptied
        Recycle Bin from, 347
    reducing amount of files on seized, 338
    separating storage in network
        appliances, 83
hardening
    client operating systems, 448
    defined, 90
    error handling vs., 103
    mobile, hand-held devices, 120
    operating system procedures, 103–104
    public Web server, 445–446
    using SSH vs. Telnet for, 100
    VPNs, 241
    Windows system, 438–439
    wireless routers, 107
hardware
    cloud computing using less, 126
    fault tolerance, 315
    server virtualization requiring less, 448
    tokens, 190–191, 454

hardware security module (HSM), 128, 445–446
hardware threats
    defined, 78
    keyloggers, 80
    USB security. *see* USB security
hash tables, reducing files on seized disks, 338
Hash-based Message Authentication Code (HMAC), 240
hashes. *see* file hashes
hashing algorithms
    MD5 as, 455
    RIPEMD and HMAC as, 240
heat
    causing patched server failure, 271
    hot and cold aisles in server room, 273
Heating Ventilation Air Conditioning. *see* HVAC (Heating Ventilation Air Conditioning)
help file, on CD-ROM accompanying this book, 461
hexadecimal addresses, IPv6, 12
HIDS (host-based intrusion detection system)
    defined, 441
    installing on hosts where needed, 386
    looking for network abnormalities, 124–125, 126, 128
    protecting laptops disconnected from LANs, 385–386
high availability, ensuring e-commerce, 318
high-gain antennas, 422
HIPS (host intrusion prevention system)
    defined, 142, 441
    monitoring specific applications on hosts with, 393
    stopping attacks in progress, 386
HMAC (Hash-based Message Authentication Code), 240
home office configuration
    securing with WPA2 PSK, 363
    securing with WPA2 PSK and WPA, 175
honeynets
    example of, 362
    honeypots vs., 151, 359
honeypots
    configuring on secured hosts, 382–383
    configuring to identify offender, 151
    honeynets vs., 362
    tracking malicious activity to host in DMZ with, 359
host intrusion prevention system. *see* HIPS (host intrusion prevention system)

host-based firewalls
    allowing/denying network traffic, 125
    offering protection from network attacks, 112
    preventing non-compliant devices from connecting using NAC, 152
host-based intrusion detection system. *see* HIDS (host-based intrusion detection system)
hosts
    configuring honeypots on secured, 382–383
    defined, 68
    determining open ports on, 366
    DNS redirection attacks and, 63
    honeynets configuring intentionally vulnerable, 362
    honeypots tracking malicious activity in DMZ to, 359
    load balancers distributing network traffic to, 417
    moving virtualized servers to other physical, 425
    storing log files on centralized logging, 389
    tracking performance metrics for several servers, 387
hot and cold aisles, 273
hot sites, 313–314
hot spots, identifying in large data center, 273
HSM (hardware security module), 128, 445–446
HTTP (Hypertext Transfer Protocol)
    as application protocol, 15
    connecting and configuring wireless router with, 169
    encrypting with SSL, 230
    TCP port 80 used by, 12
    Web application firewalls stopping inappropriate activity on, 149
HTTPS (Hypertext Transfer Protocol Secure)
    configuring web server security, 257–258
    protecting e-mail confidentiality, 230
    securing HTTP traffic with SSL, 425
    securing wireless network beyond HTTP, 169
    TCP port 443 used by, 12
hubs
    capturing network traffic using, 417
    not performing packet inspection, 17, 421
    single broadcast domains of, 420

human resource policies. *see* acceptable use policies
humidity, monitoring, 273–274
HVAC (Heating Ventilation Air Conditioning)
    hot and cold aisles vs., 273
    mitigating server failure from heat, 271
    risk analysis of power reliability, 297
    for server room rack mount servers, 431
hybrid password attacks, 69
Hypertext Transfer Protocol. *see* HTTP (Hypertext Transfer Protocol)
Hypertext Transfer Protocol Secure. *see* HTTPS (Hypertext Transfer Protocol Secure)

ICMP (Internet Control Message Protocol)
    example of, 424
    network attacks and, 3
    not used for security, 238
    PING and TRACERT utilities using, 10
identification
    access control methods not using, 274
    defined, 20
    e-mail address example of, 28–29
    entering logon name for, 189
    proving with authentication. *see* authentication
    proving with driver's license and passport, 30
IDS (intrusion detection system)
    defined, 141
    host-based. *see* HIDS (host-based intrusion detection system)
    network. *see* NIDS (network intrusion detection system)
IGMP (Internet Group Message Protocol), 424
imaging
    capturing system image to another disk, 339
    not affecting slow and unstable performance, 391
    RAID 5 array in computer forensics, 336
IMAP, as TCP/IP mail protocol, 9
impact analysis
    mitigation solutions vs., 301
    in risk analysis, 291
    risk management vs., 295

implicit denial, 150, 210
inbox, not related to outbound SMTP
traffic, 336–337
incident response policies
alarms, 102
business impact analysis, 431–432
function of first responder, 335
not implying collection of
evidence, 432
incremental backups, 315, 317
infrared remotes, relying on line of
sight, 172
initial baseline configuration, mitigating
security threats, 100
initialization vector (IV) attacks,
WEP, 171
in-progress network attacks
stopping with HIPS, 386
stopping with NIPSs, 381
input validation
alarms vs., 102
example of ignoring, 106
hardening public Web server with,
445–446
preventing SQL injection attacks, 67
instant messaging, examining hard disk in
forensics, 343–344
insurance coverage, 292–293
integrity
CAs issuing certificates for, 246
confidentiality vs., 28
custodian role in maintaining, 27
defined, 26
digital signatures for message, 242
enabling for backups stored offsite, 317
enabling WPA on WLAN for, 164
MD5 encryption providing, 232
PKI providing, 262
of shielded computer rooms, 29
violating, 34
integrity algorithms, 456
intellectual property, social networking
risk, 48
internal patch update servers, minimizing
network utilization, 445
internal threats, risk analysis, 290
Internet
redundant links, 318
securing network traffic using
VPNs, 423
tracking criminals using
IP addresses, 44
Internet connectivity
authenticating using proxy
servers, 140

preventing clients connecting to
internal computers, 140
protecting laptops with personal
firewalls, 121
SLAs defining expected level of
service for, 46
troubleshooting TCP/IP settings on
workstation, 13
Internet Control Message Protocol. *see*
ICMP (Internet Control Message
Protocol)
Internet Group Message Protocol
(IGMP), 424
Internet service providers (ISPs), 154
intrusion detection system (IDS)
defined, 141
false positives in, 151
host-based. *see* HIDS (host-based
intrusion detection system)
network. *see* NIDS (network
intrusion detection system)
intrusion prevention system (IPS)
defining, 141
host. *see* HIPS (host intrusion
prevention system)
network. *see* NIPSs (network
intrusion prevention systems)
receiving security alerts as false
positives, 388–389
IP addresses
analyzing network traffic as legitimate
or spoofed, 345–346
assigning to workstations, 18
determining web server, 365–366
DNS reverse lookups using, 12
forging, 340
getting from DHCP server, 16
internal networks using NAT with,
141, 417
IPv4 format, 12
IPv6 format, 12
ISPs disclosing persons associated
with, 154
not at risk in social networking, 48
not tracking mobile devices using, 122
not within issued certificates of PKI
server, 253
resolving to network card hardware
addresses, 18
spoof attacks modifying, 62
troubleshooting TCP/IP on
workstation, 13
VLANs interconnecting with other
VLANs using, 418–419
workstations connecting to servers, 418

IPCONFIG, 16
IPS (intrusion prevention system)
defining, 141
hosts. *see* HIPS (host intrusion
prevention system)
networks. *see* NIPSs (network
intrusion prevention systems)
receiving security alerts as false
positives, 388–389
IPSec (IP Security)
NAT vs., 142
not applicable to physical site
security, 272
not detecting malicious activity in
SQL database server, 125
not detecting or preventing
intrusions, 141
preventing ARP poisoning attack
with, 440
RADIUS vs., 423
securing all internal LAN traffic with,
424–425
unable to use SSL, 238, 456–457
using encryption and integrity
algorithms, 231, 456
iris scanning, 190
isolation mode, wireless, 165
ISPs (Internet service providers), 154
IV (initialization vector) attacks, WEP, 171

job rotation, 29, 451
JPEGs, forensic analysis of, 344
junk e-mail. *see* spam

Kerberos authentication protocol, 187, 449
key escrow, 255
keyloggers
example of, 80
mitigated by virus scanners, 447
obtaining forensic evidence with, 347

landline phones, 127
LANs
configuring PKI certificates for, 426
firewall rule set for, 143

IPSec securing, 234, 424–425
plugging wireless router into internal, 140
preventing ARP poisoning attacks, 440
preventing unauthorized access using NAC, 185
protecting laptops disconnected from, 385–386
using DMZ networks, 146
VPN concentrator placement for travelers, 146–147
VPNs accessing private, 151
laptops
authentication methods, 450
configuring WLAN access in Windows 7, 167
creating rogue access points in Windows 7, 169
preventing hacking of OS passwords, 436
preventing theft with cable locks, 124, 217
protecting when disconnected from LANs, 385–386
protecting with personal firewall software, 121
providing secure access to LAN with VPN, 421
risk of infecting isolated networks, 48–49
USB device encryption on, 104
use of PII, 44
large attack surface, vulnerabilities of computers with, 361
laser security system, 274
law enforcement, tracking Internet offender using IP address, 44
Layer 2 (Data Link Layer) filtering, based on MAC addresses, 439
LDAP (Lightweight Directory Access Protocol)
for Linux clients, 188
overview of, 449
port 389 used by, 195, 449
SSO vs., 453
transmitting clear text credentials with TCP port 389, 195
LEAP (Lightweight Extensible Authentication Protocol), 167
LearnKey technical support, 461
least privilege
allowing rights to perform task, 45, 451
defined, 29
example of, 46
violating principle of, 207, 453

legalities
cloud computing full data disclosure, 120
financial data security, 124
folder encryption not required for all companies, 28
forensic analysis, 345
ISPs disclosure of persons associated with IP addresses, 154
obtaining forensic evidence with warrants, 347
POS software storage of magnetic data, 50–51
licensed software
cost of, 368–369
not transferring to others, 429
Lightweight Directory Access Protocol. *see* LDAP (Lightweight Directory Access Protocol)
Lightweight Extensible Authentication Protocol (LEAP), 167
Linux
hardening computers on network, 445–446
SSH allowing secured remote access to host, 230
Live Migration, Microsoft Hyper-V, 425
LMHOSTS file, 68
load balancers
distributing network traffic among mirrored servers, 417
distributing traffic on available web server, 10
for high availability for e-commerce site, 318
improving web site response time, 314
reducing risk, 292
local computer certificates, WPA2 wireless networks, 192
local security policy, 100
locking server chassis, 277
logging access electronically, proximity cards, 272
logging servers, never intentionally unpatching, 151
logic bombs
botnets vs., 80, 86
defined, 437
Michelangelo virus, 85
privilege escalation vs., 79
login
e-mail tricking users for information on, 436

with fingerprint scanner on laptop, 44
never copying disks on seized computers using, 343–344
logs
access, 212, 382
audit, 384, 387–388
backing up, 392
checking for slow and unstable performance, 391
event viewer, 102–103
firewall. *see* firewall log
identifying client computers controlled by RDP from Internet, 390–391
monitoring with HIDS, 125
motion sensor, 274–275
not revealing deleted data, 344
preventing tampering of, 389
tracking users of inappropriate sites, 392
VPN security, 44–45
web server, 336–337, 389
loop protection, 148–149

MAC (mandatory access control)
defined, 451
example of, 207–208
as user-driven, 209
using data classifications and security clearances, 212–213
MAC (Media Access Control) addresses
in ARP poisoning, 434
assigning to specific switch ports, 17
causing unlit link light on network card in new workstation, 147
connecting wireless clients with, 99
detecting rogue access points with, 174
forging, 340
format, 12
Layer 2 filtering based on, 439
network cards tied to, 8
network connectivity devices using, 15
not for tracking mobile devices, 122
unique in each virtual machine, 125
viewing switch MAC address table, 420
MAC address filtering
blocking unauthorized access, 175
controlling systems connecting to wireless network, 164, 422
physical port security with, 441

MAC flood attacks, 10–11
mail servers
    log revealing excessive SMTP
        outbound traffic, 336–337
    ports used by, 362
    receiving e-mail using SMTP on TCP
        port 25, 419
malicious software
    adware, 78–79, 87
    backdoors, 80–81, 86–87
    botnets. see botnets
    cell phone threats, 82
    computer viruses. see viruses
    defined, 78
    logic bombs. see logic bombs
    privilege escalation. see privilege
        escalation
    rootkits. see rootkits
    spam. see spam
    spyware. see spyware
    Trojans. see Trojans
    worms. see worms
malpractice, due care vs., 32
malware
    training users in, 434–435
    web security gateways detecting and
        dealing with, 142
man hour expenses, forensic budgets, 346
mandatory access control. see MAC
    (mandatory access control)
mandatory vacations
    exposing improper activity in job
        role, 46, 451
    IT benefit of, 210–211
    purpose of enforcing, 52
man-in-the-middle attacks
    DDoS attack vs., 66
    defined, 435
    DoS attack vs., 65
    example of, 68
    preventing, 439–440
mantraps
    limiting tailgating with, 60
    not applicable to post analysis of
        security breach, 274
    trapping perpetrators with, 274
MasterExam, 460–461
mathematically related keys, RSA, 232
maximum password age, 214, 433
MD5 (Message Digest 5)
    data integrity provided by, 232
    data not encrypted by, 230
    as hashing integrity algorithm, 455
Media Access Control addresses. see MAC
    (Media Access Control) addresses

memory, spyware consuming, 86
metadata analysis, computer forensics, 344
Michelangelo virus, 85
Microsoft Challenge Handshake
    Authentication Protocol
    (MS-CHAP), 242
Microsoft HCL, 44–45
Microsoft Office upgrade, 363
Microsoft Word, forensic analysis of
    metadata, 344
microwave ovens, 802.11g network
    interference, 172
minimum password age
    increasing in password policy, 214
    preventing users from reusing old
        passwords, 433
    reviewing during security audit,
        369–370
mobile, hand-held devices
    cell phone voice encryption
        software, 127
    hardening, 120
    protecting data after loss or theft, 122
    tracking location with GPS, 122
modems, for remote connectivity to
    networks, 6
monitoring and auditing
    audit log, viewing firewall
        configuration changes in, 387–388
    audit results, viewing in Windows, 382
    audit settings, deploying quickly in
        AD, 390
    behavior-based detection, 383
    certification objectives, 373
    changes to user accounts, 385
    clients controlled by RDP from
        Internet, 390–391
    detailed verbose logging, 391
    false positives obtained in, 388–389
    honeypots on secured hosts for,
        382–383
    lack of RAM causing degraded
        performance, 392–393
    log entries for slow and unstable
        performance, 391
    log file backups, 392
    log files, preventing tampering of, 389
    missing files on FTP server, 382
    overview of, 374
    performance metrics for several
        servers, 387
    signature-based detection, 383
    storage retention policies, 386
    tracking users of inappropriate
        sites, 392

tracking web surfing activity with
    proxy servers, 385
unauthorized WLAN access, 381
user access and rights reviews, 384
using firewall log, 387–388
using HIDSs for, 386
using HIPS for, 393
using NIDs for, 385–386, 390
using NIPSs, 381
using Performance Monitor, 384
web server log irregularities, 389
motherboard photograph, not useful in
    computer forensics, 337
motion sensor logs, 274–275
MS-CHAP (Microsoft Challenge
    Handshake Authentication
    Protocol), 242
multifactor authentication
    defined, 178
    dual-factor authentication vs., 189
    example of, 184, 190
    SSO vs., 453

N

NAC (Network Access Control)
    ensuring health compliancy of
        connecting devices, 152
    preventing unauthorized access with,
        185, 217
    single sign-on vs., 194
named accounts, administrative, 367
NAS (network-attached storage)
    devices, 83, 84
NAT (Network Address Translation)
    ACLs vs., 145
    allowing multiple computers to gain
        network access with single IP
        address, 141, 417
    functionality of, 153
    not authenticating connections, 140
    not performing packet inspection for
        authentication, 421
    not preventing e-mail from getting to
        its destination, 153
    not providing secure access to LAN
        for travelers, 421
    as single point of failure, 430
    tracking users of inappropriate sites, 392
    VLANs vs., 142–143
NetBIOS computer names, 8
NETSTAT, 16
Network Access Control. see NAC
    (Network Access Control)

Network Address Translation. *see* NAT (Network Address Translation)
network bandwidth, spyware consuming, 86
network cards
    MAC addresses tied to specific, 8
    resolving IP addresses with ARP, 18
    unlit link light on, 147
network infrastructure
    allowing and denying traffic with ACLs, 144–145
    authenticating workstations before LAN access, 147–148
    connections between networks, 150–151
    DMZs, 140–141, 146
    false positives, 152
    honeynets, 151
    implicit denial, 150
    intrusion prevention system. *see* IPS (intrusion prevention system)
    legitimate e-mail flagged as junk mail, 153
    loop protection, 148–149
    NAC. *see* NAC (Network Access Control)
    NAT. *see* NAT (Network Address Translation)
    obtaining person linked to IP address in illegal Internet activity, 154–155
    packet encryption concerns, 155
    protocol analyzers, 143–144
    proxy servers. *see* proxy servers
    sniffers and NIDS, 145
    SYN flood protection, 148
    TFTP security, 144
    unauthorized administrative access to wireless routers, 154
    unlit link light in new workstation, 147
    URL filtering, 149–150
    VLANs, 142–143
    VPN concentrator placement, 146–147
    VPNs accessing private LANs, 151
    Web application firewalls, 149
    web security gateways, 142
network intrusion detection system. *see* NIDS (network intrusion detection system)
network intrusion prevention systems. *see* NIPSs (network intrusion prevention systems)
network load balancers. *see* NLBs (network load balancers)
network mapping
    defined, 359–360
    determining network server types, 368
    penetration testing vs., 361

network operating systems (NOSs), time of day access control with, 209
Network Policy Server (NPS) role, enforcing, 101
network scanning, 166
Network Time Protocol (NTP), synchronizing computers, 13–14, 342–343
network traffic
    analyzing for malicious packets with NIDS, 385–386
    blocking specific HTTP, 149
    distributing among mirrored servers with load balancer, 417
    encrypting all with single IPSec policy, 425
    Ethernet switches unable to capture all, 342
    implicit denial example, 150
    mail server log analyzing excessive SMTP outbound, 336–337
    only from certain hosts, 144–145
    protocol analyzers viewing, 144, 358
    reducing using proxy server, 422–423
    sniffers and NIDS analyzing, 145
    SSH encryption of, 230
    SYN flood protection from DoS attacks, 148
    VPNs accessing private LANs, 151
    web security gateways filtering, 142
network-attached storage (NAS) devices, 83, 84
New Technology File System. *see* NTFS (New Technology File System)
New Technology LAN Manager (NTLM v2), 242
NIDS (network intrusion detection system)
    admitting packet captures as evidence, 342–343
    configuring alerts and notifications, 385–386
    data loss prevention solutions vs., 127–128
    defined, 441
    detecting but not preventing suspicious activity, 422
    excessive network traffic for TCP port 389, 449
    false positives reported by, 152, 432
    HIDS vs., 125
    NAT vs., 142
    network traffic analysis in, 145, 385–386
    NIPSs vs., 381
    not detecting malicious activity in SQL database server, 125

not tracking web surfing activity, 385
    packet sniffers vs., 390
NIPSs (network intrusion prevention systems)
    blocking suspicious traffic entering network, 386
    configuring signature-based detection, 383
    detecting and preventing network attacks, 441
    stopping in-progress network attacks, 381, 421
NLBs (network load balancers)
    distributing network traffic among mirrored servers, 417
    distributing traffic on available web server, 10
    ensuring high availability for e-commerce, 318
    improving web site response time, 314
    reducing risk, 292
non-repudiation
    CAs issuing certificates for, 246
    defined, 31
    overview of, 236
    PKI providing, 262
NOSs (network operating systems), time of day access control with, 209
notifications, configuring with NIDS, 385–386
NPS (Network Policy Server) role, enforcing, 101
NTFS (New Technology File System)
    disk encryption vs. permissions of, 118
    enabling EFS encryption, 129
    share permissions combined with, 452–453
    TPM chips vs., 122
NTLM v2 (New Technology LAN Manager), 242
NTP (Network Time Protocol), synchronizing computers, 13–14, 342–343
numerical data, qualitative and quantitative risk assessment, 293

omnidirectional antennae, 168
one-time pads, transmitting messages during wartime, 240
online data storage, DRP, 320
online fraud, 347

operating system defects, patching, 123
operating system hardening
    disabling unneeded services, 97,
        103–104
    for financial software, 105
    for laptops using USB devices, 104
order of volatility
    collecting data evidence in, 336, 432
    defined, 335
    starting from power-dependent
        locations, 338
OS fingerprinting, 364
"Other Networks," in Windows 7, 167

P2P (Peer to Peer) files
    propagating Trojans via, 87
    risk of infection from, 48–49
packet analysis, 432
packet captures
    analyzing network traffic as legitimate
        or spoofed, 345–346
    ensuring date and time for admission
        as evidence, 342–343
    tracking users of inappropriate
        sites, 392
packet filtering firewalls
    allowing or restricting packets, 421
    configuring packet encryption for
        internal networks, 155
    not able to prevent SYN floods, 148
    not analyzing packet payloads, 142
    not controlling network access, 185
    not performing packet inspection for
        authentication, 421
    not stopping in-progress network
        attacks, 381
    not tracking web surfing
        activity, 385
packet headers, encrypting internal
    networks, 155
Packet Internet Groper. see PING (Packet
    Internet Groper)
packet sniffers
    bluesnarfing vs., 171
    detecting and controlling, 172
    initiating MAC flood attacks with,
        3, 10–11
    NIDS vs., 390
    port scanners vs., 359
PAP (Password Authentication Protocol),
    241–242

paper documents
    clean desk policy for, 52
    mitigating physical threats by
        shredding, 78, 435–436
    policy to shred sensitive, 66
passive security testing, 364
passphrase
    for encrypted disk in online fraud, 347
    symmetric encryption, 243
password attacks
    account lockout impeding, 369
    brute-force attacks as, 60
    dictionary attacks as, 61
    hybrid, 69
    mitigating dictionary, 98
Password Authentication Protocol (PAP),
    241–242
password cracking, 109, 358
password hints, 98, 108, 206
password length
    password policies controlling,
        44–45, 50
    reducing security with minimum, 450
Password Never Expires option, for service
    accounts, 216
password policies
    clean desk policy vs., 52
    defined, 44
    encouraging proper adherence to, 50
    increasing minimum password age, 214
    reviewing during security audit,
        369–370
    on service accounts, 215–216
    specific criteria for, 45
passwords
    as authentication, 34
    changing service account, 364
    EAP supporting, 166
    eliminating strict requirements in
        new laptops, 450
    example of, 193
    maximum password age, 214, 433
    minimum password age, 214,
        369–370, 433
    mitigating attacks against user
        accounts, 108
    mitigating dictionary attacks with
        strong, 70, 211
    mitigating password attacks with
        strong, 98
    not sending over network with
        CHAP, 192
    preventing hacking of OS on
        laptops, 436
    preventing users from reusing old, 433

securing wireless routers, 154
    setting console port, 278–279
    SSO eliminating multiple prompts
        for, 191, 212
    storing with reversible encryption, 370
    strong (complex). see strong passwords
    TFTP server storing files without
        requiring, 13
patching
    fuzzing vs., 97
    hardening Linux computers, 445–446
    hardening operating systems, 103–104
    hardening public Web servers, 445–446
    hardening vs., 97
    invoked snapshots vs. currently
        running virtual machines, 119
    management of, 360
    mitigating buffer overflow attacks, 64
    not preventing ARP cache poisoning,
        64, 106
    not preventing password attacks, 70
    operating systems, 105, 123
    security audit considerations, 368–369
payroll, ensuring confidentiality, 28
PBXs (private branch exchanges), 83–84
PDFs, forensic analysis of metadata, 344
PEAP (Protected Extensible
    Authentication Protocol), 166
Peer to Peer (P2P) files
    propagating Trojans via, 87
    risk of infection from, 48–49
penetration testing
    black box, 364–365
    defined, 363
    determining security of
        computers, 109
    ensuring network security, 363
    example of, 361
performance
    baselines, 44–45, 109
    checking log entries for slow and
        unstable, 391
    of computers with large attack
        surface, 361
    counters, 387
    detailed verbose logging degrading, 391
Performance Monitor
    defined, 359–360
    example of, 384
    tracking performance metrics for
        several servers, 387
performance monitors, 381
perimeter fencing, 276
perimeter firewalls, 419, 440
periodic network testing, 363

permissions
 allowing or denying access, 35
 assigning new users to groups, 206
 implicit denial, 213–214
 NTFS combined with share, 452–453
 principle of least privilege, 46
 RBAC assigning to roles, 213
 user access and rights reviews, 384
personal firewalls
 impeding success of port scanners, 359
 for laptops, 121
Personally Identifiable Information. see PII
 (Personally Identifiable Information)
personnel
 administrative control of hiring
  policy for, 218
 assigning tasks to in disaster recovery
  plan, 319
 authorizing access using ID badges
  for, 276
 first responder to incident
  determining needed, 335
 internal threats from, 290
 training in disaster recovery plan, 320
 training in security awareness, 47
 training to reduce risk, 292
PGP (Pretty Good Privacy), 241
phishing scams
 avoiding, 47
 example of, 62
 overview of, 433–434
 spam vs., 119
 tailgating vs., 49
 tricking users out of account/login
  information, 436
physical security
 access control that does not identify
  persons, 274
 analyzing security breaches, 274–275
 cipher locks, 271
 countering ARP poisoning with, 64
 EMI shielding for entire facility, 272
 fail safe UPS, 277
 fail secure systems, 275
 Faraday cages, 276–277
 hardware keys, 274
 hardware locks, 274
 heat causing patched server failure, 271
 hot and cold aisles, 273
 monitoring air flow, humidity and
  power, 273–274
 multifactor authentication vs., 184
 overview of, 266
 perimeter fencing, 276
 proximity cards, 272

retinal scans, 279
 in risk analysis, 297
 SAN disk security problem, 278
 server rooms, 277
 smoke detection waterless fire
  suppression, 273
 switches and routers, 278
physical threats
 adding CMOS hardening to server
  policies, 81
 defined, 78
 financial data security in event of
  physical breach, 124
 mitigating by shredding paper
  documents, 78
 to physical server room security, 81
 USB security. see USB security
picture ID cards, 272
PII (Personally Identifiable Information)
 defined, 38
 gathering with spyware, 123
 methods of masking, 429
 personal signatures on checks as, 48
 POS software storage of magnetic
  data and, 50–51
 proper usage of, 44
PING (Packet Internet Groper)
 checking if host is online, 16
 not relying on seeing all network
  traffic, 11
 using ICMP, 10, 424
ping of death, 83
PINs, for hardware tokens, 454
PKI (public key infrastructure) certificates
 accessing 802.1x network with, 193
 CA role in, 264
 CAs, departmental subordinate,
  262–263
 common name error, 259–260
 computer authentication, 426
 computer digital certificates, 259
 containing private keys, 258
 digital certificates not containing IP
  addresses of PKI server, 253
 digital signatures, CA using private
  key to create, 263
 digital signatures, in document
  workflow, 254
 digital signatures, inability to sign
  e-mail, 253
 EAP supporting, 166
 e-mail encryption, 233
 enabling EAP-TLS, 173
 enabling SSL, 259
 example of, 193

hardening, 254
 integrity and non-repudiation, 262
 key escrow, defined, 255
 keys for e-commerce sites, 263
 never sharing your private key, 261
 PEAP using server-side, 166
 RADIUS vs., 423
 removing warning stating web site
  not to be trusted, 256–257
 renewing expired X.509
  certificates, 256
 restricting workstation access, 258
 root CAs, installing in different
  cities, 260
 securing hard disk data in case of
  theft, 261–262
 SSL encryption using, 456
 system authentication using, 30–31
 time frame for revoked certificates, 255
 verifying identity of requestors,
  255–256
 web server security, 257–258
 WPA2 network authentication
  using, 192
plaintiff, 339
point of sale (POS) software, 50–51
policies. see security policies
POP (Post Office Protocol)
 defined, 438
 TCP port 110 used by, 419
 as TCP/IP mail protocol, 9
pop-up advertisements, from adware,
 78–79
port scanners
 bluesnarfing vs., 171
 identifying open ports on hosts with,
  359, 366
 network mapping vs., 368
 not analyzing all network traffic,
  11, 145
 not determining impact of open port,
  359–360
 protocol analyzers vs., 144
 vulnerability scanners vs., 358, 442
ports
 disabling unused, for network
  security, 8
 disabling unused, for routers and
  switches, 278–279
 disabling unused, preventing ARP
  poisoning, 440
 disabling USB, 82
 port scanners testing for open. see
  port scanners
 security of physical, 441

POS (point of sale) software, 50–51
Post Office Protocol. *see* POP
   (Post Office Protocol)
power
   keeping doors locked during
      outages, 275
   monitoring to minimize IT
      infrastructure disruption, 273–274
   order of volatility and, 336, 338
   risk analysis of, 297
   UPS device providing temporary, 275
Power User, 32
power-on passwords, 118
preserving evidence, in chain of
   custody, 339
Pretty Good Privacy (PGP), 241
principle of least privilege. *see* least privilege
printers, security concerns, 279
privacy laws, disclosing persons associated
   with IP addresses, 154
privacy policies
   clean desk policy vs., 52
   defined, 44
   password policies vs., 45
   secure equipment disposal
      policies vs., 47
private branch exchanges (PBXs), 83–84
private keys
   CAs creating digital certificates with,
      246, 263
   CAs digitally signing certificates
      with, 264
   certificates lacking, 253
   creating digital signatures, 242–243
   CRL publishing list of untrusted, 256
   decrypting client session key with,
      454–455
   decrypting received messages, 242–243
   describing certificates
      containing, 258
   in e-commerce sites, 263
   elliptic curve cryptography
      defining, 237
   never sharing with others, 261
   PKI e-mail encryption, 232
   Pretty Good Privacy, 241
   verifying message sender authenticity,
      339–340
privilege escalation
   botnets vs., 84
   defined, 27
   example of, 79
   preventing in Windows networking
      service, 84
   rootkits vs., 80–81
   User Account Control addressing, 86

privileges, user access and rights
   reviews, 384
probability values, calculating ALE,
   296, 301
property restoration specialist, 319
Protected Extensible Authentication
   Protocol (PEAP), 166
protecting evidence, chain of
   custody, 339
protocol analyzers
   capturing and viewing network
      traffic, 144
   network mapping vs., 368
   security audit using, 358
   seeing own transmissions when
      using, 417
   violating principle of confidentiality, 31
   vulnerability scanners vs., 358, 442
   wireless access point logs vs., 381
proximity cards, 272
proxy servers
   ACLs vs., 145
   controlling outbound network
      connections, 421
   masking personally identifiable
      information with anonymous, 429
   never leaving intentionally
      vulnerable, 362
   not analyzing network traffic, 381
   not applicable to WLANs, 381
   not balancing network traffic
      workloads, 417
   not improving web site response
      time, 314
   performing packet inspection for user
      authentication, 421
   reducing network traffic, 422–423
   retrieving external content for
      internal clients, 140, 148
   tracking web surfing activity, 385
PSTN (public switched telephone
   network), 18
public key infrastructure. *see* PKI (public
   key infrastructure) certificates
public keys
   in e-commerce sites, 263
   elliptic curve cryptography
      defining, 237
   encrypting e-mail with
      recipient's, 455
   not protected, 340
   not verifying identity of certificate
      requestor, 256
   PKI e-mail encryption, 232
   Pretty Good Privacy using, 241
   SSH authentication using, 425

qualitative risk analysis
   overview of, 293
   quantitative vs., 296
   ranking risks by likelihood, 296
   ranking threats and asset valuation
      in, 296–297, 433
quantitative risk analysis
   based on dollar figures, 433
   ranking risks by likelihood, 296
   using ALE value. *see* ALE (annual
      loss expectancy) value

RA (registration authority), 255–256
RACE Integrity Primitives Evaluation
   Message Digest (RIPEMD)
   algorithm, 240
RADIUS (Remote Authentication Dial
   In User Service) server
   as alternative to TACAS+, 187
   authenticating connecting users
      to, 165
   authenticating remote users prior to
      network access, 186
   centralized authentication for wireless
      networks, 371, 423
   Diameter protocol for, 191
   disabling unused user accounts
      on, 98–99
   examples of clients, 186
   functionality of, 448–449
   TCP ports 1812 and 1813 used by, 449
RAID (redundant array of inexpensive
   disks)
   implementing availability with, 35
   not related to confidentiality, 35
RAID 0
   defined, 312
   RAID 5 vs., 316–317
   as single point of failure, 430
   striping data across multiple disks, 386
RAID 1 disk mirroring
   configuring hard disks for availability,
      33, 427
   example of, 312
   providing fault tolerance, 386
   RAID 5 vs., 316–317
   removing single points of failure, 430
RAID 5
   defined, 312
   example of, 316–317

imaging array in computer forensics, 336
providing fault tolerance, 315
RAID 5+1, 312, 316–317
RAM (random access memory)
collecting forensic evidence in order of volatility from, 336, 338
degraded performance from lack of, 392–393
random access memory. see RAM (random access memory)
ranking of potential threats, qualitative risk analysis, 296–297
ranking risks by likelihood, disaster recovery plan, 299, 318–319
raw disk partitions, virtual machines, 425
RBAC (role-based access control)
defined, 208
discretionary access control vs., 209
granting users access to administrative tasks, 451
RC4
as stream cipher, 239, 456
as symmetric algorithm, 232, 455
RDP (Remote Desktop Protocol)
ACL configuration on Cisco router with, 216
connecting to LAN computers with, 143
determining availability of, 366
explicit denial of traffic, 450
identifying client computers controlled from Internet by, 390–391
TCP port 3389 used by, 232, 362, 449
recovery agents, hardening PKI with, 254
recovery key, TPM chips, 443
Recycle Bin, recovering deleted files from emptied, 347
redundant Internet links, for high availability, 318
registration authority (RA), 255–256
regulations, storage retention policies, 386
remediation, 101, 102
Remote Authentication Dial In User Service. see RADIUS (Remote Authentication Dial In User Service) server
Remote Desktop Protocol. see RDP (Remote Desktop Protocol)
remote garage door openers, frequency range of, 172
remote wipes
protecting smart phones, 442
protecting stolen hand-held device data, 122

removable media boot, preventing in event of breach, 277
research, as due diligence action, 33
Restricted security labeling, 47–48
return on investment (ROI) analysis
completing risk analysis before, 296
defined, 293
not using for disaster recovery plan, 319–320
revenue loss, justifying warm sites, 321
reverse lookups, DNS, 12
reversible encryption, storing passwords, 370
revoked certificates
for compromised CA, 260
frame for, 255
role of CA in PKI, 264
serial numbers, 458
rights
assigning new users to groups, 206
RBAC assigning to roles, 213
RIPEMD (RACE Integrity Primitives Evaluation Message Digest) algorithm, 240
risk acceptance, 299
risk analysis
asset identification, 289
baseline analysis vs., 360
business impact analysis vs., 312–313, 432
calculating ALE, 293–294
calculating ALE after identifying threats and valuing assets, 300
calculating ALE for server downtime, 292
calculating ALE using probability values that vary, 296
calculating plausible risks, 289
confidentiality, 291
disaster recovery plan vs., 317–318
identifying assets, threats and risk, 359–360
impact analysis, 291
insurance coverage, 292
internal threats, 290
mitigation solutions, 301
new business location, 297
of number of server hard disks, 292
overview of, 282
preventive measures, 292
qualitative, 293, 296–297
quantitative, 292–293
quantitative using ALE, 296
quantitative vs. qualitative, 301–302
ranking risks by likelihood, 299
risk acceptance, 299

risk avoidance, 298
risk management. see risk management
risk transference, 297–298
service level agreements, 295
threat assessment vs., 290
risk assessment
code review in, 360
defined, 289, 363
as due diligence action, 33
penetration testing vs., 361
potential sources of virus infection, 289–290
risk management vs., 301
risk avoidance, 298–299
risk management
ALE figures in, 298
business continuity vs., 316
overview of, 295
risk assessment vs., 301
strategy, 300
risk mitigation, 289
risk reduction, 299
risk transference
defined, 297–298
risk acceptance vs., 299
risk avoidance vs., 298
Rivest Shamir Adleman. see RSA (Rivest Shamir Adleman)
rogue access points
creating in laptop with Windows 7, 169
detecting, 174
evil twin configuration vs., 170
security problem of 2.4 GHz range, 169
ROI (return on investment) analysis
completing risk analysis before, 296
defined, 293
not using for disaster recovery plan, 319–320
role-based access control (RBAC)
defined, 208
discretionary access control vs., 209
granting users access to administrative tasks, 451
roles. see security roles
root CAs, 260
rootkits
botnets vs., 84
defined, 78
making backdoors accessible, 81
privilege escalation vs., 80–81
in Stuxnet attack, 85

rotation of duties policy, 52
routers
    configuring to only allow traffic from
        certain hosts, 144–145
    filtering network traffic, 17
    hardening wireless, 107
    not retaining MAC address
        information, 420
    PBXs vs., 84
    physical security of, 278–279
    reviewing compliance with security
        policies, 144
    separating networks into smaller
        broadcast domains, 420
    wireless. see wireless routers
RSA (Rivest Shamir Adleman)
    asymmetric encryption algorithm, 455
    as block cipher, 456
    CCMP vs., 168
    encryption strength of, 232–233
    securing LANs with IPSec, 234
    as stream cipher, 239
    using two mathematically related
        keys, 233

SAM file, 63
Samba, 188
SANs (storage area networks)
    potential security problem of, 278
    spread of worm virus and, 346
    virtualized environments not
        requiring, 425
scalability, cloud computing, 126
scheduling
    differential backups, 315
    nightly data replication, 314
    server backups, 392
SCP (Secure Copy)
    built on SSH, 238
    encrypting data transmissions, 15
screen locks, hardening mobile devices,
    120, 448
screenshots, on computers seized for
    forensics, 337
secure coding guideline, error handling
    as, 103
Secure Copy (SCP)
    built on SSH, 238
    encrypting data transmissions, 15
secure equipment disposal policies, 47
Secure File Transfer Protocol (SFTP), 238

secure hash algorithm (SHA), 230, 235
Secure Shell (SSH)
    allowing secured remote access to
        Unix host, 230
    encrypting data transmissions, 15
    hardening using, 100
    LDAP vs., 188
    not encryption solution, 231
    remote network appliance
        administration, 425
    Secure Copy protocol built on, 238
    TCP port 22 used by, 12, 425
    viewing switch MAC address table
        with, 420
Secure Sockets Layer. see SSL (Secure
    Sockets Layer) encryption
security assessments and audits
    802.1x for open wireless networks, 368
    AD account lockout policies, 369
    baseline analysis, 360
    black box penetration testing,
        364–365
    certification objectives, 349
    code review, 360
    computers with large attack surface, 361
    design review, 362–363
    determining if RDP is running, 366
    honeynets, 362
    honeypots, 359, 371
    locating web server IP address/
        determining use of SSL, 365–366
    network mapping determining
        network server types, 368
    overview of, 350
    passive security testing, 364
    password policy review, 369–370
    penetration testing, 361
    periodic network testing, 363
    port scanner, 359
    price of server licensing not included
        in, 368–369
    protocol analyzers, 358
    RADIUS centralized
        authentication, 371
    renaming or disabling administrator
        accounts, 367
    risk analysis, 359–360
    service account configuration, 364
    vulnerability scanners, 358, 362,
        370–371
    white box testing, 370
    WPA2 as most secure wireless
        network encryption, 366–367
    WPA2 PSK for home wireless
        network, 363

security audit
    defined, 312–313
    risk management vs., 295
    using protocol analyzer, 358
security awareness training, 47
security clearances, 212–213, 219
security data labeling, 47–48
security guards, 275–276
security log, 382, 387–388
security passes, preventing tailgating, 49
security policies
    acceptable use. see acceptable use
        policies
    clean desk policy, 51–52
    continuous monitoring of, 101
    Data Owner enforcing, 28
    disaster recovery, 386
    impeding password attacks in AD
        with administrative account
        lockout, 369
    mandatory vacations, 46, 52
    password. see password policies
    performing due care by following, 34
    privacy. see privacy policies
    rotation of duties, 52
    secure equipment disposal, 47
    storage retention, 386
    USB flash drive encryption, 50
    VPN. see VPN security policies
security roles
    Custodian security role, 26–27, 32
    Data Owner, 28
security templates
    applying security baseline with, 108
    penetration testing vs., 109
security terminology
    auditing, 35
    authentication. see authentication
    authorization. see authorization
    availability. see availability
    confidentiality. see confidentiality
    due care. see due care
    due diligence. see due diligence
    exploits. see exploits
    identification. see identification
    integrity. see integrity
    roles. see security roles
security threats. see threats; threats,
    mitigating
security thresholds, using warning
    alarms, 102
separation of duties
    as administrative control, 218
    defined, 26
    example of, 429–430

least privilege vs., 46, 207
modifying firewall logs, 45
reducing likelihood of fraud or
    embezzlement, 451
violating principle of, 207
server administrator, 427
server audit logs, 384
Server Backup Operator role, Custodian
    as, 26–27
server restoration specialist, disaster
    recovery plan, 319
server room
    HVAC for rack mount servers in, 277
    physical security of, 81
    securing data in event of breach, 277
    security audit consideration, 368–369
    virtualization requiring less space
        in, 448
servers
    adding CMOS hardening to, 81
    choosing for storage of router
        configuration files, 13
    clustering software between two, 314
    configuring network load balancer to
        distribute traffic, 10
    hardening by disabling unneeded
        services, 109
    hardening public Web, 445–446
    internal patch updates, 445
    releasing from digital signatures and
        encryption, 128
    SAN potential security problem, 278
    tracking performance metrics for
        several, 387
    virtualized, 425, 447–448
    workstations connecting to, 418
service accounts
    configuring for security, 364
    password issues, 215–216
    using Active Directory accounts
        as, 364
service level agreements (SLAs)
    defining expected level of service, 46
    in risk analysis, 295
services
    hardening operating system by
        disabling unneeded, 97, 104
    hardening Windows server by
        disabling, 109
services file, 63
session hijacking attack, 69
session keys, in e-commerce sites, 263
severity, worm virus, 346
SFTP (Secure File Transfer Protocol), 238
SHA (secure hash algorithm), 230, 235

SHA-256 cryptographic hashing
    algorithm, 230
SHA-512 cryptographic hashing
    algorithm, 230
share permissions, combined with NTFS,
    452–453
shielded computer rooms, 29
shoulder surfing
    defined, 78
    tailgating vs., 49
"show mac-address-table" command, 420
shut down, of Ethernet switches to control
    worm virus, 346
signature-based detection, 383
SIM (Subscriber Identification Module)
    cards, cell phones
    difficulty of forging, 340
    gathering evidence from, 341
    not using for tracking mobile
        devices, 122
    seized mobile wireless devices and,
        341–342
Simple Mail Transfer Protocol. *see* SMTP
    (Simple Mail Transfer Protocol)
Simple Network Management Protocol.
    see SNMP (Simple Network
    Management Protocol)
single loss expectancy. *see* SLE (single loss
    expectancy)
single points of failure
    identifying in DRP risk analysis, 324
    physical host as, 322
    removing, 430
    removing with fault tolerance. *see*
        fault tolerance
single sign-on authentication. *see* SSO
    (single sign-on) authentication
single-factor authentication, 189
SLAs (service level agreements)
    defining expected level of service, 46
    in risk analysis, 295
SLE (single loss expectancy)
    calculating ALE, 293–294
    calculating ALE for server downtime,
        294, 430
    not ranking risks using, 299
smart phones, securing, 448
smartcards
    cipher locks vs., 271
    defined, 47
    EAP supporting, 166
    enabling EAP-TLS, 173
    example of authentication, 193
    hardware keyloggers vs., 80
    hardware security module vs., 128

identifying users with, 274
insecurity of, 279
for laptop authentication, 450
not likely sources of malware, 289
smoke detection waterless fire suppression
    system, 273
SMTP (Simple Mail Transfer Protocol)
    defined, 438
    encrypting with SSL, 230
    TCP port 25 used by, 419
    as TCP/IP mail protocol, 2, 9
    uninstalling when TCP port 25 is in
        listening state, 9
smurf attack, as DDoS attack, 65–66
snapshots, implementing system
    security, 119
sniffers, network traffic analysis using, 145
SNMP (Simple Network Management
    Protocol)
    as network management protocol, 9
    using UDP for transport, 10
    using UDP port 161, 419
social engineering attack
    defined, 435
    DoS attack vs., 65
    phishing scam vs., 434
social networking sites, security risks of, 48
software
    clustering between two servers, 314
    purpose of disk forensic, 340
    threats. *see* malicious software
source code, analyzing security in code
    review, 360
spam
    antispam software incorrectly
        identifying, 153
    example of, 82–83
    filtering with antispam software, 123
    as unsolicited junk mail, 433–434,
        437–438
    from work e-mail address when
        surfing web, 119
spoof attacks, 62, 436
spyware
    adware vs., 79
    affecting memory and network
        bandwidth, 86
    as cell phone threat, 82
    defined, 78, 437
    gathering personal information and
        computer usage habits, 123
    HIDS vs., 125
SQL injection attacks
    buffer overflow attacks vs., 63
    countermeasures, 67

SQL injection attacks (*Cont.*)
 cross-site scripting vs., 67
 defined, 61
 example of, 61
 spam vs., 119
 spoof attacks vs., 62
SSH (Secure Shell)
 allowing secured remote access to
  Unix host, 230
 encrypting data transmissions, 15
 hardening using, 100
 LDAP vs., 188
 not encryption solution, 231
 remote network appliance
  administration, 425
 Secure Copy protocol built on, 238
 TCP port 22 used by, 12, 425
 viewing switch MAC address table
  with, 420
SSID (Station Set Identifier)
 changing name of wireless network,
  164, 363
 identifying wireless network, 8
SSID (Station Set Identifier), disabling
 broadcasting
 enhancing wireless network
  security, 422
 not securing wireless home
  networks, 363
 not securing wireless routers, 154
 suppressing wireless network name,
  167, 172
SSL (Secure Sockets Layer) encryption
 defined, 125
 determining whether site is using,
  365–366
 for e-commerce site, 259
 FTPS using, 238
 handled by HSM, not external
  device, 445–446
 for higher-level protocols, 230–231
 HTTPS using, 230
 IPSec vs., 425
 of network traffic, 185, 317
 PKI certificates used in, 456
 RADIUS vs., 423
 TCP port 443 used by, 362
 TLS superseding, 231, 426
 for web server security, 257–258
SSO (single sign-on) authentication
 eliminating multiple password
  prompts, 212
 enabling once for multiple
  applications, 231, 453
 preventing multiple logons with, 191

SSH vs., 230
 using same username and password for
  internal web sites with, 194
static ARP entries, countering ARP
 poisoning, 64
steganography
 concealing message within file, 236
 encryption vs., 278
 identifying forensic evidence on USB
  flash drives, 347–348
storage
 cloud computing security issues, 120
 disaster recovery plan using online
  data, 320
 network-attached storage
  devices, 83, 84
 retention policies, 386, 428
storage area networks (SANs)
 potential security problem of, 278
 spread of worm virus and, 346
 virtualized environments not
  requiring, 425
stream ciphers
 AES as, 456
 defined, 238
 RC4 as, 239, 456
 RSA as, 239
strong passwords
 hacking by booting locally from
  removable media, 436
 mitigating dictionary attacks with,
  70, 211
 mitigating password attacks with, 98
 not securing stolen hard disks, 118
 password length related to, 433
 password policies controlling, 45
 remembering with password hints,
  108, 206
 reviewing during security audit,
  369–370
 securing smart phones with, 448
Stuxnet attack, 85
subnet masks, 418–419
subnets, ACLs vs., 145
Subscriber Identification Module (SIM)
 cards, cell phones
 difficulty of forging, 340
 gathering evidence from, 341
 not using for tracking mobile
  devices, 122
 seized mobile wireless devices and,
  341–342
succession planning, 315–316
suspicious network activity, configuring
 NIPS for, 386, 421

swap files, collecting as forensic
 evidence, 338
switches
 seeing own transmissions when using
  protocol analyzer, 417
 single broadcast domains of, 420
switches, Ethernet
 capturing network traffic with, 342
 configuring security for, 17
 correcting incorrectly linked, 148–149
 disabling unused ports, 8
 examining MAC addresses, 17
 not authenticating connections, 140
 not improving web site response
  time, 314
 PBXs vs., 84
 physical security of, 278–279
 powering down to control spread of
  worm virus, 346
 preventing ARP cache poisoning by
  disabling unneeded ports, 105
 tied to specific physical network
  cards, 8
 using MAC addresses for network
  connectivity, 15
symmetric algorithms, identifying, 455
symmetric block ciphers, 235
symmetric encryption
 AES, 456
 defined, 222
 example, 239–240, 243
 securing LANs with IPSec using AES
  and 3DES, 234
SYN flood protection, 148
sysprepped image, 100
system requirements, on CD-ROM
 accompanying this book, 460
System Restore, 391
system restore points, 384
system security
 antispam software, 123
 cell phone encryption software, 127
 cloud computing benefits, 126
 cloud computing issues, 120
 detecting abnormal behavior, 127
 enabling EFS with NTFS, 129
 enabling TPM, 128–129
 encrypting drives, 121–122
 encrypting hard disks, 118
 file system auditing, 126
 financial data laws, 124
 hardening mobile, hand-held
  devices, 120
 hardware security module, 128
 HIDS, 124–125

laptop theft prevention, 124
overview of, 112
patching defects, 123
personal firewalls for laptops, 121
preventing leakage of e-mail with
  DLP, 127–128
recovering files encrypted for old
  accounts, 118
remote wipes for stolen/lost
  hand-held devices, 122
spam, 119
spyware, 123
tracking location of mobile devices, 122
USB flash drive encryption, 121
virtual machines, features of, 125–126
virtual machines, point-in-time
  snapshots, 119
system.dat file, 68

T

TACAS, 187
TACAS+ (Terminal Access Controller
  Access Control System), 187–188
tailgating
  defined, 436
  implementing controls to prevent, 60
  preventing with security passes, 49
tape backups, 274
tattoos, as personally identifiable
  information, 429
TCO (total cost of ownership) analysis
  ALE value vs., 293
  defined, 290
  not using for disaster recovery plan,
    319–320
TCP (Transmission Control Protocol)
  port 110 used by POP3, 419
  port 22 used by SSH, 12, 230, 425
  port 25 for SMTP, 419
  port 25 in listening state, 2, 9
  port 25 used by SMTP to receive
    mail, 419
  port 3389 used by RDP, 232, 362, 449
  port 389 used by LDAP, 195, 449
  port 443 used by HTTPS, 4, 12
  port 443 used by SSL, 231–232, 362
  port 53 mitigating DNS poisoning,
    106–107
  port 80 used by HTTP, 12, 230, 232
  port 80 used by web servers, 362, 419
  port 989 used by FTPS, 12
  port 990 used by FTPS, 12

port scanners, determining open
  ports, 359
ports 135-139, File and Print Sharing
  using, 359
ports 1812 and 1813 used by
  RADIUS, 449
protocol analyzers allowing traffic
  filters for, 417
SYN flood protection preventing DoS
  attacks on, 148
as transport protocol, 15, 187, 424
TCP/IP
  encrypting data transmissions, 14–15
  ensuring computers are on different
    networks, 11
  mail protocols, 9
  remote command prompt to network
    service, 14
  synchronizing time between
    computers, 13–14
  transport protocols, 15
  troubleshooting workstation settings, 13
technical controls, for secure access, 218
technical support, for electronic book or
  MasterExam, 461
TELNET
  as application protocol, 15
  not identifying transmission
    problems, 16
  as remote command prompt to
    network service, 14
  uses of, 187
  using SSH for hardening vs., 100
templates
  applying security, 108
  limitations of freely downloadable
    DRP, 319–320
Temporary Key Integrity Protocol. see
  TKIP (Temporary Key Integrity
  Protocol)
Terminal Access Controller Access
  Control System (TACAS+), 187–188
testing
  black, white and gray box, 365
  financial software, 105
  for open ports on hosts. see port
    scanners
  passive security, 364
  penetration. see penetration testing
  periodic network, 363
TFTP (Trivial FTP)
  security problem with routers using, 144
  storing files without requiring
    usernames or passwords, 13
  UDP port 69 used by, 14

thermal imaging, identifying hot spots, 273
threat analysis, 289, 301
threat assessment, risk analysis, 290
threats
  adware, 78–79, 87
  backdoors, 80–81, 86, 87
  blocking in behavior-based network
    monitoring, 383
  botnets. see botnets
  cell phone, 82
  certification objectives, 71
  changing boot order, 81
  computer viruses. see viruses
  hardware keyloggers, 80
  identifying and categorizing in
    qualitative risk analysis, 293
  identifying before calculating
    ALE, 300
  logic bombs. see logic bombs
  overview of, 72
  physical, 78
  privilege escalation. see privilege
    escalation
  qualitative risk analysis ranking
    potential, 296–297
  risk analysis by specifying
    internal, 290
  risk analysis identifying, 359–360
  spam. see spam
  Stuxnet attack, 85
  Trojans. see Trojans
  USB security. see USB security
  worms. see worms
threats, mitigating
  with account lockouts, 108
  with alarms, 102
  with application pools, 109–110
  ARP cache poisoning, 105–106
  with authentication before allowing
    network access, 107–108
  certification objectives, 89
  cross-site request forgeries, 101–102
  dictionary password attacks, 98
  disabling unused user accounts, 98–99
  DNS poisoning, 106–107
  with error handling, 103
  with fuzzing, 97
  with hardening, 97
  with hardening operating system,
    103–104
  with hardening using SSH, 100
  with hardening Windows server, 109
  with initial baseline
    configuration, 100
  with input validation, 106

threats, mitigating (*Cont.*)
    laptops with USB devices, 104
    overview of, 97
    with penetration testing, 109
    with remediation, 101
    with restriction on connecting
        wireless clients, 99
    with security templates, 108
    with trend analysis, 102–103
time, correlating captured packets for
    evidence, 342–343
time of day access control, 208, 209
time offset, validating digital forensic
    evidence, 335
timestamped, packet captures as,
    342–343
TKIP (Temporary Key Integrity Protocol)
    enhancing wireless security to
        WEP, 231
    using with WPA for added
        security, 371
    WPA using for encryption, 173
    WPA2 Enterprise vs., 165
TLS (Transport Layer Security)
    HTTPS using, 230
    not related to SSL, 456–457
    superseding SSL, 231, 238, 426
    unable to check for file
        tampering, 237
token cards, as authentication, 34
tokens, hardware, 190–191, 454
Top Secret security labeling, 47–48
total cost of ownership (TCO) analysis
    ALE value vs., 293
    defined, 290
    not using for disaster recovery plan,
        319–320
TPM (Trusted Platform Module) chips
    backing up keys, 128–129
    drive encryption, 121–122
    embedded on motherboards, 445–446
    integrity and non-repudiation of, 262
    not applicable to high
        availability, 318
    securing data in server room
        with, 277
    using separate recovery key for, 443
TRACERT (Trace Route) utility
    identifying transmission problems, 16
    using ICMP, 10
training
    employees in disaster recovery plan, 320
    as IT forensic budget item, 346
    reducing risk with employee, 292
    for security awareness, 47
    users in malware, 434–435

Transmission Control Protocol. *see* TCP
    (Transmission Control Protocol)
transmission of unwelcome bulk messages,
    82–83
transmit power level, reducing wireless
    coverage area, 169
Transport Layer Security. *see* TLS
    (Transport Layer Security)
transport protocols, TCP/IP, 5
travel expenses, as IT forensic budget
    item, 346
trend analysis
    baseline analysis vs., 360
    mitigating security threats with,
        102–103
3DES (Triple Digital Encryption
    Standard)
    encryption strength of, 232–233
    hot hashing function, 240
    securing LANs with IPSec, 234
    symmetric encryption algorithm, 232
Trivial FTP. *see* TFTP (Trivial FTP)
Trojans
    in downloaded pirated software, 434
    firewall log revealing machine under
        malicious control, 388
    hardware keyloggers vs., 80
    logic bomb vs., 85
    malicious code appearing as innocent
        software, 87, 428
    mitigated by virus scanners, 447
    not self-replicating, 437
    privilege escalation vs., 79
    zero-day exploits vs., 49
Trusted OS (operating system), 211
Trusted Platform Module. *see* TPM
    (Trusted Platform Module) chips
trusted root certificates, 445–446
trusted third party with decryption keys, as
    key escrow, 255
2.4 GHz range, Wi-Fi, 169–170, 172
TwoFish, 235

U

UAC (User Account Control), Windows,
    86
UDP (User Datagram Protocol)
    defined, 188
    as OSI layer 4 transport protocol, 424
    port 123 used by NTP, 14
    port 161 used by SNMP, 419
    port 53 showing only DNS traffic, 419
    port 69 used by TFTP, 14

port scanners, determining open
    ports, 359
protocol analyzers allowing traffic
    filters for, 417
RADIUS user authentication with, 188
as transport protocol, 15
Unix networks
    authenticating with Kerberos, 187
    SSH allowing secured remote access
        to host, 230
upgrades, Microsoft Office, 363
UPS (uninterruptible power supply)
    configuring for fail safe, 277
    fail secure systems vs., 275
    protecting data on stolen USB flash
        drives, 278
URL filtering, preventing access to
    forbidden sites, 149
USB flash drives
    collecting data in order of volatility
        from, 336
    documents easily forged on, 340
    encrypting for data confidentiality,
        33, 121
    encrypting for data handling, 50
    encrypting for secure data, 443
    encrypting in case of theft or loss, 278
    internal threat of users plugging in
        personal, 290
    obtaining incriminating evidence on,
        347–348
    as potential source of virus infection,
        289–290
    security concerns of, 279
USB security
    configuring device encryption on
        laptops, 104
    creating policy for, 82
    for hardware keyloggers on
        keyboards, 80
USB write-blocking devices, 341
user access and rights reviews, 384
User Account Control (UAC),
    Windows, 86
user accounts
    mistakenly deleting, then newly
        creating, 118, 209
    mitigating attacks against
        passwords, 108
    mitigating threats by disabling
        unused, 98–99
    setting expiration date for
        temporary, 454
    symmetric encryption using
        passphrase, 243
    tracking changes with auditing, 385

tricking users for information on, 436
user access and rights reviews of, 384
User Datagram Protocol. *see* UDP (User Datagram Protocol)
user education and awareness
    clean desk policy, 51–52
    encrypting data on USB flash drives, 50
    infection from files downloaded through P2P, 49
    mandatory vacation policy, 52
    POS software storage of magnetic data, 50–51
    preventing tailgating, 49
    providing training, 47
    secure equipment disposal policies, 47
    social networking risks, 48
    users not securing own computers, 51
    zero-day exploits, 49
usernames
    as authentication, 34
    example of authentication, 193
    TFTP server storing files without requiring, 13

validation
    of digital forensic evidence with time offset, 335
    preventing cross-site scripting attacks, 98, 441
ventilation. *see* HVAC (Heating Ventilation Air Conditioning)
video surveillance
    analyzing security breaches, 274–275
    as evidence in computer forensics, 337
    security guard advantages over, 275
virtual local area networks. *see* VLANs (virtual local area networks)
virtual private networks. *see* VPNs (virtual private networks)
virtualization
    benefits of server, 447–448
    features of, 125
    reverting to older snapshots, 119
virtualized server security, 425, 442–443
virus scanners
    attacks not mitigated by, 447
    network mapping vs., 368
    not detecting zero-day exploits, 371
    not related to confidentiality, 31
    not testing for open ports on hosts, 366

securing smart phones with, 448
vulnerability scanners vs., 442
viruses. *see also* worms
    carried by worms, 78
    controlling spread of worm, 346
    description of, 79
    exploits vs., 427–428
    identifying potential sources of infection, 289–290
    as malicious code that can copy itself, 428
Visio network diagram, in computer forensics, 337
VLANs (virtual local area networks)
    creating separate broadcast domains with, 142
    ensuring computers are on different networks, 3, 11
    grouping all switch ports into, 342
    not verifying client health compliance, 152
    virtual machines connecting to different, 125
    VLANs interconnecting with other VLANs, 418–419
VMotion, VMWare, 425
Voice over Internet Protocol. *see* VoIP (Voice over Internet Protocol)
voiceprint scans, insecurity of, 190, 279
VoIP (Voice over Internet Protocol)
    cell phone voice encryption software vs., 127
    identifying network traffic, 10
    reducing telephony costs with, 185
VPN concentrator, 146–147
VPN security logs, 44–45
VPN security policies
    defined, 44–45
    for employees working at home, 51
    as technical controls, 218
VPNs (virtual private networks)
    accessing private LANs using, 151
    defined, 217
    encryption for WANs, 231
    hardening, 241
    not retaining MAC address information, 420
    not tied to SSL as only solution, 456–457
    providing secure access to LAN for traveling user with, 421
    remote access to corporate database servers, 184
    renewing expired X.509 certificates on, 256

securing network traffic from users using, 423
single sign-on vs., 194
solutions with SSL and, 231
using hardware tokens, 454
VLANs vs., 142–143
vulnerability
    of computers with large attack surface, 361
    configuring intentionally with honeynets, 359, 362
    configuring intentionally with honeypots, 359, 362
    due care vs., 33–34
    due diligence vs., 33
    exploits taking advantage of, 427–428
    zero-day exploit vs., 49
vulnerability assessment
    business impact analysis vs., 432
    penetration testing vs., 361
    risk analysis, 359–360
vulnerability scanners
    detecting security misconfigurations with, 442
    for known security threats, 358, 370–371
    port scanners vs., 359
    protocol analyzers vs., 144
    showing open TCP ports 135-139, 362

WANs, VPN encryption for, 231
war chalking, 166, 170
war dialing, 166
war driving, 165–166, 170
warm sites
    example of, 313–314
    justifying cost of, 321
warrants, obtaining forensic evidence with, 347
Web application firewalls, 149
web security gateways, 142
web server logs, identifying irregularities on, 389
web servers
    determining IP addresses of, 365–366
    using private keys to decrypt client session key, 454–455
    using TCP port 80, 419
    using TCP port 80 or 443, 362

WEP (Wired Equivalent Privacy)
   CCMP vs., 168
   easily broken encryption of, 367
   not as secure for wireless networks, 368
   not providing centralized
      authentication, 371
   securing home wireless network with
      WPA2 PSK vs., 363
   TKIP enhancing wireless security
      to, 231
   WPA2 Enterprise vs., 165
whaling, 436
white box testing, 365, 370
Wi-Fi networks
   correcting unstable wireless 802.11g
      connectivity, 169–170
   defined, 158
   eavesdropping on, 440
Wi-Fi Protected Access. *see* WPA (Wi-Fi
   Protected Access)
Windows 7
   authenticating workstations before
      LAN access, 147–148
   creating rogue access point on laptop
      in, 169
   scanning for other networks in, 167
   self-assigned IPv6 addresses in, 424
Windows Guest account, disabling for
   security, 364
Windows Mail, 9
Windows networking service, preventing
   privilege escalation in, 84
Windows Server Update Services
   (WSUS), 364, 445
Windows Update
   not affecting slow and unstable
      performance, 391
   not disabling to minimize network
      utilization, 445
Wired Equivalent Privacy. *see* WEP
   (Wired Equivalent Privacy)
wired networks, connecting to with MAC
   address, 8
wireless access point logs, in unauthorized
   WLAN access, 381
wireless encryption protocol, security
   audits, 368–369
wireless networking
   802.1x securing open, 368
   authenticating connections using
      proxy servers, 140
   authenticating users to RADIUS
      server, 165
   authentication with 802.1x, 174
   authentication with EAP, 166

authentication with PEAP,
   166–167
Bluejacking, 170, 175–176
Bluesnarfing, 171
CCMP encryption protocol,
   167–168
centralized authentication using
   RADIUS, 371
connections between networks,
   150–151
control of systems connecting
   to, 164
correcting unstable 802.11g
   connectivity, 169–170
creating rogue access point in
   Windows 7, 169
detecting rogue access points, 174
disabling SSID broadcasting, 422
enabling EAP-TLS, 173
enabling MAC address filtering, 422
enabling WPA, 164
evil twin configuration, 170
home office configuration, 175
isolation mode, 165
IV attacks in WEP, 171
MAC address filtering blocking
   unauthorized access, 175
microwave oven interference with
   802.11g, 172
omnidirectional antennae
   location, 168
personal firewalls for laptops, 121
preventing devices from seeing
   WLAN name, 172
reducing coverage area, 169
scanning for other networks in
   Windows 7, 167
securing wireless routers, 154
shared bandwidth on 802.11g,
   173–174
VPNs accessing private LANs, 151
war driving, 165–166
WPA using TKIP, 173
wireless routers
   authenticating users to RADIUS
      server, 165
   authentication prior to network
      access, 457
   connecting clients to Internet, not
      internal computers, 140
   correcting unstable wireless 802.11g
      connectivity, 169–170
   as example of RADIUS client, 186
   hardening of, 107
   with omnidirectional antennae, 168

preventing users from administrative
   access to, 154
RBAC for, 451
removing due to violation of due
   care, 32
transmit power level, 169
wireless scanners, 366
WLAN (wireless LANs), enabling WPA
   on, 164
workstations
   assigning IP addresses to, 18
   authenticating in Windows 7 before
      LAN access, 147–148
   client-side certificates restricting
      access to, 258
   problems connecting to server, 418
   security concerns, 279
   tracking users of inappropriate
      sites, 392
   troubleshooting TCP/IP settings, 13
   unlit link light on network card in
      new, 147
   updating with WSUS, 364
worms
   botnets vs., 80
   carrying viruses, 78
   controlling spread of, 346
   exploits vs., 427–428
   logic bombs vs., 85
   propagating to other systems, 78
   as self-replicating malicious code,
      428, 437
   spam vs., 83
   Stuxnet attack using, 85
   zero-day exploits vs., 49
WPA (Wi-Fi Protected Access)
   addressing weaknesses of WEP, 367
   EAP options for, 166
   enabling on WLAN, 164
   using TKIP for encryption, 173
WPA (Wi-Fi Protected Access)
   Personal, 165
WPA2 (Wi-Fi Protected Access) PSK
   (Preshared Key), 368
WPA2 (Wi-Fi Protected Access version 2)
   Enterprise
   authenticating connecting users to
      RADIUS server, 165
   authentication for laptop
      implementing PKI, 192
   EAP options for, 166
   as most secure wireless network
      encryption, 366–367
   not for wireless home networks, 363
   overview of, 165

WPA2 (Wi-Fi Protected Access version 2)
PSK (Preshared Key)
home office configuration, 175
not providing centralized
authentication, 371
securing home wireless network with
WEP vs., 363
write protection, 278
written consent, prior to penetration
testing, 361
WSUS (Windows Server Update
Services), 364, 445

X.509 standard, 256, 263
XSS (cross-site scripting) attack
adware vs., 79
botnets vs., 84
DNS poisoning vs., 107
example of, 66–67
fuzzing vs., 97
mitigating with validation, 98
phishing vs., 434
preventing by validating user input
before submissions, 441

zero-day exploits
defined, 428
example of, 68
honeypots logging, 371
logic bombs vs., 85
no current remedy for, 49
zombies, 437–438

New Online Resources for IT Professionals!
Certification Shows You Know IT—Now Share IT
Join the IT Pro Community to network and engage with professionals from around the world. You can also post your resume on the CompTIA IT Job Board—an employment website designed for CompTIA certified professionals. Highlight your certification status so you'll come up first when employers search for qualified candidates.
Get Involved. Get Smart.
Get on the Path to Success.
CompTIA
JOIN TODAY!
IT Pro Community http://itpro.comptia.org
CompTIA IT Job Board http://itcareers.comptia.org
2010 CompTIA, Inc. All rights reserved. CompTIA and its logo are trademarks of CompTIA, Inc.

The Best in Security Certification Prep

CISSP Boxed Set
Shon Harris
0-07-176845-9

**CISSP All-in-One Exam Guide,
Fifth Edition**
Shon Harris
0-07-160217-8

CISSP Practice Exams
Shon Harris
0-07-170139-7

CSSLP Certification All-in-One Exam Guide
Wm. Arthur Conklin and Daniel Shoemaker
0-07-176026-1

**CISA Certified Information Systems Auditor
All-in-One Exam Guide, Second Edition**
Peter Gregory
0-07-176910-2

Learn more. McGraw Hill Do more.
MHPROFESSIONAL.COM

Available in print and ebook formats.

Follow us @MHComputing

LICENSE AGREEMENT

.ODUCT (THE "PRODUCT") CONTAINS PROPRIETARY SOFTWARE, DATA AND INFORMATION (INCLUDING
.MENTATION) OWNED BY THE McGRAW-HILL COMPANIES, INC. ("McGRAW-HILL") AND ITS LICENSORS. YOUR
.HT TO USE THE PRODUCT IS GOVERNED BY THE TERMS AND CONDITIONS OF THIS AGREEMENT.

.CENSE: Throughout this License Agreement, "you" shall mean either the individual or the entity whose agent opens this package. You
are granted a non-exclusive and non-transferable license to use the Product subject to the following terms:
(i) If you have licensed a single user version of the Product, the Product may only be used on a single computer (i.e., a single CPU). If you
licensed and paid the fee applicable to a local area network or wide area network version of the Product, you are subject to the terms of the
following subparagraph (ii).
(ii) If you have licensed a local area network version, you may use the Product on unlimited workstations located in one single building
selected by you that is served by such local area network. If you have licensed a wide area network version, you may use the Product on
unlimited workstations located in multiple buildings on the same site selected by you that is served by such wide area network; provided,
however, that any building will not be considered located in the same site if it is more than five (5) miles away from any building included in
such site. In addition, you may only use a local area or wide area network version of the Product on one single server. If you wish to use the
Product on more than one server, you must obtain written authorization from McGraw-Hill and pay additional fees.
(iii) You may make one copy of the Product for back-up purposes only and you must maintain an accurate record as to the location of the
back-up at all times.

COPYRIGHT; RESTRICTIONS ON USE AND TRANSFER: All rights (including copyright) in and to the Product are owned by
McGraw-Hill and its licensors. You are the owner of the enclosed disc on which the Product is recorded. You may not use, copy, decompile,
disassemble, reverse engineer, modify, reproduce, create derivative works, transmit, distribute, sublicense, store in a database or retrieval
system of any kind, rent or transfer the Product, or any portion thereof, in any form or by any means (including electronically or otherwise)
except as expressly provided for in this License Agreement. You must reproduce the copyright notices, trademark notices, legends and logos
of McGraw-Hill and its licensors that appear on the Product on the back-up copy of the Product which you are permitted to make hereunder.
All rights in the Product not expressly granted herein are reserved by McGraw-Hill and its licensors.

TERM: This License Agreement is effective until terminated. It will terminate if you fail to comply with any term or condition of this
License Agreement. Upon termination, you are obligated to return to McGraw-Hill the Product together with all copies thereof and to purge
all copies of the Product included in any and all servers and computer facilities.

DISCLAIMER OF WARRANTY: THE PRODUCT AND THE BACK-UP COPY ARE LICENSED "AS IS." McGRAW-HILL, ITS
LICENSORS AND THE AUTHORS MAKE NO WARRANTIES, EXPRESS OR IMPLIED, AS TO THE RESULTS TO BE OBTAINED
BY ANY PERSON OR ENTITY FROM USE OF THE PRODUCT, ANY INFORMATION OR DATA INCLUDED THEREIN AND/OR
ANY TECHNICAL SUPPORT SERVICES PROVIDED HEREUNDER, IF ANY ("TECHNICAL SUPPORT SERVICES").
McGRAW-HILL, ITS LICENSORS AND THE AUTHORS MAKE NO EXPRESS OR IMPLIED WARRANTIES OF
MERCHANTABILITY OR FITNESS FOR A PARTICULAR PURPOSE OR USE WITH RESPECT TO THE PRODUCT.
McGRAW-HILL, ITS LICENSORS, AND THE AUTHORS MAKE NO GUARANTEE THAT YOU WILL PASS ANY
CERTIFICATION EXAM WHATSOEVER BY USING THIS PRODUCT. NEITHER McGRAW-HILL, ANY OF ITS LICENSORS NOR
THE AUTHORS WARRANT THAT THE FUNCTIONS CONTAINED IN THE PRODUCT WILL MEET YOUR REQUIREMENTS OR
THAT THE OPERATION OF THE PRODUCT WILL BE UNINTERRUPTED OR ERROR FREE. YOU ASSUME THE ENTIRE RISK
WITH RESPECT TO THE QUALITY AND PERFORMANCE OF THE PRODUCT.

LIMITED WARRANTY FOR DISC: To the original licensee only, McGraw-Hill warrants that the enclosed disc on which the Product is
recorded is free from defects in materials and workmanship under normal use and service for a period of ninety (90) days from the date of
purchase. In the event of a defect in the disc covered by the foregoing warranty, McGraw-Hill will replace the disc.

LIMITATION OF LIABILITY: NEITHER McGRAW-HILL, ITS LICENSORS NOR THE AUTHORS SHALL BE LIABLE FOR ANY
INDIRECT, SPECIAL OR CONSEQUENTIAL DAMAGES, SUCH AS BUT NOT LIMITED TO, LOSS OF ANTICIPATED PROFITS
OR BENEFITS, RESULTING FROM THE USE OR INABILITY TO USE THE PRODUCT EVEN IF ANY OF THEM HAS BEEN
ADVISED OF THE POSSIBILITY OF SUCH DAMAGES. THIS LIMITATION OF LIABILITY SHALL APPLY TO ANY CLAIM OR
CAUSE WHATSOEVER WHETHER SUCH CLAIM OR CAUSE ARISES IN CONTRACT, TORT, OR OTHERWISE. Some states do
not allow the exclusion or limitation of indirect, special or consequential damages, so the above limitation may not apply to you.

U.S. GOVERNMENT RESTRICTED RIGHTS: Any software included in the Product is provided with restricted rights subject to
subparagraphs (c), (1) and (2) of the Commercial Computer Software-Restricted Rights clause at 48 C.F.R. 52.227-19. The terms of this
Agreement applicable to the use of the data in the Product are those under which the data are generally made available to the general public
McGraw-Hill. Except as provided herein, no reproduction, use, or disclosure rights are granted with respect to the data included in the
nd no right to modify or create derivative works from any such data is hereby granted.

is License Agreement constitutes the entire agreement between the parties relating to the Product. The terms of any Purchase
fect on the terms of this License Agreement. Failure of McGraw-Hill to insist at any time on strict compliance with
hall not constitute a waiver of any rights under this License Agreement. This License Agreement shall be construed
ance with the laws of the State of New York. If any provision of this License Agreement is held to be contrary to law,
enforced to the maximum extent permissible and the remaining provisions will remain in full force and effect.